Introduction to Property Valuation in Australia

This book provides an easy-to-follow introduction to the principal methods of property valuation in Australia within the context of International Valuation Standards, so bridging the gap between traditional property valuation methods and the modern era of global valuation governance.

Providing a framework for valuation practice, the book outlines the property asset class, the role of valuation, concepts of value and valuation standards before focusing on the instructing, undertaking and reporting aspects of the valuation process. The market approach to valuation is addressed through the comparative method of valuation, with the income approach addressed through the capitalisation of income, discounted cash flow and profits methods of valuation and the cost approach addressed through the replacement cost, reproduction cost and residual or hypothetical development methods of valuation.

As an introductory textbook on property valuation methods, this book is a companion to Australia's leading advanced valuation textbook, *Principles and Practice of Property Valuation in Australia*, edited by the same author and also published by Routledge, which is a more advanced text considering key principles underlying property valuation and current techniques and issues in the practice of property valuation for major sectors of the Australian property market.

The most up-to-date valuation textbook for the Australian market, this book will appeal to both valuation practitioners and undergraduate/postgraduate students as well as to accountants, auditors, lawyers, lenders and all professionals dealing with property valuation issues.

Dr. David Parker is an internationally recognised real estate industry expert and highly regarded real estate academic (www.davidparker.com.au); being the author of *Principles and Practice of Property Valuation in Australia* (2022) and *The Routledge REITs Research Handbook* (2018). He is a regular contributor to property and valuation academic journals, a Visiting Professor at the Henley Business School, University of Reading and a Visiting Fellow at the University of Ulster.

Introduction to Property Valuation in Australia

David Parker

Routledge
Taylor & Francis Group

LONDON AND NEW YORK

Cover image: © Getty Images

First published 2024
by Routledge
4 Park Square, Milton Park, Abingdon, Oxon OX14 4RN

and by Routledge
605 Third Avenue, New York, NY 10158

Routledge is an imprint of the Taylor & Francis Group, an informa business

British Library Cataloguing-in-Publication Data
A catalogue record for this book is available from the British Library

Library of Congress Cataloging-in-Publication Data
Names: Parker, David, 1949 September 28– author.
Title: Introduction to property valuation in Australia / David Parker.
Description: New York, NY : Routledge, 2024. | Includes bibliographical references and index.
Identifiers: LCCN 2023035931 (print) | LCCN 2023035932 (ebook) | ISBN 9781032503165 (hardback) | ISBN 9781032498515 (paperback) | ISBN 9781003397922 (ebook)
Subjects: LCSH: Real property—Valuation—Australia. | Valuation—Australia.
Classification: LCC HD1036.5 .P37 2024 (print) | LCC HD1036.5 (ebook) | DDC 333.33/20994—dc23/eng/20230818
LC record available at https://lccn.loc.gov/2023035931
LC ebook record available at https://lccn.loc.gov/2023035932

ISBN: 978-1-032-50316-5 (hbk)
ISBN: 978-1-032-49851-5 (pbk)
ISBN: 978-1-003-39792-2 (ebk)

DOI: 10.1201/9781003397922

Typeset in Times New Roman
by Apex CoVantage, LLC

To my partner and my twin millennials.
May the future with Ed recompense for that foregone.

Contents

About the author

David Parker is an internationally recognised real estate industry expert and highly regarded real estate academic, being a director and adviser to real estate investment groups, including listed real estate investment trusts, unlisted funds and private real estate businesses (www. davidparker.com.au).

Dr. Parker is Visiting Professor at the Henley Business School, University of Reading and Visiting Fellow at the University of Ulster. He is Acting Commissioner of the Land and Environment Court of New South Wales, the former Valuer General of New South Wales and the inaugural Professor of Property at the University of South Australia.

With over 40 years of experience in property funds management, real estate investment trusts, valuation standards and statutory valuation, Dr. Parker previously held senior executive positions with Schroders Property Fund and ANZ Funds Management.

Holding a BSc, MComm, MPhil, MBA and PhD degrees, Dr. Parker is Fellow of the Royal Institution of Chartered Surveyors, the Australian Institute of Company Directors, the Australian Property Institute, the Australian Institute of Management and Senior Fellow of the Financial Services Institute of Australasia. He is a member of the Society of Property Researchers, the American Real Estate and Urban Economics Association and the European, American and Pacific Rim Real Estate Societies.

Author of *Principles and Practice of Property Valuation in Australia* (2022) and editor of *The Routledge REITS Research Handbook* (2018), Dr. Parker is also the author of *International Valuation Standards: A Guide to the Valuation of Real Property Assets* (2016) and *Global Real Estate Investment Trusts: People, Process and Management* (2011). Dr. Parker has published numerous papers in academic and industry journals and is a regular conference presenter around the world, being an Editorial Board Member for the highly ranked *Journal of Property Research* and *Journal of Property Investment and Finance*.

Dr. Parker may be contacted by email at davidparker@davidparker.com.au.

Foreword

For all students and practitioners of real estate valuation, *Property Valuation in Australia* is essential reading.

This book provides a contemporary update of real estate valuation principles and is a worthy successor to *Principles and Practices of Valuation* by J F N Murray and *Land Valuation and Compensation in Australia* by R O Rost and H G Collins.

These principles are the cornerstone of your practice in real estate valuation and a point of reference that will be invaluable throughout your career.

Over time your practice may focus on a specific class of real estate; however, this does not diminish the need to fully understand valuation principles and practices as they provide the essential intellectual base and discipline.

Governing your valuation practice are the valuation standards requiring compliance, including the International Valuation Standards, RICS Red Book and API guidance papers, with each providing guidance in relation to valuation theory and practice. The synergy between practice and compliance is inseparable and fundamental to a successful career as a real estate valuer. These standards do not attempt to provide a detailed or exhaustive list of what to do in every situation. They represent a framework for professional conduct and aim to provide assistance and clarification in addition to the accumulated knowledge and experience of valuers engaging in professional services.

This excellent publication deals with the fundamental proposition of market value and the valuation methods that should be applied in the proper assessment of market value.

Valuation methods, including direct comparison, capitalisation of income, residual or hypothetical development and the discounted cash flow method of valuation, which is the principal method of valuation for multi-tenanted investment properties, are all discussed in detail in this publication. Your detailed market analysis and understanding of the assumptions adopted by vendors and purchasers from your enquiries of market participants will guide you to the most appropriate method to be applied. Your enquiries that disclose how the market actually functions must be applied consistently in your analysis and valuation assessment, adopting the valuation principles set out in this publication.

This publication sets out the foundations and cornerstone of valuation practice, which should be adopted throughout your valuation career as you build your skills, knowledge and experience, which are then applied objectively and independently.

This book is a significant contribution to the body of knowledge not only for students but also for existing practitioners. It is also an invaluable reference point for accountants, lawyers and other professionals dealing with property valuation issues.

Peter Dempsey FAPI
Director
Dempsey Valuation and Advisory
June 2023

Preface

This book provides the reader with an introduction to the fundamentals of property valuation, outlining the principal methods of property valuation in Australia within the context of International Valuation Standards.

With International Valuation Standards focusing on the market approach, income approach and cost approach, this book recasts the traditional five methods of property valuation within the relevant International Valuation Standards approaches and so bridges the gap between traditional property valuation methods and the modern era of global valuation governance.

This book is premised on the acceptance of International Valuation Standards as the principal guiding principles for valuation globally, supplemented as necessary by regional and national principles statements and replacing Court decisions as the principal guiding principles for valuation in Australia. Relegating *Spencer* to its twenty-first-century role as a significant precedent for statutory valuation purposes represents a major change in the Australian approach to valuation.

Outlining the structure of the property asset class, this book examines the traditional characteristics of property (including heterogeneity, durability, illiquidity and so forth) and the traditional risks of property (including location, building, tenant risk and so forth) through the lenses of systematic, unsystematic and idiosyncratic risk, so aligning property valuation with capital market theory.

Concepts of value are explored, reconciling the International Valuation Standards' definition of market value to the concept of market value in *Spencer v Commonwealth* (1907) with a detailed examination of International Valuation Standards, the RICS Red Book and API guidance papers. Through a review of the self-supporting process of instructing, undertaking and reporting valuations, this book examines how this process inter-relates to the choice of valuation approach, valuation method and the purpose of the valuation.

The market approach to valuation is addressed through the comparative method of valuation, with the income approach addressed through the capitalisation of income, discounted cash flow and profits methods of valuation and the cost approach addressed through the replacement cost, reproduction cost and residual or hypothetical development methods of valuation. The book concludes with a consideration of future perspectives, including the role of uncertainty, data, optionality ESG, space use and indigenous issues.

As an introductory textbook on property valuation methods, this book is a companion to Australia's leading advanced valuation textbook, *Principles and Practice of Property Valuation in Australia,* edited by the same author and also published by Routledge, which is a more advanced text considering key principles underlying property valuation and current techniques and issues in the practice of property valuation for major sectors of the Australian property market.

David Parker
Sydney
June 2023

1 Introduction to the property asset class

1.1 Introduction

This book is an introduction to the fundamentals of property valuation, outlining the principal methods of property valuation in Australia within the context of International Valuation Standards, so bridging the gap between traditional property valuation methods and the modern era of global valuation governance.

This chapter seeks to outline the structure of the property asset class, examining the traditional characteristics of property (including heterogeneity, durability, illiquidity and so forth) and the traditional risks of property (including location, building, tenant risk and so forth) through the lenses of systematic, unsystematic and idiosyncratic risk, so aligning property valuation with capital market theory.

Chapter 2 considers the evolution of property valuation in Australia, the role of the valuer and the diverse activities of the valuation profession, followed by a detailed examination of the inter-acting framework provided by valuation standards and ethical standards promulgated by IVSC, RICS and API.

Chapter 3 explores concepts of value and normative and positive definitions of value, dissecting the International Valuation Standards' definition of market value with a reconciliation to the concept of market value in *Spencer v Commonwealth* (1907) and examining such contemporary valuation issues as valuation lag, variance, accuracy, negligence and valuer rotation.

Chapter 4 introduces International Financial Reporting Standards and International Accounting Standards with a detailed examination of the key provisions of International Valuation Standards, the RICS Red Book and API guidance papers that impact on valuation practice in Australia.

Chapter 5 outlines conceptual approaches to the valuation process with a review of the self-supporting process of instructing, undertaking and reporting valuations under the International Valuation Standards, RICS Red Book and API guidance papers, examining how this process inter-relates to the choice of valuation approach, valuation method and the purpose of the valuation.

Chapter 6 addresses the market approach to valuation through the comparative method of valuation, including the key steps of accumulation, analysis, adjustment and application of comparable sales evidence to the subject property being valued, with an example.

Chapter 7 considers the income approach to valuation addressed through the static methods of the capitalisation of income and the profits methods of valuation, including an examination of the key inputs for each method with examples and a consideration of both marriage value and the surrender and renewal of leases.

DOI: 10.1201/9781003397922-1

Chapter 8 considers the income approach to valuation addressed through the dynamic method of the discounted cash flow method of valuation, including an examination of the key inputs and a focus on the derivation of the discount rate and consideration of the role of sensitivity and scenario analysis, with an example.

Chapter 9 considers the cost approach to valuation addressed through the replacement cost, reproduction cost, summation and residual or hypothetical development methods of valuation, with an example.

Finally, Chapter 10 concludes the book with a consideration of future perspectives, including the role of uncertainty, data, automated valuation models, artificial intelligence, optionality, environmental, social and governance issues, retail and office space use and indigenous issues.

This book is based on those standards and guidance documents published in IVSC (2021) and RICS (2021) and on the API website (accessed January to May 2023). Given their nature, standards and guidance documents are dynamic, being regularly updated and with the most recently published versions replacing previously published versions. Accordingly, readers should not rely on this book as a current statement of a standard or guidance document and should visit www.ivsc.org, www.rics.org and/or www.api.org.au to find the most recent version.

As an introductory textbook on property valuation methods in Australia, this book is a companion to Australia's leading advanced valuation textbook, *Principles and Practice of Property Valuation in Australia,* edited by the same author and also published by Routledge, which is a deeper analysis of key principles underlying property valuation and current techniques and issues in the practice of property valuation for major sectors of the Australian property market.

Accordingly, this chapter will now consider:

- the property market, including key property market sectors and property uses;
- the characteristics of the property asset class;
- the risks within the property asset class;
- risk classification; and
- securitisation.

1.2 The property market

The property market comprises a complex and disparate amalgam of different types of property used for different purposes. While it may be referred to as a single market, it is, in reality, a large number of different markets. There is a wide range of different types of property or property sectors, including residential, office, retail and so forth, that are considered further in what follows. Similarly, there is a wide range of purposes for which property may be used, including owner occupation, investment and development, which are also considered further in what follows.

Gilbertson (2002) famously summarised the property market scenario facing valuers:

Deals happen. There is not a perfect market. This imperfection makes a valuer's task very difficult. The valuer has to interpret where the market is going. A valuation is like a snapshot in time.

Imagine a photograph containing a ball in flight. Is it actually going up or down? That's what the client wants to know. He would really like to know where the ball will be after an agreed period of time, but that is probably too difficult for all but the crystal ball gazers.

As a market, the property market functions in the same way economically as any other market, with the confluence of supply and demand determining pricing. For example, in the transaction (buy/sell) market, if three apartment buildings are completed at the same time, the supply of new apartments in the market may exceed the demand for new apartments, with the result that new apartment prices may fall. Similarly, in the leasing market, if three high-rise office buildings are completed at the same time, the supply of office space for lease may exceed the demand for office space resulting in an increased vacancy rate with the result that the rent for new office space may fall, in simple terms (although in reality, new office building owners may try to preserve rents by offering potential lessees incentives to lease office space, effectively moving the vacancy and decreasing rents to older, existing office buildings).

The property market suffers from a significant level of economic inelasticity. Land is a scarce resource and may take considerable time to acquire in response to demand for a particular form of development, such as residential or office development. Development itself may take a considerable time with the requirement for planning approvals and time taken for construction. Demand may be dependent on the buoyancy of the economy and exist when a development commences but no longer exist when the development is completed. Accordingly therefore, the property market may be considered relatively inelastic, exhibiting difficulties aligning supply and demand with relatively small changes in quantities potentially having a disproportionate effect on price/rent.

A useful lens when considering the value of property in the context of the property market is whether the property is located where you would expect it to be located. Blackledge (2017) outlines the evolution of land use theories and principles over the last 300 years, concluding with the work of Lean and Goodall (1966), who identified five concentric zones or regions, being:

- the central business district (CBD), being the core of the city from which transportation routes radiate, giving the highest level of accessibility facilitating dense, high-order development such as high-rise office buildings;
- the zone of transition surrounding the CBD with high land values and mixed development uses;
- suburban areas with less intense development and lower land values, usually for residential development with complementary uses (shopping centres, small offices, etc.);
- rural-urban fringe where residential uses mix with agricultural uses, often being identified in planning instruments for long-term residential development; and
- rural areas being used for agriculture, forestry, open space and similar uses.

In broad terms, the value of land and buildings decreases as land use moves from the CBD outwards towards rural areas. In an Australian context, this is best visualised with application to larger country cities such as Bendigo, Griffith or Rockhampton, where the commercial core forms the centre of the city and the uses diminish in intensity as they radiate outwards in broadly concentric circles, mountains, water and physical geographic features permitting.

While generally applicable to the capital cities in Australia, their locations next to ocean and the existence of other natural features, such as mountains, tend to result in broadly concentric crescents rather than circles. Further, the evolution of capital cities in Australia has seen the development of satellite centres such as Dandenong, Parramatta and Loganholme, which each have their own concentric zones radiating outwards.

The property market may be considered in terms of both property market sectors (section 1.2.1, following) and property uses (section 1.2.2, following).

1.2.1 Property market sectors

The property market comprises a complex and disparate amalgam of different types of property used for different purposes. While it may be referred to as a single market, it is, in reality, a large number of different markets. While there is a wide range of different types of property or property sectors in Australia, the principal sectors comprise residential, office, retail, industrial, leisure and rural, which are considered further in what follows.

1.2.1.1 Residential sector

The residential sector comprises housing in its many and varied forms. The sector includes all forms of houses ranging from detached houses, semi-detached houses or duplexes and townhouses to beach shacks and dongas. The sector also includes apartments which may be highrise, medium-rise or low-rise.

In the December quarter of 2022, there were 10,911,000 residential dwellings in Australia, with a total value of $9.6 trillion (ABS, 2022a). The total value movement over the period 2017–2022 is shown in Figure 1.1.

As of the date of the 2021 census, 70% of private dwellings were separate houses, 13% were townhouses and 16% were apartments, with 31% owned outright, 35% owned with a mortgage and 31% rented (ABS, 2022b).

Heffernan (2016) notes that the residential sector represents one of the most complex property sectors within the economic, community, political and built environment landscape of Australia due to a range of features including:

• the very large scale of the sector, representing approximately one-third of the value of the entire Australian built environment;
• the interface of this sector and the assets produced with the economically critical development, building and financial sectors;
• the diversity of ownership and high level of home ownership or home subject to mortgage;

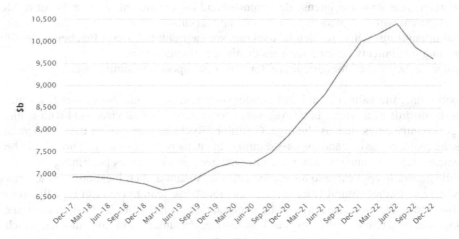

Figure 1.1 Total value of dwelling stock, Australia

Source: ABS (2022a)

- the electoral interest and sensitivity in securing home ownership and related issues, leading to public policy and government financial support and taxation concessions that favour home ownership but create long-term, complex economic supply/demand aberrations;
- the regional and physical diversity of housing assets and the uniqueness of each individual asset within the umbrella of meeting the fundamental need for shelter;
- the ability of the same housing asset to provide the basic human requirement of shelter but also to transfer seamlessly into a source of income (through rent) and potential capital gain to the owner; and
- the concept of home ownership lying deep in the aspirations and ethos of Australian households, being fundamental to identity and socio-economic standing within most of the Australian community (page 158–159).

Key factors affecting residential property valuation include:

- size of property, number of bedrooms, bathrooms, garages, etc.;
- size of land upon which the property is situated;
- views and aspect;
- proximity to local schools and shopping centres;
- proximity to transport facilities including bus, train or ferry; and
- proximity to community facilities, places of worship, hospitals, etc.

A more detailed consideration of the valuation of residential property may be found in Kininmonth in Parker (2022).

1.2.1.2 Office sector

The office sector comprises all such property as may be used as an office, such as high-rise CBD office towers, low-rise suburban office buildings and office parks or campuses.

Approximately 19 million sqm of office space is located within the CBDs of Australia's capital cities, benefitting from a clustering effect providing proximity for a wide range of interactive businesses, with a further approximately 7.8 million sqm of office space in non-CBD locations.

The Property Council of Australia defines four grades of office quality, with the presentation of each being described as follows:

Premium buildings

A landmark office building located in major CBD office markets, which is a trendsetter in establishing rents, includes expansive views and outlook, ample natural light, prestige quality access from an attractive street setting, prestige lobby and lift finishes, premium quality lift ride, premium quality amenities, premium presentation and maintenance.

Grade A buildings

High-quality office building including high-quality views, outlook and natural light, high-quality access from an attractive street setting, high-quality lobby and lift finishes, high-quality lift ride, high-quality amenities, high-quality presentation and maintenance.

Grade B buildings

Good quality office building with a good standard of finish and maintenance.

Grade C buildings

Adequate quality office space with further descriptive criteria for environmental, mechanical, electrical, lifts, security, amenities and so forth (Property Council of Australia, 2019).
Key factors affecting office property valuation include:

- location relative to other office buildings;
- proximity of public transport;
- quality of building, including façade, ceiling height and sustainability features;
- views from upper floors;
- level of car parking within the building;
- end of trip facilities and tenant amenities; and
- prestige attached to property.

A more detailed consideration of the valuation of office property may be found in Dempsey in Parker (2022).

1.2.1.3 Retail sector

The retail sector comprises all such property as may be used for retailing from super-regional shopping centres, regional shopping centres, sub-regional shopping centres, neighbourhood shopping centres and suburban shopping strips to freestanding shops in country towns.
Key factors affecting retail property valuation include:

- location relative to other competing shopping centres;
- size and extent of the catchment area for shoppers;
- demographic and socio-economic profile of shoppers within the catchment area;
- extent of car parking available;
- split between major tenants (department stores, discount department stores, supermarkets, etc.) and specialty retailers;
- relativity of focus on discretionary and non-discretionary retailing;
- extent of provision of experiential retailing (such as restaurants, cinemas, gyms, etc.); and
- proximity of public transport.

With a gross lettable area of approximately 24.5 million sqm, Sweeney in Parker (2022) notes that there is a wide variety of types and sizes of shopping centres that are grouped or "classified" for comparison of various data. The following classifications from Property Council of Australia (2015) are endorsed by the Shopping Centre Council of Australia:

1.2.1.3.1 CITY CENTRES

Retail premises within an arcade or mall development owned by one company, firm or person and promoted as an entity within a major Central Business District (CBD).

Total Gross Leasable Area—Retail (GLAR) exceeds 1,000 sqm.
Key features:

* dominated by specialty shops;
* likely to have frontage on a mall or major CBD street;
* generally do not include supermarkets; and
* often co-exist with large department stores.

1.2.1.3.2 SUPER-REGIONAL SHOPPING CENTRES

A major shopping centre typically incorporating two full-line department stores, one or more full-line discount department stores (DDS), two supermarkets and around 250 or more specialty shops.
Total GLAR exceeds 85,000 sqm.
Key features:

* one-stop shopping for all needs;
* comprehensive coverage of the full range of retail needs (including specialised retail), containing a combination of full-line department stores, supermarkets, services, chain and other specialty retailers;
* typically include a number of entertainment and leisure attractions such as cinemas, game arcades and soft play centres; and
* provide a broad range of shopper facilities (car parking, food court) and amenities (restrooms, seating).

1.2.1.3.3 MAJOR REGIONAL SHOPPING CENTRES

A major shopping centre typically incorporating at least one full-line department store, one or more full-line discount department stores, one or more supermarkets and around 150 specialty shops.
Total GLAR generally ranges between 50,000 and 85,000 sqm.
Key features:

* one-stop shopping for all needs;
* extensive coverage of the full range of retail needs (including specialised retail), containing a combination of full-line department stores, full-line discount department stores, supermarkets, services, chain and other specialty retailers;
* typically include a number of entertainment and leisure attractions such as cinemas, game arcades and soft play centres; and
* provide a broad range of shopper facilities (car parking, food court) and amenities (restrooms, seating).

1.2.1.3.4 REGIONAL SHOPPING CENTRES

A shopping centre typically incorporating one full-line department store, a full-line discount department store, one or more supermarkets and around 100 or more specialty shops.
Total GLAR typically ranges between 30,000 and 50,000 sqm.

In some instances, all other characteristics being equal, a centre with two full discount department stores but without a department store can serve as a regional centre.

Key features:

- extensive coverage of a broad range of retail needs (including specialised retail), however, not as exhaustive as major regional centres;
- contains a combination of full-line department stores, full-line discount department stores, supermarkets, banks, chain and other specialty retailers; and
- provide a broad range of shopper facilities and amenities.

1.2.1.3.5 SUB-REGIONAL SHOPPING CENTRES

A medium-sized shopping centre typically incorporating at least one full-line discount department store, a major supermarket and approximately 40 or more specialty shops.

Total GLAR will typically range between 10,000 and 30,000 sqm.

Key features:

- provides a broad range of sub-regional retail needs; and
- typically dominated by a full-line discount department store or major supermarket.

1.2.1.3.6 NEIGHBOURHOOD SHOPPING CENTRES

A local shopping centre comprising a supermarket and approximately 35 specialty shops.

Total GLAR will typically be less than 10,000 sqm.

Key features:

- typically located in residential areas;
- services immediate residential neighbourhood;
- usually have extended trading hours; and
- cater for basic day-to-day retail needs.

1.2.1.3.7 BULKY GOODS CENTRES

A medium to large-sized shopping centre dominated by bulky goods retailers (furniture, white goods and other homewares), occupying large areas to display merchandise. Typically contain a small number of specialty shops.

Total GLAR will typically be greater than 5,000 sqm.

Key features:

- generally located adjacent to large regional centres or in non-traditional retail locations (i.e., greenfield sites and industrial areas); and
- purpose designed, built and operated, generally with a layout of outlets around a central, landscaped area and an overall design and colour theme to promote the appearance of an integrated development.

1.2.1.3.8 RETAIL TENANCY LEGISLATION

Heffernan (2016) notes that practically all State jurisdictions in Australia have enacted specific shop-lease legislation to regulate the relationship between landlord and tenant beyond that contained in the lease document and to address the power imbalance between shopping centre owner and retailer. While the legislation varies between States, Heffernan (2016) notes common themes include the following:

- specific methodologies for assessing market rent, including the designation of specialist retail valuers;
- provisions for the allocation of outgoings;
- provision of disclosure statements by landlords;
- cooling-off periods prior to leases taking effect;
- the establishment of mediation procedures and tribunals to assist in resolving disputes; and
- the emergence of provisions to outlaw unconscionable conduct by any party in undertaking a lease (pages 150–151).

A more detailed consideration of the valuation of retail property may be found in Sweeney in Parker (2022).

1.2.1.4 Industrial sector

The industrial sector comprises a very wide range of properties including:

- traditional industrial property where manufacturing, fabrication, assembly or other forms of production are undertaken;
- warehouses where goods are stored;
- distribution centres where goods are stored for dispatch to businesses;
- fulfillment centres or high-tech warehouses facilitating e-commerce, where goods are stored and collated for dispatch to customers;
- business and science parks, often with a high level of technology, laboratory and/or office space; and
- industrial estates comprising a range of buildings of differing sizes for differing uses.

Preliminary estimates of the size of the industrial sector indicate approximately 66 million sqm comprising buildings in excess of 3,000 sqm.

Heffernan (2016) notes that local government land use zoning plans have, for many decades, recognised various sub-categories of land, including:

- light industry;
- service industry;
- heavy or general industry;
- noxious, offensive or hazardous industry;
- extractive industries (to preserve and protect deposits of minerals and construction materials);
- future industry (land reserved for industrial use into the future as demand requires); and
- special zoning or development control areas to accommodate uses such as ports and airports (page 151).

Key factors affecting industrial property valuation include:

- land and building size;
- land and building shape;
- level of natural light and requirement for artificial light;

- access road network generally, rail network, ports, airports;
- egress road network specifically;
- style of construction—clear span portal frame, columns;
- load-bearing capacity of floors;
- maximum and minimum slab-to-roof clearances;
- roller doors;
- docking/loading;
- crane services;
- fire ratings and certifications; and
- proximity to supply of suitable labour.

A more detailed consideration of the valuation of industrial property may be found in Korda in Parker (2022).

1.2.1.5 Leisure sector

The leisure sector comprises all such property as may be used for leisure purposes, such as hotels, motels, pubs, bars, nightclubs, reception centres, conference centres, casinos, theme parks, backpacker hostels and campsites.

As McIntosh and Milsom in Parker (2022) note, it is essential that the valuer understands the nature of the business and the property, as well as the opportunities and risks. This requires more than a simple understanding of real estate. It requires, amongst other things, knowledge of the business operations, the demand drivers and the buyers' rationale and motivation. There are several characteristics that distinguish leisure properties from commercial real estate, including:

- the short-term nature of the income (usually daily) compared with leased properties;
- the resultant relative volatility of the income;
- the even greater volatility of the net income since many of the costs are fixed and comprise a higher proportion of revenue than for commercial buildings;
- the need for active management—even if there is a manager, the asset management relates to the business, not just the maintenance of the property; and
- the need for regular capital expenditure at a much higher level than for commercial property.

The valuation of leisure property is both complex and specialist. While this book considers the profits method of valuation, the valuation of leisure property is considered in greater depth by McIntosh and Milsom in Parker (2022).

1.2.1.6 Rural sector

The rural sector comprises all forms of agricultural, horticultural and aquacultural land uses for a diverse range of cropping and grazing purposes, including feedlots, poultry enterprises, orchards and vineyards and timberland.

As Parker (2022) notes, issues for consideration in rural property valuation are complex and specialist. The market for rural land is regionally influenced and may fluctuate depending on seasonal conditions, commodities outlook, general economic circumstances and rural property market participant perceptions. To value rural property, the valuer needs to fully understand the marketplace for the land, the nature of the land and farming practices.

Key factors affecting rural property valuation include:

- climate, which varies by district, with rainfall, seasonal distribution, temperatures, evaporation rates, drought, wind and patterns, frost and major storms and cyclones being important considerations together with the impact of climate change;
- topography which commonly determines the use of rural land with land capable of being ploughed used to grow crops, while unarable land usually comprises land with remnant native vegetation or hilly to steep land which cannot be economically or safely cultivated;
- soil type and quality are an integral part of the agricultural production process and different soil types or land classes may result in different values. Soil characteristics across most districts fall into the following main categories such as sands, loams, non-cracking clays, cracking clays, calcareous earths, massive earths, structured earths with either smooth or rough ped fabric, duplex soils—red, brown, yellow, yellow-grey, black and grey—and organic soils;
- water plays a critical part in agriculture, with areas of low rainfall often boosted by irrigation from river storages, surface water catchment or underground sources. Throughout most regions of Australia, the use of irrigation water is controlled by Government through licensing. In recent times, Water Licences have been "unbundled" from the land in most districts, meaning they form a separate legal (personal) asset. Where the water "Entitlement" has been separated from the land, any intending financier should register an interest in the asset;
- tenure of rural property, which may be freehold, Crown Land (being land that is not freehold and still held by the Crown, being regulated by the relevant State Government) or pastoral leases, which cover approximately 44% of Australia's mainland, allowing the use of land for grazing traditional livestock and more recently for tourism and non-traditional livestock such as kangaroos and camels; and
- productivity, a measure that can be used to compare rural land relatively. Productivity can be measured on various bases and will vary depending on what type of enterprise is to be undertaken—such as "green acres" (being a term used to describe the area of irrigated land), carrying capacity for a grazing property or production or yields within a dryland cropping or irrigation property. The productivity will be closely aligned with the land types, level of improvement and infrastructure, climate and rainfall and management practices (Parker, 2022).

The valuation of rural property is both complex and specialist and is not considered in this book. A more detailed consideration of the valuation of rural property may be found in Baxter and Cohen (2009) and Parker (2022).

1.2.1.7 Summary—property market sectors

While there is a wide range of different types of property or property sectors in Australia, the principal sectors may be contended to comprise residential, office, retail, industrial, leisure and rural. While information on the valuation of other sectors may be difficult to find, the valuation of retirement and aged care property is addressed by Towart in Parker (2022).

1.2.2 Property uses

The property market comprises a complex and disparate amalgam of different types of property used for different purposes. While it may be referred to as a single market, it is, in reality, a large number of different markets. There is a wide range of different types of property or property sectors, including residential, office, retail and so forth, that were considered in what came before.

Similarly, there is a wide range of purposes for which property may be used, including owner occupation, investment and development that are considered further in what follows.

1.2.2.1 Property for owner occupation

Property for owner occupation comprises that property which is occupied by the owner, the most common example being residential property though other types of property such as office, retail and industrial may also be owner occupied.

In the residential sector, as of the date of the 2021 census, approximately 66% of private dwellings were owner-occupied, comprising 31% of private dwellings owned outright and 35% owned with a mortgage (ABS, 2022b). While owner occupation of office, retail and industrial property has decreased over the last few decades as banks and major corporates sold and then leased back property, Harvey Norman Holdings Limited still owner occupies a portfolio comprising 121 properties valued at $3.74 billion as of 30 June 2022 (source: http://clients.weblink. com.au/news/pdf/02575137.pdf, accessed 9 June 2023).

As owner-occupied property, especially residential, is generally relatively stable and benefits from deep markets that generate extensive comparable sales evidence, property for owner occupation may generally be less complex to value than property for investment and property for development.

1.2.2.2 Property for investment

Property for investment comprises that property which is, generally, owned by one party and occupied by another party. This may include residential property, such as an apartment owned by one party and rented to another party to occupy. Property investment is very common in the office, retail and industrial sectors where owners such as REITs (including Dexus, Scentre and Goodman), property funds (including Australian Prime Property Fund and Cromwell Direct Property Fund), superannuation funds (including Cbus and Aware), insurance companies (including Zurich and MLC), private investors and foreign investors may own a property and lease it to one or more occupiers, such as large firms of solicitors or accountants (such as Herbert Smith Freehills or KPMG), retailers (such as Coles or Athlete's Foot) or distributors (such as Amazon or UPS).

The essential nature of any investment is the foregoing of a capital sum now in return for a regular income and/or growth in capital value over a future period. This income can arise from the payment of a rate of interest each year or, with property, from the receipt of rent paid by a tenant in occupation (Blackledge, 2017).

Wyatt (2023) notes that property is regarded as a financial asset in the investment market, where rational investors seek to maximise returns on a range of assets and compare the risks of holding property against other investment opportunities such as shares or bonds. Investors aim to maximise their level of return for an acceptable level of risk, with the investment market driven by the opportunity cost of capital.

As the risk-return attractiveness of property relative to other asset classes varies over time, property for investment generally requires valuations that have regard to other asset classes and the prevailing level of risk and return, both within the property asset class and relative to other asset classes.

Property investment is a complex area with numerous specialist textbooks, including Brown and Matysiak (2000), Hoesli and Macgregor (2000) and Pagliari (1995), to which readers are referred.

1.2.2.3 Property for development

Property for development comprises that property that is owned for the purpose of changing it into another form of property through the development process. This may include a group of houses held for demolition and redevelopment into a high-rise apartment building, a brownfield site held for redevelopment into a retail warehouse or vacant land being a greenfield site held for redevelopment into a distribution centre.

Property for development generally requires valuations that are forward-looking and deal with significant uncertainty. While the existing building or site may be known, that which will be constructed, the time and cost taken to undertake construction and the value and saleability of the development on completion are unknown, will occur at some point in the future and are inherently uncertain.

Property development is a complex area with numerous specialist textbooks, including Baum et al. (2018) and Wyatt (2023), to which readers are referred.

1.2.2.4 Summary—property uses

While there is a wide range of different types of property or property sectors, including residential, office, retail and so forth, that were considered previously, there is also a wide range of purposes for which property may be used with the principal uses comprising owner occupation, investment and development.

1.3 Characteristics of the property asset class

The property asset class, being all property sectors considered together, exhibits a range of fundamental characteristics that impact upon the risk-return profile of property relative to other asset classes, such as shares and bonds, including the following:

1.3.1 Heterogeneity

It is generally accepted that property is heterogenous, with each property being unique and no two properties being exactly the same. The usual claims for homogeneity in property, such as terrace houses or a row of industrial units, can never be entirely homogenous as the location of each property will be marginally different such as being marginally closer to a corner shop or to the entrance to an industrial estate.

Similarly, with high-rise apartment buildings, while each apartment may have the same layout and be facing in the same direction, no two apartments will be exactly the same as their height or precise outlook will differ.

1.3.2 Durability

A fundamental characteristic of land is that it is indestructible and perpetual, and of property is that it lasts for a very long period of time, with the usual assumption for the life of a modern office building being around 60 years and many cities around the world having properties that are several hundred years old.

However, while property is durable, it is also subject to depreciation due to obsolescence which is usually considered to take three forms, physical, functional and external or economic obsolescence.

1.3.3 Illiquidity

Liquidity usually refers to the ease with which an asset may be converted into cash. Due to the time taken and difficulty in selling property, it is generally considered to be an illiquid asset taking a long time to convert into cash.

Compared to shares and bonds that can be traded online in a matter of minutes and converted to cash in a matter of days, it may take several months to market and sell a house with a further period before settlement, at which point the asset is turned into cash.

1.3.4 Indivisibility

Indivisibility usually refers to the inability to divide a property into smaller units. Generally, as the lot size of a property investment gets larger, the pool of potential purchasers gets smaller, and this impacts the risk-return profile of property relative to highly divisible asset classes such as shares and bonds.

Generally, it is not possible to buy part of an investment property, and so, property is considered to be indivisible. Indivisibility may be addressed by the joint acquisition of a property as joint tenants or tenants in common, the development of property within a strata title or community title structure allowing the sale of individual apartments or offices or through securitisation, but each is expensive and time-consuming to facilitate.

1.3.5 Market imperfection

The nature of landed property, the method, cost and time taken to conduct transactions all contribute to the imperfections of the property market (Shapiro et al., 2019). Property is rarely sold instantly online, usually requiring a marketing campaign leading to an auction, sale by tender or sale by private treaty, which can take several weeks or months. While online conveyancing has reduced the time taken to complete transactions in some property sectors, for larger office, retail and industrial assets, the time taken remains significant.

A sale and purchase transaction for property will often involve an agent and a solicitor for both the seller and the buyer, resulting in significant costs. Further, the buyer will generally be liable for stamp duty on the purchase, further increasing transaction costs.

1.3.6 Market inefficiency

Seminal research by Fama (1970) proposed three levels or forms of market efficiency, being:

- weak form efficiency—where prices reflect historic information, such as previous prices and sale dates, so that no investor can earn excess returns from trading rules based on a past series of prices;
- semi-strong form efficiency—where prices reflect all publicly available information, such as a recent planning consent or new letting data, so that no investor can earn excess returns based on publicly available information; and
- strong form efficiency—where prices reflect all information, including information only known to corporate insiders and specialists, such as insider information, so that no investor can earn excess returns from any information, whether publicly available or not (Parker, 2011).

The property market is generally considered to be weak-form efficient (or, effectively, inefficient), with the use of a time series of returns or historic market trends being unlikely to, for example, lead to the generation of abnormal returns.

Limited information has long been held to be a significant problem preventing efficiency in the property market. While the advent of technology has dramatically increased the amount of public information relating to transactions that is available online for residential property, public information for transactions in other property sectors remains limited, underlining the importance of personal relationships in the property profession and industry as a source of information.

1.3.7 Intermediaries

For the sale or purchase of office, retail or industrial property, an agent or representative of the buyer and the seller are likely to be involved in bringing the parties together and then undertaking the negotiation process as intermediaries, so incurring costs. For other asset classes, such as shares and bonds, such intermediaries are not required, with the transaction able to be undertaken online at little cost.

For the sale of residential property in Australia, while the involvement of a vendor's agent is common, it is not unknown for a vendor to sell a property him or herself or for the sale process to be undertaken online.

1.3.8 Scarcity

The supply of land is effectively finite, with additions to land through reclamation representing a very small percentage of total land area. Similarly, some types of property, such as harbour-front mansions in Sydney or super-regional shopping centres, are limited in supply with significant impediments to the creation of more supply.

Accordingly, property is generally considered to be scarce, with larger or more specialist property becoming increasingly scarcer. While it may sound unlikely, an investor wishing to spend $1 billion on a major office tower in the CBD of a State capital would have a relatively limited range of properties from which to choose, of which only a small proportion may be available for sale.

1.3.9 Fixed geographical location

Property is immoveable, as elegantly captured by the French word for real estate, *immobilier*. Whereas shares or bonds can be moved around by an investor and taken wherever the investor may wish to go, property cannot as it is irrevocably fixed to land.

Accordingly, property is subject to the political and economic trends prevailing in its geographic location and is not immune from their effects. Similarly, if a property happens to be in the way of a proposed highway, it cannot simply be moved to accommodate the highway, but a portion or all of the property will have to be acquired for the highway to be developed.

1.3.10 Proof of ownership

In most Western economies, sophisticated land titling systems make establishing proof of ownership of land and buildings relatively straightforward. However, even in some Western economies, there may be land subject to old forms of title that have not been transferred to a land titling system, making proof of ownership more challenging.

Difficulties often arise in countries lacking sophisticated land titling systems or operating under a form of customary law and title where clear and definitive proof of ownership may be difficult to establish. Such problems do not arise with shares and bonds, where the registration of ownership is usually automated or on a bearer system allowing easy proof of ownership.

1.3.11 Lot size

Related to indivisibility and heterogeneity as a characteristic of the property asset class, lot size refers to the amount of money required to acquire a particular piece of property or "lot". Property does not come in convenient small, medium, large and extra-large sizes like other assets but tends to come in one size only, being its actual size.

Accordingly, if an investor wishes to buy a super-regional shopping centre, it is likely to only exist in a lot size of around $2–$3 billion, with smaller versions simply not available. This is very different from shares and bonds where, generally, there is no minimum lot size other than one unit and a maximum lot size usually governed by corporate regulation.

1.3.12 Prestige

Shares and bonds offer little in the way of prestige to an investor or owner. However, property has the potential to provide a high level of prestige to an investor or owner.

Prestige commonly arises with large residential properties where the owner gains satisfaction by being the owner of a large and very expensive house. Similarly, foreign investors often gain satisfaction from owning an office building that is visible on a capital city skyline and can be pointed out to friends and colleagues.

1.3.13 Government intervention

Unlike shares and bonds, property is highly susceptible to government intervention at a federal, state and local level, such as through foreign ownership rules, taxation and development control.

Such intervention is not static but dynamic, often changing with new governments or in response to public outcry. While a property owner may know the tax status or planning status of a property on acquisition, changes in statute or regulation may change this while being beyond the property owner's control.

1.3.14 No single market

As Millington (2000) notes, the property market does not consist of one large market but a series of smaller markets, each of which is local in nature and each of which suffers from constrained information.

While the property market is the sum of the residential market, the office market, the retail market, the industrial market and every other property sector market, each such sector market is the sum of a series of sub-sector markets. For example, the residential market in a given suburb or town is the sum of the local house market, townhouse market, apartment market and so forth, with the retail market in a State being the sum of the super-regional shopping centre market, regional shopping centre market, sub-regional shopping centre market and neighbourhood shopping centre market.

1.3.15 Number of buyers and sellers

In a perfectly competitive market, there are a large number of buyers and sellers. However, in the property market, there are generally a limited number of buyers and sellers of particular types of property at a specific point in time.

Accordingly, part of the contribution of intermediaries is to ensure that a property is widely exposed to the market and to identify as many potential buyers as possible in order to ensure a healthy level of competition and price bidding. Similarly, part of the contribution of intermediaries is to source potential sellers when their buyer client is seeking a particular type of property, generally through their network of market contacts, given that the seller may not be actively considering sale at that point in time.

1.3.16 Frequency of transactions

In a perfectly competitive market, transactions take place frequently—for example, on the share market, multiple transactions may take place every minute of the trading day. However, in the property market, transactions may be very much less frequent, with some property types rarely trading.

The greatest frequency of transactions takes place in the residential property sector, where there is a relatively high turnover of houses, apartments and so forth. In the smaller lot size end of the office, retail and industrial market, there is usually a steady flow of transactions over the course of a year which may be counted in the dozens. However, in the larger lot size end of the office, retail and industrial market transactions are usually infrequent and may be counted in single digits when the market is subdued and in the low tens each year when the market is more active.

1.3.17 Transaction costs

Transaction costs for property in Australia are very high and vastly higher than transaction costs for other asset classes. For example, buying $2 million of Goodman Property Group units on CommSec will incur brokerage costs and taxes of approximately $2,402, indicating that transaction costs for acquisition in the shares asset class are approximately 0.12%.

Buying a $2 million apartment in Sydney will incur transaction costs of approximately $96,600, including stamp duty of $94,200, legal/conveyancing fees of $1,500 and a strata report at $900, indicating that transaction costs for acquisition in the property asset class are approximately 4.85%.

On disposal, a $2 million parcel of shares would incur approximately the same transaction costs plus capital gains tax, if applicable. However, on disposal, a $2 million dollar property would incur agent's fees (around 1–2% of the sale price) and marketing and advertising costs (approximately $10,000–15,000) plus capital gains tax, if applicable. This indicates total transaction fees for buying and selling a $2 million parcel of shares to be approximately 0.24% compared to approximately 6.95% for a $2 million parcel of property.

The same principles apply to the purchase and sale of office, retail, industrial and other forms of property, which has an impact on the purchaser's target returns, net of costs, and holding periods contributing to the popular notion that property is a long-term asset.

1.3.18 Summary—characteristics of the property asset class

A key feature of the property asset class is its number of characteristics, which is significant as this directly impacts market participants' view of the risk of the property asset class and the resultant return that they seek to compensate for the risk taken relative to other asset classes such as shares or bonds.

The wide range of characteristics requiring compensation often appears to be overlooked when property sub-markets enter periods of exuberance, with transaction prices escalating and suggesting low-risk premiums when analysed. Invariably, when the particular property sub-market then declines, this wide range of characteristics emerges as reasons to explain falls in value when what has really changed is market participants' confidence and perceptions of risk.

1.4 Risks within the property asset class

While major investors such as superannuation funds and insurance companies focus on the risk of property at the portfolio level, determining the resultant return that they seek to compensate for the risk taken relative to other asset classes such as shares or bonds, valuation tends to focus on risk within the property asset class (such as that arising from the characteristics of the property asset class as a whole), that which affects all properties within a given sector (such as shopping centres in the retail sector) and risk at the individual property level.

Further, there is a wide range of risks at the individual property level, comprising those that affect every property (such as taxation risk), those that affect all properties within a given grouping (such as economic risks of retail spending, unemployment and consumer sentiment affecting all shopping centres) and those that only impact a specific property (such as the public policy risk of heritage affecting a historic office building).

Accordingly, risk should be considered as a pervasive web that reaches far and wide with varying levels of impact that have a direct effect on the value of a specific property. While risk may be dissected and classified in a wide range of ways, the following are contended to include the principal sources of risk relevant to the valuation of property.

1.4.1 Legal risk

Legal risk can take various forms, including:

- tenure risk—such as indefeasibility of title for freehold interests, validity of leases for lease-hold interests, period of certainty for periodic tenancy interests and disharmony for strata title or community title interests;
- lease risk—such as the validity of terms and conditions of leases, efficacy of rent review clauses, lease renewal and options clauses and integrity of use, assignment/sub-letting, repair, maintenance and make good clauses;
- statute risk—such as amendments to existing statutes and the introduction of new statutes. When laws are changed, or new law is introduced, some property may benefit and some may be disadvantaged;
- case law risk—such as decisions by the Courts that either clarify a grey area of law or create a precedent or new rule for application, being particularly common in taxation cases and planning cases; and
- regulatory risk—such as the introduction of new regulations or amendment of existing regulations by Government, including foreign investment regulation at the Federal level, heritage regulation at the State level and building regulation at a local Council level.

1.4.2 Public policy risk

Hutley in Parker (2022) identifies the following public policy risks:

- infrastructure risk—public policy towards infrastructure impacts property values, including transport infrastructure (such as roads, railways and airports) and social infrastructure (such as schools, hospitals, libraries, swimming pools and parks);
- utilities risk—including public policy concerning access to and cost of water, energy, waste and telecommunications, with access to utilities generally being value positive, though proximity to sewerage plants, telecommunications towers and heavy overhead cabling can be value negative;
- water risk—public policy concerning access to water and availability of water is significant for a wide range of property, including rural property and broadacre residential subdivision land;
- environment and climate change risk—public policy impacts on property from environment and climate change are very diverse, including building regulation regarding energy, water and waste efficiency, extreme weather events impacting coastal property, river plain property, bushfire areas and cyclone areas;
- contamination risk—public policy on the identification and management of contamination on land is extensive, with the requirement for major remediation being potentially very expensive;
- heritage and conservation risk—Government at all levels impose controls on the determination and treatment of heritage properties, ranging from allowable external paint colour schemes to the requirement to retain and maintain an entire building;
- social housing risk—public policy on the provision of social (public and community) housing for various groups, including disadvantaged groups and key workers, is dynamic and evolving with particular impact on residential property developers who may be required to incorporate the provision of social housing in a proposed development; and
- native title risk—Australian law recognises that native title exists where indigenous groups have maintained a traditional connection to their land and waters, on a continuous basis, since sovereignty and where acts of Government have not removed it, with significant parts of rural, metropolitan and remote Australia subject to ongoing native title claims.

1.4.3 Taxation risk

Taxation is pervasive in property, with Hutley in Parker (2022) identifying the following at different levels of Government:

- Federal Government level—including the negative gearing tax concession, capital gains tax and superannuation;
- State Government level—including stamp duty and land tax; and
- Local Government level—including rates and Council charges.

Property values are very sensitive to any changes in the taxation regime and may also respond to the prospect of changes in the taxation regime, with the residential market particularly sensitive to not only amendments to the negative gearing concession but also to any proposals to amend the negative gearing tax concession.

As Millington (2000) notes, while valuation is usually undertaken without regard to tax, when differing groups are contemplating property acquisition or disposal, their tax position may be a major consideration with very different tax regimes applying for individuals, companies, trusts and superannuation entities. The author also notes the impact of development land tax and inheritance tax on the operation of the UK property market, both of which taxes are generally absent in Australia (except Windfall Gains Tax in Victoria).

1.4.4 Compulsory acquisition risk

Hutley in Parker (2022) notes that all levels of Government in Australia have statutory powers to make compulsory acquisitions of land or interests in land, generally for a public purpose such as the development of a highway or railway or for an easement. Public policy has seen massive ongoing investment by Government, particularly at the Federal and State levels, in infrastructure across Australia, including western Sydney's Nancy-Bird Walton airport, Melbourne's West Gate Tunnel Project and Brisbane's Cross River Rail Project.

1.4.5 Technology risk

As technology becomes ever more pervasive in the property sector, technology risk rises. Many of the services within major investment properties, such as high-rise office towers, major shopping centres and distribution/fulfillment warehouses, are technology dependent, including lifts, escalators, air-conditioning, fire and security systems.

1.4.6 Economic risk

While some aspects of the international economy, the national economy and the local economy impact all property sectors, other aspects may have a greater impact on a specific sector. For example, key economic variables such as inflation, currency, GDP and the bond rate impact all property sectors, whereas retail spending, unemployment and consumer sentiment have a more direct impact on the retail sector and the Reserve Bank cash rate has a very direct impact on the residential sector of the property market.

1.4.7 Demographic risk

Millington (2000) notes that increases and decreases in both national and local population, changes in the age distribution of the population and changes in the proportion of single-person families to multi-person families can significantly impact property markets and property values.

While directly evident in the residential property market (such as an increasing number of single-person families driving a trend to smaller apartments and houses), the availability of blue-collar labour is a significant determinant of location for industrial and warehouse properties and an ageing population has a long term effect on the retail property market and shopping centre tenancy mix.

1.4.8 CSR and sustainability risk

Isaac and O'Leary (2012) identify the risks associated with the emerging concept of corporate social responsibility (CSR) that will increasingly mean that properties that are developed, purchased or leased must achieve some wider social and environmental benefits, as well as satisfying economic criteria.

Significant risk is already emerging for buildings that do not meet sustainability criteria, particularly in the office sector. In order to hold their value or outperform their peer group, properties will increasingly need to demonstrate through a recognised accreditation (such as a LEED, BREAM or NABERS rating) that they are sustainable (Isaac and O'Leary, 2012).

1.4.9 Security risk

Security risk may be considered in terms of security of capital and security of income. Security of capital is a relative measure that varies between asset classes, with Government backed bonds generally considered safest or least risk offering a Government backed return of capital.

Shares as an asset class are generally considered the riskiest, with a greater likelihood of not receiving a return of capital than the property asset class. However, return of capital is not guaranteed for the property asset class, with properties selling for less than their cost of acquisition for a wide range of reasons, including market downturns, tenants vacating and building obsolescence.

Security of income is generally linked to the ability of a tenant to pay their rent and other charges, which, in turn, is linked to the quality of the lease document (legal risk) and the creditworthiness of the tenant (tenant risk).

1.4.10 Supply/demand risk

As considered previously, among the characteristics of property are indivisibility and lot size, with one impact of such characteristics being that it takes a long period of time to develop major assets such as high-rise office towers and apartment buildings.

Accordingly, market forecasts may indicate strong economic conditions and thus demand for office space or apartments in a given city when a development is being launched but during the long period of time taken for development, economic conditions may deteriorate and market demand weaken significantly resulting in major over-supply at completion of the development. This is generally known as the property market cycle, which usually comprises sequential booms and busts, with the lumpy nature of the supply of property exacerbating the boom and the resultant over-supply exacerbating the bust.

Such supply/demand risk may manifest in high vacancy rates and/or incentives in the office sector or significant price reductions to clear stock in the residential sector. Supply/demand risk may be referred to as the state of the property market, being capable of factual assessment and objective measurement, which should be distinguished from sentiment risk.

1.4.11 Sentiment risk

Distinct from risks arising from the state of the property market or supply/demand risk, which are a factual, objective or measured view of the current or previous market, sentiment risk comprises a range of metaphysical issues such as optimism, pessimism, perceptions and feelings which may be rational or irrational and positive or negative. Sentiment may be described as a particular disposition of the mind, being a subjective perception of the property market or of a given property in the past, now or in the future.

Negative market sentiment usually describes a generally adverse view of a particular market sub-sector, and positive market sentiment usually describes a generally benign view of a particular market sub-sector. While there may be reasons beneath such views (for example, interest rate forecasts impacting residential market sentiment), sentiment may exhibit a compounding or cumulative impact and become very positive or very negative remarkably quickly, often aided by the 24-hour news cycle and uninformed social media. As such, sentiment is highly subjective and highly contagious, having the propensity to override more objective and rational considerations.

1.4.12 Planning risk

Planning risk may manifest in two principal forms, temporal and spatial. The time taken to prepare an application, lodge an application, wait for Council to consider the application and challenge an adverse Council decision is extensive and presents a major risk in the development process for all property sectors.

Spatially, for example, if a development is to be viable, then a greater density or height of development than that allowed in the Council's planning instruments may be required. This presents considerable risk to a developer who faces not only temporal risk but also spatial risk as his/her development may not be approved or may be approved with unattractive or unacceptable conditions.

1.4.13 Fashion risk

Tastes change over time, and that which was once fashionable may, at some point in the future, be unfashionable. This may be evident in the residential property market sector, where preferences for the number of bedrooms, the number of bathrooms, the number of garages and so forth vary over time. The advent of the COVID pandemic led to significant changes in taste for residential property, with the demand for home-office spaces leading to design changes in both apartment and house development.

Similar changes may be seen in the office sector with trends to full height glass windows and open plan floor spaces as well as in the retail sector with changes in the design of shopping centres to include wider malls with greater ceiling heights, larger atriums and so forth.

1.4.14 Location risk

Location is at the heart of heterogeneity as a fundamental characteristic of property, as no two properties can have exactly the same location. As noted previously, the usual claims for homogeneity in property, such as terrace houses or a row of industrial units, can never be entirely homogenous as the location of each property will be marginally different such as being marginally closer to a corner shop or the entrance to an industrial estate.

Location risk varies in significance between property sectors. Within the residential sector, the value differences between panoramic water views, water views and water glimpses are potentially massive. In the office sector, the exact location within the CBD is of paramount importance not only for proximity to transportation and retail services but also for adjacency to prestige office towers. In the retail sector, the location of a shop along a mall or suburban strip may have a significant impact on value, with proximity to anchor retailers (such as a department store or supermarket) and transportation of vital importance. For the industrial sector, relativity to major highways, rail hubs, ports and airports are key locational determinants.

It should be noted that location may vary over time. The oft-quoted example is Sydney, where, around 1900, the area around Central Station was considered a prime commercial location in

Sydney, with the area around Circular Quay considered less desirable. A century later, around 2000, this was reversed, with the area around Circular Quay considered a prime commercial location in Sydney and the area around Central Station considered less desirable.

Similarly, the emergence of Barangaroo in Sydney, Docklands in Melbourne and North Quay in Brisbane have each significantly reshaped the concept of location in each city.

1.4.15 Building risk

The physical construction and condition of the built envelope is a significant source of risk for property. Generally, as buildings age, they become more obsolete and depreciate accordingly, with some buildings faring better than others.

In broad terms, particularly for the residential, office and industrial sectors, as a building ages, the quality of accommodation and services will deteriorate, leading to lower rental value with less rental growth, likely resulting in weakening capitalisation and discount rates giving reduced increases in value or reductions in value.

This may be offset by refurbishment with, for example, the upgrading of kitchens and bathrooms, often preserving or enhancing value in the residential sector. The retail and leisure sectors tend to see a much greater frequency of refurbishment than other sectors, leading to value maintenance or increases.

1.4.16 Tenant risk

Linked to the security of income risk, the tenant is the primary source of income return and income growth for property investment such that tenant default is a major risk. In addition to carefully drafted leases and the provision of securities (such as bonds) and guarantees, the principal safeguard against tenant risk is the financial strength of the tenant, usually referred to as quality of covenant.

In general terms, Government is considered the highest quality of covenant as it is unlikely to become insolvent and can raise taxes to pay its bills. Major listed corporations (such as banks, insurance companies and retailers) and large professional practices (such as lawyers and accountants) are considered to be high-quality covenants with smaller listed companies, unlisted businesses and smaller professional practices considered to be weaker covenants.

There are, of course, exceptions to such a generalisation, with some small businesses being financially very robust and easily capable of paying their rent, whereas some larger corporates, such as Ansett Airlines, HIH, ABC Learning Centres and Dick Smith, have collapsed.

1.4.17 Summary—risks within the property asset class

Rather than risk relative to other asset classes, valuation tends to focus on risk within the property asset class (such as that arising from the characteristics of the property asset class as a whole), that which affects all properties within a given sector (such as shopping centres in the retail sector) and risk at the individual property level.

As considered previously, there is a wide range of risks at the individual property level, comprising those that affect every property (such as taxation risk), those that affect all properties within a given grouping (such as economic risks of retail spending, unemployment and consumer sentiment affecting all shopping centres) and those that only impact a specific property (such as the public policy risk of heritage affecting a historic office building). Accordingly, risk should be considered as a pervasive web that reaches far and wide with varying levels of impact that have a direct effect on the value of a specific property.

1.5 Risk classification

Having identified the risks arising from the fundamental characteristics of property that impact upon the risk return profile of property and hence the value of property, previously, it is helpful to adopt a framework within which to classify such risks.

For the pricing of assets, capital market theory asserts that it is not the total risk that is important but the level of risk that cannot be diversified away through combining assets within a portfolio, with investors not being willing to pay a premium for bearing risk that can be diversified away (Parker, 2011).

Further, the risk inherent within an asset is asserted to be a combination of systematic risk, unsystematic risk and idiosyncratic (or specific) risk. Systematic risk comprises those risks endemic to the system, being generally considered to be economic risks, such as inflation, which cannot be diversified away. Unsystematic risk comprises those risks that are common to as asset class or sub-set of an asset class, such as regulatory planning risk. Idiosyncratic or specific risk comprises those risks that are specific to an individual asset, such as location (Parker, 2011).

Modern portfolio theory asserts that by combining properties within a portfolio, the impact of unsystematic and idiosyncratic risks may be significantly reduced or neutralised through diversification, in theory, though the significance of unsystematic and idiosyncratic risk in practice for property renders this challenging (Parker, 2011).

Essentially, it may be contended that unsystematic risk and idiosyncratic risk are likely to be greater for property than for shares and bonds, and their complete neutralisation through diversification may be unlikely.

This contention is evident when considering the risks inherent between different property sectors (such as retail vs. office), between different property sub-sectors (such as grade A office vs. grade C office) and between individual properties (such as 1 Farrer Place vs. 1 Bligh Street in Sydney).

In the valuation process, the consideration of relative risks arises when contemplating a pool of analysed comparable sales and making adjustments to determine an appropriate capitalisation rate or discount rate for application—which of the risks are common to all properties in the pool and which are different between properties and so require recognition through the adjustment process?

Inherent within making adjustments to comparable sales is that risks for consideration are from the perspective of individual properties within one property sub-sector only. The adjustment process is not considering retail vs. office risks or grade A vs. grade C office risks but considering the risks between individual properties, such as 1 Farrer Place vs. 1 Bligh Street in Sydney.

Table 1.1 provides a matrix showing how the fundamental characteristics of property and the wide range of risks arising from property that impact upon the risk return profile of property may be classified in the context of individual office properties such as 1 Farrer Place, Sydney and 1 Bligh Street, Sydney.

Table 1.1 shows that if considering the adjustment of the capitalisation rate or discount rate from an analysed comparable sale at, for example, 1 Farrer Place, Sydney, for application to the valuation of 1 Bligh Street, Sydney:

- those risks listed in the systematic risks column will be common to both properties and reflected in the capitalisation rate and discount rate of each;
- those risks listed in the unsystematic risks column will be common to both properties and reflected in the capitalisation rate and discount rate of each; but

Table 1.1 Risk classification matrix

Systematic Risks	Unsystematic Risks	Idiosyncratic or Specific Risks
Risks affecting all office properties in the Sydney CBD	Risks affecting all grade A office properties in the Sydney CBD	Risks differing between 1 Farrer Place vs. 1 Bligh Street, specifically
Taxation risk	Public policy risk	Legal risk
Compulsory acquisition risk	CSR and sustainability risk	Technology risk
Demographic risk	Security risk	Location risk
Economic risk	Supply/demand risk	Building risk
	Sentiment risk	Tenant risk
	Planning risk	
	Fashion risk	

Source: Author

- those risks listed in the idiosyncratic or specific risks column will differ between each property and so require reflection in the adjustments made to the capitalisation rate and discount rate.

Accordingly, the valuer would focus most on the differences in location, building quality, tenant profile, legal issues and technology between 1 Farrer Place, Sydney and 1 Bligh Street, Sydney when determining the adjustment to be made to the analysed capitalisation rate or discount rate from 1 Farrer Place, Sydney for application in the valuation of 1 Bligh Street, Sydney.

1.6 Securitisation

Securitisation is the term usually used to refer to the subdivision of a physical investment asset into a large number of units, evidenced by pieces of paper or certificates. For example, assume a large office building has a sale price of $500 million. The number of potential purchasers for an asset of this size will be limited. However, if 500 million $1 units in a fund are created, the number of potential purchasers of a $1 unit in the fund is potentially far greater.

The 2022 Annual Financial Report for Scentre Group, a long-established Australian real estate investment trust (AREIT) that owns 42 Westfield Shopping centres, indicates total assets of $35 billion held through 5.18 billion securities with each security trading on 8 June 2023 at $2.63 on the ASX. Therefore, through securitisation, an investor may buy one unit in Scentre Group for $2.63 and participate in the performance of a portfolio of 42 shopping centres, none of which could be individually acquired by the investor.

Securitisation may be undertaken through AREITs listed on the stock exchange (such as Dexus, Vicinity or Centuria Industrial), through unlisted property trusts or funds (such as Australian Prime Property Fund, Healthcare Property Trust or Cromwell Funds Management) or through syndicates where a small group of like-minded parties comes together to own a property.

While the process of securitisation and the law and regulations attaching to AREITs and managed investment products are complex and beyond the scope of this book, it is important to note that securitisation offers the ability to address some of the key problems with the characteristics of property as an asset class such as indivisibility and lot size.

1.7 Summary and conclusions

This chapter outlined the structure of the property asset class, examining the traditional characteristics of property (including heterogeneity, durability, illiquidity and so forth) and the traditional risks of property (including location, building, tenant risk and so forth) through the lenses of systematic, unsystematic and idiosyncratic risk, so aligning property valuation with capital market theory.

The complex and disparate amalgam that is the property market was considered through the principal sectors of residential, office, retail, industrial, leisure and rural, with the key factors affecting the valuation of each reviewed, together with property uses which were classified into three principal groupings, being owner occupation, investment and development.

The number of characteristics of the property asset class was identified as a key feature in market participants' view of the risk of the property asset class and the resultant return that they seek to compensate for the risk taken relative to other asset classes, such as shares or bonds. Various forms of risk were identified, with some affecting the entire property market, some affecting a given sector of the property market and some affecting specific properties, though all primarily seeking reflection through the capitalisation rate or discount rate applied in the valuation process.

Viewing such risks through the lenses of systematic, unsystematic and idiosyncratic risk seeks to align property valuation with capital market theory, focusing the valuer's attention on idiosyncratic risks in the adjustment of analysed sales evidence for application to a subject property being valued. In the context of the office property valuation considered as an example, this focused attention on the role of location, building, tenant, legal and technology risk in the adjustment of analysed capitalisation rate or discount rate evidence for application in the valuation of the subject property.

While the process of securitisation and the law and regulations attaching to AREITs and managed investment products are complex and beyond the scope of this book, it is important to note that securitisation has been incredibly successful in addressing indivisibility and lot size, two of the key problem characteristics of property as an asset class, as well as providing a steady flow of transaction support and financial statement work for the property valuation profession in Australia.

The next chapter will consider the evolution of property valuation in Australia, the role of the valuer and the diverse activities of the valuation profession, followed by a detailed examination of the inter-acting framework provided by valuation standards and ethical standards promulgated by IVSC, RICS and API.

Chapter 3 explores concepts of value and normative and positive definitions of value, dissecting the International Valuation Standards' definition of market value with a reconciliation to the concept of market value in *Spencer v Commonwealth* (1907) and examining such contemporary valuation issues as valuation lag, variance, accuracy, negligence and valuer rotation.

Chapter 4 introduces International Financial Reporting Standards and International Accounting Standards with a detailed examination of the key provisions of International Valuation Standards, the RICS Red Book and API guidance papers that impact on valuation practice in Australia.

Chapter 5 outlines conceptual approaches to the valuation process with a review of the self-supporting process of instructing, undertaking and reporting valuations under the International Valuation Standards, RICS Red Book and API guidance papers, examining how this process inter-relates to the choice of valuation approach, valuation method and the purpose of the valuation.

Chapter 6 addresses the market approach to valuation through the comparative method of valuation, including the key steps of accumulation, analysis, adjustment and application of comparable sales evidence to the subject property being valued, with an example.

Chapter 7 considers the income approach to valuation addressed through the static methods of the capitalisation of income and the profits methods of valuation, including an examination of the key inputs for each method with examples and a consideration of both marriage value and the surrender and renewal of leases.

Chapter 8 considers the income approach to valuation addressed through the dynamic method of the discounted cash flow method of valuation, including an examination of the key inputs and a focus on the derivation of the discount rate and consideration of the role of sensitivity and scenario analysis, with examples.

Chapter 9 considers the cost approach to valuation addressed through the replacement cost, reproduction cost, summation and residual or hypothetical development methods of valuation.

Finally, Chapter 10 concludes the book with a consideration of future perspectives, including the role of uncertainty, data, automated valuation models, artificial intelligence, optionality, environmental, social and governance issues, retail and office space use and indigenous issues.

References

ABS (2022a) *Latest release—total value of dwellings—December quarter 2022*, Australian Bureau of Statistics, Canberra.

ABS (2022b) *Latest release—housing: census 2021*, Australian Bureau of Statistics, Canberra.

Baum, A, Mackmin, D and Nunnington, N (2018) *The income approach to property valuation*, Routledge, Abingdon.

Baxter, JS and Cohen, RK (2009) *Rural valuation*, Australian Property Institute, Deakin.

Blackledge, M (2017) *Introducing property valuation*, Routledge, Abingdon.

Brown, GR and Matysiak, GA (2000) *Real estate investment—a capital market approach*, Pearson Education Limited, Harlow.

Dempsey, P (2022) 'Office property valuation', in Parker, D (Ed) *Principles and practice of property valuation in Australia*, Routledge, Abingdon.

Fama, EF (1970) 'Efficient capital markets: A review of theory and empirical work', *Journal of Finance*, Vol XXV, No 2, p. 383.

Gilbertson, B (2002, February) 'Valuation or appraisal: an art or a science?', *Australian Property Journal*, Vol 37, No 1, pp. 11–13.

Heffernan, MJ (2016) *Real property in Australia*, Mackenzie Green Publishing, Buderim.

Hoesli, M and MacGregor, BD (2000) *Property investment*, Pearson Education Limited, Harlow.

Hutley, N (2022) 'Policy principles', in Parker, D (Ed) *Principles and practice of property valuation in Australia*, Routledge, Abingdon.

Isaac, D and O'Leary, J (2012) *Property valuation principles*, Palgrave Macmillan, Basingstoke.

IVSC (2021) *International valuation standards*, International Valuation Standards Council, London.

Kininmonth, D (2022) 'Residential property valuation', in Parker, D (Ed) *Principles and practice of property valuation in Australia*, Routledge, Abingdon.

Korda, R (2022) 'Industrial property valuation', in Parker, D (Ed) *Principles and practice of property valuation in Australia*, Routledge, Abingdon.

Lean, W and Goodall, B (1966) *Aspects of land economics*, Estates Gazette, London.

McIntosh, R and Milsom, W (2022) 'Leisure property valuation', in Parker, D (Ed) *Principles and practice of property valuation in Australia*, Routledge, Abingdon.

Millington, A (2000) *An introduction to property valuation*, Routledge, Abingdon.

Pagliari, JL (Ed) (1995) *The handbook of real estate portfolio management*, Vols 1 and 2, Irwin, Burr Ridge.

Parker, D (2011) *Global real estate investment trusts: people, process and management*, Wiley-Blackwell, Chichester.

Parker, D (2022) *Principles and practice of property valuation in Australia*, Routledge, Abingdon.

Property Council of Australia (2015) *Operating cost benchmarks 2015: shopping centres*, Property Council of Australia, Sydney.

Property Council of Australia (2019) *A guide to office building quality*, 3rd edition, Property Council of Australia, Sydney.

RICS (2021) *RICS valuation—global standards*, Royal Institution of Chartered Surveyors, London.

Shapiro, E, Mackmin, D and Sams, G (2019) *Modern methods of valuation*, Routledge, Abingdon.

Sweeney, B (2022) 'Retail property valuation', in Parker, D (Ed) *Principles and practice of property valuation in Australia*, Routledge, Abingdon.

Towart, L (2022) 'Retirement and aged care property valuation', in Parker, D (Ed) *Principles and practice of property valuation in Australia*, Routledge, Abingdon.

Wyatt, P (2023) *Property valuation*, Wiley Blackwell, Chichester.

2 Role of valuation

2.1 Introduction

This book is an introduction to the fundamentals of property valuation, outlining the principal methods of property valuation in Australia within the context of International Valuation Standards, bridging the gap between traditional property valuation methods and the modern era of global valuation governance.

Chapter 1 outlined the structure of the property asset class, examining the traditional characteristics of property (including heterogeneity, durability, illiquidity and so forth) and the traditional risks of property (including location, building, tenant risk and so forth) through the lenses of systematic, unsystematic and idiosyncratic risk, so aligning property valuation with capital market theory.

This chapter seeks to consider the evolution of property valuation in Australia, the role of the valuer and the diverse activities of the valuation profession, followed by a detailed examination of the inter-acting framework provided by valuation standards and ethical standards promulgated by IVSC, RICS and API.

Chapter 3 explores concepts of value and normative and positive definitions of value, dissecting the International Valuation Standards' definition of market value with a reconciliation to the concept of market value in *Spencer v Commonwealth* (1907) and examining such contemporary valuation issues as valuation lag, variance, accuracy, negligence and valuer rotation.

Chapter 4 introduces International Financial Reporting Standards and International Accounting Standards with a detailed examination of the key provisions of International Valuation Standards, the RICS Red Book and API guidance papers that impact on valuation practice in Australia.

Chapter 5 outlines conceptual approaches to the valuation process with a review of the self-supporting process of instructing, undertaking and reporting valuations under the International Valuation Standards, RICS Red Book and API guidance papers, examining how this process inter-relates to the choice of valuation approach, valuation method and the purpose of the valuation.

Chapter 6 addresses the market approach to valuation through the comparative method of valuation, including the key steps of accumulation, analysis, adjustment and application of comparable sales evidence to the subject property being valued, with an example.

Chapter 7 considers the income approach to valuation addressed through the static methods of the capitalisation of income and the profits methods of valuation, including an examination of the key inputs for each method with examples and a consideration of both marriage value and the surrender and renewal of leases.

DOI: 10.1201/9781003397922-2

Chapter 8 considers the income approach to valuation addressed through the dynamic method of the discounted cash flow method of valuation, including an examination of the key inputs and a focus on the derivation of the discount rate and consideration of the role of sensitivity and scenario analysis, with examples.

Chapter 9 considers the cost approach to valuation addressed through the replacement cost, reproduction cost, summation and residual or hypothetical development methods of valuation.

Finally, Chapter 10 concludes the book with a consideration of future perspectives, including the role of uncertainty, data, automated valuation models, artificial intelligence, optionality, environmental, social and governance issues, retail and office space use and indigenous issues.

This book is based on those standards and guidance documents published in IVSC (2021) and RICS (2021a) and on the API website (accessed January to May 2023). Given their nature, standards and guidance documents are dynamic, being regularly updated and with the most recently published versions replacing previously published versions. Accordingly, readers should not rely on this book as a current statement of a standard or guidance document and should visit www.ivsc.org, www.rics.org and/or www.api.org.au to find the most recent version.

As an introductory textbook on property valuation methods in Australia, this book is a companion to Australia's leading advanced valuation textbook, *Principles and Practice of Property Valuation in Australia,* edited by the same author and also published by Routledge, which is a deeper analysis of key principles underlying property valuation and current techniques and issues in the practice of property valuation for major sectors of the Australian property market.

Accordingly, this chapter will now consider:

- the evolution of valuation in Australia and the century-long transition from a statutory-based framework to a standards-based framework;
- what is a valuation, the valuation profession, a valuer, the role of a valuer and valuation professional bodies;
- globalisation, IVSC and RICS valuation standards and API guidance; and
- IVSC, RICS and API ethical frameworks in valuation.

2.2 Evolution of valuation in Australia

Valuation in Australia is firmly rooted in statutory valuation practice, being valuation for rating, taxation and compulsory acquisition. A conventional career in valuation over a century ago would have included starting as a cadet in an office of one of the State Valuer Generals, developing professional skills and experience and then either remaining with the State Valuer General's office for an entire career or moving to work in the private sector where practice would have had a heavy emphasis on land subdivision, residential development and mortgage lending.

Murray (1963) records that Tasmania enacted *The Property Valuation Act* in 1857, with a *Land Tax Act* coming into operation in New South Wales in 1896 and the Valuer General's Department established in 1916 with the enactment of the *Valuation of Land Act* 1916. Further, Victoria imposed land tax from 1877, South Australia from 1884, Western Australia from 1907 and Queensland from 1915.

Squirrel (2000) notes that Australian academic education in valuation started in 1920 in the South Australian Government Valuation Department with the Commonwealth Institute of Valuers (a forebear of the Australian Property Institute), then developing part-time valuation courses in all State Divisions and providing part-time lecturers and comprehensive correspondence notes for the next 40 years. As Westwood (1997) notes:

Since the foundation of the Australian Institute of Valuers and Land Economists in 1926, the Institute has accepted a public role in providing instruction and educational material to students and members of the valuation profession.

(iii)

Given the centrality of the role of the State Valuer General offices and statutory valuation, the *Spencer* definition of market value was paramount and that not supported by case law was treated with skepticism. This is reflected in Australia's first locally produced and seminal valuation text book, *Principles and Practice of Valuation* by Dr. Murray, published by the Commonwealth Institute of Valuers in January 1949, which focuses heavily on land valuation and compulsory acquisition with relatively little attention to investment property valuation.

Squirrel (2000) further notes that, in the late 1960s, the Commonwealth Institute of Valuers started to hand over their valuation courses to State technical schools with the second, seminal Australian valuation textbook, *Land Valuation and Compensation in Australia* by Rost and Collins, first published in 1971. The title and content of this seminal work echo the emphasis of Murray, focusing heavily on land valuation and compulsory acquisition though now including chapters on compound interest tables and capitalisation of rental values.

From the mid-1970s, the provision of valuation education evolved around Australia to become a degree-level offering, including the Royal Melbourne Institute of Technology (a forebear of RMIT University), the University of Queensland offering the longstanding course at the Gatton Agricultural College, the University of Western Sydney offering the longstanding course at the Hawkesbury Agricultural College and the University of South Australia offering the longstanding course at the South Australian Institute of Technology. Over time, further Universities started to offer degree-level valuation courses, including QUT, Sunshine Coast, Bond, UNSW and Deakin.

An emphasis on statutory valuation practice in University valuation courses is now long gone, with most University programs now including economics, marketing, accounting, law, finance, building, planning and valuation, with a focus on valuation standards, together with first and final year industry socialisation and application courses with the property specific content monitored by API and/or RICS through the accreditation process.

The third seminal Australian valuation textbook, Whipple's magnum opus *Property Valuation and Analysis,* was published in 1995 and adopted a very different approach with extensive coverage of investment property valuation and discounted cash flow, aligning much more closely with the principal textbooks published in the UK and USA.

A fourth Australian valuation textbook, *Specialist Valuations in Australia and New Zealand* was published by API in 1996, with the fifth Australian valuation textbook, *Valuation Principles and Practice*, edited by Westwood, published in 1997, being a multi-authored text written by practitioners with the second edition published in 2007.

This reflected the shift in predominant employment of valuers from the State Valuer General's offices to the private sector and the shift in emphasis of practice from a statutory-based framework to a standards-based framework. Finally, in 2007, an Australian version of the US Appraisal Institute's *The Valuation of Real Estate—the Australia Edition* was published.

This book is an introductory text following in the style of Murray and Rost and Collins, being a companion to the third edition of *Principles and Practice of Property Valuation in Australia,* a multi-authored text edited by the author and also published by Routledge in 2022, which is a deeper analysis of key principles underlying property valuation and current techniques and issues in the practice of property valuation for major sectors of the Australian property market.

Reflecting the century-long transition from a statutory-based framework to a standards-based framework, this book is the first Australian valuation textbook to place valuation within the context of the International Valuation Standards, relegating *Spencer* to a value definition of relevance only for statutory valuation matters and acknowledging the primacy of discounted cash flow for investment property valuation.

Interestingly, the historical supremacy of the *Spencer* definition of market value may be argued to have delayed the adoption of valuation standards by the Australian valuation profession with the skepticism towards that not supported by case law delaying the adoption of discounted cash flow by the Australian valuation profession for many years until clients insisted on its use.

A century on and entry to the valuation profession is commonly through completion of a three-year degree program at a University accredited by API and/or RICS followed by completion of a professional practice program administered by API or RICS. The number of valuers practicing in the offices of State Valuer Generals is now very low, with the vast majority now working in private practice either as sole principals, in small firms, in larger state or national firms or within multi-national firms such as CBRE, JLL and Colliers. Accordingly, statutory valuation practice, being valuation for rating, taxation and compulsory acquisition, has now become a specialism warranting a separate textbook, with this textbook focusing on valuation for the current principal forms of practice being valuation for secured lending purposes and valuation for financial reporting purposes.

2.3 What is a valuation?

In a joint publication with the PCA and REI, the API defines valuation as follows:

(*a*) *the process of estimating value;*
(*b*) *the prediction of the value of an asset at a point in time, depending on the purpose for which the valuation is required.* (API, 2007, page 122)

However, in the modern world of valuation standards, that definition of valuation adopted within the standards is paramount.

Valuation is defined in the IVS Glossary (IVSC, 2021) as follows:

The act or process of determining an opinion or conclusion of value of an asset on a stated basis of value at a specified date in compliance with IVS.

(20.24, page 8)

The IVS definition of a valuation is framed as a process leading to an outcome but does not specify what the elements of the process should be. However, the IVS Framework (IVSC, 2021) notes:

In order for a valuation to be compliant with IVS the valuer must comply with all the requirements contained within IVS.

(10.2, page 10)

The RICS Red Book (RICS, 2021a) definition of valuation goes further to include both verbal and written valuations, with the latter anticipated to include elements of inspection, investigation, enquiries, formation of an opinion and provision of a written form:

> *An opinion of the value of an asset or liability on a stated basis, at a specified date. If supplied in written form, all valuation advice given by members is subject to at least some of the requirements of the Red Book Global Standards—there are no exemptions. Unless limitations are agreed in the terms of engagement, a valuation will be provided after an inspection, and any further investigations and enquiries that are appropriate, having regard to the nature of the asset and the purpose of the valuation.*
>
> (page 13)

The RICS Red Book (RICS, 2021a) further clarifies *specified date* with the following definition of valuation date:

> *The date on which the opinion of value applies. The valuation date should also include the time at which it applies if the value of the type of asset can change materially in the course of a single day.*
>
> (page 13)

which may be distinguishable from the date of the valuation report being defined in the RICS Red Book as

> *The date on which the valuer signs the report.*
>
> (RICS, 2021a, page 8)

with VPS3 in the RICS Red Book noting:

> *If there has been a material change in market conditions, or in the circumstances of a property, asset or portfolio, between the valuation date (where this is earlier than the date of the report) and the date of report, the valuer should draw attention to this.*
>
> (RICS, 2021a, page 55)

A valuation may be distinguished from a valuation review, with IVSC historically defining a valuation review as follows:

> *The act or process of considering and reporting on a valuation undertaken by another party, which may or may not require the reviewer to provide their own valuation opinion.*
>
> (IVSC, 2013, page 9)

In a joint publication with the PCA and REI, the API amplifies the definition of valuation review as follows:

> *The principal characteristic all valuation reviews have in common is that one Valuer exercises impartial judgment in considering the work of another Valuer. A valuation review may support the same valuation conclusion in the valuation under review or it may result in disagreement with that value conclusion. Valuation reviews provide a credibility check*

on the valuation as well as a check on the strength of the work of the Valuer who developed it, as regards the Valuer's knowledge, experience, and independence.

(API, 2007, page 122)

Therefore, while that which is a valuation review appears clear, that which is a valuation appears less clear. It may be contended that a valuation includes elements of inspection, investigation, enquiries, formation of an opinion and provision of an opinion. However, the form of the inspection may be external or internal and the provision of an opinion may be verbal or written, though criteria apply if the valuation is to be compliant with IVS and/or the RICS Red Book.

2.4 The valuation profession

The valuation profession is comprised, unsurprisingly, of valuers who may be assembled within the valuation professional bodies.

2.4.1 What is a valuer?

In a joint publication with the PCA and REI, the API defines a valuer as follows:

A person who is:

(a) registered/licensed/approved to carry out property or plant and machinery valuations under any State, Territory or Commonwealth legislation; and/or
(b) a member of the Australian Property Institute who is accredited as a Certified Practising Valuer. (API, 2007, page 123)

However, today only Queensland and Western Australia still operate a valuer registration system (www.vrbq.qld.gov.au and www.commerce.wa.gov.au/consumer-protection/licensing-land-valuers) and, in the modern world of valuation work based on valuation standards, it is the definition of a valuer that is adopted within the standards which are paramount.

Valuer is defined in the IVS Glossary (IVSC, 2021) as follows:

A "valuer" is an individual, group of individuals or individual within an entity, regardless of whether employed (internal) or engaged (contracted/external), possessing the necessary qualifications, ability and experience to execute a valuation in an objective, unbiased, ethical and competent manner. In some jurisdictions, licensing is required before one can act as a valuer.

(20.30, page 9)

The RICS Red Book Glossary (RICS, 2021a) further defines internal valuer as:

A valuer who is in the employ of either the enterprise that owns the assets, or the accounting firm responsible for preparing the enterprise's financial records and/or reports. An internal valuer is generally capable of meeting the requirements of independence and professional objectivity in accordance with PS2 section 3, but may not always be able to satisfy additional criteria for independence specific to certain types of assignment, for example under PS 2 paragraph 3.4.

(page 10)

and external valuer as:

> *A valuer who, together with any associates, has no material links with the client, an agent acting on behalf of the client or the subject of the assignment.*

(page 9)

The IVSC definition of valuer is further explained in *A Competency Framework for Professional Valuers* (IVSC, 2012b). To demonstrate competence, a professional valuer must be able to demonstrate:

(a) *professional knowledge;*
(b) *professional skills; and*
(c) *professional values, ethics, and behaviour.*

(page 4)

which are gained through initial professional development and continuing professional development.

The IVSC competency framework requirements for professional knowledge and professional skills comprise:

Initial professional development

1. University-level degree education or equivalent such as an extended period of practical experience accompanied by formal or informal study to a level required to obtain a degree;
2. education on valuation that includes at least the following subjects:
   a. economic theory and principles;
   b. financial markets;
   c. recognised valuation concepts and principles;
   d. theory and application of valuation methods used in the market in which the person intends to operate;
   e. legal framework relevant to that market; and
   f. the technical standards and guidance relevant to that market; and
3. training in the fundamental principles of ethical conduct as identified in the IVSC *Code of Ethical Principles for Professional Valuers* (considered further below); and
4. experience in applying the matters in 2 and 3 in a supervised work environment with a minimum period of 1,500 hours over two years suggested; and

Continuing professional development

Demonstrated commitment to a program of CPD throughout their period of practice, which is relevant to their chosen area of practice. This may be accomplished by a combination of attendance at training events and self-study, with a minimum of 50 hours of structured professional development recommended in any three-year period. (pages 5–6)

The IVSC competency framework requirements for professional values, ethics and behaviour comprise:

Character—an individual shall be able to demonstrate that they are of good character and reputation;

Conduct—a professional valuer will conduct themselves in accordance with ethical principles as identified in the IVSC *Code of Ethical Principles for Professional Valuers*;

Accountability—a professional valuer will be accountable for any failure to comply with the ethical principles of conduct or the competent application of professional knowledge and skills; and

Legal compliance—a professional valuer will comply with the conditions of any statutory system of licensing or other regulatory requirements relating to the market or sector in which they operate. (page 7)

Therefore, in an Australian context, a person who has completed an accredited degree and completed the professional practice assessment of API or RICS and who complies with the ethical and CPD requirements of the relevant body may be considered to have fulfilled the IVSC requirements to be a valuer.

A valuation reviewer is defined in the IVSC Glossary (IVSC, 2021) as follows:

> A *"valuation reviewer" is a professional valuer engaged to review the work of another valuer. As part of a valuation review, that professional may perform certain valuation procedures and/or provide an opinion of value.*
>
> (20.28, page 8)

with a valuation reviewer needing to first be a professional valuer as considered previously.

2.4.2 Role of the valuer

Concerning the role of a valuer, Shapiro et al. (2019) succinctly note that those involved with property might need to know the value of that property, and so may require the services of a valuer to provide a valuation of that property, with valuers potentially instructed to advise:

- owners on the price or rent that they should ask for their property;
- buyers on offer prices;
- tenants on the rent that they should pay;
- lenders on the value of property for loan security;
- owners dispossessed under compulsory powers on their right to compensation; and
- owners on their liability for property taxation.

Millington (2000) notes that valuers are able to apply local knowledge to the determination of value but within the context of a wide range of local, state, national and international issues that affect value. Shapiro et al. (2019) consider the services of a professionally qualified valuer to be essential because:

- the market for property is imperfect;
- landed property is heterogenous;
- the legal interests therein are complex; and
- the laws relating to landed property are complicated,

to which Millington (2000) adds that the role of the valuer includes exercising judgment on the value impact of differences, such as may arise from legal issues.

Blackledge (2017) notes that valuers not only provide valuations but may also advise clients on policy or strategy, recommend actions and negotiate with counter parties with the main tasks undertaken by valuers including:

- receiving and confirming instructions;
- inspecting the property and its location;
- liaising with the client's other professional advisors where necessary, such as accountants, lawyers and management consultants;
- researching and analysing all relevant information;
- undertaking calculations;
- arriving at an opinion of value;
- reporting the results of the research and providing the valuation;
- if required, negotiating with the other party's representatives to reach an agreement;
- if required, instructing solicitors on behalf of a client or employer; and
- if required, providing investment and property advisory and management services (page 25).

which may, in addition to providing valuations, assist clients in various ways including:

- landlord and tenant matters—including rent review, lease renewal and associated dispute resolution;
- investment and fund management matters—including sale and purchase, portfolio selection and management and creation and implementation of investment strategy;
- property management matters—including maintenance and repair and insurance;
- research matters—including market research and specific topic research;
- agency matters—including marketing and sale or letting of all types of property;
- planning matters—including development, sustainability and regeneration to optimize a property's potential; and
- facilities management and management consulting matters—including service delivery and business strategy application to property for corporate clients (page 26).

The advice of a valuer is likely to be a combination of advice concerning three principal elements—a property market sector, a geography and a valuation purpose.

2.4.2.1 Property market sector

The major property market sectors were outlined in Chapter 1, including:

- residential sector;
- office sector;
- retail sector;
- industrial sector;
- leisure sector; and
- rural sector.

A valuer may choose to practice across several property sectors (such as regional office, retail and industrial), to focus on one sector (such as CBD office including all grades) or to specialise in a sub-set of one sector (such as international five-star hotels).

2.4.2.2　*Geography*

Property market sectors exist across all geographies—from State capital CBD to metropolitan suburb to regional city to country town to rural village—with the nature and combination of property market sectors varying by settlement size and the nature of valuation practice similarly generally trending from specialist through focused to generalist.

A valuer may choose to practice in the CBD, the metropolitan suburbs, regional cities or rural villages or may choose to transcend geographies by focusing on one sector (such as regional shopping centres in State capital cities) or specialise in one sub-set of a sector (such as data centres across Australia).

2.4.2.3　*Valuation purpose*

Valuation purposes may be contended to comprise valuation for owner occupation, investment, development, financial reporting, secured lending and other purposes.

2.4.2.3.1　VALUATION FOR OWNER OCCUPATION

A valuation for owner occupation is a valuation of a property for a client who owns and occupies the subject property being valued.

Valuations for owner occupation may occur in any property sector in any geography, with the most common being valuations for private individuals for residential property or rural property or for businesses for smaller commercial, retail or industrial property.

As many owner-occupied properties are debt-financed or held on balance sheets (consolidated statements of financial position) by businesses, valuations for owner occupation may often arise through valuations for secured lending or through valuations for financial reporting purposes.

2.4.2.3.2　VALUATION FOR INVESTMENT

A valuation for investment is a valuation of a property for a client who owns a property that is leased to other parties as an investment.

Valuations for investment may occur in any property sector in any geography, with the most common being valuations of office, retail and industrial property for private individuals, businesses, property funds, superannuation funds and AREITs.

As many investment properties are debt-financed or held on balance sheets (consolidated statements of financial position) by businesses, valuations for investment may often arise through valuations for secured lending or through valuations for financial statements.

Valuations for investment purposes may be complex, with readers referred to Baum et al. (2018) and Wyatt (2023) for greater detail.

2.4.2.3.3　VALUATION FOR DEVELOPMENT

A valuation for development is a valuation of a property for a client who owns a property that is to be developed, which may include vacant land upon which a property is to be constructed and occupied or leased or an existing property that is to be demolished for redevelopment or refurbished for occupation or leasing.

Valuations for development may occur in any property sector in any geography, with the most common being valuations of residential, office, retail and industrial property for private individuals, businesses, property developers, property funds, superannuation funds and AREITs.

As many development properties are debt-financed or held on balance sheets (consolidated statements of financial position) by businesses, valuations for development may often arise through valuations for secured lending or through valuations for financial reporting purposes.

Valuations for development purposes are complex and specialist, with readers referred to Wyatt (2023) and Isaac and O'Leary (2013) for greater detail and to IVS410 *Development property* (IVSC, 2021).

2.4.2.3.4 VALUATION FOR FINANCIAL REPORTING PURPOSES

A valuation for financial reporting purposes is a valuation of a property for a client to include in financial statements.

Valuations for financial reporting purposes may occur in any property sector in any geography, with the most common being valuations of property for medium and large businesses, both Australian and multi-national such as Harvey Norman or Coca-Cola.

Valuations for financial reporting purposes are complex and specialist, with readers referred to *Valuations for financial reporting purposes* by Stewart in Parker (2022), VPGA1 *Valuations for inclusion in financial statements* in the Red Book (RICS, 2021a) and AVGP302 *Valuations of Real Property, Plant and Equipment for Use in Australian Financial Reports* (API, 2021a) for greater detail.

2.4.2.3.5 VALUATION FOR SECURED LENDING PURPOSES

A valuation for secured lending purposes is a valuation of a property for a lender who will be using the property as security for a loan to a borrower.

Valuations for secured lending purposes may occur in any property sector in any geography, with the most common being valuations of property for international lenders, large Australian lenders and smaller lending institutions such as HSBC, NAB and Bank of Queensland.

Valuations for secured lending purposes are complex and specialist, with readers referred to *Valuations for secured lending purposes* by Turner in Parker (2022), to VPGA2 *Valuations of interests for secured lending* in the Red Book (RICS, 2021a) and ANZVGP112 *Valuations for Mortgage and Loan Security Purposes* (API, 2021b) for greater detail.

2.4.2.3.6 VALUATION FOR OTHER PURPOSES

While there is a wide range of other purposes for which a valuation may be required, the most common may be contended to be for acquisition/disposal and statutory purposes.

A valuation for acquisition/disposal purposes is a valuation of a property for a client who is contemplating either buying or selling a property. A valuation for statutory purposes is a valuation for either property taxation (such as land tax or as the basis for rates or levies) or compulsory acquisition where the Government acquires land for infrastructure development (such as building an airport, highway, hospital or school) and pays the dispossessed owner compensation.

Valuations for acquisition/disposal and statutory purposes may occur in any property sector in any geography, with valuations for acquisitions/disposal being for a wide range of clients, including private individuals, small and large businesses, Government and the not-for-profit sector. Valuations for statutory purposes may include unusual property sectors such as churches, banana plantations, river and sea beds and mountain sides in remote locations, with clients usually being either the land owner or a Government instrumentality such as the Department of Defence, Transport for NSW or Brisbane City Council.

Valuations for statutory purposes are complex and specialist, with readers referred to *Valuations for statutory purposes* by Parker in Parker (2022) and ANZVGP113 *Valuations for Compensation and Compulsory Acquisition* (API, 2021c) for greater detail.

2.4.2.4 Combination of property market sector, geography and valuation purpose

The combination of property market sector, geography and valuation purpose provides an enormously wide range of diverse career opportunities for valuers. For example, a valuer may choose to undertake residential valuation in the western suburbs of Sydney for debt lending purposes, internet fulfillment logistics property valuations in each State capital city for financial statement purposes or resort valuations for acquisition/disposal anywhere in Australia.

However, as Isaac and O'Leary (2012) note, where valuers tend to become specialists in a particular type of work and in a particular geographic area, when they step outside those bounds, they have a professional obligation to consider their ability to undertake such a valuation task or whether they require assistance from a relevant specialist. Accordingly, a valuer who specialises in office valuations in Brisbane may not be appropriately skilled to undertake a shopping centre valuation in Melbourne and so should seek specialist assistance from a Melbourne shopping centre valuer or decline the instruction.

2.4.3 Valuation professional bodies

For the purposes of a practicing valuer in Australia, the principal professional bodies are the national professional body, the Australian Property Institute (API), and the international professional body, the Royal Institution of Chartered Surveyors (RICS).

API was founded in Adelaide in 1926 and is the professional body representing residential, commercial and plant and machinery valuers, analysts, fund managers and property lawyers. API has close to 8,000 members with offices in each State capital city. API publishes standards, guidance documents and a code of ethics to which members are required to adhere and administers a regulatory function to address non-adherence (www.api.org.au).

RICS was founded in London in 1868 and is the international professional body representing those working in the built environment, construction, land, property and real estate. RICS has over 130,000 members with offices across the world, including Sydney. RICS publishes standards, guidance documents and Rules of Conduct to which members are required to adhere and administers a regulatory function to address non-adherence (www.rics.org).

The principal route of entry to each professional body is common, comprising completion of an accredited degree followed by a period of supervised professional practice, with each body offering reciprocity of membership.

Further details on each professional body may be found at www.api.org.au and www.rics.org.

2.4.4 Summary—the valuation profession

The world of the IVSC-defined valuer is inextricably linked to the worlds of the principal professional bodies, API and RICS, who supervise the education programs and professional experience programs that facilitate qualification as a valuer and then provide standards, ethics and regulation that facilitate the operation of the valuation profession. Interestingly, while there is clarity as to what a valuer is, that which is a valuation is less clear.

2.5 Valuation standards

Following the trend to globalisation, the second half of the last century saw a journey towards one common basis for valuation worldwide, resulting in the relevant valuation standards for valuers practising in Australia being those promulgated by the International Valuation Standards Council (IVSC), RICS and API.

The following draws heavily on Parker (2016), which is duly acknowledged here rather than individually referenced through the section and to which readers are referred for a deeper consideration.

2.5.1 Globalisation and valuation

Globalisation increasingly gained pace following the end of the Second World War, with the Bretton Woods Agreement on international monetary policy, commerce and finance, the emergence of container shipping and the growth in international air travel as examples of global developments facilitating increasing international integration in trade and commerce. The late twentieth-century developments in communications, computing and the advent of the internet facilitated even greater globalisation in banking, finance and investment, contributing to the current very high level of interconnectedness between the world's major economies.

The establishment of the International Monetary Fund, World Bank and Basel Committee on Banking Supervision provide examples of the impact of globalisation in the financial markets, with groups such as the G20 providing an example of governmental globalisation. The creation of the European Union led to the free movement of labour and capital across Europe and a common currency, with the fall of the Berlin Wall leading to the creation of independent eastern European states, which further enhanced European movement of labour and capital.

A series of bilateral and later regional trade agreements between countries, the formation of GATT and the World Trade Organisation have each fostered the development of international trade and the growth of multinational corporations such as HSBC and Airbus, making it economically feasible for a European-based company to manufacture goods in China or India and sell to world markets in USA or Africa, either directly through the supply chain leading to the world's shopping centres or indirectly through fulfilment of internet orders.

The increasing impact of globalisation has the effect of reducing the significance of national and political borders and increasing the significance of economic integration. The interconnectedness of the world's major economies was glaringly apparent during the Global Financial Crisis towards the end of the first decade of the twenty-first century, when problems arising in the US property, banking and finance markets rapidly became problems for the property, banking and finance markets of each of the world's major economies.

In the context of property, the growth in multinational corporations has significantly increased the amount of property in other countries held by businesses for the purposes of operations. As a result of globalisation, such multinational corporations as HSBC and Airbus have become significant property owners and occupiers in a vast number of countries around the world. Similarly, property investment has rapidly globalised in the last fifty years with the emergence of sovereign wealth funds in the 1970s building diversified global property portfolios and many pension funds, superannuation funds, REITs and other property fund managers seeking to invest outside their country of origin, resulting in many of the major office, shopping centre, hotel and warehouse properties of large cities around the world now being owned by foreign investors.

The globalisation of property has been mirrored by the globalisation of property services groups, with the UK Richard Ellis merging with the US Coldwell Banker to become CBRE and the UK Jones Lang Wootton merging with the US LaSalle Partners in 1999 to become Jones Lang LaSalle or JLL, with 30,000 staff in 750 locations in 60 countries (Babawale, 2012a).

Consistent with trends in other parts of the economy worldwide, the emergence of both multinational corporations and international property investors has created the demand for international valuation services, and the merger of major national firms into international property services groups has created the supply of international valuation services.

2.5.1.1 *International Financial Reporting Standards*

In an increasingly global marketplace, international comparability of information is essential to enable the effective allocation of scarce resources. Accordingly, global businesses require a common basis for company accounts that is understandable, comparable, reliable and relevant for internal and external users across different countries.

As globalisation evolved, it became apparent that national accounting standards would be both inadequate for and complicate international business and investment. The apparent need for international accounting standards led to the formation of the International Accounting Standards Committee (IASC) in 1973 by accounting bodies from Australia, Canada, France, Germany, Mexico, the Netherlands, the United Kingdom, Ireland and the United States. The aim of the IASC was to achieve consistency internationally in definitions, measurement and treatment of transactions in the course of business or investment to enable financial reporting that permitted cross-country comparability and appreciation. (Dugeri et al., 2012) Those standards issued by the IASC between 1973 and 2001 comprise the International Accounting Standards (IAS).

Since 2001, the International Accounting Standards Board (IASB) succeeded the IASC and assumed the full standard-setting role for the accountancy profession worldwide, with those standards issued by the IASB from 2001 comprising the International Financial Reporting Standards (IFRS). (Dugeri et al., 2012) The objectives of the IASB include:

* to develop, in the public interest, a single set of high-quality, understandable, enforceable and globally accepted financial reporting standards based on clearly articulated principles;
* to promote the use and rigorous application of those standards;
* to take account of the needs of a range of sizes and types of entities in diverse economic settings; and
* to promote and facilitate the adoption of IFRS through the convergence of national accounting standards and IFRSs (IFRS, 2013, para 6, page A10).

The IASB achieves its objectives primarily by developing and publishing IFRSs and promoting their use (IFRS, 2013, para 7, page A10). IFRSs set out recognition, measurement, presentation and disclosure requirements dealing with transactions and events that are important in general purpose financial statements (IFRS, 2013, para 8, page A11), prepared by the entity (IAS1, para 2, page A541) on the going concern assumption (IAS1, para 25, page A547).

Those IASs and IFRSs of principal relevance to the valuation of real property assets include:

IAS16	*Property, Plant and Equipment*
IAS17	*Leases*
IAS36	*Impairment of Assets*
IAS40	*Investment Property*
IFRS5	*Non-Current Assets Held for Sale and Discontinued Operations*
IFRS13	*Fair Value Measurement*

Currently, around 100 countries have adopted IFRS, including the European Union, Australia, Canada, Montenegro and Nepal. However, major economies such as the USA, Japan and India are yet to require IFRS for listed companies.

The benefits of IFRS, as a common basis for accounting worldwide, include the provision of high-quality, transparent and comparable information in financial reporting to help investors, other participants in the various capital markets of the world and other users of financial information make economic decisions. (IFRS, 2013) Such transparency and comparability aid the global flow of capital between countries, support national economies and improve international competitiveness as well as reducing financial reporting costs, improving the quality of financial reporting and providing more useful information to decision-makers.

Therefore, for such multinational corporations as HSBC and Airbus and for international property investors such as sovereign wealth funds, pension funds, superannuation funds, REITs and other property fund managers, who have become significant property owners and occupiers in a vast number of countries around the world, IFRS effectively provides one common basis for accounting worldwide facilitating the ultimate "apples with apples" comparison for the purposes of decision making.

2.5.1.2 *Impact on valuation*

While IFRS effectively provides one common basis for accounting worldwide, in order for IFRS to provide a reliable decision-making basis in the context of property, the provision of those inputs concerning property valuation also needs to be undertaken on one common basis worldwide.

The global client base driving the adoption of international standards in accounting and banking also required the same for valuation, given that valuation is the basis for lending decisions, financial reporting of multinational companies, cross-border property investment, securitisation of real estate and so forth (Babawale, 2012b).

Essentially, the principal drivers for the introduction and adoption of international valuation standards include:

- the requirement of Governments for valuations of publicly owned assets for the purpose of accountability, measurement of performance and financial transparency;
- the trend towards the privatisation of Government enterprises;
- the development of international accounting standards;
- emerging economies with no established skill or depth in real estate appraisal;
- the Basle Committee on bank lending;
- world trade agreements, designed to balance world trade practices;
- the move towards a fair value accounting model;
- the activities of the United Nations Conference on Trade and Development, which is working towards the harmonisation of accounting and other professional practices; and
- the need for performance measurement of both investment property and owner-occupied property to contribute to the measurement of property, portfolio and company management performance (Edge, 2001).

While it may be contended that the principal benefit of converging valuation regulation internationally with accounting regulation is the efficient and effective functioning and stability of global capital and debt markets, several further benefits of global regulatory convergence may be identified including:

- improving the comparability of financial information, with consistent valuation practices supporting the transparency and credibility of valuations in financial reporting globally, so increasing the potential mobility of capital across national borders and providing all decision-makers with consistent, high-quality, reliable information with which to make informed investment, resource and policy decisions;

- improving the auditability of financial statements, with the adoption and application of globally consistent valuation standards providing auditors with clear benchmarks to assess whether valuations included in financial statements are reasonably founded;
- reducing the effects of systemic risk, with a reduction in the threats to the global financial systems of such behaviours as over confidence in rising markets and extreme risk aversion in falling markets which may heighten systemic risk in globally connected markets such as banking, insurance and securities;
- reducing information costs, with multinational companies and global property investors being able to measure assets consistently in different countries, which reduces the cost of preparing financial statements and the need to reconcile differing valuation approaches;
- decreasing the opportunities for regulatory arbitrage by removing opportunities for pricing differentials that do not have a basis in economic fundamentals but instead arise from different valuation practices;
- providing an underpinning for a global regulatory system, through which global bodies such as the G20 can develop global solutions to address global issues with regulatory convergence facilitating intergovernmental co-operation, greater institutional linkages and international policy integration; and
- providing additional benefits for developing and emerging economies through the adoption and implementation of existing high-quality, internationally accepted standards recognised by international bodies, governments, investors, corporations, lenders and so forth (IVSC, 2014).

The development of international valuation standards that are consistent with IFRS contributes to achieving such benefits and provides investors, regulators, and users of valuations with that which they seek, being consistency, clarity, reliability and transparency in valuation reporting worldwide (Edge, 2001) as:

> *Clients need to understand that a valuation produced in Massachusetts, Manchester, Melbourne, Moscow or Matabeleland is reliable in its standards and its methodologies.*
>
> (Gilbertson, 2002, page 12)

Like the journey to achieve one common basis for accounting worldwide through IFRS, the journey to achieve one common basis for valuation worldwide was an evolutionary process spanning almost half a century.

2.5.2 Evolution of valuation standard setting

The journey to achieve one common basis for valuation worldwide has been an evolutionary process spanning almost half a century, being a journey fraught with the booms and busts of independent and interdependent cyclical national property markets worldwide that has been contended to comprise the following principal phases: (Dugeri et al., 2012; Edge, 2001; Mackmin, 1999; Babawale, 2012a, 2012b; French, 2003; Mallinson and French, 2000; IVSC, 2015; Banfield, 2014)

1. **initial development of valuation standards in the UK;**

   arising from the 1970s' UK recession and the 1974 UK property crash, which precipitated a loss of credibility for the valuation profession, RICS established a joint working party with the Institute of Chartered Accountants in England and Wales in 1973 to report on the valuation of property assets, followed by the formation of the Asset Valuation Standards Committee in 1974 which developed guidance notes;

following Greenwell's (1976) criticism of traditional capitalisation of income methods as incorrect, illogical and by deduction, leading to inaccurate valuations, RICS responded by establishing a research programme into valuation methods and published *Guidance Notes on the Valuation of Assets* in 1976, the original RICS Red Book, being endorsed by the Bank of England, London Stock Exchange, City Panel on Takeovers and Mergers, banking associations and others;

the Red Book has been regularly updated since, including reflection of the RICS-initiated Trott Report, Mallinson Report (incorporated in 1996 RICS Red Book) and Carsberg Report;

2. **followed by the development of regional European valuation standards:**

the European Group of Valuers of Fixed Assets (TEGOVOFA) was created in 1977, now The European Group of Valuer Associations (TEGoVA), which created a set of regional European valuation standards published in 1981 as the Blue Book or Guide Bleu;

3. **and development of valuation standards internationally:**

the International Assets Valuation Committee (TIAVSC) was created in 1981/82, which metamorphosed into the International Valuation Standards Committee in 1996 and the International Valuation Standards Council (IVSC) in 2008, having published the first International Valuation Standards in 1985;

since 2000, IVSC published IVSs reviewed in accordance with IFRS, reflecting international regulatory convergence, with the process coming full circle as the 2003 edition of the RICS Red Book adopted and supported IVS's; and

in 2014, IVSC Trustees commissioned an independent assessment *to ensure the organisation is equipped for the next phase of its development.* (IVSC, 2015) A Review Group was created, which assessed the governance, financial stability, processes and outputs of IVSC and made recommendations for improvements for implementation.

Therefore, valuation standards developed out of valuation practice rather than out of valuation theory, having evolved independently of economic theory, finance theory and capital market theory. Significantly, the development of valuation standards worldwide was initially undertaken by national valuation professional bodies independently or in association and then internationally for around thirty years, but in a property vacuum until 2000 when convergence with the common basis for accounting worldwide was undertaken, reflecting the demands of globalisation and leading to the evolution of one common basis for valuation worldwide.

2.5.3 IVSC standards

The IVSC is an independent, non-profit organisation incorporated in the USA that has two principal functions:

- to develop and promulgate globally recognised financial standards, acceptable to the world's capital market organisations, regulators and market participants; and
- to act as a global focus for the valuation profession,

which came into sharp focus following the Global Financial Crisis of 2007–2009 when G20 leaders called for standard setters to improve valuation principles and to achieve clarity and consistency worldwide (IVSC, 2009).

The objective of the IVSC is to build confidence and public trust in the valuation process by creating a framework for the delivery of credible valuation opinions by suitably trained valuation professionals acting in an ethical manner (IVSC, 2013).

In its policy paper on *Global Regulatory Convergence and the Valuation Profession*, IVSC (2014) succinctly stated:

> *With many corporations and financial institutions now operating globally, convergence of the diverse systems of national regulation of the financial markets is essential for both effective regulation and to facilitate economic growth.*
>
> *Consistent and effective regulation is important in promoting the comparability of financial information, minimising the effects of systemic economic risks, and helping to create a level playing field for international competition.*
>
> *For the valuation profession, regulatory convergence includes the global adoption and implementation of high-quality internationally accepted standards for the undertaking and reporting of those valuations that are relied upon by investors and regulators of the global financial markets.*
>
> (p. 1)

Acting in the public interest, IVSC contends that valuation is a key input into financial information relied upon by investors and used to support decisions in financial markets, such as financial reporting, managing the solvency of financial institutions, supporting lending or other investment decisions and pricing units in collective investment schemes, that each have a direct impact on the public interest and that each will benefit from global regulatory convergence (IVSC, 2014).

IVSC operates by consulting with valuation users to identify their concerns, working with professional valuers to identify issues and projects and then developing and promoting solutions (such a standards, valuation applications or technical information papers) following an established process of public exposure and consultation. Enforcement of compliance with IVSs is, however, not undertaken by IVSC but by those regulators and national valuation professional organisations adopting the IVSs (IVSC, 2012a).

This book is based on the International Valuation Standards effective 31 January 2022 (IVSC, 2021) which comprises the following key sections:

- Introduction—including the core principles of valuation;
- Glossary—defining terms used in IVS which must then be read as having that meaning attributed by IVSC in the definition;
- IVS Framework—consisting of general principles for valuers following IVS regarding compliance, objectivity, judgment, competence and acceptable departures from IVS;
- General Standards—setting forth the requirements for the conduct of all valuation assignments:

    - IVS101   Scope of Work;
    - IVS102   Investigation and Compliance;
    - IVS103   Reporting;
    - IVS104   Bases of Value;
    - IVS105   Valuation Approaches and Methods; and

- Asset Standards—setting forth requirements related to specific assets, including the following of relevance to property valuation:

  - IVS300   Plant and Equipment;
  - IVS400   Real Property Interests; and
  - IVS410   Development Property.

International valuation standards are dynamic, being regularly amended and updated such that primary reliance should always be placed on the most recent standards, which may be found at www.ivsc.org.

2.5.4 RICS standards

RICS publishes a vast amount of valuation guidance, research and information, which is too extensive to consider in full in this book but may be found by searching the RICS website at www.rics.org.

The principal valuation standards publication by RICS is *RICS Valuation—Global Standards* (RICS, 2021a), commonly referred to as the Red Book, first published in 1976. This book is based on the edition effective 31 January 2022, which comprises the following sections:

- Introduction—including the purpose, coverage and structure of the Red Book;
- Glossary—defining terms used in the Red Book, which must then be read as having that meaning attributed by RICS in the definition;
- Professional Standards—being mandatory (unless otherwise stated) for all RICS members providing written valuations:

  - PS1   Compliance with standards where a written valuation is provided;
  - PS2   Ethics, competency, objectivity and disclosures;

- Valuation technical and performance standards—containing specific, mandatory (unless otherwise stated) requirements and related implementation guidance directed to the provision of a valuation that is IVS compliant:

  - VPS1   Terms of engagement (scope of work);
  - VPS2   Inspections, investigations and records;
  - VPS3   Valuation reports;
  - VPS4   Bases of value, assumptions and special assumptions;
  - VPS5   Valuation approaches and methods; and

- Valuation applications—being advisory and not mandatory, providing further implementation guidance in the following specific areas:

  - VPGA1   Valuation for inclusion in financial statements;
  - VPGA2   Valuation of interests for secured lending;
  - VPGA3   Valuation of business and business interests;
  - VPGA4   Valuation of individual trade-related properties;
  - VPGA5   Valuation of plant and equipment;
  - VPGA6   Valuation of intangible assets;
  - VPGA7   Valuation of personal property, including arts and antiques;
  - VPGA8   Valuation of real property interests;
  - VPGA9   Identification of portfolios, collections and groups of properties; and
  - VPGA10   Matters that may give rise to material valuation uncertainty.

The RICS Red Book is fully compliant with and consistent with IVS standards, which are included at the back of the RICS Red Book (RICS, 2021a). The RICS Red Book is regularly amended and updated such that primary reliance should always be placed on the most recent version, which may be found at www.rics.org.

2.5.5 API guidance papers and protocols

The API does not publish valuation standards but adopts IVS in full. Since 1 July 2021, API publishes Guidance Papers and Protocols, with Guidance Papers not being mandatory, providing a guide and measure of acceptable professional practice and conduct by an API member conveying elements of what is considered competent professional practice (www.api.org.au).

While not mandatory, a departure from or non-compliance with a Guidance Paper must be stated in an API member's report or advice, including:

- the reasons for the departure or non-compliance; and
- any impact that the departure or non-compliance may have on the content of the report,

with members advised to seek legal and/or other advice before departing from practice recommended in a Guidance Paper.

Thirty-nine Guidance Papers are listed on the API website as of 11 May 2023, including the following valuation guidance papers:

ANZVGP 101	Retrospective Valuations
ANZVGP 102	Market Value of Property, Plant and Equipment in a Business
ANZVGP 103	Addressing the Concept of Forced Sale
ANZVGP 104	Valuations for Insurance Purposes
ANZVGP 105	Valuation of Self Storage Facilities
ANZVGP 106	Valuation of Partial Interests of Property held within Co-ownership Structures
ANZVGP 107	Valuation of Accommodation Hotels
ANZVGP 108	Valuations for use in Offer Documents
ANZVGP 109	Valuation of Rural and Agribusiness Properties
ANZVGP 110	Considerations when forming an opinion of value when there is a shortage of market transactions
ANZVGP 111	Valuation Procedures—Real Property
ANZVGP 112	Valuations for Mortgage and Loan Security Purposes
ANZVGP 113	Valuations for Compensation and Compulsory Acquisition
ANZVGP 115	Contamination Issues
AVGP 301	Rental Valuations and Advice
AVGP 302	Valuations of Real Property, Plant and Equipment for Use in Australian Financial Reports
AVGP 304	Rental Determinations

API Guidance Papers and Protocols are regularly amended and updated such that primary reliance should always be placed on the most recent version, which may be found at www.api.org.au.

2.5.6 Summary—valuation standards

With emergence following the trend of globalisation and spurred by economic and market collapses, international valuation standards have now evolved into a compatible suite of documents that are aligned with international accounting standards and international financial reporting standards. As valuation professional organisations aligned to IVSC, both API and RICS adopt IVSC valuation standards in full, complemented by their own additional compatible and consistent standards and guidance papers, to provide the standards framework applicable to valuation practitioners in Australia today.

2.6 Ethical frameworks in valuation

Traditionally, valuation textbooks would include a discussion about the *art vs. science* debate, noting that the practice of valuation contains judgment which is an *art* as well as calculation which is a *science*, usually concluding that both are required to effectively practice valuation.

Today, while the role of spreadsheets and specialist valuation software programs have significantly increased the role of *science*, judgment is still required, and it is judgment that can make the largest difference to a valuation outcome. For example, after accumulating, analysing and adjusting comparable capitalisation rate evidence, the application requires a judgment as to whether the capitalisation rate for use in the valuation should be 4.5% or 4.75%, with the difference between the two resulting in a significant financial difference in the valuation.

Given the central importance of *art* or judgment in the valuation process, users of valuation services must have total confidence in the valuer exercising judgment which, by its nature, cannot be governed by quantitative requirements but only by qualitative requirements that are relevantly manifest in the codes of ethics promulgated by IVSC, RICS and API. Through the valuer's adherence to ethical standards, the users of valuation services can have confidence in a valuer's exercise of judgment.

2.6.1 IVSC code of ethical principles for professional valuers

In the Introduction to IVS, IVSC state 14 core principles of valuation, which include:

1. *Ethics—valuers must follow the ethical principles of integrity, objectivity, impartiality, confidentiality, competence and professionalism to promote and preserve the public trust and*
2. *Competency—at the time the valuation is submitted, valuers must have the technical skills and knowledge required to appropriately complete the valuation assignment.* (IVSC, 2021, page 2).

Ethics are further addressed in the IVSC publication *Code of Ethical Principles for Professional Valuers* (IVSC, 2011), supporting the IVSC's objective:

> to build confidence and public trust in the valuation process by creating a framework for the delivery of credible valuation opinions by suitably trained valuation professionals acting in an ethical manner.
>
> (IVSC, 2011, page 1)

IVSC achieves this objective by the provision of IVS and technical and professional guidance and by promoting the development of the valuation profession and ethical practices globally through the *Code of Ethical Principles for Professional Valuers*.

The *Code of Ethical Principles for Professional Valuers* comprises four elements:

* fundamental principles;
* fundamental principles—guidance;
* threats and safeguards (Appendix 1); and
* discussion of fundamental principles (Appendix 2).

2.6.1.1 Fundamental principles

The *Code of Ethical Principles for Professional Valuers* states:

> *It is fundamental to the integrity of the valuation process that those who rely on valuations have confidence that those valuations are provided by valuers who have the appropriate experience, skill and judgment, who act in a professional manner and who exercise their judgment free from any undue influence or bias.*
>
> (IVSC, 2011)

The fundamental principles consist of five principles of conduct to which a professional valuer is expected to adhere when providing a valuation service (IVSC, 2011):

- integrity—to be straightforward and honest in professional and business relationships, including statements or omissions of information that are materially false or misleading or made recklessly;
- objectivity—not to allow perceived or actual bias, conflict of interest, or undue influence or bias to override professional or business judgment, including acting for both parties in a transaction and providing a valuation for a third party on behalf of a major client;
- competence—to maintain, through continuing professional development, the professional knowledge and skill required to ensure that a client or employer receives a service that is based on current developments in practice, legislation, and valuation techniques;
- confidentiality—to respect the confidentiality of information acquired as a result of professional and business relationships and not to disclose such information to third parties without proper and specific authority (unless there is a legal or professional right or duty to disclose), nor to use information for the personal advantage of the professional valuer or third parties with particular awareness of inadvertent disclosure in a social environment; and
- professional behaviour—to act diligently and to produce work in a timely manner in accordance with applicable legal requirements, technical and professional standards. To always act in the public interest and to avoid any action that discredits the profession or makes disparaging references or unsubstantiated comparisons to the work of others (IVSC, 2011, page 3).

Each of the five principles of conduct is further explained in detail in Appendix 2 of the *Code of Ethical Principles for Professional Valuers (IVSC, 2011)*. Significantly, in terms of personal conduct outside of a professional work environment, Appendix 2 further states:

> *A professional valuer should avoid any action that may discredit the profession . . . this includes any action that a reasonable and informed third party, weighing all the specific facts and circumstances available to the professional valuer at that time, would be likely to conclude adversely affects the good reputation of the profession.*
>
> (IVSC, 2011, page 14)

2.6.1.2 Threats and safeguards

When a professional valuer identifies a potential threat to their ability to comply with the fundamental principles, they should evaluate the significance of that threat. Some threats may be capable of elimination or reduction to an acceptable level by taking appropriate safeguards, with appropriate being determined through the eyes of a reasonable and informed third party weighing all the specific facts and circumstances available at the time. If the threat to the professional valuer's ability to comply with the fundamental principles cannot be eliminated or reduced to an acceptable level, the valuation assignment should be declined or discontinued (IVSC, 2011, page 4).

The threats and safeguards in Appendix 1 identify the principal categories of threat that may compromise a professional valuer's ability to comply with the fundamental principles and the types of safeguards that may be appropriate to avoid or mitigate those threats (IVSC, 2011). The threats identified comprise:

- self-interest threat—where self-interest may inappropriately influence professional judgment;
- self-review threat—where a previous judgment may not be objectively reviewed;
- client conflict threat—where two or more clients may have opposing or conflicting interests in the outcome of a valuation;
- advocacy threat—where a professional valuer may promote their client's position such that objectivity is compromised;
- familiarity threat—where a long or close relationship with a client or employer may affect objective judgment; and
- intimidation threat—where a professional valuer may be deterred from acting objectively because of actual or perceived pressure, including attempts to exercise undue influence over the valuation opinion (IVSC, 2011, page 6).

The safeguards identified comprise:

- safeguards contained in statutes or regulations relating to the purpose for which the valuation is undertaken;
- safeguards contained in the rules of conduct issued by a Valuation Professional Organisation (such as RICS or API) to which the professional valuer belongs; and
- safeguards contained in a firm's internal working procedures and quality controls such as operational separation of functions, register of personal interest, controls on gifts and hospitality and internal peer review of valuations (IVSC, 2011, page 7).

Further safeguards may include an effective and well-publicised complaint system operated by the valuation firm, professional body or regulator and an explicitly stated duty by professional valuers to report breaches of ethical requirements (IVSC, 2011, page 8).

2.6.2 RICS rules of conduct

RICS addresses ethics principally through the *Rules of Conduct* (RICS, 2021b), which apply to all members and PS2 *Ethics, competency, objectivity and disclosures* in the RICS Red Book (RICS, 2021a), which is mandatory.

2.6.2.1 Rules of Conduct

The *Rules of Conduct* are based on the ethical principles of honesty, integrity, competence, service, respect and responsibility. The five *Rules of Conduct* apply globally and provide a structure for making ethical decisions about how to behave as a professional, with members required to use professional judgment to apply the principles to situations that arise. While the rules are primarily about professional conduct, personal conduct may be relevant to the rules where there may be damage to public confidence in the profession (RICS, 2021b).

Reflecting their international application, the five *Rules of Conduct* are of a high level, comprising broad statements of obligations which are effectively indisputable:

- Rule 1: members and firms must be honest, act with integrity and comply with their professional obligations, including obligations to RICS—with example behaviours including not misleading by act or omission, improper influence by others, conflicts of interest, honest and objective advice, transparency and protection of confidential information;
- Rule 2: members and firms must maintain their professional competence and ensure that services are provided by competent individuals who have the necessary expertise—with example behaviours including only undertaking work for which you have the knowledge, skills and resources to carry out competently, supervise employees and subcontractors and undertake CPD;
- Rule 3: members and firms must provide good-quality and diligent service—with example behaviours including understanding client needs, agreeing the scope of service, undertaking work in a timely manner with due care, skill and diligence, communicating clearly with clients, keeping proper records and encouraging solutions that are sustainable;
- Rule 4: members and firms must treat others with respect and encourage diversity and inclusion—with example behaviours including no discrimination, bullying, victimisation or harassment and checking that supply chains do not involve modern slavery; and
- Rule 5: members and firms must act in the public interest, take responsibility for their actions and act to prevent harm and to maintain public confidence in the profession—with example behaviours including questioning practices and decisions that they suspect are not right, not making public statements that undermine public confidence in the profession, promptly, openly and professionally responding to complaints, considering the impact of health conditions on competence and managing professional finances responsibly (RICS, 2021a).

Appendix A to the *Rules of Conduct* sets out the core professional obligations of members to RICS that are mandatory for RICS members:

- members must comply with CPD requirements set by RICS;
- members must cooperate with RICS; and
- members must promptly provide all information reasonably requested by the Standards and Regulation Board or those exercising delegated authority on its behalf (RICS, 2021b).

Appendix A further sets out core obligations of firms to RICS that are mandatory for RICS members, including the provision of a complaints-handling procedure, maintenance of professional indemnity insurance coverage and cooperation with RICS.

2.6.2.2 *PS2 Ethics, competency, objectivity and disclosures*

PS2 is a mandatory standard for RICS members, applying the IVS Framework, recognising the International Ethical Standards and specifying additional mandatory requirements for RICS members, being prefaced by the following statement:

> *As it is fundamental to the integrity of the valuation process, all members practicing as valuers must have the appropriate experience, skill and judgment for the task in question*

and must always act in a professional and ethical manner free from any undue influence, bias or conflict of interest.

(RICS, 2021a)

PS2 comprises eight sections, being:

- professional and ethical standards;
- member qualification;
- independence, objectivity, confidentiality and the identification and management of conflicts of interest;
- maintaining strict separation between advisers;
- disclosures where the public has an interest or upon which third parties may rely;
- reviewing another valuer's valuation;
- terms of engagement (scope of work); and
- responsibility for valuation.

PS2 is very detailed, and readers are encouraged to read the standard in full, with the following comprising a brief overview rather than a comprehensive summary.

2.6.2.2.1 PROFESSIONAL AND ETHICAL STANDARDS

As RICS members operate to the highest professional and ethical standards, RICS members must meet or exceed the standards for conduct and competency promoted by IVSC with observance monitored and enforced through RICS Regulation.

Accordingly, PS2 sets a very high threshold:

Members must at all times act with integrity and avoid any actions or situations that are inconsistent with their professional obligations. They must bring the required levels of independence and objectivity to bear on individual assignments, applying professional scepticism to information and data where it is to be relied on as evidence. Professional scepticism is an attitude that includes a questioning mind, critically assessing evidence relied on in the valuation process and being alert to conditions that may cause information provided to be misleading. Members must not allow conflicts of interest to override their professional or business judgment and obligations, and must not divulge confidential information.

(RICS, 2021a, 1.5)

2.6.2.2.2 MEMBER QUALIFICATION

RICS members must ensure that services are provided by competent individuals who have the necessary expertise, being capable of satisfying the following criteria:

- appropriate academic/professional qualifications, demonstrating technical competence;
- membership of a professional body, demonstrating a commitment to ethical standards;
- sufficient current local, national and international (as appropriate) knowledge of the asset type and its particular market, and the skills and understanding necessary, to undertake the valuation competently;
- compliance with any country or state legal regulations governing the right to practice valuation; [which includes valuer's registration in Queensland and Western Australia] and

- where applicable, compliance with RICS Valuers Registration (VR) requirements (RICS, 2021a, 2.1). .

If a member does not have the required level of expertise, assistance should be sought from other members of the valuation firm or from other professionals with the express agreement of the client.

2.6.2.2.3 INDEPENDENCE, OBJECTIVITY, CONFIDENTIALITY AND THE IDENTIFICATION AND
         MANAGEMENT OF CONFLICTS OF INTEREST

PS2 is very clear on the importance of the following fundamental ethical issues:

> *Bringing the required levels of independence and objectivity to bear on individual assignments, respecting and maintaining confidentiality, and identifying and managing potential or actual conflicts of interest are of crucial importance.*
>
> (RICS, 2021a, 3.3)

PS2 further notes that the duty of confidentiality is continuous and ongoing and includes current, past and even potential clients (RICS, 2021a, 3.8).

PS2 notes that independence and objectivity are inextricably linked to the proper observance of the confidentiality of information and to the wider issue of the identification and management of conflicts of interest, with members required to follow the mandatory requirements within the RICS professional statement, *Conflicts of interest* which contains two fundamental requirements:

- *an RICS member or regulated firm must not advise or represent a client where doing so would involve a Conflict of Interest or a significant risk of a Conflict of Interest; other than where all of those who are or may be affected have provided their prior Informed Consent. Informed Consent may be sought only where the RICS member or regulated firm is satisfied that proceeding despite a Conflict of Interest is:*
  - *in the interests of all of those who are or may be affected and*
  - *is not prohibited by law,*

  and that the conflict will not prevent the member or regulated firm from providing competent and diligent advice to those that may be affected (RICS, 2022, 1.1); and
- *keep records of the decisions made in relation to whether to accept (and where relevant, to continue) individual professional assignments, the obtaining of Informed Consent, and any measures taken to avoid Conflicts of Interest arising* (RICS, 2022, 1.2b).

Examples provided of situations where a threat to independence or objectivity may arise include:

- acting for the buyer and seller of a property in the same transaction;
- acting for two or more parties competing for an opportunity;
- valuing for a lender where advice is also being provided to the borrower or the broker;
- valuing a property previously valued for another client of the same valuer or firm;
- undertaking a valuation for third party consumption where the valuer's firm has other fee earning relationships with the client; and
- valuing both parties' interests in a leasehold transaction (RICS, 2022, 3.9).

Members are advised to be wary of discussing the outcome of a valuation with a client or other party before its completion, which, while not improper, may threaten objectivity (3.10). In providing a client with preliminary advice or a draft valuation report in advance of completion, the member must state that:

- the opinion is provisional and subject to completion of the final report;
- the advice is provided for the client's internal purposes only; and
- if any matters of fundamental importance are not reflected, their omission must be declared (RICS, 2022, 3.12),

with file notes made of discussions held (3.14).

2.6.2.2.4 MAINTAINING STRICT SEPARATION BETWEEN ADVISERS

Dealing with "Chinese walls", PS2 notes that RICS has strict guidelines on minimum standards that must be adopted to ensure that arrangements established are robust enough to offer no chance of information or data passing from one set of advisers to another, with "reasonable steps" being insufficient (RICS, 2021a, 4.1).

Having obtained informed consent for separation of advisers from the client(s), the arrangements must satisfy each of the following requirements:

- the individuals acting for conflicting clients must be different, including support staff;
- such individuals or teams must be physically separated in different parts of a building or different buildings;
- any information or data must not be accessible to the other side at any time and must be kept in separate locked accommodation;
- an independent compliance officer should be appointed to oversee the arrangements; and
- there should be appropriate education and training within the firm on the principles and practices relating to the management of conflicts of interest (RICS, 2021a, 4.2).

2.6.2.2.5 DISCLOSURES WHERE THE PUBLIC HAS AN INTEREST OR UPON WHICH THIRD PARTIES MAY RELY

This relates to valuations that may be relied upon by other parties, such as valuations for published financial statements, prospectus or stock exchange reliance, investment schemes and takeovers and mergers. Where the valuation is of an asset previously valued by the valuer or their firm for any purpose, disclosure must be made in the terms of engagement of the relationship, rotation policy (if the member has provided a series of valuations over a period of time (5.4.1)), time as signatory (where a member has continuously been the signatory to a valuation for the same purpose (5.4.4)) and proportion of fees (being total client fees as a proportion of total member firm fee income during the preceding year, with less than 5% being considered "minimal", 5%-25% "significant" and above 25% "substantial" (5.7)) (RICS, 2021a, 5.1.1).

Further, where a member or member's firm has been involved with the purchase of one or more of the assets for the client within the period of 12 months preceding the date of instruction, the receipt of an introductory fee or the negotiation of that purchase on behalf of the client must be disclosed (RICS, 2021a, 5.3.2) with the interpretation of client being wide and including subsidiaries of an instructing holding company and third parties as agents for different legal entities (5.3.7).

2.6.2.2.6 REVIEWING ANOTHER VALUER'S VALUATION

A critical review of a valuation may be distinguished from an audit of a valuation or an independent valuation of a property included in another valuer's report (6.2), with a review seeking to:

- *form opinions as to whether the analysis in the work under review is appropriate;*
- *consider whether the opinions and conclusions are credible; and*
- *consider whether the report is appropriate and not misleading* (RICS, 2021a, 6.3),

with a member reporting opinions and conclusions together with the reasons for any disagreement (6.4).

2.6.2.2.7 TERMS OF ENGAGEMENT (SCOPE OF WORK)

By the time that the valuation is concluded, but prior to the issue of the report, all matters material to the report must have been brought to the client's attention and appropriately documented to ensure that the report is consistent with the terms of engagement (RICS, 2021a, 7.1).

2.6.2.2.8 RESPONSIBILITY FOR VALUATION

PS2 is clear that each valuation to which the standard applies must be prepared by, or under the supervision of, an appropriately qualified and named valuer who accepts responsibility for it (RICS, 2021a, 8.1). Notably, unlike IVS, RICS does not allow a valuation to be prepared by a firm, though the use of "for and on behalf of" under the responsible valuer's signature is acceptable (8.3).

PS2 cautions against permitting valuations to be used for purposes other than those originally agreed, lest the valuation be misunderstood or taken out of context or a potential conflict of interest arise that may not have been relevant to the original assignment (8.5).

2.6.3 API code of ethics

API addresses ethics principally through the *API Code of Ethics* (API, 2021d) which apply to all members, the *API Rules of Professional Conduct* (API, 2021e) (previously referred to as the *API Code of Professional Conduct*) and the *API Professional Conduct Policy* (API, 2020) which are mandatory.

2.6.3.1 API Code of Ethics

The API Code of Ethics:

> *aims to protect the public by ensuring all members work to a minimum standard of professional conduct, have the appropriate experience, skill, and judgement, act professionally and exercise their judgement free from any undue influence or bias.*
>
> (API, 2021d, 1.2)

The Code sets out the principles, values, behaviours and standards expected of members and assists members to act ethically and in accordance with standards of professional practice while also informing the public about the ethical standards by which members must abide (API, 2021d, 1.3).

The Code sets out five fundamental overarching principles that API members must abide by:

- professional behaviour—members must not by act or omission take action that is likely to discredit them or bring the property profession or the API into disrepute and must always act ethically and with professional courtesy towards other members of the API and profession;
- conflicts of interest—members have an individual obligation to disclose any actual or perceived conflict of interest in a timely manner. If the conflict cannot be removed or mitigated, the member shall withdraw from the matter unless the parties and the member mutually agree in writing;
- integrity—members must act ethically, honestly and fairly when undertaking professional services and must base their professional advice on relevant, valid and objective evidence, not allowing bias, conflict of interest or undue influence of others to override professional or business judgment.

Referring to information generally, the Code states:

> *Members must not knowingly use any information they become aware of during the provision of professional services in a manner that is contrary to accepted valuation practice or any applicable law.*
>
> (API, 2021d, 7.4)

though "contrary to accepted valuation practice" is neither defined nor explained;

- professional competence—members shall take steps to ensure that their practice is consistent with evolving ethical principles and professional standards, undertaking CPD and acting with due care and diligence in the provision of professional services. Further, members shall provide services for which they are competent and qualified, shall be open and accessible and shall provide relevant documentation, including terms of engagement in plain language and shall present the results of data and analysis clearly and without improper manipulation; and
- confidentiality—members must act confidentially, protect confidential client information and not disclose confidential information without prior permission unless required by law or regulation (API, 2021d).

2.6.3.2 API Rules of Professional Conduct

The *API Rules of Professional Conduct* are an interpretation and expansion of the *API Code of Ethics*, the purpose of which is to ensure high standards of professional behaviour are observed by all members through providing a framework for professional conduct which must be complied with by every member of the API (API, 2021e).

While the *API Rules of Professional Conduct* should be read in full, the following should be considered:

- professional and personal conduct—including requirements such as acting ethically, honestly, competently, in good faith, without bias and in a manner that upholds the values and reputation of the API. Further requirements address compliance with Rules, not making false or misleading claims in advertising, operating within the limits of qualifications and experience, confirming instructions in writing, taking steps to maintain and improve knowledge and skill, confidential information, attributing information relied upon within a report and the critical requirements that the fee payable to a member must not depend on a client nominated outcome and that the member must not influence the provision of work through any payment, gift, favour or otherwise;

- relationships with clients—including the requirement to act promptly and efficiently in the servicing of client instructions with communication concerning any delays;
- conflict of interest—including seeking to identify and avoid any real, perceived or potential conflict of interest, bringing such conflict to the attention of the instructing party, and decline or not proceed with an instruction where there is or may be a conflict or only proceed with express written instructions acknowledging the conflict;
- impartiality—including the requirement to strictly maintain independence and impartiality when providing professional services, not to act as an advocate and an expert in the same matter or as an advocate/expert when another member of the same firm is acting as an advocate/expert in the same matter and not rely on critical client supplied information without appropriate confirmation or qualification in the report;
- members and the API—including not saying or doing anything that may bring the API into disrepute or adversely impact other members of the API;
- plagiarism—including not using the intellectual property of another person without appropriate acknowledgment;
- disclosure requirements—including disclosure of unverified facts or information and disclosure of the extent of involvement when counter-signing a report;
- maintaining records—including maintaining adequate records to substantiate reports, opinions, advice, instructions and other records upon which an opinion or advice was based;
- departure or non-compliance provisions—in the event of a departure or non-compliance, the member's report, advice or opinion must include a written statement of reasons and impact;
- property valuations—including compliance with IVS, applicable legislation and API requirements and statement of membership category and certification held when signing a report, advice or opinion;
- undertaking valuations—including the following critical requirements:

> *For the avoidance of doubt, valuations include full personal inspections by the Valuer as well as limited on-site inspections and kerbside inspections by the Valuer.*
> *When undertaking a valuation, unless otherwise instructed in writing by the client, a Valuer, who is the Primary Valuer, must:*
> *(a) complete inspections and other investigations to enable the Valuer to satisfy themselves as to all material valuation considerations; and*
> *(b) conduct inspections and other investigations to enable the Valuer to complete the valuation in accordance with accepted valuation practice* (API, 2021e, 11.2),

and

> *If the asset is not fully and personally inspected by the Valuer or only subject to a limited or restricted inspection, in accordance with the written instructions from the client or the client representative, the Valuer must disclose in the valuation report, opinion or advice:*
> *(a) the extent of the restricted or limited inspection undertaken; and*
> *(b) that the property was not personally inspected by the Valuer or only subject to a limited or restricted inspection in accordance with the written instructions from the client or the client's representative; and*

(c) *the effect* that *non-inspection or a limited or restricted inspection may have on the valuation provided* (API, 2021e, 11.3),

and

a Valuer, who is the Primary Valuer, must include in the valuation report, opinion or advice:

(a) details of the extent/form of physical inspection, of the asset, personally undertaken by the Valuer and;

(b) a statement of all assumptions made in arriving at an opinion of value and all conditions;

(c) any requirements or limitations arising from the client's instructions;

(d) any requirements or limitations arising due to any other circumstances;

(e) where all facts or information have not been ascertained or verified, written disclosure of this, together with a statement of the extent, if any, to which the failure to ascertain or verify the facts or information in question qualifies or affects the valuation provided; and

(f) the degree of reliance, if any, on information and/or professional opinion from others (API, 2021e, 11.5);

- plant, machinery and equipment valuations—including the requirement for inspection of a representative sample of assets and the review and comparison of identified data sources;
- statutory valuations—including the requirement to comply with the requirements of the statutory body; and
- student and provisional members—including allowance to assist in undertaking a valuation and preparing a valuation report but not the signature of a report, opinion or advice excepting restricted assessments conducted by a Provisional Member who is certified as a Residential Property Valuer and undertaken in accordance with the API Restricted Assessment Supporting Memorandum.

2.6.3.3 API Professional Conduct Policy

This policy provides complainants with the opportunity to bring to the attention of the API circumstances which may give rise to a finding of professional misconduct against an API member and provides the API CEO with an opportunity to undertake a disciplinary assessment of the conduct of a member (API, 2020).

The API has no authority to determine negligence, assess the accuracy of a valuation, determine the outcome of a dispute, request an amendment to a report, award compensation or a fee refund or overturn a decision of a court, tribunal or other association or regulatory body.

2.6.4 Summary—ethical frameworks in valuation

The provisions of the IVSC *Code of ethical principles for professional valuers*, the RICS *Rules of Conduct* and PS2 *Ethics, competency, objectivity and disclosures*, the *API Code of Ethics*, *API Rules of Professional Conduct* and *API Professional Conduct Policy* are both extensive and overlapping, but demonstrably essential for the maintenance of public confidence and trust in the valuation system. Codifying acting ethically invites both the monitoring of adherence by the valuer and/or valuation firm for quality control and by the professional bodies for regulation, adding further layers of time and cost to the provision of valuation services.

2.7 Summary and conclusions

Chapter 1 outlined the structure of the property asset class, examining the traditional characteristics of property (including heterogeneity, durability, illiquidity and so forth) and the traditional risks of property (including location, building, tenant risk and so forth) through the lenses of systematic, unsystematic and idiosyncratic risk, so aligning property valuation with capital market theory.

This chapter considered the evolution of property valuation in Australia, the role of the valuer and the diverse activities of the valuation profession, followed by a detailed examination of the inter-acting framework provided by valuation standards and ethical standards promulgated by IVSC, RICS and API.

Emerging through the offices of the State Valuer Generals, the valuation profession in Australia was firmly based in statutory valuation and the definition of value provided in *Spencer v Commonwealth* (1907), which prevailed for much of the twentieth century. The decline of State Valuer Generals as the principal employer of valuers, the growth of the private sector valuation profession and the transfer of valuation education into the University environment mirrored the transition of the valuation profession from a statutory-based framework to a standards-based framework.

Interestingly, while that which is a valuation review appears clearly defined, that which is a valuation appears less clear. With regard to the IVSC's *A Competency Framework for Professional Valuers* (IVSC, 2012b), a person who has completed an accredited degree and completed the professional practice assessment of API or RICS and who complies with the ethical and CPD requirements of the relevant body may be considered to have fulfilled the IVSC requirements to be a valuer in an Australian context.

Drawing on the broad knowledge and experience of the education and training process, a valuer is equipped to undertake a very wide role, providing advice for a diverse range of purposes to a diverse range of parties. The development of knowledge and experience as a route to membership is supervised by the principal professional bodies for valuers in Australia, the Australian Property Institute and the Royal Institution of Chartered Surveyors, with both providing standards, ethical codes and regulations for the valuation profession.

Globalisation of trade, commerce, investment, banking and finance brought down national boundaries and necessitated not only international accounting standards and international financial reporting standards but also international valuation standards, given that valuation is the basis for lending decisions, financial reporting of multinational companies, cross border property investment, securitisation of real estate and so forth. For a relatively small economy like Australia which is heavily dependent on international trade and investment, the adoption of international standards was essential to maintain global competitiveness. By aligning with IVSC and adopting international valuation standards in full, complemented by their own additional compatible and consistent standards and guidance papers, API and RICS have contributed to a locally relevant and applicable valuation standards framework for the valuation profession in Australia today.

The numerous ethical statements published by IVSC, RICS and API provide a vast and inter-woven codification for the management and regulation of the "*art*" of valuation, being the exercise of judgment required during the valuation process. While managing issues such as confidentiality and conflict of interest are paramount to maintaining public confidence in the valuation system and so are indisputable, the granularity of prescription may be serving to move the focus towards a checklist approach rather than placing an onus on the valuer to keep ethics at the front of mind in all professional and personal activities.

The next chapter will explore concepts of value and normative and positive definitions of value, dissecting the International Valuation Standards' definition of market value with a reconciliation to the concept of market value in *Spencer v Commonwealth* (1907) and examining such contemporary valuation issues as valuation lag, variance, accuracy, negligence and valuer rotation.

Chapter 4 introduces International Financial Reporting Standards and International Accounting Standards with a detailed examination of the key provisions of International Valuation Standards, the RICS Red Book and API guidance papers that impact on valuation practice in Australia.

Chapter 5 outlines conceptual approaches to the valuation process with a review of the self-supporting process of instructing, undertaking and reporting valuations under the International Valuation Standards, RICS Red Book and API guidance papers, examining how this process inter-relates to the choice of valuation approach, valuation method and the purpose of the valuation.

Chapter 6 addresses the market approach to valuation through the comparative method of valuation, including the key steps of accumulation, analysis, adjustment and application of comparable sales evidence to the subject property being valued, with an example.

Chapter 7 considers the income approach to valuation addressed through the static methods of the capitalisation of income and the profits methods of valuation, including an examination of the key inputs for each method with examples and a consideration of both marriage value and the surrender and renewal of leases.

Chapter 8 considers the income approach to valuation addressed through the dynamic method of the discounted cash flow method of valuation, including an examination of the key inputs and a focus on the derivation of the discount rate and consideration of the role of sensitivity and scenario analysis, with examples.

Chapter 9 considers the cost approach to valuation addressed through the replacement cost, reproduction cost, summation and residual or hypothetical development methods of valuation.

Finally, Chapter 10 concludes the book with a consideration of future perspectives, including the role of uncertainty, data, automated valuation models, artificial intelligence, optionality, environmental, social and governance issues, retail and office space use and indigenous issues.

References

API (2007) *Glossary of property terms*, API, PCA and REI, Deakin.

API (2020) *Professional conduct policy*, API, Deakin.

API (2021a) *AVGP302 valuations of real property, plant and equipment for use in Australian financial reports*, API, Deakin.

API (2021b) *ANZVGP112 valuations for mortgage and loan security purposes*, API, Deakin.

API (2021c) *ANZVGP113 valuations for compensation and compulsory acquisition*, API, Deakin.

API (2021d) *Code of ethics*, API, Deakin.

API (2021e) *Rules of professional conduct*, API, Deakin.

Babawale, GK (2012a) 'Paradigm shift in investment property valuation theory and practice: Nigerian practitioner's response', *Mediterranean Journal of Social Sciences*, Vol 3, No 3.

Babawale, GK (2012b) 'An assessment of the current standard of real estate valuation practice in Nigeria', *Social Science*, Vol 47.

Banfield, A (2014) *A valuer's guide to the RICS red book*, RICS, London.

Baum, A, Mackmin, D and Nunnington, N (2018) *The income approach to property valuation*, Routledge, Abingdon.

Blackledge, M (2017) *Introducing property valuation*, Routledge, Abingdon.

Dugeri, TT, Gambo, YL and Ajayi, CA (2012) 'Internalising international valuation standards: relevance and applicability issues in the Nigerian context', *ATBU Journal of Environmental Technology*, Vol 5, No 1.

Edge, JA (2001, January) 'The globalisation of real estate appraisal: a European perspective', *The Appraisal Journal*, Vol 69, No 1, pp. 84–94.

French, N (2003) 'The RICS valuation and appraisal standards', *Journal of Property Investment and Finance*, Vol 21, No 6.

Gilbertson, B (2002, February) 'Valuation or appraisal: an art or a science?', *Australian Property Journal*, Vol 37, No 1, pp. 11–13.

Greenwell, W (1976) 'A call for new valuation methods', *Estates Gazette*, Vol 238, p. 481.

IFRS (2013) *International financial reporting standards*, International Accounting Standards Board, London.

Isaac, D and O'Leary, J (2012) *Property valuation principles*, Palgrave Macmillan, Basingstoke.

Isaac, D and O'Leary, J (2013) *Property valuation techniques*, Palgrave Macmillan, Basingstoke.

IVSC (2009) *Setting the standard*, IVSC, London.

IVSC (2011) *Code of ethical principles for professional valuers*, IVSC, London.

IVSC (2012a) *Raising the bar for the valuation profession*, Roundtable Discussion, IVSC, London.

IVSC (2012b) *A competency framework for professional valuers*, IVSC, London.

IVSC (2013) *International valuation standards 2013*, IVSC, London.

IVSC (2014) *Global regulatory convergence and the valuation profession*, IVSC, London.

IVSC (2015) *IVSC review group report—engagement paper*, IVSC, London.

IVSC (2021) *International valuation standards*, International Valuation Standards Council, London.

Mackmin, D (1999) 'Valuation of real estate in global markets', *Property Management*, Vol 17, No 4.

Mallinson, M and French, N (2000) 'The nature and relevance of uncertainty and how it might be measured and reported', *Journal of Property Investment and Finance*, Vol 18, No 1.

Millington, A (2000) *An introduction to property valuation*, Routledge, Abingdon.

Murray, JFN (1963) *Principles and practice of valuation*, Commonwealth Institute of Valuers, Sydney.

Parker, D (2016) *International valuation standards: a guide to the valuation of real property assets*, Wiley-Blackwell, Chichester.

Parker, D (2022) *Principles and practice of property valuation in Australia*, Routledge, Abingdon.

RICS (2021a) *RICS valuation—global standards*, Royal Institution of Chartered Surveyors, London.

RICS (2021b) *Rules of conduct*, Royal Institution of Chartered Surveyors, London.

RICS (2022) *Professional statement—conflicts of interest*, Royal Institution of Chartered Surveyors, London.

Shapiro, E, Mackmin, D and Sams, G (2019) *Modern methods of valuation*, Routledge, Abingdon.

Squirrel, M (2000) 'The history of the pacific rim real estate society', in Parker, D (Ed) *Property into the next millennium*, PRRES, Sydney.

Stewart, R (2022) 'Valuation for financial reporting purposes', in Parker, D (Ed) *Principles and practice of property valuation in Australia*, Routledge, Abingdon.

Westwood, R (Ed) (1997) *Valuation principles and practice*, Australian Institute of Valuers and Land Economists, Deakin.

Wyatt, P (2023) *Property valuation*, Wiley Blackwell, Chichester.

3　Value

3.1 Introduction

This book is an introduction to the fundamentals of property valuation, outlining the principal methods of property valuation in Australia within the context of International Valuation Standards, bridging the gap between traditional property valuation methods and the modern era of global valuation governance.

Chapter 1 outlined the structure of the property asset class, examining the traditional characteristics of property (including heterogeneity, durability, illiquidity and so forth) and the traditional risks of property (including location, building, tenant risk and so forth) through the lenses of systematic, unsystematic and idiosyncratic risk, so aligning property valuation with capital market theory.

Chapter 2 considered the evolution of property valuation in Australia, the role of the valuer and the diverse activities of the valuation profession, followed by a detailed examination of the inter-acting framework provided by valuation standards and ethical standards promulgated by IVSC, RICS and API.

This chapter seeks to explore concepts of value and normative and positive definitions of value, dissecting the International Valuation Standards' definition of market value with a reconciliation to the concept of market value in *Spencer v Commonwealth* (1907) and examining such contemporary valuation issues as valuation lag, variance, accuracy, negligence and valuer rotation.

Chapter 4 introduces International Financial Reporting Standards and International Accounting Standards with a detailed examination of the key provisions of International Valuation Standards, the RICS Red Book and API guidance papers that impact on valuation practice in Australia.

Chapter 5 outlines conceptual approaches to the valuation process with a review of the self-supporting process of instructing, undertaking and reporting valuations under the International Valuation Standards, RICS Red Book and API guidance papers, examining how this process inter-relates to the choice of valuation approach, valuation method and the purpose of the valuation.

Chapter 6 addresses the market approach to valuation through the comparative method of valuation, including the key steps of accumulation, analysis, adjustment and application of comparable sales evidence to the subject property being valued, with an example.

Chapter 7 considers the income approach to valuation addressed through the static methods of the capitalisation of income and the profits methods of valuation, including an examination of the key inputs for each method with examples and a consideration of both marriage value and the surrender and renewal of leases.

DOI: 10.1201/9781003397922-3

Chapter 8 considers the income approach to valuation addressed through the dynamic method of the discounted cash flow method of valuation, including an examination of the key inputs and a focus on the derivation of the discount rate and consideration of the role of sensitivity and scenario analysis, with examples.

Chapter 9 considers the cost approach to valuation addressed through the replacement cost, reproduction cost, summation and residual or hypothetical development methods of valuation.

Finally, Chapter 10 concludes the book with a consideration of future perspectives, including the role of uncertainty, data, automated valuation models, artificial intelligence, optionality, environmental, social and governance issues, retail and office space use and indigenous issues.

This book is based on those standards and guidance documents published in IVSC (2021) and RICS (2021) and on the API website (accessed January to May 2023). Given their nature, standards and guidance documents are dynamic, being regularly updated and with the most recently published versions replacing previously published versions. Accordingly, readers should not rely on this book as a current statement of a standard or guidance document and should visit www.ivsc.org, www.rics.org and/or www.api.org.au to find the most recent version.

As an introductory textbook on property valuation methods in Australia, this book is a companion to Australia's leading advanced valuation textbook, *Principles and Practice of Property Valuation in Australia,* edited by the same author and also published by Routledge, which is a deeper analysis of key principles underlying property valuation and current techniques and issues in the practice of property valuation for major sectors of the Australian property market.

Accordingly, this chapter will now consider:

- concepts of value and normative and positive definitions of value;
- the definition of market value arising from the landmark case of *Spencer v Commonwealth* (1907) 5 CLR 418;
- the IVSC definition of market value with an analysis of each key element; and
- contemporary valuation issues including valuation lag, frequency, variance, accuracy, negligence and valuer rotation.

3.2 Concepts of value

Value derives not from the land or property thereupon itself, but from the benefits that the rights to hold such land or property confer. Such benefits may be economic, social, cultural, religious, spiritual or environmental and each may have a different value (Wyatt, 2023). This book is primarily concerned with value arising from the economic benefits of the right to hold land or property.

Wyatt (2023) notes that if the rights provide an ability to use the land, then a value in use arises. Further and more significantly for the purposes of this book, if the rights are transferable, then a value in exchange may arise. As exchange of such rights normally take place in markets, value in exchange is often referred to as market value.

As Millington (2000) validly points out, for such an exchange to occur there needs to be a party willing to sell and a party willing to buy at a price that they both agree, with each having the right to walk away. This simple concept is the foundation for market value.

This book focuses on value arising from the economic benefits of the right to hold land or property. However, value arising from non-economic benefits, such as social value arising from a public monument such as a Shrine of Remembrance or cultural value arising from a property with cultural significance such as a cave with ancient indigenous rock art, while also important, is challenging to determine and beyond the scope of this book.

Gilbertson (2002) famously summarised the dilemma facing valuers:

Valuers have to reflect, not make, the market. A valuation could be a surrogate pricing process. Whereas, worth is what the purchaser is prepared to pay. What is value? Does value exist? Can value really be measured or is it ethereal?

Does a valuer work in the property market, or measure the market in property?

(Page 12)

with Wyatt (2023) noting that the estimation of market value is based on price discovery and the analysis of market evidence, such that:

the market learns from itself and valuers learn from the market.

(page 14)

3.3 Normative and positive definitions of value

Whipple's (2006) seminal text correctly draws attention to the fundamental distinction between normative and positive definitions of value, with:

* normative concerning what ought to be, through the prescription of rules; and
* positive concerning what is, being that which has to be accepted as we find it.

Further, Whipple (2006) provides the following examples:

The statement "the government shouldn't pay $100,000 in compensation for this lot" is a normative one which expresses the value judgement that the community should not have to pay that much for it on resumption. As it is a product of the speaker's ethical views, it does not admit of testing.

The proposition "this lot cannot be sold for $100,000" is a positive statement which can be tested. How? By ascertaining the prices fetched recently for similar lots (an appeal to the facts) or by placing it in the market and advertising it for sale.

What I in fact get for my land (positive) may not be what I think I ought (normative) to get for it.

(page 88)

Significantly, Whipple (2006) notes that the origins of normative definitions of value appear to emanate from public policy through compulsory acquisition being premised on the normative definition question *what should the owner receive by way of compensation for the compulsory taking of this lot?* which is different to the positive definition question *what will this lot sell for?*

This is important in Australia as the widely used definition of value during the twentieth century was that based on a compulsory acquisition case, the *Spencer* case (considered in what follows). Accordingly, the normative definition of value effectively became the de facto definition of value in Australia and gained a level of permanency without an appreciation of its being normative. Indeed, as Whipple (2006) notes, the *Spencer case has had a profound influence on the valuation profession in Australia* (page 89).

Whipple (2006), citing Ratcliff in Graaskamp (1977, page 8), states a positive definition of value as follows:

The most probable price is that selling price which is most likely to emerge from a trans-action involving the subject property if it were exposed for sale in the current market for a reasonable time at terms of sale which are currently predominant for properties of the subject type.

(page 106)

Essentially, this is a definition of value being that which is, without restrictive assumptions about the seller and buyer. This positive definition is echoed by the IVSC in their definition of value:

The opinion resulting from a valuation process that is compliant with IVS. It is an estimate of either the most probable monetary consideration for an interest in an asset or the eco-nomic benefits of holding an interest in an asset on a stated basis of value.

(IVSC 2021, page 9)

Again, this is a definition of value being that which is, without restrictive assumptions about the seller and buyer or the state of the market—both are as is, not as should be. Accordingly, there may be unequal bargaining positions between buyer and seller and the market may not be in equilibrium, both of which may be assumed away in a normative definition of value.

However, as will be considered in what follows, the IVSC definition of market value (which is different to the IVSC definition of value) is a normative definition based very closely on the definition of value enunciated in *Spencer*.

3.4 *Spencer v Commonwealth* (1907) 5 CLR 418

This section draws heavily on Parker (2016) which is duly acknowledged here rather than individually referenced through the section and to which readers are referred for a deeper consideration.

The landmark decision of the High Court of Australia in *Spencer v Commonwealth* (1907) 5 CLR 418 (*Spencer*) was a major milestone for valuation theory and practice in Australia. Following the cessation of colonial status with the creation of the Commonwealth of Australia upon Federation on 1 January 1901 and separation from Great Britain, the High Court of Australia was only a few years old when it heard an appeal on a compulsory acquisition matter.

The appeal concerned the compulsory acquisition by the Commonwealth of six acres, one rood and two perches of virtually vacant land in North Fremantle for the construction of a fort, being described as follows:

The land consists of sand-hummocks overlooking the Indian Ocean. It has no grass; and it is useless in its present condition for any purpose of production.

with the valuation date set as 1 January 1905.

The Commonwealth offered Spencer £2,641 in compensation and Spencer sought compensation of £10,000. Spencer brought an action in the High Court claiming compensation of £10,000 and the Commonwealth paid £3,000 into the Court without denying liability. The originating action was heard by Higgins J with the appeal against his decision heard by Griffith CJ, Barton J and Isaacs J who awarded Spencer the £3,000 already paid to the Court.

The bench was particularly notable, comprising Griffith CJ who was generally claimed to be the principal author of the Constitution of Australia and the first Chief Justice of Australia, Barton J who had previously been the first Prime Minister of Australia from 1901 to 1903 and Isaacs J who became the first Australian born Governor General of Australia in 1930.

It is important to note that the High Court was considering value in the context of compulsory acquisition. Spencer and the Commonwealth would presumably have had a period of negotiation to try and agree a value for the land. Such a negotiation would have presumably allowed Spencer to contend that which he considered to be the value of the land to him in order to entice him to sell and the Commonwealth would contend that which they thought should be paid for the land. As a compulsory acquisition process, there was no opportunity for the property to be marketed and for the parties to see what, if any, bids may be made for the land as would occur in a normal sale process. Further, the negotiations could not continue indefinitely as the fort project needed to proceed. Accordingly, as the two positions did not meet, the negotiation presumably would have been unsuccessful.

As the parties were unable to agree, it ultimately came to the High Court to determine. By this point, title would presumably have transferred from Spencer to the Commonwealth and all that was required to be decided was the value of the land that was to be paid as compensation. Significantly, the High Court did not contemplate the value of the land to Spencer nor the value of the land to the Commonwealth, nor did it contemplate that value at which Spencer and the Commonwealth may have been able to agree (which would have been positive definitions of value), but instead formulated its own approach to the determination of value (which was a normative definition of value) attempting to strive for a balance that was fair to both parties—to Spencer as the dispossessed owner and to the Commonwealth which represents its taxpayer citizens being the community at large.

The significance of the decision lies in the way in which the Judges constructed the concept of value:

In my judgement, the test of value of land is to be determined, not by inquiring what price a man desiring to sell could actually have obtained for it on a given day, ie, whether there was in fact on that day a willing buyer, but by inquiring "What would a man desiring to buy the land have had to pay for it on that day to a vendor willing to sell it for a fair price but not desirous to sell?" It is, no doubt, very difficult to answer such a question, and any answer must be to some extent conjectural. The necessary mental process is to put yourself as far as possible in the position of persons conversant with the subject at the relevant time, and from that point of view to ascertain what, according to then current opinion of land values, a purchaser would have had to offer for the land to induce such a willing vendor to sell it, or, in other words, to inquire at what point a desirous purchaser and a not unwilling vendor would come together.

(Griffiths CJ)

And I should say, in view of the many authorities cited and upon the sense of the matter, that a claimant is entitled to have for his land what it is worth to a man of ordinary prudence and foresight, not holding his land for merely speculative purposes, nor, on the other hand, anxious to sell for any compelling or private reason, but willing to sell as a business man would be to another such person, both of them alike uninfluenced by any consideration of sentiment or need.

(Barton J)

To arrive at the value of the land on that date, we have, as I conceive, to suppose it sold then, not by means of a forced sale, but by voluntary bargaining between the plaintiff and a purchaser, willing to trade, but neither of them so anxious to do so that he would over-look any ordinary business consideration. We must further suppose both to be perfectly acquainted with the land, and cognizant of all circumstances which might affect its value, either advantageously or prejudicially, including its situation, character, quality, proxim-ity to conveniences or inconveniences, its surrounding features, the then present demand for land, and the likelihood, as then appearing to persons best capable of forming an opinion, of a rise or fall for what reason soever in the amount which one would otherwise be willing to fix as the value of the property.

(Isaacs J)

together with:

In order that any article may have an exchange value, there must be presupposed a person willing to give the article in exchange for money and another willing to give money in exchange for the article.

(Griffiths CJ)

value implies the existence of a willing buyer as well as of a willing seller.

(Griffiths CJ)

Prosperity unexpected, or depression, which no man would ever have anticipated, if hap-pening after the date named, must be alike disregarded.

(Isaacs J)

the all important fact on that day is the opinion regarding the fair price of the land, which a hypothetical prudent purchaser would entertain, if he desired to purchase it for the most advantageous purpose for which it was adapted. The plaintiff is to be compensated; therefore he is to receive the money equivalent to the loss he has sustained by deprivation of his land, and that . . . cannot exceed what such a prudent purchaser would be prepared to give him.

(Isaacs J)

Within the Judges construction of the concept of value, the following elements may be identified:

- an estimated amount: *could actually have obtained for it, have had to pay* (Griffith CJ), *value of the land, the fair price of the land* (Isaacs J);
- an exchange: *a man desiring to buy the land have had to pay for it . . . to a vendor willing to sell, may have an exchange value* (Griffith CJ), *willing to trade* (Isaacs J);
- a valuation date: *on a given day, on that day* (Griffith CJ), *on that date, prosperity unex-pected, or depression . . . if happening after the date named* (Isaacs J);
- a willing buyer: *a man desiring to buy the land, a desirous purchaser, willing buyer* (Griffith CJ), *voluntary bargaining, willing to trade, hypothetical prudent purchaser* (Isaacs J);
- a willing seller: *a vendor willing to sell it for a fair price, a not unwilling vendor* (Griffith CJ), *voluntary bargaining, willing to trade* (Isaacs J);
- a knowledgeable and prudent buyer and seller: *to a man of ordinary prudence and foresight, willing to sell as a business man would be to another such person* (Barton J), *perfectly acquainted with the land, hypothetical prudent purchaser* (Isaacs J);
- an absence of compulsion: *but not desirous to sell* (Griffith CJ), *nor, on the other hand, anxious to sell for any compelling or private reason, uninfluenced by any consideration of*

sentiment or need (Barton J), *not by means of a forced sale, overlook any ordinary business consideration* (Isaacs J); and

- an assumption of highest and best use: *the most advantageous purpose for which it was adapted* (Isaacs J).

Accordingly, at the beginning of the last century within the judgments in *Spencer*, the key elements of the concept of that which is now known as market value may be identified, in the form of a normative definition. Whipple (2006) provides a detailed discussion of *Spencer* to which readers are referred for a deeper consideration.

It should, however, be noted that the judgments were in the context of a vacant block of land on the coast of Western Australia in 1905 such that, while as a concept it is still of relevance today, care is required in the interpretation of language in this century—for example, *perfectly acquainted with the land* should be interpreted relative to a vacant coastal block in 1905 rather than in the context of the application of the efficient market hypothesis to a high rise office investment property in 2023.

While emanating from a compulsory acquisition case, the normative definition of value became the de facto definition of market value that was adopted in Australia for the balance of the twentieth century. Indeed, as Whipple (2006) notes, the Spencer case *has had a profound influence on the valuation profession in Australia* (page 89).

It was not until the codification of valuation standards by RICS in the UK in the 1970s that a formal definition of market value was developed. Significantly, this was also a normative definition that, over time, evolved into the current IVSC definition of market value.

3.5 IVSC definition of market value

This section draws heavily on Parker (2016), which is duly acknowledged here rather than individually referenced through the section and to which readers are referred for a deeper consideration.

IVSC defines value (which IVSC distinguishes from market value) as a positive definition:

The opinion resulting from a valuation process that is compliant with IVS. It is an estimate of either the most probable monetary consideration for an interest in an asset or the economic benefits of holding an interest in an asset on a stated basis of value.

(IVSC, 2021, page 9)

However, IVSC define market value as a normative definition:

Market value is the estimated amount for which an asset or liability should exchange on the valuation date between a willing buyer and a willing seller in an arm's length transaction, after proper marketing and where the parties had each acted knowledgably, prudently and without compulsion.

(IVSC, 2021, IVS104, 30.1; RICS, 2021, Glossary)

The definition includes most key elements identified previously from the concept of market value in *Spencer*, being:

- an estimated amount;
- an exchange;
- a valuation date;

- a willing buyer;
- a willing seller;
- a knowledgeable and prudent buyer and seller; and
- an absence of compulsion

but does not explicitly include an assumption of highest and best use, though this is fundamental to the proper application of the definition and will be considered in what follows.

However, the IVS definition also adds the following to the concept of market value in *Spencer*:

- an arm's length transaction; and
- a period of marketing.

Significantly, neither the IVS definition of *market value* nor the judgments in *Spencer* explicitly address an assumption concerning transaction costs, which will also be considered further in what follows.

Reflecting the fundamental nature and centrality of the definition of market value to IVSs, extensive instruction concerning interpretation and application is provided by IVSC:

> *The definition of market value must be applied in accordance with the following concep-*
> *tual framework:*
>
> (IVSC, 2021, IVS104, 30.2)

with nine elements addressed, each of which is considered in the following sub-sections. Application of the definition of market value in this way is mandatory (*must*), being obligatory, not optional, with application otherwise not providing an assessment of market value. As a conceptual framework, the elements are proposed as a series of overarching principles or scaffolding for the valuation process, capable of interpretation and application to different types of property interests in different countries at different times, thus being an effective example of principles-based standard setting for international application.

3.5.1 Estimated amount

The *conceptual framework* states:

> (*a*) *"The estimated amount" refers to a price expressed in terms of money payable for the asset in an arm's length market transaction. Market value is the most probable price reasonably obtainable in the market on the valuation date in keeping with the market value definition. It is the best price reasonably obtainable by the seller and the most advantageous price reasonably obtainable by the buyer. This estimate specifically excludes an estimated price inflated or deflated by special terms or circumstances such as atypical financing, sale and leaseback arrangements, special considerations or concessions granted by anyone associated with the sale, or any element of value available only to a specific owner of purchaser.*
>
> (IVS104, 30.2(a))

The use of the term *estimated* reinforces that a valuation is a matter of opinion rather than a matter of fact, with the *estimated amount* being an assessment of *price* or *most probable price*. Effectively, *price* or *most probable price* is the intersection between the hypothetical purchaser's assessment of worth to them (*most advantageous price*) and the hypothetical vendor's assessment of worth to them (*best price*).

The specification of *arm's length market transaction* adds the element of separation and independence of the parties to the concept expressed in *Spencer*, while the *market transaction* confirms the estimated amount to be an amount in exchange in a given market.

For both hypothetical parties, the *price* or *most probable price* is *reasonably obtainable*, requiring an assumption of reasonableness by the parties in the price-setting process. Effectively, this is consistent with the hypothetical purchaser's *most advantageous price* and the hypothetical vendor's *best price*, the price obtainable without being unreasonable.

However, the *price* or *most probable price* is assumed to not be influenced by issues that may make the hypothetical purchaser's *most advantageous price* and the hypothetical vendor's *best price* assessments of worth unlikely to converge, such as special terms, financing, leaseback or concessions. It is challenging, given the assumption of hypothetical parties, to understand how any element of value available only to *a specific owner or purchaser* may arise. Effectively, a "plain vanilla" or "normal" transaction, presumably with "typical" financing, is to be assumed with no abnormal or unusual features that may affect the pricing of the transaction, though that which may be "plain vanilla" or "normal" may differ between property sectors and property markets around the world.

3.5.2 An asset should exchange

The *conceptual framework* states:

> (b) *"An asset or liability should exchange" refers to the fact that the value of an asset or liability is an estimated amount rather than a predetermined amount or actual sale price. It is the price in a transaction that meets all the elements of the market value definition at the valuation date.*
>
> (IVS104, 30.2(b))

The use of the phrase *should exchange* rather than "would" is consistent with the hypothetical nature of the transaction and the *estimated amount*, reflecting the notion of the hypothetical purchaser's *most advantageous price* and the hypothetical vendor's *best price* assessments of worth coming together at a point of agreement that satisfies (*meets*) all (not most or some) of the assumptions of *market value* on a specified date.

3.5.3 On the valuation date

The *conceptual framework* states:

> (c) *"On the valuation date" requires that the value is time-specific as of a given date. Because markets and market conditions may change, the estimated value may be incorrect or inappropriate at another time. The valuation amount will reflect the market state and circumstances as at the valuation date, not those of any other date.*
>
> (IVS104, 30.2(b))

The assessment of value is temporal, being reflective of market conditions at that time and only applicable on the *valuation date,* thus requiring care when market conditions may be changing rapidly either upwards or downwards and even greater care when market conditions may be at an inflection point.

Consistently, if a valuation is being prepared retrospectively, care is required concerning regard to proximate changes in market conditions or the happening of a reasonably forseeable event subsequent to the *valuation date* or to evidence of transactions at the *valuation date* that emerge subsequently.

3.5.4 Between a willing buyer

The *conceptual framework* states:

> (*d*) *"Between a willing buyer" refers to one who is motivated, but not compelled to buy. This buyer is neither over eager nor determined to buy at any price. This buyer is also one who purchases in accordance with the realities of the current market and with current market expectations, rather than in relation to an imaginary or hypothetical market that cannot be demonstrated or anticipated to exist. The assumed buyer would not pay a higher price than the market requires. The present owner is included among those who constitute "the market".*
>
> (IVS104, 30.2(c))

The characterisation of the willing buyer as *motivated, but not compelled*, not *over eager nor determined to buy at any price* is consistent with the rational investor assumption that underlies capital market theory and finance theory but inconsistent with the behavioural characteristics often observed in property transactions when parties become emotionally involved with buyers rarely, if ever, being unmotivated. Effectively, the definition requires the assumption of a willing buyer who is both rational and emotionally detached.

While the buyer is not explicitly stated to be hypothetical and so may be actual (such as the *present owner*), care is required to avoid infecting the assumption of *willing* with the characteristics of a specific party. While the buyer may be hypothetical, the market in which they are assumed to be transacting is real, both in terms of current conditions and expectations of that which may happen in the foreseeable future. Accordingly, it is not some form of normalised market or long-term average market but the actual market as of the *valuation date*.

Further, the impermissibility of an *imaginary or hypothetical market* requires a focus on that market that exists with those buyers who exist. Accordingly, in a depressed market when debt financing is generally unavailable, a market of equity-funded buyers could be assumed and the participation of debt-funded buyers could not be assumed unless it could be *demonstrated or anticipated to exist*.

Consistent with economic theory, there will always be a price at which a market will clear. As Banfield (2014) notes:

> For there to be a sale there has to be a purchaser and in reality whatever the state of the market there is always a figure at which somebody will deal—remember the present owner is included among those who constitute the market.
>
> (Banfield, 2014, page 122)

3.5.5 And a willing seller

The *conceptual framework* states:

> (*e*) *"And a willing seller" is neither an over-eager nor a forced seller prepared to sell at any price, nor one prepared to hold out for a price not considered reasonable in the*

current market. The willing seller is motivated to sell the asset at market terms for the best price attainable in the open market after proper marketing, whatever that price may be. The factual circumstances of the actual owner are not a part of this consideration because the willing seller is a hypothetical owner.

(IVS104, 30.2(e))

The characteristics of the *willing seller* mirror those of the *willing buyer*, being *neither over eager nor a forced seller, nor one prepared to hold out for a price not considered reasonable.* Effectively, the definition requires the assumption of a willing seller who is also both rational and emotionally detached, consistent with a willingness to sell *for the best price attainable, whatever that price may be, after proper marketing.*

Similarly, the market is assumed to be the *current market*, consistent with the assumptions for the *willing buyer*. Further, the conditions and circumstances of the actual owner are assumed irrelevant as the hypothetical scenario requires a focus on what a hypothetical owner would do as a *willing seller*, not what the actual owner may do.

3.5.6 *In an arm's length transaction*

The IVS definition adds the assumption of *in an arm's length transaction* to the concept of market value in *Spencer,* with the *conceptual framework* stating:

(f) "In an arm's length transaction" is one between parties who do not have a particular or special relationship, eg, parent and subsidiary companies or landlord and tenant, that may make the price level uncharacteristic of the market or inflated. The market value transaction is presumed to be between unrelated parties, each acting independently.

(IVS104, 30.2(f))

Summarised in the last sentence, the *arm's length transaction* assumption concerns each party being assumed to be independent or not related and operating in isolation. More obvious examples of a lack of independence would be if the parties were assumed to have some form of relationship or connection that may lead to paying more or less than the price level of the market.

Effectively, the parties are assumed to be stand-alone market participants engaging in a unique transaction, which is consistent with the assumption of parties acting rationally but inconsistent with the nature of the property market, where parties may be likely to transact with each other on multiple occasions over time and so not operate in isolation.

3.5.7 *After proper marketing*

The IVS definition adds the assumption of *after proper marketing* to the concept of market value in *Spencer,* with the *conceptual framework* stating:

(g) "After proper marketing" means that the asset has been exposed to the market in the most appropriate manner to effect its disposal at the best price reasonably obtainable in accordance with the market value definition. The method of sale is deemed to be that most appropriate to obtain the best price in the market to which the seller has access. The length of exposure time is not a fixed period but will vary according to the type of asset and market conditions. The only criterion is that there must have been sufficient time to allow the asset to be brought to the attention of an adequate number of market participants. The exposure period occurs prior to the valuation date.

(IVS104, 30.2(g))

Significantly, the transaction is assumed to occur *after* marketing, and such marketing is assumed to be *proper*, or marketing that is *the most appropriate manner to effect its disposal at the best price reasonably obtainable*. Accordingly, the *proper* marketing for a large office property investment for sale by tender may differ from that for a large manufacturing facility for sale by auction, but each is assumed to have occurred before the *valuation date*.

Both the marketing and the method of sale are to be *most appropriate* to achieve the *best price*, such that it may be prudent, in the case of larger or unusual properties, for the valuer to state the assumed form of marketing and method of sale in the valuation report.

The duration of the marketing period may vary depending on the nature of the property, the state of the market and the profile of market participants, being of greatest significance when it comes to large or unusual properties in declining or depressed markets or for properties for which market participants are challenging to identify. Conversely, with properties for which there are very few but easily identifiable market participants, an *adequate number* may be canvassed in a short period. As previously stated, it may be prudent, in such cases, for the valuer to state the assumed duration of the marketing period in the valuation report.

IVS104 further adds:

> The concept of market value presumes a price negotiated in an open and competitive market where the participants are acting freely. The market for an asset could be an international market or a local market.
>
> The market in which the asset is presumed exposed for sale is the one in which the asset notionally being exchanged is normally exchanged.
>
> (IVS104, 30.3)

Significantly, IVS104 focuses the notion of market on that which is usual for that type of asset. Accordingly, if the asset is a high-rise office tower in the centre of the Melbourne CBD, the market may be expected to be both international and local and to comprise the sub-market for high-rise CBD office towers, not the entire market for any form of office property, with such sub-market generally comprising such hypothetical buyers as REITs, wholesale funds, superannuation funds, overseas buyers, sovereign wealth funds and so forth.

3.5.8 *Where the parties had each acted knowledgably, prudently*

The *conceptual framework* states:

> (*h*) "Where the parties had each acted knowledgably, prudently" presumes that both the willing buyer and the willing seller are reasonably informed about the nature and characteristics of the asset, its actual and potential uses, and the state of the market as of the valuation date. Each is further presumed to use that knowledge prudently to seek the price that is most favourable for their respective positions in the transaction. Prudence is assessed by referring to the state of the market at the valuation date, not with benefit of hindsight at some later date. For example, it is not necessarily imprudent for a seller to sell assets in a market with falling prices at a price that is lower than previous market levels. In such cases, as is true for other exchanges in markets with changing prices, the prudent buyer or seller will act in accordance with the best market information available at the time.
>
> (IVS104, 30.2(h))

Acting knowledgably and prudently is not explicitly defined but may be implied to be related to information. Knowledge would appear to be awareness of the information, and prudence would appear to be the use of that information to seek an optimal price, which is generally consistent with the notion of prudence as carefulness and risk aversion.

The phrase *acted knowledgably, prudently* is limited to both parties being assumed to be *reasonably informed* (which is somewhat less than fully informed) about only three nominated issues:

- *the nature and characteristics of the asset;*
- *its actual and potential uses;* and
- *the state of the market as of the valuation date,*

which may be contended to be a much lower level of knowledge than may be possessed by an actual major investor or major occupier prior to making a decision on a property transaction.

Significantly, the assessment of prudence is temporal, being in the context of the state of the market at the *valuation date* and disregarding anything that may have happened thereafter. Accordingly, that which may be considered prudent at the peak of a property boom just before the collapse may not be judged to have been prudent retrospectively six months after the collapse, but this should be disregarded. The assessment of prudence by the willing parties is, therefore, a snapshot as at the valuation date rather than a video.

3.5.9 And without compulsion

The *conceptual framework* states:

(i) *"And without compulsion" establishes that each party is motivated to undertake the transaction, but neither is forced or unduly coerced to complete it.*

(IVS104, 30.2(i))

The use of the term *and* firmly links *without compulsion* to the definition as a requirement for both parties, being consistent with the notion of *willing* and the reference to *motivated*. While this qualification removes such scenarios as forced sales or pressure to buy/sell from third parties, the reference to undue coercion also potentially precludes reflection of some common property market behavioural characteristics such as peer pressure.

3.5.10 Highest and best use assumption

The assumption of highest and best use is identified as an element in the concept of market value in the judgments in *Spencer* and is addressed in IVS104:

The market value of an asset will reflect its highest and best use. The highest and best use is the use of an asset that maximises its potential and that is possible, legally permissible and financially feasible. The highest and best use may be for continuation of an asset's existing use or for some alternative use. This is determined by the use that a market participant would have in mind for the asset when formulating the price that it would be willing to bid.

(IVS104, 30.4)

The interpretation of *possible* focuses on that use which would be considered reasonable by market participants, requiring consideration of such physical issues as being capable of real-world creation given such constraints as the location, size and topography of the land. Similarly, the inclusion of *legally permissible* focuses on planning aspects (such as use, nature of development, density, height and so forth) but may also include permissibility within the form of title held, which is particularly significant for leasehold interests, licenses and other forms of title that are not freehold title. Further, the inclusion of *financially feasible* focuses on the acceptability of return as a relative measure (being relative to the *existing use*) rather than as an absolute measure, consistent with the assumption of the rational hypothetical buyer.

It should be noted that all three constraints are applicable to an assessment of highest and best use, such that a proposed use that is (physically) possible and legally permissible may not be the highest and best use if it is not financially feasible. Effectively, the IVSs require the assumption of highest and best use to reflect a real-world scenario that could actually occur rather than a hypothetical scenario that would be unlikely to or would not occur in reality.

Significantly, the assessment of highest and best use is through the eyes of a *market participant*, usually the assumed rational hypothetical buyer, who reflects all aspects of the assessment of highest and best use in the price it would attribute to the property. However, such an assumed rational hypothetical buyer is not necessarily a single party but is indicative or representative of a small group of assumed rational hypothetical buyers comprising that market or sub-market.

3.5.11 Transaction costs assumption

An assumption concerning transaction costs may not be found in either the IVS definition of *market value* or the judgments in *Spencer* but is addressed in IVS104 as follows:

> *Most bases of value represent the estimated exchange price of an asset without regard to the seller's costs of sale or the buyer's costs of purchase and without adjustment for any taxes payable by either party as a direct result of the transaction.*
>
> (IVS104, 210.1)

Accordingly, transaction costs may be interpreted to include:

* *costs of sale* and *costs of purchase*—being such costs as agency fees, marketing costs, legal fees and so forth for the seller and due diligence costs, legal fees and so forth for the buyer; and
* *any taxes payable by either party as a direct result of the transaction*—being such commonly levied taxes as stamp duty on transfer, title registration fees and so forth,

as being excluded from the estimated exchange price of an asset, though such costs and taxes may be included as inputs in some valuation methods, such as discounted cash flow and the residual method.

While the exclusion of *costs of sale* and *costs of purchase* may be applied commonly and consistently to all purchaser groups, the exclusion of *taxes payable* requires greater care. Some purchaser groups (such as institutions, REITs and so forth) may be liable for taxes directly resulting from the transaction, whereas other purchaser groups (such as charities, public bodies and some religious groups) may be exempt and other purchaser groups (such as private individuals) may receive concessional treatment. Accordingly, where the assumed rational hypothetical buyer is identifiable as a specific group, the exclusion of taxes may be anticipated to have a common effect on price formation. However, where the assumed rational hypothetical buyer is identifiable as potentially being one or more specific groups with differing tax status, the distinction between *market value* and *investment value* may require greater attention.

3.5.12 *Market value in practice*

For completeness, IVS104 (IVSC, 2021) reinforces several issues for application in practice:

- the nature and source of valuation inputs must be consistent with the basis of value, which must, in turn, have regard to the valuation purpose. Therefore, the market approach to determine market value will use market-derived inputs and assumptions that would be adopted by market participants (IVS104, 30.5);
- the data available and the circumstances relating to the market for the asset being valued must determine which valuation method or methods are most relevant and appropriate (IVS104, 30.6); and
- market value does not reflect attributes of an asset that are of value to a specific owner or purchaser that are not available to other buyers in the market, consistent with the assumption of a willing party, not a particular willing party (IVS104, 30.7).

3.6 Contemporary valuation issues

Over the last few decades, the gulf between statutory valuation and non-statutory valuation has widened significantly, with statutory valuation becoming a specialism within valuation practice. Non-statutory valuation, generally being valuation under the provisions of the IVSC, RICS Red Book and API guidance papers, has grown exponentially, leading to a range of issues emerging, including valuation lag, frequency, rotation, variance, accuracy and negligence which will be considered further in what follows.

This section draws heavily on Parker (2022), which is duly acknowledged here rather than individually referenced through the section and to which readers are referred for a deeper consideration.

3.6.1 *Valuation lag*

A critical issue in the valuation process in periods of cyclical upturn and cyclical downturn is valuation lag, whereby a valuation cannot reflect value at exactly the date of valuation but only value at the date of the most recent relevant comparable transactions. Accordingly, during a cyclical upturn, values may be increasing faster than recent sales suggest and during a cyclical downturn, values may be falling faster than recent sales suggest.

For example, as markets rise, a sale/purchase transaction of an office building may commence negotiation on 1 January 2023 and be contracted on 1 July 2023, which is primary evidence of value levels in the office market on 1 January 2023. However, the transaction may not settle until 1 September 2023 such that it may not be considered reliable evidence for valuation purposes until 1 September 2023 and merely indicative in the interim. If a valuation of another office building is undertaken on 1 January 2024, it may have regard to the previous sale but by this point, the previous sale will be evidence of market conditions twelve months prior. Therefore, due to the nature of the comparable sales process, valuations are always lagging the market.

The situation may be more challenging in a falling market where no transactions are being undertaken, as occurred during the Global Financial Crisis. While market participants may agree that the value of office properties in a market is falling, in the absence of transactions, the rate of fall and prevailing value levels are unobservable such that the lag between a valuation and the most recent prior transaction may become very lengthy.

While valuation lag may appear to represent a fundamental flaw in the valuation process, which is essentially reliant on a continuous flow of up-to-date information on prevailing pricing levels in a market, the application of judgement by the valuer based on experience as to the extent to which a market may have risen or fallen since the last transaction is not precluded.

3.6.2 Valuation frequency and valuer rotation

Closely linked to the issue of valuation lag is the issue of valuation frequency. In most office, retail and industrial property markets, transaction numbers are relatively small and spread out over any given time period. While the underlying property market may be in a constant state of change, in a cyclical upturn or cyclical downturn, evidence of value levels through transactions in that market is only intermittently available.

Generally, valuations for financial reporting purposes will be undertaken annually, though some property funds may seek half-yearly and quarterly updates. It is generally held that annual revaluation represents a reasonable balance between sufficient frequency and sufficient availability of transaction evidence to observe movements in the market. If occurring more often than annually, any transaction evidence may be insufficient to clearly show a market trend, whereas longer than annually may see the market straying unacceptably far from the last valuation estimate.

Also linked to the issue of valuation lag and valuation frequency is the issue of valuer rotation, which comes sharply into focus in periods of cyclical upturn and cyclical downturn. Valuation theory purists argue that a truly independent view on the value of a property will only be obtained if a different valuer undertakes the valuation each time, removing any risk of serial bias in valuation estimates. The alternative argument suggests that there are economies in having the same valuer undertake the valuation repeatedly, as the valuer becomes familiar with the property and its place in the market, but the issue then becomes how many repeat valuations are acceptable before a valuer becomes too familiar with the property and potentially complacent?

Within the RICS Red Book (RICS, 2021), PS 2 *Ethics, competency, objectivity and disclosures* addresses valuer rotation policy in section 5.4. PS 2 acknowledges that a valuer who undertakes the valuation of the same property for many years may become familiar with the asset or the client such that a perception may arise that the valuer's independence or objectivity may have been compromised, with this risk addressed by arranging rotation of the valuers undertaking the valuation task (RICS, 2021, 5.4.2).

PS2 notes that the method of rotation and the choice of valuer are for the firm to decide after discussion with the client, if appropriate, though RICS recommends that the individual responsible for signing the report should have that responsibility *for a limited number of years* with the exact period depending on:

- the frequency of valuation;
- any control and review procedures in place, such as a valuation panel within the firm, which assist both the accuracy and objectivity of the valuation process; and
- good business practice

with rotation at intervals not exceeding seven years to be *good practice* (RICS, 2021, 5.4.3).

The period of time for which a valuer has continuously been a signatory to valuations for the same purpose, the period for which the valuer's firm has been carrying out valuations for the same client and the extent and duration of their relationship (including other than the valuation instruction in question) should be disclosed to third parties (RICS, 2021, 5.5.1).

Similarly, valuation of the asset for the same purpose by the valuer or firm or involvement with the purchase of the asset within the prior 12 months should be disclosed to expose any potential conflict of interest (RICS, 2021, 5.6.1) together with a statement whether the client's contribution to the total fees of the firm is minimal (less than 5%), significant (5%-25%) or substantial (above 25%) (RICS, 2021, 5.7.1).

Specific disclosure rules also apply for valuations provided for inclusion in a published document in which the public has an interest or upon which third parties may rely (RICS, 2021, 5.6.2), such as a product disclosure statement for a financial product.

3.6.3 *Valuation variance, valuation accuracy and valuation negligence*

Given that the process of valuation includes the exercise of judgment by the valuer, it is highly likely that two valuers could value the same property interest for the same purpose at the same valuation date and produce two different numbers. Similarly, given the imperfect nature of the property market, it is highly likely that a valuer could determine the market value of a property interest at a given date, and the same property may sell for a different price at that date.

This does not necessarily mean that any of the valuers were wrong but that their exercise of judgment led them to a different value conclusion. However, if the gap between valuers or between the valuation and the sale price is too wide, confidence in the valuation profession would be damaged and trust by users of valuation services would be lost.

There has, therefore, been extensive research and litigation into how wide the gap can be between valuers or between a valuation and a sale price before the valuation is considered to be wrong, which may be approached in three groupings:

- valuation variance—which is the difference between two valuers valuing the same property interest for the same purpose at the same valuation date and producing two different numbers;
- valuation accuracy—which is the difference between a valuer's assessment of the market value of a property interest at a given date and the sale price of that property at that date; and
- valuation negligence—which is a failure to take reasonable care by the valuer that results in the valuer's assessment of the market value of a property interest at a given date being different from the sale price of that property at that date, usually resulting in financial loss.

3.6.3.1 *Valuation variance*

Valuation variance is the difference between two valuers valuing the same property interest for the same purpose at the same valuation date and producing two different numbers.

Valuation variance may commonly arise in two situations, including the check valuation of a sample where a portfolio of properties is being valued by another valuer and the valuations produced by two expert witnesses in Court proceedings.

Wyatt (2023) cites a study by Hutchison et al. (1996) of valuation variation between national and local valuation firms, which found the average overall variation to be 9.53% from the mean

Table 3.1 Valuation Variance

Case/Court	Difference Between Experts
Cash Resources Aust Pty Ltd v Ken Gaetjens Real Estate Pty Ltd (Supreme Court, SA)	11.11%
Flemington Properties Pty Ltd v Raine & Home Commercial (Federal Court, NSW)	10.67%
MGICA (1992) Ltd v Kenny and Good Pty Ltd (Federal Court, NSW)	7.14%
Average difference	9.64%

Source: Author based on findings of Crosby et al. (1998)

valuation of each property, with national practices producing a lower level of variation (8.63%) to local practices (11.86%).

Research by Crosby et al. (1998) identified a range of valuation variance between expert witnesses in Australian Court cases, which is summarised in Table 3.1.

Accordingly, as a very broad guide, a difference of up to around 10% between two valuers valuing the same property interest for the same purpose at the same valuation date may not be unexpected.

3.6.3.2 Valuation accuracy

Valuation accuracy is the difference between a valuer's assessment of the market value of a property interest at a given date and the sale price of that property at that date.

Wyatt (2023) cites a study by Walvekar and Kakka (2020) of valuation accuracy around the world, which found the weighted average absolute difference in 2019 to be +9.5% globally—being valuations below sale prices by a global average of 9.5%.

In an Australian context, Parker (1999) reported the findings of a case study where an Australian institutional vendor offered a portfolio of seven commercial, retail and industrial properties located along the eastern seaboard of Australia for sale by tender closing in November 1995. Each of the properties was independently valued by one major, national firm of valuers as at the date of close of tenders, with offers to purchase each received from seven different purchasers, which remained unchanged to settlement at a total of $105.2 million.

The case study is unusual in that the sale date and valuation date are the same, such that no adjustment is required for effluxion of time or changes in market conditions. The variation in valuation and sale price for each of the seven properties is summarised in Table 3.2.

For the portfolio overall, the average level of valuation accuracy appears very high, with valuations exceeding market price by a dollar-weighted average of only 2.5%. However, at the sectoral level, the industrial properties exhibited lower accuracy, with valuations exceeding market price by a dollar-weighted average of 8.3%. Further, at the individual property level, accuracy ranged widely from -1.6% to market price, exceeding valuation by 14.3%.

Accordingly, as a very broad guide, a difference up to +/-10% between a valuer's assessment of the market value of a property interest at a given date and the sale price of that property at that date may not be unexpected.

Table 3.2 Valuation Accuracy

Property	Location	No. of tenants	Val. Accuracy
Commercial	Victoria metro	1	−6.06%
Commercial	NSW metro	24	+14.29%
		Arithmetic avg	+4.11%
		$ wghtd avg	−1.15%
Retail	NSW country	27	−6.73%
Retail	NSW metro	45	−1.64%
		Arithmetic avg	−2.55%
		$ wghtd avg	−0.49%
Industrial	NSW metro	2	−8.33%
Industrial	NSW metro	16	−8.20%
Industrial	NSW metro	1	−8.82%
		Arithmetic avg	−8.45%
		$ wghtd avg	−8.32%
Portfolio		**Arithmetic avg**	−3.17%
		$ wghtd avg	−2.46%

Source: Author after Parker (1999)

3.6.3.3 Valuation negligence

Valuation negligence is where a failure to take reasonable care by the valuer results in the valuer's assessment of the market value of a property interest at a given date being different from the sale price of that property at that date, usually resulting in financial loss.

In an Australian context, Crosby et al. (1998) note:

> In the light of these and other authorities, the Australian legal position has been summarised by Joyce and Norris as follows: a court faced by an apparent overvaluation should not immediately conclude that the valuer has been negligent, but should look behind the figure in order to see how it was arrived at. Only if this enquiry reveals no explanation for the overvaluation, for example because the valuer does not provide any evidence as to the methodology or calculations, is the court entitled, though not bound, to infer negligence.
>
> (Crosby et al., 1998, page 165)

Valuation negligence is a highly specialised area, with findings of negligence by the Courts turning on the exact details of a specific case. Readers are referred to the seminal text, *Valuers Liability* by Joyce and Norris (1994) for a deeper consideration.

A common source of valuation negligence claims arises from the valuation of development land for secured lending purposes on behalf of second and third-tier lender clients following a property market downturn. As the valuation of development land includes many variables that are determined by valuer judgment, with small changes in any variable potentially resulting in a large change in the final valuation, such valuations are fertile ground for client claims of failure to take reasonable care if a client suffers a significant loss due to a property market downturn when development land is often one of the more volatile sectors.

There have been numerous valuation negligence cases that have served to create a body of precedent, including landmark cases such as *Singer and Friedlander Ltd v John D Wood & Co* (1977) 243 EG 212 and *Titan Europe 2006–3 plc v Colliers International UK plc (in liquidation)* (2014) EWHC 3106. While the House of Lords decision in *South Australia Asset Management Corporation v York Montague Ltd* (1997) AC 1914 established the principle that loss attributable to a fall in the market will not be recoverable, each other case turns on its specific facts with Blackledge (2017) succinctly summarising the various decisions as:

- establishing the concept of a bracket or margin of error around the correct valuation;
- which is around +/-5% for straightforward valuations (such as standard residential property); but
- which may extend to +/-10–15% or higher for complex valuations (such as a property with exceptional features).

Many clients require valuers to carry professional indemnity insurance such that if the client suffers a loss as a result of the valuer's valuation, the valuer will be indemnified by the insurer in the event of a claim by the client against the valuer for the loss. Professional indemnity insurance is often very expensive for a valuation practice to take out but, as a client requirement with proof of currency of cover commonly required when tendering for valuation work, is usually unavoidable.

The personal toll on a valuer of a professional negligence claim is tremendous, including stress, anxiety and depression. Such claims often take years to litigate and require enormous amounts of time to be spent by the valuer in litigation preparation. While professional indemnity insurance may cover any damages claim and legal costs, the valuer may still face disciplinary proceedings by a professional body, reputational damage and the prospect of no longer being able to practice as a valuer.

3.6.4 Statutory valuation

While this book focuses on valuation under the provisions of the IVSC, RICS and API standards and guidance papers, valuers may also be required to undertake valuations under the provisions of specific statutes.

In Australia, such statutory valuations will most commonly be for the purposes of rating and land tax or for the compulsory acquisition of land and property. Each State and Territory has different statutes for rating and land tax valuation and for valuation for the purposes of compulsory acquisition. For example, in New South Wales, valuations for rating and taxing are under the provisions of the *Valuation of Land Act* 1916 and valuations for compulsory acquisition are under the provisions of the *Land Acquisition (Just Terms Compensation) Act* 1991.

Statutory valuation is a specialised area of valuation with a wide range of complexities arising from statutory interpretation and the application of case law, with valuers practising in statutory valuation tending to be statutory valuation specialists.

3.6.5 Summary—contemporary valuation issues

As statutory valuation has evolved into a specialism over the last few decades, the exponential growth in non-statutory valuation has led to a range of issues arising for consideration by valuers.

For those valuers practising in non-statutory valuation, not only does attention need to be given to the provisions of the IVSC, RICS and API standards and guidance papers and valuation lag in the undertaking of an individual valuation, but attention also needs to be given at a firm level to valuation frequency and valuer rotation as well as valuation variance, valuation accuracy and valuation negligence, adding further layers of complexity to valuation practice.

While the parameters of valuation variance, valuation accuracy and valuation negligence are fluid and case-specific, as a broad guide:

- valuation variance of up to in the order of 10% may not be unexpected;
- valuation accuracy of up to in the order of +/-10% may not be unexpected; and
- valuation negligence may not be unexpected beyond the brackets of around +/-5% for straightforward valuations and around +/-10–15% or higher for complex valuations.

3.7 Summary and conclusions

Chapter 1 outlined the structure of the property asset class, examining the traditional characteristics of property (including heterogeneity, durability, illiquidity and so forth) and the traditional risks of property (including location, building, tenant risk and so forth) through the lenses of systematic, unsystematic and idiosyncratic risk, so aligning property valuation with capital market theory.

Chapter 2 considered the evolution of property valuation in Australia, the role of the valuer and the diverse activities of the valuation profession, followed by a detailed examination of the inter-acting framework provided by valuation standards and ethical standards promulgated by IVSC, RICS and API.

This chapter explored concepts of value and normative and positive definitions of value, dissecting the International Valuation Standards' definition of market value with a reconciliation to the concept of market value in *Spencer v Commonwealth* (1907) and examining such contemporary valuation issues as valuation lag, variance, accuracy, negligence and valuer rotation.

With value arising from the benefits of rights to hold land and property rather than from the land and property itself, it is the economic benefits of transferable rights that are the key focus of this book. Value may be posited in a normative definition concerning what ought to be through the prescription of rules or a positive definition concerning what is, being that which has to be accepted as we find it. Significantly, for the evolution of valuation in Australia, the first widely accepted definition of value was normative following the High Court decision in *Spencer*.

Spencer provides the key elements of a normative definition of market value, being an estimated amount, an exchange, a date, a willing buyer and a willing seller who are knowledgeable and prudent, an absence of compulsion and an assumption of highest and best use. While formulated for a virtually vacant block of coastal land in 1905, the key elements remain applicable to the valuation of all types of property today, subject to allowance for developments in theory and practice over the last century, continuing to manifest not only in statutory valuation but also in the IVSC definition of market value.

The IVSC definition of market value adds marginally to the *Spencer* key elements and provides a framework within which all of the key elements may operate cohesively and consistently. The IVSC definition may be optimally approached by considering, first, who is the most likely hypothetical purchaser group and then contemplating that group standing outside the subject property and forming a view on what they might hypothetically bid. Such an approach allows the key elements of properly marketed, knowledgeable, prudent and without compulsion to be placed in context, providing focus and clarity in the valuation process.

Contemporary issues in valuation, such as valuation lag, frequency, rotation, variance, accuracy and negligence, have all emerged as the market moved from a statutory valuation-based environment to a standards-based environment. While each has been addressed through guidance by regulatory and/or professional bodies and/or by the Courts, all are essentially manifestations of some form of valuer judgment, further reinforcing the importance of the numerous ethical statements published by IVSC, RICS and API.

The next chapter will introduce International Financial Reporting Standards and International Accounting Standards with a detailed examination of the key provisions of International Valuation Standards, the RICS Red Book and API guidance papers that impact on valuation practice in Australia.

Chapter 5 outlines conceptual approaches to the valuation process with a review of the self-supporting process of instructing, undertaking and reporting valuations under the International Valuation Standards, RICS Red Book and API guidance papers, examining how this process inter-relates to the choice of valuation approach, valuation method and the purpose of the valuation.

Chapter 6 addresses the market approach to valuation through the comparative method of valuation, including the key steps of accumulation, analysis, adjustment and application of comparable sales evidence to the subject property being valued, with an example.

Chapter 7 considers the income approach to valuation addressed through the static methods of the capitalisation of income and the profits methods of valuation, including an examination of the key inputs for each method with examples and a consideration of both marriage value and the surrender and renewal of leases.

Chapter 8 considers the income approach to valuation addressed through the dynamic method of the discounted cash flow method of valuation, including an examination of the key inputs and a focus on the derivation of the discount rate and consideration of the role of sensitivity and scenario analysis, with examples.

Chapter 9 considers the cost approach to valuation addressed through the replacement cost, reproduction cost, summation and residual or hypothetical development methods of valuation.

Finally, Chapter 10 concludes the book with a consideration of future perspectives, including the role of uncertainty, data, automated valuation models, artificial intelligence, optionality, environmental, social and governance issues, retail and office space use and indigenous issues.

References

Banfield, A (2014) *A valuer's guide to the RICS red book* 2014, RICS, London.

Blackledge, M (2017) *Introducing property valuation*, Routledge, Abingdon.

Crosby, N, Lavers, A and Murdoch, J (1998) 'Property valuations: the role of the margin of error test in establishing negligence', *Western Australian Law Review*, Vol 27, pp. 156–194.

Gilbertson, B (2002, February) 'Valuation or appraisal: an art or a science?', *Australian Property Journal*, Vol 37, No 1, pp. 11–13.

Graaskamp, JA (1977) *The appraisal of 25 North Pinckney*, Landmark Research, Madison.

Hutchison, N, MacGregor, B and Nanthakumaran, N (1996) *Variations in the capital valuations of UK commercial property*, Royal Institution of Chartered Surveyors, London.

IVSC (2021) *International valuation standards*, International Valuation Standards Council, London.

Joyce, L and Norris, K (1994) *Valuers liability*, Australian Institute of Valuers and Land Economists, Deakin.

Millington, A (2000) *An introduction to property valuation*, Routledge, Abingdon.

Parker, D (1999) 'A note on valuation accuracy: an Australian case study', *Journal of Property Investment and Finance*, Vol 17, No 4, pp. 40–411.

Parker, D (2016) *International valuation standards: a guide to the valuation of real property assets*, Wiley-Blackwell, Chichester.

Parker, D (2022) 'Addressing cyclicality through international financial standards', in d'Amato, M and Coskun, Y (Ed) *Property valuation and market cycle*, Springer, New York.

RICS (2021) *RICS valuation—global standards*, Royal Institution of Chartered Surveyors, London.

Walvekar, G and Kakka, V (2020) *Private real estate: valuation and sale price comparison 2019*, MSCI, New York.

Whipple, RTM (2006) *Property valuation and analysis*, Lawbook Co, Sydney.

Wyatt, P (2023) *Property valuation*, Wiley Blackwell, Chichester.

4 Valuation standards

Acknowledgement

This chapter draws heavily on the following:

- Parker, D (2016) *International valuation standards: a guide to the valuation of real property assets*, Wiley-Blackwell, Chichester.
- Parker, D (2022) 'Addressing cyclicality through international financial standards', in d'Amato, M and Coskun, Y (Ed) *Property valuation and market cycle*, Springer, New York.
- Stewart, R (2022) 'Valuation for financial reporting purposes', in Parker, D (Ed) *Principles and practice of property valuation in Australia*, Routledge, Abingdon.

The authors are duly acknowledged here rather than individually referenced through the chapter and readers are referred to these works for a deeper consideration.

4.1 Introduction

This book is an introduction to the fundamentals of property valuation, outlining the principal methods of property valuation in Australia within the context of International Valuation Standards, bridging the gap between traditional property valuation methods and the modern era of global valuation governance.

Chapter 1 outlined the structure of the property asset class, examining the traditional characteristics of property (including heterogeneity, durability, illiquidity and so forth) and the traditional risks of property (including location, building, tenant risk and so forth) through the lenses of systematic, unsystematic and idiosyncratic risk, so aligning property valuation with capital market theory.

Chapter 2 considered the evolution of property valuation in Australia, the role of the valuer and the diverse activities of the valuation profession, followed by a detailed examination of the inter-acting framework provided by valuation standards and ethical standards promulgated by IVSC, RICS and API.

Chapter 3 explored concepts of value and normative and positive definitions of value, dissecting the International Valuation Standards' definition of market value with a reconciliation to the concept of market value in *Spencer v Commonwealth* (1907) and examining such contemporary valuation issues as valuation lag, variance, accuracy, negligence and valuer rotation.

This chapter seeks to introduce International Financial Reporting Standards and International Accounting Standards with a detailed examination of the key provisions of International

DOI: 10.1201/9781003397922-4

Valuation Standards, the RICS Red Book and API guidance papers that impact valuation practice in Australia.

Chapter 5 outlines conceptual approaches to the valuation process with a review of the self-supporting process of instructing, undertaking and reporting valuations under the International Valuation Standards, RICS Red Book and API guidance papers, examining how this process inter-relates to the choice of valuation approach, valuation method and the purpose of the valuation.

Chapter 6 addresses the market approach to valuation through the comparative method of valuation, including the key steps of accumulation, analysis, adjustment and application of comparable sales evidence to the subject property being valued, with an example.

Chapter 7 considers the income approach to valuation addressed through the static methods of the capitalisation of income and the profits methods of valuation, including an examination of the key inputs for each method with examples and a consideration of both marriage value and the surrender and renewal of leases.

Chapter 8 considers the income approach to valuation addressed through the dynamic method of the discounted cash flow method of valuation, including an examination of the key inputs and a focus on the derivation of the discount rate and consideration of the role of sensitivity and scenario analysis, with examples.

Chapter 9 considers the cost approach to valuation addressed through the replacement cost, reproduction cost, summation and residual or hypothetical development methods of valuation.

Finally, Chapter 10 concludes the book with a consideration of future perspectives, including the role of uncertainty, data, automated valuation models, artificial intelligence, optionality, environmental, social and governance issues, retail and office space use and indigenous issues.

This book is based on those standards and guidance documents published in IVSC (2021) and RICS (2021) and on the API website (accessed January to May 2023). Given their nature, standards and guidance documents are dynamic, being regularly updated and with the most recently published versions replacing previously published versions. Accordingly, readers should not rely on this book as a current statement of a standard or guidance document and should visit www.ivsc.org, www.rics.org and/or www.api.org.au to find the most recent version.

As an introductory textbook on property valuation methods in Australia, this book is a companion to Australia's leading advanced valuation textbook, *Principles and Practice of Property Valuation in Australia,* edited by the same author and also published by Routledge, which is a deeper analysis of key principles underlying property valuation and current techniques and issues in the practice of property valuation for major sectors of the Australian property market.

Accordingly, this chapter will now consider:

- International Financial Reporting Standards (IFRS) and International Accounting Standards (IAS);
- International Valuation Standards (IVS) (IVSC, 2021);
- the RICS Red Book (RICS, 2021); and
- API guidance papers,

which all inter-relate and are harmonised and consistent, sitting beneath each other in a hierarchy. Accordingly, IVS are consistent with IFRS/IAS beneath which they sit and RICS standards and API guidance papers are consistent with IVS beneath which they sit and, therefore, are also consistent with IFRS/IAS.

4.2 International Financial Reporting Standards

The overarching goal of international financial reporting, accounting and valuation standards is the facilitation of capital mobility globally, which is a particularly important issue for international property investment and worldwide corporate real estate (Parker, 2022).

IFRS and IAS are set by the International Accounting Standards Board, which is a not-for-profit public-interest organisation with oversight by a monitoring board of public authorities, with a mission to bring transparency, accountability and efficiency to the financial markets around the world, fostering trust, growth and long term financial stability in the global economy. (Elder, 2018)

While IFRS 5 *Non-Current Assets Held for Sale and Discontinued Operations* is of relevance for the valuation of property, the principal IFRS of direct relevance for the valuation of property in Australia is IFRS 13 *Fair Value Measurement* (IASB, 2011) which provides a framework for the measurement of fair value and the requirements for disclosure in financial statements, based on the fundamental premise that fair value is a market-based measurement not an entity-specific measurement (Parker, 2022). For the purposes of the preparation of financial statements, IFRS 13 defines fair value as:

> *The price that would be received to sell an asset, or paid to transfer a liability, in an orderly transaction between market participants at the measurement date.*

This definition is identically stated in AASB13 *Fair Value Measurement* (AASB, 2015). This effectively defines the basis of value to be adopted for financial statements, with AASB13 further describing what should be taken into account, including:

- characteristics—like condition and location of the asset and restrictions, if any, on the sale or use of the asset;
- assumptions—those that market participants would use when pricing the asset or liability, assuming that market participants act in their economic best interest;
- purchase or sale price—the exit price under current market conditions i.e., sale price, regardless of whether that price is directly observable or estimated using another valuation technique;
- market for the asset—principal (or most advantageous) market;
- use of the asset—highest and best use;
- techniques—use of valuation techniques consistent with [market, cost or income]approaches to measure fair value; and
- inputs—maximise the use of relevant observable inputs and minimise the use of unobservable inputs (Stewart, 2022).

AASB 13 categorises inputs on a scale of 1 to 3 as follows:

- Level 1 inputs—being quoted prices (unadjusted) in active markets for identical assets or liabilities that the entity can access at the measurement date (para 76). Valuers will seldom be engaged if the entity has access to these inputs for the asset in question;
- Level 2 inputs—being inputs other than quoted prices included within Level 1 that are observable for the asset or liability, either directly or indirectly (para 81). Examples include comparable prices or market yields; and

- Level 3 inputs—being inputs that are unobservable in a market. Examples might include future income forecasts or cost analyses (Stewart, 2022).

Generally, property valuers will use a mix of Level 2 and 3 inputs, with the entity required to disclose the technique used, the type of inputs used and, where recurring valuations are used with Level 3 inputs, how much changes in those valuations have affected profit (Stewart, 2022).

RICS considers the definition of fair value in IFRS to be generally consistent with the definition of market value in the RICS Red Book:

Indeed the references in IFRS 13 to market participants and a sale make it clear that for most practical purposes the concept of fair value is consistent with that of market value, and so there would ordinarily be no difference between them in terms of the valuation figure reported.

(RICS, 2021, VPS4, section 7.3)

Therefore, while the number of International Financial Reporting Standards of direct relevance to the valuation of property in Australia may be low, they are very significant for the valuation of property for financial reporting purposes.

4.3 International Accounting Standards

The overarching goal of international financial reporting, accounting and valuation standards is the facilitation of capital mobility globally, which is a particularly important issue for international property investment and worldwide corporate real estate (Parker, 2022).

IFRS and IAS are set by the International Accounting Standards Board, which is a not-for-profit public-interest organisation with oversight by a monitoring board of public authorities, having a mission to bring transparency, accountability and efficiency to the financial markets around the world, fostering trust, growth and long term financial stability in the global economy. (Elder, 2018)

The principal IASs of relevance for the valuation of property are:

- IAS 16 *Property, Plant and Equipment*;
- IAS 36 *Impairment of Assets*; and
- IAS 40 *Investment Property*.

As valuers in Australia will commonly be instructed to prepare reports under Australian Accounting Standards, particular regard should be given to AAS116, 136 and 140, with Stewart (2022) identifying those Australian Accounting Standards where valuation is a central concern (Table 4.1).

The standards listed here are just those for companies and private sector organisations, but they cover many different assets. Generally, fair value is used in these standards to establish initial transaction values and then restate them annually (Stewart, 2022).

The public sector also has its own standards, similar to those in Table 4.1, called IPSAS. These follow a similar pattern in relation to valuation issues as the previously listed standards. The most relevant of these for valuers is IPSAS 17, *Property Plant and Equipment*. This is quite similar to AASB117, with some specific differences in relation to heritage and infrastructure assets (Stewart, 2022).

Table 4.1 Australian Accounting Standards and Valuation Issues

AASB No.	Title	Key valuation issue
2	Share-based Payments	Securities issued as consideration for service to be fair valued (para 10, specially defined in Appendix B)
3	Business Combinations	All assets and liabilities to be fair valued and separately allocated as part of Purchase Price allocation on a business combination (para 18)
5	Non-current Assets Held for Sale and Discontinued Operations	Assets held for sale to be held at lower of carrying amount or fair value less costs to sell (para 15)
9	Financial Instruments	Financial instruments to be carried at fair value (para 5.2.1)
16	Leases (supersedes AASB 117 for periods on or after 1 January 2019)	Rights of use and leases can be fair valued at the present value of lease payments (para 26)
116	Property, Plant and Equipment	Assets can be revalued at fair value (para 31) and applies AASB 136 (para 63)
136	Impairment of Assets	Assets may be impaired, i.e. written down if higher of fair value less costs to sell (para 25) and value in use (para 30) is less than carrying amount.
138	Intangible Assets	Can revalue intangible assets at fair value, if an active market exists (para 75)
140	Investment Property	Investment property must be carried at fair value (para 33)
141	Agriculture	Biological assets (para 12, e.g. an orchard) and agricultural produce (para 13, e.g. a crop) must be valued at fair value
1051	Land Under Roads	May elect to value land under roads at fair value (para 13)
1056	Superannuation Entities	Assets held by (and liabilities of) superannuation funds must be held at fair value (para 13)

Source: Stewart (2022)

Concerning accounting standards, Stewart (2022) notes:

- standards are law: for most valuations, basis of value, approaches, methods and disclosure are a matter of professional practice. For financial reporting, the standards bind clients with legal force (Australian Accounting Standards are mandatory by law) which effectively binds the valuer regardless of their professional background;
- accounting standards have primacy: valuation standards and guidance are secondary to accounting standards and standards should be followed if members of professional bodies are bound to do so. Because of the legal force of the accounting standards, where there is a conflict, the accounting standard prevails. However, for matters where there is no conflict, even if a valuer is not bound to do so, it would be considered good practice to adopt the standards; and
- valuation basis and other valuation issues prescribed: in most valuation engagements, the valuation basis, method, approaches, disclosures and so forth are defined by valuation standards, but the valuer and their client are free to agree which are to be used in the particular assignment. For financial reporting, the requirements of AASB13 means that this is not the case.

Therefore, while International Accounting Standards are applicable, Australian Accounting Standards are of primary relevance for the valuation of property in Australia.

4.4 International Valuation Standards

The overarching goal of international financial reporting, accounting and valuation standards is the facilitation of capital mobility globally, which is a particularly important issue for international property investment and worldwide corporate real estate (Parker, 2022).

IVS are set by the International Valuation Standards Council, which is an independent not-for-profit organisation that produces and sets standards for the valuation of assets around the world in the public interest, with a mission to establish and maintain effective, high-quality international valuation and professional standards to contribute to the development of the global valuation profession, thereby serving the public interest (Elder, 2018). Importantly, departures from IVS to comply with legislative and regulatory requirements in a jurisdiction that are in conflict with the standards are allowed (IVSC, 2021, page 2).

International Valuation Standards (IVSs) are, by definition, of international application, being aligned with IAS and IFRS, sitting above regional and national standards. It is through application that IVSs gain their status as, when a statement is made that a valuation has been performed in compliance with IVS, it is implicit that all relevant standards are complied with and due account is taken of any supporting guidance issued by IVSC. Accordingly, unlike some national and regional standards issued by valuation professional organisations for their valuer members, IVSs are not mandatory on valuers unless they state that they are undertaking a valuation in accordance with IVSs.

IVSC's role in promulgating international valuation standards and acting as a global focus for the valuation profession is largely operationalised through engagement with valuation professional organisations (VPOs—currently totalling around 50 and including RICS and the Australian Property Institute), regulators and other groups around the world who enforce implementation and who may also develop complementary and consistent regional and/or national standards which sit below IVSs.

Such VPOs are generally the national professional body for their country that advance the adoption and implementation of IVSs in that country, produce regional or national standards or guidance consistent with and harmonised with IVSs as may be required for that jurisdiction, act to regulate individual valuers either through self-regulation or shared regulation with Government and promote the benefits of IVSs to their Government and regulators (IVSC, 2014).

For the valuation of real property assets, the structure of IVSs may be summarised as comprising:

- Glossary (following);
- IVS Framework (4.4.2);
- IVS General Standards (4.4.3.1); and
- IVS Asset Standards (4.4.3.2);

supported by the IVS scaffolding (4.4.4), underpinned by the IVS Core Principles of Valuation (4.4.1) (IVSC, 2021).

Within IVSs, defined terms (usually italicised) are important and should be read in accordance with the definition in the Glossary, including:

- **may**—describing actions and procedures that valuers have a responsibility to consider with implementation dependent on the exercise of professional judgment (20.15);
- **must**—indicating an unconditional responsibility that must be fulfilled (20.16); and

- **should**—indicating responsibilities that are presumptively mandatory and must be complied with except in rare circumstances where the valuer demonstrates that alternative actions that were followed under the circumstances were sufficient to achieve the objectives of the standards (20.20) (IVSC, 2021).

4.4.1 IVS core principles of valuation

IVSC specifies 14 core principles of valuation (IVSC, 2021, page 3), which, as may be expected, transcend time and jurisdiction:

1. **ethics**—valuers must follow the ethical principles of integrity, objectivity, impartiality, confidentiality, competence and professionalism to promote and preserve public trust;
2. **competency**—at the time the valuation is submitted, valuers must have the technical skills and knowledge required to appropriately complete the valuation assignment;
3. **compliance**—valuers must disclose or report the published valuation standards used for the assignment and comply with those standards;
4. **basis** (i.e. type or standard) of value—valuers must select the basis (or bases) of value appropriate for the assignment and follow all applicable requirements. The basis of value (or bases) must be either defined or cited;
5. **date of value** (i.e. effective date/date of valuation)—valuers must disclose or report the date of value that is the basis of their analyses, opinions or conclusions. Valuers must also state the date they disclose or report the valuation;
6. **assumptions and conditions**—valuers must disclose significant assumptions and conditions specific to the assignment that may affect the assignment result;
7. **intended use**—valuers must disclose or report a clear and accurate description of the intended use of the valuation;
8. **intended user(s)**—valuers must disclose or report a clear and accurate description of the intended user(s) of the valuation;
9. **scope of work**—valuers must determine, perform and disclose or report a scope of work that is appropriate for the assignment that will result in a credible valuation;
10. **identification of subject of valuation**—valuers must clearly identify what is being valued;
11. **data**—valuers must use appropriate information and data inputs in a clear and transparent manner so as to provide a credible valuation;
12. **valuation methodology**—valuers must properly use the appropriate valuation methodology(ies) to develop a credible valuation;
13. **communication of valuation**—valuers must clearly communicate the analyses, opinions and conclusions of the valuation to the intended user(s); and
14. **record keeping**—valuers must keep a copy of the valuation and a record of the valuation work performed for an appropriate period after completion of the assignment.

By adhering to these core valuation principles, valuers may avoid many of the problems that arise when valuations are challenged and so minimise the risk of litigation.

4.4.2 IVS framework

The IVS framework is a preamble to the IVS, consisting of general principles for valuers regarding objectivity, judgment, competence and acceptable departures from IVS (IVSC, 2021, page 10).

Stating that a valuation had been undertaken in accordance with IVS implies that the valuation has been prepared in compliance with all relevant standards issued by IVSC (10.1). Therefore, in order for a valuation to be compliant with IVS, the valuer must comply with all the requirements contained in IVS (10.2) and may only depart as described in section 60 of the IVS Framework (10.3), with departure being narrowly defined as follows:

> A "departure" is a circumstance where specific legislative, regulatory or other authoritative requirements must be followed that differ from some of the requirements within IVS.
>
> (IVSC, 2021, 60.1)

As such, a departure is mandatory, so the valuer may still state that the valuation was performed in accordance with IVS (60.1) with the departure identified in the scope of work and report (60.3). Departures that are not the result of legislative, regulatory or other authoritative requirements are not permitted in valuations performed in accordance with IVS (60.4).

The IVS Framework further addresses objectivity and competence:

- **objectivity**—the process of valuation requires the valuer to make impartial judgments as to the reliability of inputs and assumptions. For a valuation to be credible, such judgments must be made in a way that promotes transparency and minimises the influence of subjectivity. Judgment used in a valuation must be applied objectively to avoid biased analyses, opinions and conclusions (40.1); and
- **competence**—those involved in the preparation of a valuation must possess the necessary qualifications, ability and experience to execute a valuation in an objective, unbiased, ethical and competent manner having the appropriate technical skills, experience and knowledge of the subject of the valuation, the market(s) in which it trades and the purpose of the valuation (50.1). If competence is lacking in any aspect, the valuer may seek assistance from specialists provided this is disclosed in the scope of work and the report (50.2), but the valuer must have the technical skills, experience and knowledge to understand, interpret and utilise the work of any specialists (50.3).

4.4.3 IVS general standards and asset standards

For the valuation of real property assets, the structure of IVSs may be summarised as comprising:

- Glossary (considered previously);
- IVS Framework (considered previously);
- IVS General Standards (considered in what follows); and
- IVS Asset Standards (4.4.3.2);

supported by the IVS scaffolding (4.4.4), underpinned by the IVS Core Principles of Valuation (considered previously) (IVSC, 2021).

4.4.3.1 IVS general standards

The IVS General Standards comprise five standards, being:

- IVS101   *Scope of Work*;
- IVS102   *Investigations and Compliance*;
- IVS103   *Reporting*;

- IVS104   *Bases of Value*; and
- IVS105   *Valuation Approaches and Methods.*

IVS General Standards set forth the requirements for the conduct of all valuation assignments, being designed to be capable of application to valuations of all types of assets for any valuation purpose to which the IVSs apply (IVSC, 2021, page 3).

Considered in greater detail in Chapter 5, IVS101 *Scope of Work* specifies detailed requirements for the process of instructing the valuer. IVS102 *Investigations and Compliance* specifies detailed requirements for undertaking the valuation and IVS103 *Reporting* specifies detailed requirements for the process of reporting the valuation consistent with the original instructions.

IVS104 *Bases of Value* specifies six IVS defined bases of value and five premises of value (4.4.4.3), with IVS105 *Valuation Approach and Method* specifying the market, income and cost approach and methods (4.4.4.2).

4.4.3.2 IVS asset standards

The IVS Asset Standards comprise eight standards, including:

- IVS300   *Plant and Equipment*;
- IVS400   *Real Property Interests*; and
- IVS410   *Development Property.*

IVS Asset Standards include requirements related to specific types of assets which must be followed in conjunction with IVS General Standards when performing a valuation of a specific asset type (IVSC, 2021, page 3).

IVS Asset Standards each include *Bases of Value* and *Valuation Approaches and Methods*, with IVS300 *Plant and Equipment* specifying detailed requirements for the valuation of plant and equipment, IVS400 *Real Property Interests* specifying detailed requirements for the valuation of investment, owner-occupied and other property and IVS410 *Development Property* specifying detailed requirements for the valuation of contemplated or uncompleted development projects.

4.4.3.2.1 IVS400 REAL PROPERTY INTERESTS

In addition to the principles contained in the IVS General Standards, IVS400 *Real Property Interests* (IVSC, 2021) contains additional requirements for valuations of real property interests, being rights of ownership, control, use or occupation of land and buildings (20.2) with value attaching to the legal interest rather than to physical land and buildings (20.4).

Valuations of real property interests may be required for different purposes, including secured lending, sales and purchases, taxation, litigation, compensation, insolvency proceedings and financial reporting (20.8).

To comply with IVS101, a description of the real property interest to be valued and identification of any superior or subordinate interests that affect the interest to be valued must be included (20.5) in the scope of work.

To comply with IVS101 and IVS102, the valuer should consider:

- the evidence, if available, required to verify the real property interest and any relevant related interests;
- the extent of any inspection;
- responsibility for information on the site area, site characteristics and building floor areas;
- responsibility for confirming the specification and condition of any building;

- the extent of investigation into the nature, specification and adequacy of services;
- the existence of any information on ground conditions and soil conditions;
- responsibility for the identification of actual or potential environmental factors;
- legal permissions or restrictions on the use of the property and any buildings, as well as any expected or potential changes to legal permissions and restrictions (20.6); and
- any special assumptions that may need to be agreed upon, such as that a proposed building is valued as if complete at the valuation date or that the property is free from contamination or other environmental risks (20.7).

Concerning special considerations for real property interests, IVS400 draws valuer's attention to the following topics:

- **hierarchy of interests**—different types of real property interests may not be mutually exclusive (90.1). For example, in an Australian context, there may be a freehold interest, a head leasehold interest, a range of sub-leasehold interests and possibly some licence or other right-of-use interests. The valuer should identify the nature of the rights accruing to the holder of the interest being valued and reflect any constraints or encumbrances imposed by the existence of the other interests. Hence, each interest will have a separate value, but the sum of the individual values of interests will frequently differ from the value of the unencumbered superior interest (being, in Australia, the freehold) (90.3); and
- **rent**—when valuing the superior interest or the leasehold interest, valuers must consider the contract rent payable under the lease as well as the market rent, which may be different (100.2).

4.4.3.2.2 IVS410 DEVELOPMENT PROPERTY

For the valuation of development property, IVS General Standards and IVS400 *Real Property Interests* apply, subject to modifications and additional requirements provided in IVS410 *Development Property* (IVSC, 2021).

Development properties are defined as interests where redevelopment is required to achieve the highest and best use or where improvements are either being contemplated or are in progress at the valuation date, including the construction of buildings, provision of infrastructure on undeveloped land, redevelopment of land or the improvement/alteration of existing buildings or structures (20.1).

Valuations of development property may be required for a range of purposes, including determination of financial feasibility for a project, general consulting, tax reporting, litigation, financial reporting or statutory purposes such as compulsory acquisition (20.2).

The three principal valuation approaches of market, income and cost may be applicable for the valuation of development property and are considered in Chapters 6, 7, 8 and 9, respectively, with IVS410 noting the two main approaches to be the market approach and the residual method (considered in Chapter 9).

IVS410 *Development Property* also draws attention to the following topics:

- **existing asset**—for the valuation of development property, it is necessary to establish the suitability of the subject real property for the proposed development, which may require information or reports from other specialists, with IVS410 identifying sixteen issues that may require specific investigation (100.1);
- **special considerations for financial reporting**—including whether the reporting entity classifies the property as held for sale, for owner occupation or as investment property, which may affect the valuation requirements (110.1). It is normally appropriate to assume that any contracts (such as for construction, leasing or for sale) would pass to the buyer in the hypothetical exchange even if such contracts may not be assignable in reality (110.2); and

- **special considerations for secured lending**—while the appropriate basis of value for secured lending is normally market value, in considering the value of a development property, regard should be given to the probability that any contracts in place (such as for construction, leasing or for sale) may become void or voidable in the event that one of the parties becomes subject to formal insolvency proceedings. Regard should also be given to any contractual obligations that may have a material impact on market value, such as risk to warranties and guarantees in the event of default by the borrower. Any risks to a lender thereby arising should be highlighted (120.1).

4.4.4 IVS scaffolding

For the valuation of real property assets, the structure of IVSs may be summarised as comprising:

- Glossary (considered previously);
- IVS Framework (considered previously);
- IVS General Standards (considered previously); and
- IVS Asset Standards (considered previously);

supported by the IVS scaffolding (considered in what follows), underpinned by the IVS Core Principles of Valuation (considered previously) (IVSC, 2021).
  Considered in greater detail in sections 4.4.4.1–4.4.4.6, the IVS scaffolding includes:

- 4 key concepts (4.4.4.1);
- 3 principal valuation approaches (IVS105) (4.4.4.2);
- 6 bases of value (IVS104) (4.4.4.3);
- 5 premises of value (IVS104) (4.4.4.4);
- 5 further terms (IVS104) (4.4.4.5); and
- the valuation model (IVS105) (4.4.4.6).

The IVS scaffolding provides a framework or context within which the General Standards and Asset Standards sit, setting forth generally accepted valuation principles and concepts that are to be followed in the application of each but not including any procedural requirements.

4.4.4.1 4 key concepts—cost, price, value and worth

The IVS Glossary (IVSC, 2021) defines four key concepts, being cost, price, value and worth, which should only be used as defined and are not interchangeable nouns, considered sequentially in what follows:

4.4.4.1.1 COST

Cost is conceptually distinguishable from value and worth in IVSs, being a matter of fact rather than a matter of opinion. Further, like price, cost is observable, but that may be the extent of the useful information contributed with potentially limited insight provided into value or worth:

Cost(s): the consideration or expenditure required to acquire or create an asset.

(20.4)

The parameters of the amount required to acquire an asset are not specified and may include acquisition costs such as legal fees, due diligence costs and so forth. Similarly, the parameters of the amount required to create an asset are not specified and may include such costs to create an asset as profit and risk margin, debt costs and so forth.

As with price, the financial capabilities, motivations or special interests of particular parties are not controlled and may result in a different acquisition cost or cost to create than would arise from typical market participants, and so may not be generalisable across a market.

4.4.4.1.2 PRICE

Distinct from value or worth, which are matters of opinion, like cost, price is a matter of fact being the outcome of a contemplated or actual transaction:

> *Price: the monetary or other consideration asked, offered or paid for an asset which may be different from value.*

(20.18)

Price indicators from other transactions may occur at any point during the negotiation of a transaction, effectively being signposts, as well as an actuality at the conclusion of a transaction and may reflect the characteristics of the individual vendor and purchaser rather than the market as a whole and so not be generalisable across a market.

Accordingly, in considering price as evidence of value, valuers should investigate the vendor and purchaser's financial capabilities, motivations or special interests to determine the likelihood of replication by others in the market. While an observation of price in a single transaction may be of very limited use, multiple consistent observations of price in a series of transactions may be indicative of a market level.

4.4.4.1.3 VALUE

Value is conceptually distinguishable from price and cost in IVSs, being a matter of opinion rather than a matter of fact:

> *Value: the opinion resulting from a valuation process that is compliant with IVS. It is an estimate of either the most probable monetary consideration for an interest in an asset or the economic benefits of holding an interest in an asset on a stated basis of value.*

(20.29)

Therefore, within the IVSs, value can only be a judgment of one of two things, either the most probable price in exchange or the economic benefits of ownership, broadly according, with concepts of market value and concepts of investment value (worth), respectively.

4.4.4.1.4 WORTH (INVESTMENT VALUE)

Worth is conceptually distinguishable from price and cost in IVSs, being a matter of opinion rather than a matter of fact:

> *Investment Value: The value of an asset to the owner or a prospective owner given individual investment or operational objectives (may also be known as worth).*

(20.11)

Therefore, within the IVSs, worth may be aligned to value as the economic benefits of owner-ship but only through the lens of the owner or a prospective owner. Accordingly, while value is generalisable across a range of market participants, worth is specific to a group of market participants.

4.4.4.1.5 COST, PRICE, VALUE AND WORTH

The difference between cost, price, value and worth may be considered in the context of a can of Coca-Cola:

- the cost to produce a can of Coca-Cola is probably minimal, say $0.25;
- the price of a can of Coca-Cola in a supermarket may be, say, $1.00;
- the value of a can of Coca-Cola, when transacted between a willing hypothetical vendor and a willing hypothetical purchaser, both aware that the supermarket price may be $1.00 but unwilling to visit the supermarket, may be, say, $1.20; but
- the worth of a can of Coca-Cola to a British backpacker on Bondi Beach on a hot Christmas Day may be $2.00.

Accordingly, it is clear that the four terms are not interchangeable and should not be used inter-changeably as they each mean something conceptually quite different.

4.4.4.2 3 principal valuation approaches

The IVS scaffolding includes:

- 4 key concepts (4.4.4.1);
- 3 principal valuation approaches (IVS105) (4.4.4.2);
- 6 bases of value (IVS104) (4.4.4.3);
- 5 premises of value (IVS104) (4.4.4.4);
- 5 further terms (IVS104) (4.4.4.5); and
- the valuation model (IVS105) (4.4.4.6).

The IVS scaffolding provides a framework or context within which the General Standards and Asset Standards sit, setting forth generally accepted valuation principles and concepts that are to be followed in the application of each but not including any procedural requirements.

IVS105 (IVSC, 2021) specifies three principal valuation approaches, being the market approach, the income approach and the cost approach, requiring that consideration must be given to the relevant and appropriate valuation approach or combination of approaches (10.1).

In the selection of valuation approach, the valuer should consider, at a minimum:

- the appropriate basis(es) of value and premise(s) of value, determined by the terms and pur-pose of the valuation assignment;
- the respective strengths and weaknesses of the possible valuation approaches and methods;
- the appropriateness of each method in view of the nature of the asset and the approaches or methods used by participants in the relevant market; and
- the availability of reliable information needed to apply the method (IVS105, 10.3).

IVS105 does not require the valuer to use more than one method, particularly where the valuer has a high degree of confidence in the accuracy and reliability of the single method (10.4). Where more than one method is used, the valuation conclusion should be reasonable and the process of analysis and reconciliation, without averaging, should be described in the valuation report (10.4).

Further, IVS105 accepts that valuers may choose to use another method within the three approaches as the valuer has the responsibility to choose the appropriate method for each valuation engagement and compliance with IVS may require the valuer to use a method not defined by IVS (10.5).

4.4.4.2.1 MARKET APPROACH

The market approach is the first of the three principal valuation approaches recognised by IVS105 and is grounded in economic theory, being based on the economic principle of price equilibrium:

> *The market approach provides an indication of value by comparing the asset with identical or comparable (that is similar) assets for which price information is available.*
>
> (IVS105, 20.1)

The market approach is dependent upon there being substantially similar assets that are publicly traded with frequent and/or reasonable observable transactions (20.2), with the absence of such sales evidence rendering the approach inapplicable.

IVS105 notes that when comparable market information does not relate to the exact or substantially the same asset, the valuer must perform a comparative analysis of qualitative and quantitative similarities and differences between the comparable assets and the subject asset and make reasonable adjustments with the rationale documented (20.5).

Consistent with recent case law in the specialist Australian Courts (see, for example, *Adams v Valuer General* [2014] NSWLEC 1005), the market approach may be contended to comprise four sequential steps in the processing of sales evidence:

* the accumulation step;
* the analysis step;
* the adjustment step; and
* the application step.

4.4.4.2.2 INCOME APPROACH

The income approach is the second of the three principal valuation approaches recognised by IVS105 and is grounded in economic theory, being based on the economic principle of anticipation of benefits:

> *The income approach provides an indication of value by converting future cash flow to a single current value.*
>
> (IVS105, 40.1)

Consistent with the forward-looking nature of the underlying economic principle, the income approach conceptualises value as a single expression of future cash flows generated by the asset, masking within its simplicity a range of complex measurement issues and other related issues, including valuation accuracy, behavioural influences and so forth.

IVS105 notes that the income approach should be applied and afforded significant weight where:

- the income producing ability of the asset is the critical element affecting value from a participant's perspective; and/or
- reasonable projections of the amount and timing of future income are available for the subject asset, but there are few, if any, relevant market comparables (40.2)

Significantly, IVS105 acknowledges that a fundamental basis for the income approach (comprising both capitalisation and discounted cash flow) is that investors expect to receive a rate of return on their investments and that such rate of return should reflect the perceived risk of the investment (40.4) with return only expected for systematic risk (40.5). While regard to asset risk is often carefully and transparently considered in discounted cash flow, it is often only vaguely and opaquely considered in capitalisation.

IVS105 acknowledges that there are *many ways* to implement the income approach but contends that they are all *effectively based on discounting future amounts of cash flow to present value* and so focuses on the discounted cash flow method in detail, though the capitalisation method is widely used by the valuation profession in Australia.

The RICS Red Book (VPS 5) takes a wider view of the income approach as being based on capitalisation or the conversion of present and predicted income (cash flows) to produce a single current capital value, though noting capitalisation of conventional market-based income or discounting of a specific income projection *can both be considered appropriate depending on the type of asset and whether such an approach would be adopted by market participants* (2).

4.4.4.2.3 COST APPROACH

The cost approach is the third of three principal valuation approaches recognised by IVS105 and is grounded in economic theory, being based on the economic principle of substitution:

> *The cost approach provides an indication of value using the economic principle that a buyer will pay no more for an asset than the cost to obtain an asset of equal utility, whether by purchase or by construction, unless undue time, inconvenience, risk or other factors are involved.*
>
> (IVS105, 60.1)

Providing an indication of value, the cost approach is premised on calculating the current replacement or reproduction cost of an asset and then making deductions for physical deterioration and all other relevant forms of obsolescence (60.1).

IVS105 notes that the cost approach should be applied and afforded significant weight where:

- participants would be able to recreate an asset with substantially the same utility as the subject asset without regulatory or legal restrictions, and the asset could be recreated quickly enough that a participant would not be willing to pay a significant premium for the ability to use the subject asset immediately;
- the asset is not directly income generating and the unique nature of the asset makes using an income approach or market approach unfeasible; and/or

- the basis of value being used is fundamentally based on replacement cost, such as replacement value (60.2).

While this premise and the economic principle of substitution are relatively simple to understand, their application in practice in the context of property is much more challenging, exacerbated by the type of property for which the approach may be most relevant being where there is either no evidence of transaction prices for similar property or no identifiable actual or notional income stream that would accrue to the owner of the relevant interest. This may include specialised property such as public buildings (town halls, museums and so forth) or major operating facilities (car manufacturing plants, airports and so forth).

IVS105 considers the value of a partially completed asset as generally reflecting the costs incurred to date in creation of the asset (and whether those costs contributed to value) and the expectations of participants regarding the value of the property when completed but considering the costs and time required to complete the asset and appropriate adjustments for profit and risk (60.4).

Three cost approach methods nominated in IVS105 are the replacement cost method, the reproduction cost method and the summation method (70). With valuation being a matter of opinion rather than a matter of fact, the diversity of variables within and the complexity of the cost approach may be expected to result in a potentially wide range of opinions of value.

4.4.4.3 6 bases of value

The IVS scaffolding includes:

- 4 key concepts (4.4.4.1);
- 3 principal valuation approaches (IVS105) (4.4.4.2);
- 6 bases of value (IVS104) (4.4.4.3);
- 5 premises of value (IVS104) (4.4.4.4);
- 5 further terms (IVS104) (4.4.4.5); and
- the valuation model (IVS105) (4.4.4.6).

The IVS scaffolding provides a framework or context within which the General Standards and Asset Standards sit, setting forth generally accepted valuation principles and concepts that are to be followed in the application of each but not including any procedural requirements.

IVS104 (IVSC, 2021) considers a basis of value to describe the fundamental premise upon which the reported value will be based, which must be appropriate to the terms and purpose of the valuation assignment (10.1) and chosen by the valuer having regard to the same (20.2). Most bases of value have certain common elements, including an assumed transaction, an assumed date of transaction and assumed parties to the transaction (10.3).

IVS104 defines six bases of value being:

- market value;
- market rent;
- equitable value
- investment value/worth;
- synergistic value; and
- liquidation value (20.1(a)),

echoed by RICS (RICS, 2021) in VPS 4, which cautions that the use of an unrecognised or bespoke basis of value without good reason could breach the requirement that the valuation report not be ambiguous or misleading (2.6).

4.4.4.3.1 MARKET VALUE

As considered in Chapter 3, market value is defined in IVS104 as:

> *Market value is the estimated amount for which an asset or liability should exchange on the valuation date between a willing buyer and a willing seller in an arm's length transaction, after proper marketing and where the parties had each acted knowledgably, prudently and without compulsion.*
>
> (IVSC, 2021, 30.1)

Market value may be distinguished from equitable value, investment value/worth, synergistic value and liquidation value by its adoption of a postulated market and postulated participants, being grounded in a hypothetical on-market exchange.

The RICS Red Book (RICS, 2021) notes that market value ignores any price distortions caused by special value or marriage value (VPS 4, 4.2).

4.4.4.3.2 MARKET RENT

Market rent is defined in IVS104 as:

> *Market rent is the estimated amount for which an interest in real property should be leased on the valuation date between a willing lessor and a willing lessee on appropriate lease terms in an arm's length transaction, after proper marketing and where the parties had each acted knowledgably, prudently and without compulsion.*
>
> (IVSC, 2021, 40.1)

Accordingly, *market rent* echoes *market value* with the same conditions applying and the *appropriate lease terms*, where no lease exists, being those typically agreed in the market for the type of property on the valuation date between market participants (40.6(b)).

Market rent may be distinguished from equitable value, investment value/worth, synergistic value and liquidation value by its adoption of a postulated market and postulated participants, being grounded in a hypothetical on-market agreement.

The RICS Red Book (RICS, 2021) notes that market rent is not a suitable basis for settling the amount of rent payable under a rent review provision, where the definitions and assumptions specified in the lease have to be used (VPS 4, 5.2).

4.4.4.3.3 EQUITABLE VALUE

Equitable value is defined in IVS104 as:

> *Equitable value is the estimated price for the transfer of an asset or liability between identified knowledgeable and willing parties that reflects the respective interests of those parties.*
>
> (IVSC, 2021, 50.1)

Equitable value may be distinguished from *market value* through its basis in the actual (nominated) rather than the hypothetical (postulated). Further, *equitable value* may be distinguished from *investment value* through its dependence on participants rather than on a participant.

4.4.4.3.4 INVESTMENT VALUE (WORTH)

Investment value (often referred to in Commonwealth countries as worth and cited in the IVS Glossary as *Worth—see investment value* (20.33)) is defined in IVS104 as:

> *Investment value is the value of an asset to a particular owner or prospective owner for individual investment or operational objectives.*
>
> (IVSC, 2021, 60.1)

Investment value may be distinguished from *market value* through its basis in the actual (nominated) rather than the hypothetical (postulated).

From an Australian perspective, *investment value* as defined in IVS104 effectively accommodates notions of special value, though special value is separately defined in the RICS Red Book (RICS, 2021) as:

> *An amount that reflects particular attributes of an asset that are only of value to a special purchaser.*
>
> (RICS, 2021, page 12)

A special purchaser is defined as:

> *A particular buyer for whom a particular asset has a special value because of advantages arising from its ownership that would not be available to other buyers in a market.*
>
> (RICS, 2021, page 12)

It is often helpful to consider investment value or worth in the context of a group of market participants, with special value being relevant only to one specific market participant.

4.4.4.3.5 SYNERGISTIC VALUE

Synergistic value is defined in IVS104 as:

> *Synergistic value is the result of a combination of two or more assets or interests where the combined value is more than the sum of the separate values.*
>
> (IVSC, 2021, 70.1)

While the example often used for *synergistic value* is that value created by the combination of a freehold and long leasehold interest, it may potentially arise from any combination of two or more assets for any purpose and so requires careful distinction by the user from concepts of portfolio and aggregation in the IVSs and RICS Red Book.

Synergistic value may be distinguished from *market value* through its basis in the actual (nominated) rather than in the hypothetical (postulated). Further, *synergistic value* may be distinguished from *investment value* by its requirements for a combination of two or more assets or interests.

4.4.4.3.6 LIQUIDATION VALUE

Liquidation value is defined in IVS104 as:

> *Liquidation value is the amount that would be realised when an asset or group of assets are sold on a piecemeal basis.*

(IVSC, 2021, 80.1)

Liquidation value should take into account the costs of getting the assets into saleable condition as well as those of the disposal activity, with two different premises for determination being an orderly transaction with a typical marketing period or a forced transaction with a shortened marketing period (80.1).

Liquidation value may be distinguished from *market value* through its basis in the actual (nominated) rather than the hypothetical (postulated).

4.4.4.3.7 OTHER NON-IVS DEFINED BASES OF VALUE

IVS104 also provides a non-exhaustive list of other non-IVS defined bases of value prescribed by individual jurisdictions or recognised by international agreement (20.1(b)):

- *fair value* (International Financial Reporting Standards) (considered in section 4.2);
- *fair market value* (OECD);
- *fair market value* (US Internal Revenue Service); and
- *fair value* under:

  - the US Model Business Corporations Act; and
  - Canadian case law (Manning v Harris Steel Group Inc).

With the exception of *fair value* under International Financial Reporting Standards, such other bases of value are of limited relevance in Australia.

4.4.4.4 5 premises of value

The IVS scaffolding includes:

- 4 key concepts (4.4.4.1);
- 3 principal valuation approaches (IVS105) (4.4.4.2);
- 6 bases of value (IVS104) (4.4.4.3);
- 5 premises of value (IVS104) (4.4.4.4);
- 5 further terms (IVS104) (4.4.4.5); and
- the valuation model (IVS105) (4.4.4.6).

The IVS scaffolding provides a framework or context within which the General Standards and Asset Standards sit, setting forth generally accepted valuation principles and concepts that are to be followed in the application of each but not including any procedural requirements.

IVS104 (IVSC, 2021) specifies five premises of value, being:

- assumed use;
- highest and best use;
- current use/existing use;

- orderly liquidation; and
- forced sale,

which are considered further in what follows.

4.4.4.4.1 ASSUMED USE

Assumed use describes the circumstances of how an asset is used (IVS104, 130), being the use of the asset assumed for the purposes of valuation.

Different bases of value may require a particular premise of value or the consideration of multiple premises of value. Common premises of value include highest and best use, current use/existing use, orderly liquidation and forced sale (IVS104, 130).

4.4.4.4.2 HIGHEST AND BEST USE

Highest and best use is the use, from a participant perspective, that would produce the highest value for an asset (IVS104, 140.1).

A fundamental feature of IVS is the definition of highest and best use, which has three key elements:

The highest and best use must be physically possible (where applicable), financially feasible, legally allowed and result in the highest value.

(IVS104, 140.2)

where:

- physically possible—being what participants consider reasonable (140.5(a));
- legally allowable—having regard to existing and prospective legal and regulatory constraints (140.5(b)); and
- financially feasible—generating a sufficient return to a typical participant (140.5(c)).

Accordingly, the highest and best use cannot be a fantasy but must be capable of realisation. For example, the highest and best use of a CBD site as a 30-level five-star hotel cannot be assumed unless the hotel can physically be accommodated on the site, the project has (or will have) the relevant requisite development consents, the development will be profitable and another use does not result in a higher value.

If the highest and best use differs from the current use, the cost to convert the asset to its highest and best use may impact the value (IVS104, 140.2). If used optimally, the highest and best use of an asset may be its current or existing use (IVS104, 140.3). Further, the highest and best use of an asset valued on a stand-alone basis may be different from that as part of a group of assets when its contribution to the overall value of the group must be considered (IVS104, 140.4).

4.4.4.4.3 CURRENT USE/EXISTING USE

Current use/existing use is the current way that an asset or group of assets is used. If optimally used, current use/existing use may be the highest and best use. If not used optimally, current use/existing use may differ from the highest and best use (IVS104, 150.1).

4.4.4.4.4 ORDERLY LIQUIDATION

Orderly liquidation describes the value of a group of assets that could be realised in a liquidation sale, given a reasonable period of time to find a purchaser and with the seller being compelled to sell on an as-is, where-is basis. The reasonable period of time may vary by asset type and market conditions (IVS104, 160.1).

Essentially, orderly liquidation describes the value of an asset that has to be sold but in an orderly manner.

4.4.4.4.5 FORCED SALE

Forced sale describes a situation under which an exchange takes place rather than a distinct basis of value. Forced sale is the price (not value) of an asset under compulsion to sell that may result in a proper marketing period not being possible, with buyers potentially unable to undertake adequate due diligence (IVS104, 170.1).

If an indication of the price obtainable in a forced sale is required, the reasons requiring a forced sale and the consequences of failing to sell in the specified period should be identified as assumptions or, if they do not exist at the valuation date, must be identified as special assumptions (IVS104, 170.2).

A forced sale typically reflects the most probable price that a specified property is likely to bring under all of the following conditions:

- consummation of a sale within a short time period;
- the asset is subject to market conditions prevailing as of the date of valuation or an assumed timescale within which the transaction is to be completed;
- both the buyer and the seller are acting prudently and knowledgeably;
- the seller is under compulsion to sell;
- the buyer is typically motivated;
- both parties are acting in what they consider to be their best interests;
- a normal marketing effort is not possible due to the brief exposure time; and
- payment will be made in cash (IVS104, 170.3).

It should be noted that this is an assessment of probable price and not of value and that each of these conditions have to be met.

Sales in an inactive or falling market are not automatically forced sales simply because a seller might hope for a better price if conditions improve, unless there is a compulsion to sell by a deadline that prevents proper marketing (IVS104, 170.4) and so renders the seller potentially unwilling.

Further, forced sale transactions are generally excluded from consideration in a valuation where the basis of value is market value, though it is acknowledged that it can be difficult to verify that an arms-length transaction in a market was a forced sale (IVS104, 170.5).

Essentially, forced sale describes the price (not value) of an asset that has to be sold urgently. The RICS Red Book (2021) specifically states that the term *forced sale value* must not be used (VPS 4, 10.7). Further, the RICS Red Book (2021) considers valuations reflecting an actual or anticipated market constraint, which may take one of many different forms (VPS 4, 10.1), such as an inherent feature of the asset, of the interest being valued, of the circumstances of the client or some combination of all (VPS 4, 10.2).

API ANZVGP103 *Addressing the concept of forced sale* (API, 2022) echoes the views of IVSC and recommends that the term "forced sale value" be avoided, preferring the terms "forced sale price estimate" or "most probable forced sale price".

4.4.4.5 *Further terms*

The IVS scaffolding includes:

- 4 key concepts (4.4.4.1);
- 3 principal valuation approaches (IVS105) (4.4.4.2);
- 6 bases of value (IVS104) (4.4.4.3);
- 5 premises of value (IVS104) (4.4.4.4);
- 5 further terms (IVS104) (4.4.4.5); and
- the valuation model (IVS105) (4.4.4.6).

The IVS scaffolding provides a framework or context within which the General Standards and Asset Standards sit, setting forth generally accepted valuation principles and concepts that are to be followed in the application of each but not including any procedural requirements.

IVS104 (IVSC, 2021) considers five further terms, being:

- entity-specific factors;
- synergies;
- assumptions and special assumptions;
- transaction costs; and
- allocation of value

which are considered sequentially in what follows.

4.4.4.5.1 ENTITY-SPECIFIC FACTORS

For most bases of value, factors that are specific to a certain buyer or seller (being idiosyncratic or entity-specific) and not available to market participants generally are usually excluded from the inputs used in a market valuation (IVS104, 180.1).

Such idiosyncratic or entity-specific factors are determined on a case-by-case basis and may include:

- additional value or a reduction in value arising from the creation of a portfolio of similar assets;
- unique synergies between the asset and other assets owned by the entity;
- legal rights or restrictions applicable only to the entity;
- tax benefits or tax burdens unique to the entity; and
- an ability to exploit an asset that is unique to that entity (IVS104, 180.1).

However, if the objective of the basis of value used in a valuation is to determine the value to a specific owner, such as investment value/worth, entity-specific factors are reflected in the valuation of the asset (IVS104, 180.3).

4.4.4.5.2 SYNERGIES

Synergies refer to the benefits associated with combining assets that lead to the value of a group of assets being greater than the sum of the value of the individual assets on a stand-alone basis, commonly arising from a reduction in costs and/or an increase in revenue and/or a reduction in risk (IVS104, 190.1).

As with entity-specific factors, for most bases of value only those synergies available to participants generally will be considered (IVS104, 190.2).

4.4.4.5.3 ASSUMPTIONS AND SPECIAL ASSUMPTIONS

A fundamental feature of IVS is the definition of assumption and special assumption, with care being required to ensure proper classification.

Assumptions may be required either to clarify the state of the asset in the hypothetical exchange or the circumstances under which the asset is assumed to be exchanged and may have a significant impact on value (IVS104, 200.1).

Assumptions generally fall into one of two categories:

- assumed facts that are consistent with, or could be consistent with, those existing at the date of valuation—being assumptions (IVS104, 200.2). Assumptions are further considered and defined consistently in the RICS Red Book (RICS, 2021, VPS 4, 8); or
- assumed facts that differ from those existing at the date of valuation—being special assumptions—where the valuation conclusion is contingent upon the assumed change in circumstances or reflects a view that would not be taken by participants generally (IVS104, 200.2), such as:

  - an assumption that a property is freehold with vacant possession;
  - an assumption that a proposed building had actually been completed on the valuation date; or
  - an assumption that a specific contract was in existence on the valuation date that had not actually been completed (such as a lease) (IVS104, 200.4).

Special assumptions are further considered and defined in the RICS Red Book (RICS, 2021) as either:

- an assumption of facts that differ from those at the valuation date; or
- an assumption that would not be made by a typical market participant in a transaction on that valuation date

and may only be made if they can reasonably be regarded as realistic, relevant and valid for the particular circumstances of the valuation (RICS, 2021, VPS 4, 9) with an instruction requiring an unrealistic assumption to be declined (RICS, 2021, VPS 4, 9.3). An extensive list of possible scenarios where a special assumption may be appropriate is provided in the RICS Red Book (RICS, 2021, VPS 4, 9.4, 9.5, 9.6).

IVS104 requires that all assumptions and special assumptions:

- must be reasonable under the circumstances;
- must be supported by evidence; and
- must be relevant with regard to the purpose for which the valuation is required (IVS104, 200.5).

The RICS Red Book (RICS, 2021) further considers assumptions and special assumptions related to projected values, noting that they must be agreed upon with the client prior to reporting an opinion of projected value, with the report making reference to the higher degree of uncertainty implicit in a projected value where, by definition, comparable evidence will not be available (VPS 4, 11). Such assumptions must be supported by credible studies or economic outlook-based forecasts (11.1) and be in accordance with any applicable national or jurisdictional standard, be realistic and credible and be clearly and comprehensively set out in the report (11.2).

4.4.4.5.4 TRANSACTION COSTS

Transaction costs are generally ignored in the valuation, with most bases of value representing an estimated exchange price for an asset without regard to the seller's costs of sale or the buyer's costs of purchase and without adjustment for any taxes payable by either party as a direct result of the transaction (such as stamp duty or capital gains tax) (IVS104, 210.1).

4.4.4.5.5 ALLOCATION OF VALUE

The allocation of value is the separate apportionment of the value of an asset on an individual or component basis (IVS104, 220.1).

When apportioning value, the allocation method must be consistent with the overall valuation premise/basis and the valuer must:

- follow any applicable legal or regulatory requirements;
- set out a clear and accurate description of the purpose and intended use of the allocation;
- consider the facts and circumstances, such as the relevant characteristic(s) of the item(s) being apportioned; and
- adopt the appropriate methodology(ies) in the circumstances (IVS104, 220.2).

Valuers who are members of API should also consider ANZVGP111 *Valuation procedures— real property* (API, 2021a), section 4.20:

- sale in one line or single transaction (4.20)—the valuation of multiple properties in one development (such as lots in a subdivision) should be based on a single transaction in one line to one buyer, being the sum of individual values and may incorporate an appropriate discount to reflect marketing and sale costs, holding costs and a profit and risk factor.

4.4.4.6 *Valuation model*

The IVS scaffolding includes:

- 4 key concepts (4.4.4.1);
- 3 principal valuation approaches (IVS105) (4.4.4.2);
- 6 bases of value (IVS104) (4.4.4.3);
- 5 premises of value (IVS104) (4.4.4.4);
- 5 further terms (IVS104) (4.4.4.5); and
- the valuation model (IVS105) (4.4.4.6).

The IVS scaffolding provides a framework or context within which the General Standards and Asset Standards sit, setting forth generally accepted valuation principles and concepts that are to be followed in the application of each but not including any procedural requirements.

IVS105 (IVSC, 2021) defines a valuation model relatively widely as follows:

> *A valuation model refers collectively to the quantitative methods, systems, techniques and qualitative judgments used to estimate and document value.*
>
> (90.1)

Of significance, given the widespread use of valuation software produced by major international valuation firms and software suppliers, IVS105 requires the valuer to ensure that the valuation complies with all requirements contained within IVS (90.3), which is a particularly onerous responsibility for the valuer.

The RICS Red Book (RICS, 2021) emphasises that the valuer is *ultimately responsible for selection of the approach(es) and method(s) to be used in individual valuation assignments, unless statute or other mandatory authority imposes a particular requirement* (VPS 5, 5).

Further, when using or creating a valuation model, IVS105 requires the valuer to:

- keep appropriate records to support the selection or creation of the model;
- understand and ensure the output of the valuation model, the significant assumptions and limiting conditions are consistent with the basis and scope of the valuation; and
- consider the key risks associated with the assumptions made in the valuation model. (90.2)

4.4.4.7 *Summary—IVS scaffolding*

The IVS scaffolding is extensive and includes:

- 4 key concepts (4.4.4.1);
- 3 principal valuation approaches (IVS105) (4.4.4.2);
- 6 bases of value (IVS104) (4.4.4.3);
- 5 premises of value (IVS104) (4.4.4.4);
- 5 further terms (IVS104) (4.4.4.5); and
- the valuation model (IVS105) (4.4.4.6).

Within the IVS scaffolding is a lot of detail and carefully defined terms that effectively form the language of international valuation standards. Accordingly, as with any language, careful use of terminology is essential to avoid confusion and the potential creation of risk.

4.4.5 *Summary—International Valuation Standards*

The increasing pace of globalisation and the international flow of capital has seen the advent of International Accounting Standards, International Financial Reporting Standards and International Valuation Standards, often replacing previous regional and/or national valuation standards.

The overarching goal of international financial reporting, accounting and valuation standards is the facilitation of capital mobility globally, which is a particularly important issue for international property investment and worldwide corporate real estate (Parker, 2022). Effectively, therefore, it is International Valuation Standards that now define valuation theory and guide valuation practice in a consistent direction around the world.

Relegating the High Court decision in *Spencer* to its twenty-first-century role as a significant precedent for statutory valuation represents a major change in the Australian approach to valuation theory and practice. Valuation theory and practice are now determined by the provisions of International Valuation Standards through the IVS core principles of valuation, the IVS framework, IVS general standards and asset standards and the extensive and detailed IVS scaffolding.

4.5 RICS Red Book

The RICS Red Book (RICS, 2021) sits beneath IFRS, IAS and IVS in the hierarchy of global standards and seeks to reflect the importance of successfully combining professional, technical and performance standards in order to deliver high-quality valuation advice that meets the expectations and requirements of clients, governments, regulatory bodies, other standard-setters and of the public (RICS, 2021, page 1).

The overall purpose of the RICS Red Book is to facilitate consistency, objectivity and transparency, which are fundamental to building and sustaining public confidence and trust in valuation. In turn, their achievement depends crucially on valuation providers possessing and deploying the appropriate skills, knowledge, experience and ethical behaviour, both to form sound judgments and to report opinions of value clearly and unambiguously to clients and other valuation users in accordance with globally recognised norms (RICS, 2021, page 2).

All members of RICS providing a written valuation are required to comply with the standards set out in the RICS Red Book Global Edition (RICS Red Book) (RICS, 2021), which are mandatory while valuation practice guidance (applications—VPGAs) within the RICS Red Book are advisory (RICS, 2021, page 1).

Within the RICS Red Book, the following are of relevance for the valuation of property:

- Professional Standards—mandatory:

  - PS 1 *Compliance With Standards Where a Written Valuation is Provided*; and
  - PS 2 *Ethics, Competency, Objectivity and Disclosures*;

- Valuation, Technical and Performance Standards—mandatory:

  - VPS 1 *Terms of Engagement (Scope of Work)*;
  - VPS 2 *Inspections, Investigations and Records*;
  - VPS 3 *Valuation Reports*;
  - VPS 4 *Bases of Value, Assumptions and Special Assumptions*; and
  - VPS 5 *Valuation Approaches and Methods*;

- Valuation Applications—advisory:

  - VPGA 1 *Valuation for Inclusion in Financial Statements*;
  - VPGA 2 *Valuation of Interests for Secured Lending*;
  - VPGA 4 *Valuation of Individual Trade Related Properties*;
  - VPGA 5 *Valuation of Plant and Equipment*;
  - VPGA 8 *Valuation of Real Property Interests*;
  - VPGA 9 *Identification of Portfolios, Collections and Groups of Properties*; and
  - VPGA 10 *Matters That May Give Rise to Material Valuation Uncertainty*.

In an Australian context, the RICS Red Book is supplemented by an Australian national supplement (RICS, 2019), which includes:

- Aus VPGA1—ANZVPS;
- Aus VPGA2—Australian state and territory licensing;
- Aus VPGA3—Privacy legislation in Australia;
- Aus VPGA4—Exceptions to compliance requirements;
- Aus VPGA5—Compulsory acquisition;
- Aus VPGA6—Native title; and
- Aus VPGA7—Australian accounting standards.

Reinforcing the important role of standards, RICS actively monitors compliance through a well-established system of regulation and enforcement to provide assurance to clients, engender public confidence and ensure compliance with IVS (RICS, 2021, page 2).

4.5.1 Professional Standards—mandatory

RICS Red Book Professional Standards expressly apply to valuers and are mandatory for all RICS members providing written valuations (RICS, 2021, page 4). The Professional Standards of relevance for the valuation of property comprise:

- PS 1 *Compliance With Standards Where a Written Valuation is Provided*; and
- PS 2 *Ethics, Competency, Objectivity and Disclosures.*

4.5.1.1 PS 1 Compliance with standards where a written valuation is provided

PS1 applies IVS102, recognising the International Ethics Standards and the International Property Management Standards and specifying additional mandatory requirements for RICS members (RICS, 2021, page 5).

PS1 is extensive and beyond the scope of an introductory textbook. Readers are encouraged to read PS1 in full, which is available online. Of particular note are the following:

- the provision of an output from an AVM or a valuation modelling tool is regarded as the provision of a written valuation for the purpose of RICS standards (1.4);
- where a firm's processes expressly prevent compliance, departure is permitted provided that it does not result in misleading the client and is identified in the terms of engagement and report (2.2);
- where an RICS member is requested to provide a report that complies with jurisdictionally specific or other standards, this is permissible provided it is absolutely clear which standards are being adopted in the terms of engagement and report (4.1); and
- any departure from RICS standards must be confirmed and agreed upon with the client and a clear statement to that effect must be included in the terms of engagement and report (6.2)

4.5.1.2 PS 2 Ethics, competency, objectivity and disclosures

PS2 applies the IVS Framework, recognises the International Ethics Standards and the International Property Management Standards and specifies additional mandatory requirements for RICS members (RICS, 2021, page 22), stating:

As it is fundamental to the integrity of the valuation process, all members practising as valuers must have the appropriate experience, skill and judgment for the task in question and must always act in a professional and ethical manner free from any undue influence, bias or conflict of interest.

(page 22)

PS2 is extensive, and readers are encouraged to read it in full, available online. Reflecting the global and professionally wide ambit of RICS, the contents of PS2 are provided under the following headings:

- professional and ethical standards;
- member qualification;
- independence, objectivity, confidentiality and the identification and management of conflicts of interest;
- maintaining strict separation between advisers (Chinese walls);
- disclosures where the public has in interest or upon which third parties may rely (including rotation policy and time as a signatory);
- reviewing another valuer's valuation;
- terms of engagement (scope of work); and
- responsibility for the valuation.

4.5.2 Valuation, technical and performance standards—mandatory

RICS Red Book VPSs contain specific requirements and implementation guidance directed to the provision of a valuation that is IVS compliant (RICS, 2021, page 4).
The VPSs of relevance for the valuation of property comprise:

- VPS 1 *Terms of Engagement (Scope of Work)*—considered in Chapter 5;
- VPS 2 *Inspections, Investigations and Records*—considered in Chapter 5;
- VPS 3 *Valuation Reports*—considered in Chapter 5;
- VPS 4 *Bases of Value, Assumptions and Special Assumptions*—considered in this chapter; and
- VPS 5 *Valuation Approaches and Methods*—considered in this chapter.

4.5.3 Valuation applications—advisory

RICS Red Book VPGAs are concerned with the application and implementation of global standards in specific contexts (RICS, 2021, page 73) and seek to embody best practices.
The VPGAs of relevance for the valuation of property comprise:

- VPGA 1 *Valuation for Inclusion in Financial Statements*;
- VPGA 2 *Valuation of Interests for Secured Lending*;
- VPGA 8 *Valuation of Real Property Interests*;
- VPGA 9 *Identification of Portfolios, Collections and Groups of Properties*; and
- VPGA 10 *Matters That May Give Rise to Material Valuation Uncertainty*.

4.5.3.1 VPGA 9 Identification of portfolios, collections and groups of properties

VPGA 9 provides guidance on the identification of portfolios, collections and groups of properties for reporting in accordance with VPS 3 *Valuation Reports* (RICS, 2021, 1.1).

VPGA 9 is detailed and beyond the scope of an introductory textbook. Readers are encouraged to read VPGA 9 in full, which is available online. Specific clarification of the lotting assumption may be required in scenarios such as the following:

- physically adjoining properties that have been acquired separately by the current owner— such as site amalgamation for development;
- physically separate properties that are occupied by the same entity and where there is a functional dependence between the properties—such as a physically separate car park that is exclusively used by the occupier of a building;
- where ownership of a number of separate properties would be of advantage to a single owner or occupier, such as for economies of scale, increased market share or savings in administration or distribution as with blocks of flats or hotels; or
- where each individual property is an essential component of an operation covering a large geographical area, such as telecommunication masts (2.1).

The valuer should consider the purpose of the valuation and the need to report values individually (3.1) and the relevance of a special assumption (3.2, 3.3) as recorded in the terms of engagement and report (3.3). Consideration should be given to the impact of flooding the market, with regard given in valuations for secured lending purposes (3.6) but not in valuations for inclusion in financial statement purposes (3.5).

4.5.4 Summary—RICS Red Book

Sitting beneath IFRS, IAS and IVS in the hierarchy of global standards, the RICS Red Book is fully harmonised and consistent with IVS. Rather than repeating IVS, the RICS Red Book adds to the range of mandatory and advisory guidance available to valuers through professional standards, valuation, technical and performance standards and valuation applications. Importantly, in an Australian context, RICS also issues an Australian national supplement.

4.5 API guidance papers

According to the API website, the API publishes professional standards including, but not limited to, Guidance Papers, Standards Updates and Protocols on a variety of valuation and property-specific topics (www.api.org.au/standards/, accessed 27 January 2023).

The API's professional standards provide transparency and public accountability, with API members held accountable to the principles and rules set out within the codes for professional conduct and continuing professional development. API also publishes a code of ethics setting out expectations of members who are also required to comply with IVS as well as a suite of documents relating to residential mortgage valuation services (www.api.org.au/standards/).

API guidance papers sit beneath IFRS, IAS and IVS in the hierarchy of global standards, sitting parallel to the RICS Red Book, with the API Code of Ethics (API, 2021b) and the API Rules of Professional Conduct (API, 2021c) considered in Chapter 2.

The objective of API Guidance Papers is to clarify professional and industry processes, appropriate practices and procedures and to discuss their use and implementation (www.api. org.au/standards/ accessed 27 January 2023),

When accessed on 27 January 2023, the API website (www.api.org.au/standards/) listed 39 Guidance Papers, but no Standards Updates nor Protocols were apparent. Numerous Guidance Papers are considered in this book, with other Guidance Papers covering a wide range of topics, including contamination, partial interests in co-ownership structures, self-storage, disclaimer clauses and qualifications and preparing a property for sale.

Readers are referred to the API website (www.api.org.au/standards/) for further details.

4.6 Summary and conclusions

Chapter 1 outlined the structure of the property asset class, examining the traditional characteristics of property (including heterogeneity, durability, illiquidity and so forth) and the traditional risks of property (including location, building, tenant risk and so forth) through the lenses of systematic, unsystematic and idiosyncratic risk, aligning property valuation with capital market theory.

Chapter 2 considered the evolution of property valuation in Australia, the role of the valuer and the diverse activities of the valuation profession, followed by a detailed examination of the inter-acting framework provided by valuation standards and ethical standards promulgated by IVSC, RICS and API.

Chapter 3 explored concepts of value and normative and positive definitions of value, dissecting the International Valuation Standards' definition of market value with a reconciliation to the concept of market value in *Spencer v Commonwealth* (1907) and examining such contemporary valuation issues as valuation lag, variance, accuracy, negligence and valuer rotation.

This chapter introduced International Financial Reporting Standards and International Accounting Standards with a detailed examination of the key provisions of International Valuation Standards, the RICS Red Book and API guidance papers that impact on valuation practice in Australia.

International Financial Reporting Standards and International Accounting Standards sit above International Valuation Standards in the hierarchy of standards, with the latter being harmonised and consistent with the former. Perhaps the greatest overlap between IFRS, IAS and IVSs is in the area of valuation for financial reporting purposes, making it regrettable that fair value in the former is defined differently than in the latter while, for the purposes of property valuation, IFRS/IAS fair value is effectively deemed to be the same as IVS market value.

The key provisions of International Valuation Standards are both extensive and detailed. However, the increasing pace of globalisation and the international flow of capital results in international financial reporting, accounting and valuation standards being the facilitators of capital mobility globally, being a particularly important issue for international property investment and worldwide corporate real estate. With *Spencer* now relegated to its twenty-first-century role as a significant precedent for statutory valuation, International Valuation Standards currently effectively define valuation theory and guide valuation practice in a consistent direction around the world.

Sitting beneath IFRS, IAS and IVS in the hierarchy of global standards, the RICS Red Book is fully harmonised and consistent with IVS. Rather than repeating IVS, the RICS Red Book adds to the range of mandatory and advisory guidance available to valuers through professional standards, valuation, technical and performance standards and valuation applications. Importantly, in an Australian context, RICS also issues an Australian national supplement.

Sitting parallel to the RICS Red Book and beneath IFRS, IAS and IVS in the hierarchy of global standards, API guidance papers provide valuers with a wide range of information on professional practice issues relevant to Australia. API guidance papers such as those on native title matters, valuations for use in offer documents and land contamination issues all provide Australia-specific guidance written to address local conditions and local requirements and so complementing the globally applicable material in IVS and the RICS Red Book.

The next chapter will outline conceptual approaches to the valuation process with a review of the self-supporting process of instructing, undertaking and reporting valuations under the International Valuation Standards, RICS Red Book and API guidance papers, examining how this process inter-relates to the choice of valuation approach, valuation method and the purpose of the valuation.

Chapter 6 addresses the market approach to valuation through the comparative method of valuation, including the key steps of accumulation, analysis, adjustment and application of comparable sales evidence to the subject property being valued, with an example.

Chapter 7 considers the income approach to valuation addressed through the static methods of the capitalisation of income and the profits methods of valuation, including an examination of the key inputs for each method with examples and a consideration of both marriage value and the surrender and renewal of leases.

Chapter 8 considers the income approach to valuation addressed through the dynamic method of the discounted cash flow method of valuation, including an examination of the key inputs and a focus on the derivation of the discount rate and consideration of the role of sensitivity and scenario analysis, with examples.

Chapter 9 considers the cost approach to valuation addressed through the replacement cost, reproduction cost, summation and residual or hypothetical development methods of valuation.

Finally, Chapter 10 concludes the book with a consideration of future perspectives, including the role of uncertainty, data, automated valuation models, artificial intelligence, optionality, environmental, social and governance issues, retail and office space use and indigenous issues.

References

AASB (2015) AASB13 *fair value measurement*, Australian Accounting Standards Board, Melbourne.

API (2021a) *ANZVGP111 valuation procedures—real property*, Australian Property Institute, Deakin.

API (2021b) *Code of ethics*, Australian Property Institute, Deakin.

API (2021c) *Rules of professional conduct*, Australian Property Institute, Deakin.

API (2022) *API ANZVGP103 Addressing the concept of forced sale*, Australian Property Institute, Deakin.

Elder, B (2018) 'International standards: key to unlocking the value of green buildings?', in Wilkinson, S et al. (Ed) *Routledge handbook of sustainable real estate*, Routledge, Abingdon.

IASB (2011) *IFRS 13 fair value measurement*, International Accounting Standards Board, London.

IVSC (2014) *Global regulatory convergence and the valuation profession*, International Valuation Standards Council, London.

IVSC (2021) *International valuation standards*, International Valuation Standards Council, London.

Parker, D (2022) 'Addressing cyclicality through international financial standards', in d'Amato, M and Coskun, Y (Ed) *Property valuation and market cycle*, Springer, New York.

RICS (2019) *RICS valuation—global standards 2017: Australia national supplement 2019*, Royal Institution of Chartered Surveyors, London.

RICS (2021) *RICS valuation—global standards*, Royal Institution of Chartered Surveyors, London.

Stewart, R (2022) 'Valuation for financial reporting purposes', in Parker, D (Ed) *Principles and practice of property valuation in Australia*, Routledge, Abingdon.

5 Instructing, undertaking and reporting valuations

5.1 Introduction

This book is an introduction to the fundamentals of property valuation, outlining the principal methods of property valuation in Australia within the context of International Valuation Standards, bridging the gap between traditional property valuation methods and the modern era of global valuation governance.

Chapter 1 outlined the structure of the property asset class, examining the traditional characteristics of property (including heterogeneity, durability, illiquidity and so forth) and the traditional risks of property (including location, building, tenant risk and so forth) through the lenses of systematic, unsystematic and idiosyncratic risk, so aligning property valuation with capital market theory.

Chapter 2 considered the evolution of property valuation in Australia, the role of the valuer and the diverse activities of the valuation profession, followed by a detailed examination of the inter-acting framework provided by valuation standards and ethical standards promulgated by IVSC, RICS and API.

Chapter 3 explored concepts of value and normative and positive definitions of value, dissecting the International Valuation Standards' definition of market value with a reconciliation to the concept of market value in *Spencer v Commonwealth* (1907) and examining such contemporary valuation issues as valuation lag, variance, accuracy, negligence and valuer rotation.

Chapter 4 introduced International Financial Reporting Standards and International Accounting Standards with a detailed examination of the key provisions of International Valuation Standards, the RICS Red Book and API guidance papers that impact on valuation practice in Australia.

This chapter seeks to outline conceptual approaches to the valuation process with a review of the self-supporting process of instructing, undertaking and reporting valuations under the International Valuation Standards, RICS Red Book and API guidance papers, examining how this process inter-relates to the choice of valuation approach, valuation method and the purpose of the valuation.

Chapter 6 addresses the market approach to valuation through the comparative method of valuation, including the key steps of accumulation, analysis, adjustment and application of comparable sales evidence to the subject property being valued, with an example.

Chapter 7 considers the income approach to valuation addressed through the static methods of the capitalisation of income and the profits methods of valuation, including an examination of the key inputs for each method with examples and a consideration of both marriage value and the surrender and renewal of leases.

DOI: 10.1201/9781003397922-5

Chapter 8 considers the income approach to valuation addressed through the dynamic method of the discounted cash flow method of valuation, including an examination of the key inputs and a focus on the derivation of the discount rate and consideration of the role of sensitivity and scenario analysis, with examples.

Chapter 9 considers the cost approach to valuation addressed through the replacement cost, reproduction cost, summation and residual or hypothetical development methods of valuation.

Finally, Chapter 10 concludes the book with a consideration of future perspectives, including the role of uncertainty, data, automated valuation models, artificial intelligence, optionality, environmental, social and governance issues, retail and office space use and indigenous issues.

This book is based on those standards and guidance documents published in IVSC (2021) and RICS (2021) and on the API website (accessed January to May 2023). Given their nature, standards and guidance documents are dynamic, being regularly updated and with the most recently published versions replacing previously published versions. Accordingly, readers should not rely on this book as a current statement of a standard or guidance document and should visit www.ivsc.org, www.rics.org and/or www.api.org.au to find the most recent version.

As an introductory textbook on property valuation methods in Australia, this book is a companion to Australia's leading advanced valuation textbook, *Principles and Practice of Property Valuation in Australia,* edited by the same author and also published by Routledge, which is a deeper analysis of key principles underlying property valuation and current techniques and issues in the practice of property valuation for major sectors of the Australian property market.

Accordingly, this chapter will now consider:

- the concept of the valuation process through the lenses provided by Graaskamp (1977) and Whipple (2006);
- the instruction process through the lenses of IVS101, RICS VPS1 and API ANZVGP111;
- undertaking a valuation through the lenses of IVS102, RICS VPS2 and API ANZVGP111; and
- reporting a valuation through the lenses of IVS103, RICS VPS3 and API ANZVGP111.

5.2 The valuation process—conceptual approach

The valuation process may be conceptualised as, essentially, being the steps by which a valuer gets from the valuation question to the valuation answer comprising the steps in performing a valuation. The seminal approach to the valuation process was formulated by Graaskamp (1977) and remains relevant today, some 50 years later. More recently, the valuation process was formulated as a problem-solving process, as summarised by Whipple (2006).

It may be contended that the need for an understanding of the conceptual approach has diminished with the widespread use of extensive standardised documentation for high-volume valuation tasks (such as that provided by a bank to the valuer for residential mortgage valuations) and the adoption of IVS101 *Scope of Work* (IVSC, 2021) which frames the valuation process as providing an answer to a question.

However, in the unlikely event that a request for a valuation is not covered by standardised documentation or capable of being addressed by IVS101, the application of a conceptual approach to the valuation process remains relevant and is considered further in what follows.

5.2.1 Graaskamp's seminal approach to the valuation process

While there is a range of ways to describe or classify the valuation process, Graaskamp's (1977) seminal *Appraisal of 25 North Pinckney* was adapted by Whipple (2006) to describe or classify the valuation process as 11 sequential steps as shown in Table 5.1.

Each of the steps is both essential and timeless, being as valid today as when Graaskamp identified them almost 50 years ago. However, today, some of the steps are automatically accommodated through the application of IVS (such as notions of highest and best use (Steps 4 and 6) and most probable vendor/purchaser (Steps 5 and 7)), whereas others require direct application by the valuer (such as Step 3 which was considered in Chapter 6).

5.2.2 Whipple's problem-solving approach to the valuation process

Akin to conceptualising the valuation process as a process of answering a question, Whipple (2006) conceptualises the valuation process as solving a problem through six steps.

5.2.2.1 Step 1: Define the problem

The problem may range from a vendor who wants to know what a property may sell for to a lender who wants to know the value of a property to determine if it fits within lending criteria

Table 5.1 Valuation Process

Step	Valuation Process	
1	Problem analysis	
	Definition of value	
2	Data programme	
3	Property analysis:	
	Physical attributes	
	Legal/political attributes	
	Locational attributes	
	Psychological attributes	
	Environmental attributes	
4	Alternative uses	
5	Effective demand—competitive supply	
6	Most probable use selection	
7	Most probably buyer profile	
8	Choice and application of valuation method	
9	Data satisfactory?	Data satisfactory?
	No	Yes
	Select normative valuation method	Inference from past transactions
		Most probable buyer simulation
10	Review and adjustments for special factors:	
	Apply alternative method as check	
	Check data reflects value definition	
	Review assumptions	
	Sensitivity of result to assumptions	
	Check results consistent with probable buyer motivation	
	Check all crucial issues addressed	
11	Final value estimate:	
	Transaction zone	
	Most probable price	
	Limiting conditions	

Source: Adapted from Whipple (2006) and Graaskamp (1977)

to an investor who wants to know the value to determine if the property may provide an acceptable return to a government seeking to raise tax or acquire a property for the development of infrastructure. Each has a different problem, but the answer to each problem is the assessment of the value of a property, albeit on a differing basis of value. The problem is, therefore, defined by identifying the reason for the valuation and the relevant basis of value (Whipple, 2006).

5.2.2.2 *Step 2: Determine the most probable use*

For some properties, such as a house in the heart of an extensive residential suburb, the most probable use may be the same as the actual use. For other properties, the most probable use may differ from the actual use where, for example, planning laws allow redevelopment of a semi-derelict industrial property into a residential apartment block. Whipple (2006) wisely advises starting this step with a *productivity analysis*, being an assessment of points favourable to a property and unfavourable to a property, or the property's *utility* and *disutility*, being considered consistently through the lenses of:

- physical characteristics;
- legal characteristics;
- locational characteristics;
- psychological characteristics; and
- environmental attributes,

prior to interpreting each in terms of their implications in the marketplace. From this, the valuer may then form a view as to how the market sees the property from which a range of possible uses may be contemplated and the most probable use identified.

5.2.2.3 *Step 3: Determine the most probable buyer*

Given the most probable use identified, Whipple (2006) then suggests identifying the most probable buyer (individuals or entities rather than a singular individual or entity) or buyer type (group or market sector). For example, the most probable buyers for a high-rise CBD office investment may be a range of institutions capable of individual nomination or a buyer type, such as REITs or superannuation funds.

Determining the most probable buyer allows the valuer to forecast buyer behaviour in terms of how such a buyer would approach determining a bid for the property. The valuer will need to draw on market knowledge to identify the most probable buyers and their bargaining positions which effectively defines the market for the property being valued.

5.2.2.4 *Step 4: Select the method of valuation*

Having identified the most probable use and the most probable buyer, Whipple (2006) then suggests that the next step is to determine the price that such an entity might pay for the bundle of productivities, though through the lens of IVS, this may be preferably considered as that price which such a bundle of productivities might command.

Whipple (2006) notes that the main factors affecting the selection of the method of valuation are:

- the nature of the problem;
- the nature of the available data;

- the cost of gathering data; and
- the abilities of the individual valuer.

At a conceptual level (rather than identifying individual methods of valuation), Whipple (2006) identifies three approaches to the estimation of probable price, being:

- inference from past transactions;
- market simulation; and
- normative modelling.

5.2.2.4.1 INFERENCE FROM PAST TRANSACTIONS

This approach seeks to estimate the probable price for the subject property based on previous transactions of other similar properties, being a market-based or positive approach to price estimation.

Whipple (2006) validly notes that those past transactions to be considered should involve properties with similar productivities and buyers with similar motivations to those relevant to the subject property, though through the lens of IVS, this may be preferably considered as the motivations of a group rather than a specific individual.

A productivity analysis of each transacted property and the subject property should be undertaken and compared based on the utilities and disutilities identified by relevant market participants as featuring in their pricing process, which may be discovered through discussion with market participants.

Whipple (2006) cautions that inferences from past transactions are best used under the following circumstances:

- where there is a useful number of suitably qualified transactions to infer from;
- where the circumstances surrounding each can be ascertained;
- where they relate to the recent past;
- where market conditions are stable; and
- when the forecast of the most probable price is not required too far into the future.

Where these conditions hold, this approach is the most reliable method for estimating the probable price. Where these conditions do not hold, market simulation may be considered.

5.2.2.4.2 MARKET SIMULATION

Market simulation is the simulation of the most probable buyer's price fixing calculus, being how the most probable buyers (as a group) who are currently active in the market determine how much they might pay for the property, being a market-based or positive approach to price estimation (Whipple, 2006).

For example, for high-rise CBD office towers or super-regional shopping centres, the most probable use may be the existing use and the most probable buyer may be institutions or REITs; therefore the valuer may discuss with such market participants their likely approach to valuation, the level of input variables that they might adopt and so forth. The valuer may then analyse the feedback received and simulate the approach adopted by market participants to determine value.

5.2.2.4.3 NORMATIVE MODELLING

Inference from past transactions and market simulation asserts that the market works in a particular way based on actual market information, being market-based or positive approaches to price estimation. However, in the absence of market information, the valuer may need to adopt a normative approach whereby the valuer makes a series of assumptions about how the market should work (Whipple, 2006).

Such assumptions may include types of buyers, their decision-making process, information upon which they rely and so forth, which may culminate in the assertion of a pricing model based on an informed and supported view by the valuer (Whipple, 2006). However, caution is required that the valuer does not impose his personal opinions beyond that which may be supportable by market principles.

A normative approach may be required following a period of significant market change, such as those following booms, collapses or events such as the GFC or COVID pandemic, when transactions may be few and the past may not be a guide to the future.

Critically, in a normative approach, the valuer is effectively making the market rather than in a positive approach where a valuer is reflecting the market, which may impact transaction price levels when market activity resumes—raising the question, *did the valuer accurately forecast the market or lead the market up or down?*

5.2.2.5 Step 5: Review and adjustment for external factors

Having formed a preliminary view of the price that the subject property's bundle of productivities might command, the preliminary estimate is checked and refined through a review of the work undertaken and consideration of any special factors, potential weaknesses and inconsistencies (Whipple, 2006).

For example, special factors may include a list of issues specified in a lease for the valuer to take into account when determining rental, potential weaknesses may be identified by adopting a check method of valuation and reconciling the results and inconsistencies may include checking that all assumptions are consistent (such as rental levels with rental growth rates and the discount rate) (Whipple, 2006).

5.2.2.6 Step 6: Value conclusion and limiting conditions

Having formed a preliminary view of the price that the subject property's bundle of productivities might command, then reviewed and made appropriate adjustments, the last step comprises the derivation of a final estimate of value and any limiting conditions attaching thereto (Whipple, 2006).

Limiting conditions may include reliance on external sources of information such as the advice of other professionals, critical assumptions adopted or assumptions or information provided by the client (Whipple, 2006).

Whipple (2006) cautions that uncertainty renders the assessment of a point estimate of value challenging, advocating for advice of a value range (transaction zone), with such uncertainty arising from the complex amalgam of forces bearing on the property (locational, physical, legal, external, etc.), human reaction to the bundle of utilities and disutilities offered by the property and the resulting price estimate.

However, recognising that clients usually require a point estimate of value, Whipple (2006) recommends that the valuer report what degree of reliability can be placed on the estimate with higher confidence resulting in a narrower transaction zone and vice versa.

5.2.3 Summary

As the reader will note, there is a significant amount of commonality between Graaskamp (1977), Whipple (2006) and IVS101, 102 and 103, with the former being more conceptual and the latter being more prescriptive.

In many cases, the valuation process will be guided by the provisions of IVS101, 102 and 103. However, in those cases where IVS101, 102 and 103 may not be applicable, such as the valuation of unusual properties, the valuation processes advocated by Graaskamp (1977) and Whipple (2006) provide useful frameworks.

5.3 The valuation process: instructing, undertaking and reporting

The valuation process is addressed by IVSC in IVS101, 102 and 103, by the RICS Red Book in VPS1, 2 and 3 and by the API in ANZVGP111 as three sequential elements being instructing, undertaking and reporting. As such, the IVS standards, RICS practice standards and API guidance notes are styled to be applicable to a wide range of valuation tasks.

Rather than conceptualising the valuation process as a series of steps, IVS echo Whipple (2006) by conceptualising the valuation process as providing an answer to a question, whereby the exact nature of the question becomes a critical issue. IVS anticipate all the key elements of the valuation process as a question and include these within IVS101 *Scope of Work*, then focus on the undertaking of the valuation in IVS102 *Investigations and Compliance* before addressing the findings of the valuation in IVS103 *Reporting*. The following is based on IVSC (2021), with the versions of IVS101, 102 and 103 effective January 2022.

The RICS Red Book (RICS, 2021) adopts the same approach through VPS1 *Terms of Engagement (Scope of Work)*, VPS2 *Inspections, Investigations and Records* and VPS3 *Valuation Reports*, with the following based on the versions of VPS1, 2 and 3 effective January 2022.

The API's ANZVGP111 *Valuation Procedures—Real Property* (API, 2021a) also adopts the same approach with instructing, undertaking and reporting, incorporating IVS101 but having more operational details, with the following based on the version published on 25 June 2021.

5.3.1 Instructing—IVS101, RICS VPS1 and API ANZVGP111

The instructing part of the valuation process is addressed in IVS101 *Scope of Work*, VPS1 *Terms of Engagement (Scope of Work)* and ANZVGP111 *Valuation Procedures—Real Property*.

5.3.1.1 IVS101

IVS101 *Scope of Work* applies to a wide spectrum of valuation assignments, including valuations performed by employed valuers for their own employers, valuers engaged by clients to perform valuations and valuation reviews where the reviewer may not be required to provide their own opinion of value. All valuation advice and the work undertaken in its preparation must be appropriate for the intended purpose.

IVS101 *Scope of Work* emphasises a dialogue between the client and the valuer to ensure that both fully understand what is to be provided in the valuation and any limitations on its use before it is undertaken or reported.

To ensure such clarity, IVS101 requires communication of the scope of work by the valuer to the client to include:

- identity of the valuer, be it a group or individual with any material connections that could limit the provision of unbiased and objective valuation advice being disclosed at the outset, together with the nature and extent of any material assistance from others;

- identity of the client for whom the valuation is being produced, being important when determining the form and content of the report to ensure it contains information relevant to their needs;
- identity of any other intended users, being important when determining the form and content of the report to ensure it contains information relevant to their needs;
- identity of the asset(s) being valued;
- the valuation currency, being particularly important for valuations involving assets in multiple countries in multiple currencies;
- the purpose of the valuation must be clearly stated in order that valuation advice is not used out of context or for purposes for which it is not intended. The purpose of the valuation will usually determine the basis of value to be used;
- the basis/bases of value to be used, which must be appropriate for the purpose of the valuation;
- the valuation date, which may differ from the date of the valuation report;
- the nature and extent of the valuer's work and any limitations thereon. Any limitations or restrictions on the inspection, enquiry and/or analysis in the valuation assignment must be identified together with any assumptions or special assumptions required to be made;
- the nature and sources of information upon which the valuer relies and the extent of any verification undertaken must be identified;
- the identity of any significant assumptions and/or special assumptions must be stated;
- the type of report format to be prepared within which the valuation will be communicated must be described;
- any restrictions on the use, distribution and publication of the report, where necessary or desirable, must be clearly communicated; and
- that the valuation will be prepared in compliance with IVS and that the valuer will assess the appropriateness of all significant inputs with the nature of any departures being explained,

with any changes during the course of undertaking the valuation being communicated between the valuer and the client. The scope of work should be established and agreed upon prior to the valuer beginning work, with a written scope of work being preferable (IVSC, 2021).

5.3.1.2 RICS VPS1

The requirements of IVS101 are echoed and amplified in VPS1 *Terms of Engagement (Scope of Work)* in the RICS Red Book (RICS, 2021). Significantly, VPS1 is mandatory and applies IVS101 together with additional mandatory requirements designed to:

- enhance client understanding of the service to be provided, with clarity concerning the basis on which the fee will be calculated;
- provide assurance that work undertaken by RICS members meets high professional standards backed by effective regulation; and
- address particular aspects of implementation that may arise in individual cases.

Significantly, the *General Principles* (1.3) suggest that the terms of engagement should convey a clear understanding of the valuation requirements and processes and should be couched in terms that can be read and understood by someone with no prior knowledge of the subject asset or of the valuation process.

The format and detail of the valuation report are to be agreed upon between the valuer and the client and recorded in writing in the terms of engagement, with the report being proportionate to the task and the valuation being professionally adequate for the purpose with the standards expected to be met set out in VPS3 (1.4).

While a valuation may need to reflect an actual or anticipated marketing constraint, details of the constraint must be agreed and set out in the terms of engagement. The term "forced sale value" must not be used (1.5).

By the time that the valuation is concluded, but prior to the issue of the report, all relevant matters must have been brought to the client's attention and appropriately documented to ensure that the report does not contain any revision of the initial terms of engagement of which the client is unaware (1.6).

VPS1 accepts the role of standard forms of instruction, templates and so forth, noting that these may require amendment for compliance (2.1), stressing the vital importance of the preparation of written terms of engagement for all valuation work to avoid the risk of subsequent queries where the parameters of the valuation assignment are insufficiently documented (2.2).

The terms of engagement must (being a mandatory requirement) address the inclusions in IVS101 together with:

- the basis upon which the fee will be calculated;
- where the firm is registered for regulation by RICS, reference to the firm's complaints handling procedure;
- a statement that compliance with these standards may be subject to monitoring under RICS' conduct and disciplinary regulations; and
- a statement setting out any limitations on liability that have been agreed upon (3.1).

Reflecting the importance placed on getting clear instructions that are understood by the parties before the valuation assignment is undertaken, the RICS Red Book not only makes terms of engagement mandatory but also amplifies the IVS101 inclusions (3.2). Such amplification is extensive and readers are referred to the Red Book for the full requirements. By way of example, *identity of the valuer* is amplified to require the inclusion of a statement confirming:

- that the valuation will be the responsibility of a named individual valuer, with RICS not allowing a valuation to be prepared by a firm;
- that the valuer is in a position to provide an objective and unbiased valuation;
- whether or not the valuer has any material connection or involvement with the subject asset or the other parties to the valuation assignment, with disclosure of any factors that could limit the valuer's ability to provide an impartial and independent valuation; and
- that the valuer is competent to undertake the valuation assignment, with the nature of any material assistance from and extent of reliance on others to be clear, agreed and recorded (3.2(a)).

5.3.1.3 API ANZVGP111

ANZVGP111 Valuation Procedures—Real Property (API, 2021a) addresses instructions (3.0), noting that instructions should (not must) be confirmed in writing and include (3.1):

- details regarding access arrangements;
- identification;
- ownership;
- agreed fee;
- if applicable, the purchase price and selling agent;
- the parties intended to rely on the valuation;

- the purpose of the valuation; and
- the agreed time for completion of the report.

Significantly, this excludes specifying the valuation basis and the valuation date but, interestingly, includes specifying the purchase price despite the extensive behavioural finance literature on the effects of anchoring in the valuation process.

Despite having identified that to be included within instructions in 3.1 and noted that it is the valuer's responsibility to comply with IVS (1.0), 3.2 *Scope of Work* then states:

> Before commencing any valuation, it is important to clarify with the client what is to be included in the scope of work as per IVS101 (International Valuation Standards). Some aspects of the scope of work may be addressed in documents such as standing engagement instructions, service agreements, or a company's internal policies and procedures.

Whereas IVS101 is a simple list for application, instructing under ANZVGP111 *Valuation Procedures—Real Property* would appear more challenging. To align with *competent professional practice*, being an intention of a Guidance Paper, and to be compliant with IVS101 would appear to require the valuer to:

- include the items listed in ANZVGP111 Valuation Procedures—Real Property 3.1 in the instruction; and
- include other items from IVS101 in the instruction except where addressed in documents such as standing engagement instructions, service agreements or a company's internal policies and procedures (which, presumably, should be cross-referenced or attached as part of the instruction).

5.3.1.4 Summary—instructing

IVS101 provides a clear basis for instructing, which emphasises transparency and communication with the client to ensure a common understanding. VPS1 echoes this approach but with additional details such as fees and complaints handling procedures. While ANZVGP111, on the one hand, sits beneath and incorporates IVS101 but with additional operational details, the IVS101 instruction may not stand alone, and careful integration with standing engagement instructions, service agreements or a company's internal policies and procedures will be required.

5.3.2 Undertaking—IVS102, RICS VPS2 and API ANZVGP111

The undertaking part of the valuation process is addressed in IVS102 *Investigations and Compliance*, VPS2 *Inspections, Investigations and Records* and ANZVGP111 *Valuation Procedures—Real Property*.

5.3.2.1 IVS102

Having jointly agreed and documented a *Scope of Work*, the exact nature of the question will be settled, where the valuation process is conceptualised as providing an answer to a question, with the question then being answered through the undertaking of the valuation in IVS102 *Investigations and Compliance*, before addressing the findings of the valuation in IVS103 *Reporting*.

IVS102 *Investigations and Compliance* (IVSC, 2021) addresses the process of undertaking the valuation by the valuer, requiring any investigations made during the course of a valuation assignment to be appropriate for the purpose of the valuation assignment and the basis of value (20.1), such that sufficient evidence must be assembled by means such as inspection, inquiry, computation and analysis to ensure that the valuation is properly supported (20.2). When determining the extent of evidence necessary, professional judgment should be exercised to ensure the information is adequate for the purpose of the valuation (20.3).

Any limits agreed on the extent of the valuer's investigations must be noted in the scope of work (20.3), ensuring transparency and a clear understanding by the client of any such limits. However, such limitations cannot be so substantial that the valuer is unable to sufficiently evaluate the inputs and assumptions for appropriateness for the valuation purpose (IVS105); otherwise, the valuation cannot be performed in compliance with IVS.

The valuer should consider whether information supplied by other parties is credible and may be relied upon without adversely affecting the integrity of the valuation opinion (20.4). Significant inputs provided to the valuer by management and others should be considered, investigated and corroborated (20.4), with consideration of how such information should be used if found to be unsupported. In considering the credibility and reliability of the information provided, valuers should consider the purpose of the valuation, the significance of the information to the valuation conclusion, the expertise of the source in relation to the subject matter and whether the source is independent of either the asset being valued or the recipient of the valuation (20.5).

IVS102 further requires the valuer to keep a record of the work performed during the valuation process and the basis for the work on which the conclusions were reached for a reasonable period after completion of the assignment, having regard for any relevant statutory, legal or regulatory requirements. Such records should include all key inputs, all calculations, investigations and analyses relevant to the final conclusion together with a copy of any draft or final report(s) provided to the client (30.1).

In the event that statutory, legal, regulatory or other authoritative requirements that differ from the requirement of IVS must be followed, a valuer must follow such requirements, referred to as a *departure*, with the valuation still being performed in overall compliance with IVS (40.1).

5.3.2.2 RICS VPS2

The requirements of IVS102 are echoed and amplified in considerably greater detail in VPS2 *Inspections, Investigations and Records* in the RICS Red Book (RICS, 2021), which is mandatory and imports VPGA8 *Valuation of Real Property Interests* (RICS, 2021) concerning matters evident or to be considered during the inspection of the asset being valued.

VPS2 applies IVS102 and further specifies additional mandatory requirements for RICS members designed to enhance client understanding of the valuation process and report while also addressing particular aspects of implementation that may arise in individual cases.

VPS2 requires that inspections and investigations must always be carried out to the extent necessary to produce a valuation that is professionally adequate for its purpose. The valuer must take reasonable steps to verify the information relied upon in the preparation of the valuation and clarify with the client any necessary assumptions that will be relied upon (1).

VPS2 invokes VPS1 and VPS3 concerning the identification and recording of any limitations or restrictions on the inspection, inquiry and analysis in the terms of engagement and the report, together with any assumptions or special assumptions made as a result of the restriction.

The extent to which the subject asset is to be inspected and any investigation is to be made must be agreed upon in the terms of engagement (1.1). While the degree of inspection or investigation that is appropriate will vary depending on the nature of the asset and the purpose of the valuation, VPS2 cautions that to dispense with inspection may introduce an unacceptable degree of risk in the valuation advice to be provided (1.3).

However, a revaluation without reinspection of an interest in real property previously valued by the valuer or firm may be undertaken only where the valuer is satisfied there have been no material changes to the physical attributes of the property or the nature of its location since the last valuation (2.1), with this assumption stated in the terms of engagement (2.2) with the interval between inspections being a matter for the professional judgment of the valuer (2.4).

Measurements of inspected property must have regard to International Property Measurement Standards (1.4), and an inspection should have proper regard to the relevance and significance of those matters under the general heading of *sustainability and ESG matters* (1.5, VPGA8).

VPS2 advocates declining a valuation instruction where the relevant information is not available or an inspection may not be possible or may be limited if the valuer considers that it is not possible to provide a valuation, even on a restricted basis (1.7).

Concerning valuation records, VPS2 requires that a proper record must be kept of inspections, investigations and other key inputs in an appropriate business format (3), clearly and accurately recorded in a manner that is neither ambiguous nor misleading and does not create a false impression (3.1).

To maintain an audit trail and to be in a position to respond effectively to future enquiries, legible notes (which may include photographs) of the findings, the limits of the inspection and the circumstances in which it was carried out must be made, including a record of key inputs and all calculations, investigations and analyses considered when arriving at the valuation (3.2) together with sustainability and ESG data (3.3). Such notes and records should be in an appropriate business format and retained for an appropriate period depending on the purpose of the valuation and any statutory, legal or regulatory requirements (3.4).

5.3.2.3 *API ANZVGP111*

The API's ANZVGP111 *Valuation Procedures—Real Property* (API, 2021a) is of relevance to undertaking a valuation through section 5.0 *Inspection and Enquiry Guidelines*, where the valuer should obtain enough information and should carry out on-site observations to allow the property to be adequately identified, with the source of any identification information noted and due caution exercised before reliance thereon (5.1) and the identification of the property by street name/number confirmed (5.5).

ANZVGP111 sections 5.2, 5.3 and 5.4 consider fixtures, non-fixtures and chattels, with section 5.7 cautioning on commenting if buildings are within fenced and title boundaries with useful information contained within a contract of sale which is desirable to sight (5.6).

Notably, ANZVGP111 section 4.25 states that the valuation report shall be signed by the person who conducts the valuation, who must be the person who inspects the property. It is, therefore, mandatory for the valuer who conducts the valuation and signs the valuation report to have inspected the property.

Section 5.9 details *the preferred method of inspection and notation of that inspection* as follows:

- sketch plan of the main building, preferably to scale and with the method of measurement identified;
- 26 relevant items for description and comment, considered further in what follows;

- regard to obvious significant external and/or internal defects or items of non-compliance with regulation which fall within the valuer's area of expertise, overall general condition and any current certificates (such as white ant certificates or Council orders);
- external features including views, lines of sight and the nature of surrounding development;
- obtain a copy of the relevant plan and documents for strata, unit and community title properties; and
- take appropriate photographs of the property as a record.

The 26 relevant items for description and comment in section 5.9 provide a helpful list that can be recategorised and applied as a starting point to the inspection of many types of property:

Built envelope—external:

- wall and roof framing;
- external wall coverings;
- roof drainage;
- roof coverings;
- special design or architectural features;
- car parking facilities;
- loading and unloading facilities;

Built envelope—internal:

- flooring;
- internal linings to walls and floors;
- ceilings,
- ceiling heights;
- natural and artificial lighting;
- amenity and storage areas;
- design features—including spacing of columns or clear spans, internal height, minimum clearances to roof frame, door clearances (height and width);
- prime cost items;

Built envelope—services:

- services connected or available to the site—including water, electricity, three-phase electricity and gas;
- building services—including sprinklers, hydrants, hose reels, ventilation, air conditioning, security systems, auxiliary power and lighting, escalators and elevators;
- ventilation;
- internet access and other technologies;
- courier access;

Built envelope—surrounds:

- excavations;
- landscaping;
- ancillary structures and ground improvements;
- hard stand and storage areas;

- fencing; and
- vehicular access points and manoeuvring areas (API, 2021a).

With experience, regularity of inspection allows the valuer to become familiar with the listed items and to identify a property where an expected item may be absent or an unexpected item may be present, which may have a valuation implication. For example, in a multi-level shopping centre, upward and downward escalators would be expected items, and the replacement of one by a staircase may be an unexpected item with a valuation implication.

As section 5.9 notes, taking appropriate photographs provides a helpful record, together with notes and measurements, of the inspection and may be particularly useful when later writing the valuation report.

5.3.2.4 Summary—undertaking

The undertaking element of the valuation process illustrates a significant difference between IVSC, RICS and API in the extent of direction and guidance provided. IVS102 is a relatively high-level approach to undertaking, leaving much to the judgment and experience of the valuer. VPS2 incorporates IVS102 while focusing more closely on the inspection of the property being valued as a risk management process and introducing regard to ESG issues such as flooding, wildfires, contamination and subsidence in the context of the property being valued. ANZ-VGP111, however, provides a detailed list of issues for attention during the inspection process and specifically requires the person who undertakes the inspection to be the person who conducts the valuation and to be the person who signs the valuation report.

5.3.3 *Reporting—IVS103, RICS VPS3 and API ANZVGP111*

The reporting part of the valuation process is addressed in IVS103 *Reporting*, VPS3 *Valuation reports* and ANZVGP111 *Valuation Procedures—Real Property*.

5.3.3.1 IVS103

Having jointly agreed and documented a *Scope of Work*, the exact nature of the question will be settled, where the valuation process is conceptualised as providing an answer to a question, with the question then being answered through the undertaking of the valuation in IVS102 *Investigations and Compliance* and with the findings of the valuation then being addressed in IVS103 *Reporting* (IVSC, 2021).

IVS103 *Reporting* is unambiguous:

> It is essential that the valuation report communicates the information necessary for the proper understanding of the valuation or valuation review. A report must provide the intended users with a clear understanding of the valuation.
>
> (10.1)

While foreshadowed in IVS101, IVS103 requires (must) that the report include:

- a clear and accurate description of the scope of the assignment, its purpose and intended use (including any limitations on that use); and
- disclosure of any assumptions, special assumptions, significant uncertainty or limiting conditions that directly affect the valuation (10.2).

The level of detail appropriate for the valuation report is to be determined by the purpose of the valuation, the complexity of the asset being valued and the user's requirements (20.1).

IVS103 does not specify the form or format of the report, except that it must be sufficient to communicate to the intended users the scope of the valuation assignment, the work performed and the conclusions reached (20.2), being sufficient for an appropriately experienced valuation professional with no prior involvement with the valuation engagement to review and understand the report (20.3).

However, IVS103 does specify a minimum list of inclusions in the report, either explicitly or incorporated through reference to other documents (engagement letters, internal policies and so forth) (30.2), comprising:

- the scope of the work performed;
- intended use;
- intended users;
- the purpose;
- the approach or approaches adopted;
- the method or methods applied;
- the key inputs used;
- the assumptions made;
- the conclusion(s) of value and the principal reasons for any conclusions reached; and
- the date of the report (which may differ from the valuation date) (30.1).

Further, section 40 of IVS103 sets out the reporting requirements for valuation review reports, including the minimum content.

Essentially, under IVS103, the valuation report should simply confirm that which the valuer and the client have previously agreed would be undertaken, and so should contain no surprises for the client but merely the codification of that which was agreed would be undertaken.

5.3.3.2   RICS VPS3

The requirements of IVS103 are echoed and amplified in considerably greater detail in VPS3 *Valuation reports* in the RICS Red Book (RICS, 2021), which is mandatory.

VPS3 applies IVS103 and further specifies additional mandatory requirements for RICS members designed to enhance client understanding and use of reports while also addressing particular aspects of implementation that may arise in individual cases.

VPS3 *Valuation Reports* unambiguously asserts:

The report must:

- *clearly and accurately set out the conclusions of the valuation in a manner that is neither ambiguous nor misleading, and which does not create a false impression. If appropriate, the valuer should draw attention to, and comment on, any issues affecting the degree of certainty, or uncertainty, of the valuation . . .*
- *deal with all the matters agreed between the client and the valuer in the terms of engagement (scope of work) (see VPS1) (1).*

The valuation report should convey a clear understanding of the opinions being expressed by the valuer and should be couched in terms that can be read and understood by someone with no prior knowledge of the subject asset (1.1).

Concerning the format and detail of the valuation report, VPS3 notes that this is agreed upon between the valuer and the client in the terms of engagement, noting that it should always be proportionate to the task and professionally adequate for the purpose (1.2). Preliminary valuation advice, a draft report or a draft valuation may be provided in advance of the final report, but the preliminary or provisional status must be made clear (1.4), acknowledging the potential liability that may arise to the client or third parties (1.5).

Notably, VPS3 prohibits the use of the terms *certificate of value, valuation certificate* and *statement of value* in connection with the provision of valuation advice, although *certified* or similar words may be used where it is known that the valuation is for a purpose that requires formal certification of a valuation opinion (1.6).

VPS3 extends the list of matters that must be addressed in a valuation report, reflecting the requirements of VPS1, with valuers *strongly advised where possible to consider and follow the headings set out below, to ensure that all relevant matters are covered* (2.1):

- identification and status of the valuer;
- identification of the client and any other intended users;
- purpose of the valuation;
- identification of the asset(s) valued;
- basis(es) of value adopted;
- valuation date;
- extent of investigation;
- nature and source(s) of the information relied upon;
- assumptions and special assumptions;
- restrictions on use, distribution and publication of the report;
- confirmation that the valuation has been undertaken in accordance with the IVS;
- valuation approach and reasoning;
- amount of the valuation or valuations;
- date of the valuation report;
- commentary on any material uncertainty in relation to the valuation where it is essential to ensure clarity on the part of the valuation user; and
- a statement setting out any limitation on liability that has been agreed.

If the report is to be in a format specified by the client that omits any of these items, then these should be addressed in the initial service agreement or terms of engagement; otherwise, the valuation will not be undertaken in accordance with IVS (1.2).

The list of mandatory inclusions in the report is extensive and ensures transparency and consistency with the agreed terms of engagement. VPS3 continues to amplify each of these items, some in considerable detail, such as *identification and status of the valuer*:

The valuer can be an individual or a member of a firm. The report must include:

- *the signature of the individual responsible for the valuation assignment*
- *a statement confirming that the valuer is in a position to provide an objective and unbiased valuation and is competent to undertake the valuation assignment.*

If the valuer has obtained material assistance from others in relation to any aspect of the assignment, the nature of such assistance and the extent of reliance must be referenced in the report (2.2a).

Further clarification is provided in *Implementation*, including that a valuation is the responsibility of an individual member, that professional designation (e.g. MRICS) should be stated, that material previous involvement disclosure should be provided and that a statement should be made about sufficient current local, national or international knowledge (as appropriate) of the particular market and skills and understanding to undertake the valuation competently (2.2a).

Given the very extensive amplification provided in VPS3, readers are encouraged to read the whole of VPS3 prior to report preparation.

5.3.3.3 *API ANZVGP111*

IVS103 is addressed in section 4.0 *Report Content* in the API's ANZVGP111 (API, 2021a). As a mandatory requirement, the valuation report must include content relevant to the type of property and the style of report, unless using a proforma required by the client, with the extent of detail under any heading depending on the style of report and the nature of the property (4.0).

ANZVGP111 notes that the valuation report content usually includes (being non-mandatory):

* instructing party (4.1)—details of the instructing party and reliant parties;
* purpose (4.2)—statement of the purpose of the valuation;
* date of valuation (4.3)—usually the date of inspection unless otherwise specified (e.g. rent review, statutory valuation, retrospective valuation);
* basis of value (4.4)—having regard to IVS104;
* methodology, reconciliation and value range (4.5)—assuming more than one valuation approach is adopted, the rationale, methodology and calculations for each should be outlined, providing a valuation range together with a reconciliation to a single point figure;
* legal description (4.6)—with a copy of a current title search and noting any encumbrances and impact on the value and marketability of the property;
* nature of interest (4.7)—often being the fee simple vacant possession, fee simple subject to a tenancy or lessee's interest;
* dimensions and area (4.8)—including measurements;
* location and locality (4.9)—location is stated relative to the CBD, the nearest main town or regional centre with locality describing the positive and negative features impacting value of the immediate surrounding neighbourhood;
* town planning/resource management (4.10)—including the relevant planning instrument or authority, zoning, proposed alterations to zoning, development consents, current use, highest and best use and any public or private authority reservations, designations or proposals;
* site, services and environmental hazards (4.11)—including any significant observable/visual and/or known defects or hazards such as flooding, landslip or contamination. Further enquiries of specialist advisers and/or reports may be required, and the valuation report may need to be qualified by the valuer;
* structural improvements (4.12)—description of the structural improvements and integral plant including approximate age, area and accommodation of buildings and their general state of repair. If relevant, affectation by deleterious substances (such as asbestos) and any obvious non-compliance with relevant regulatory codes should be noted in the valuation report;
* lease or licence details (4.13)—where the property is subject to a lease, licence or occupancy agreement, an appropriately detailed synopsis of relevant terms should be included in the report. If the original document or a proper copy cannot be sighted, this should be noted in the report with an appropriate qualification that the details be confirmed before relying on the valuation;

- outgoings and recoveries (4.14)—where the property is valued by capitalisation of income, actual or estimated outgoings, operating expenses and recoveries should be noted in the valuation report with a comparison to budget and previous years' actuals and those for comparable properties;
- marketability (4.15)—the valuation report should include commentary on any inherent or external features of the property that favourably or adversely affect the marketability of the property;
- further investigation—other experts (4.16)—the valuation report should note any matters that are beyond the valuer's qualifications, experience and knowledge and which require further investigation by a relevant professional, such as contamination or flooding;
- the market (4.17)—commentary should be provided in the valuation report on the state of the market for the relevant property sub-sector;
- market evidence (4.18)—including sales and rental evidence, showing the analysis relied upon for valuation and the reasoned approach adopted to support the valuation. The valuer may (not must) comment on any sale of the subject property and any known circumstances or conditions pertaining to that sale, considered against other evidence as it has been a test of the market. An overview or summary of the market evidence and its application to the subject property is considered desirable (but not mandatory);
- single valuation figure (4.19)—the value should be expressed as a single valuation amount, and the GST status should be clearly defined;
- sale in one line or single transaction (4.20)—the valuation of multiple properties in one development (such as lots in a subdivision) should be based on a single transaction in one line to one buyer, being the sum of individual values and may incorporate an appropriate discount to reflect marketing and sale costs, holding costs and a profit and risk factor;
- proposed developments (4.21)—where a proposed development of the property is being valued, the valuation report should clearly state the source of information upon which the report is based, the valuation on an *as if complete* basis and any assumptions necessary to ensure that the basis of the report is clear;
- general market advice (4.22)—if asked to provide general market advice to clients on a specific property, the scope of work should make it clear that this is not a valuation;
- going concerns (4.23)—where a property is valued as a going concern with regard to trading figures, the valuation report should state the source of the trading figures, annex a copy of the trading figures supplied and show any adjustments made to those trading figures in the valuation process;
- disclaimers and qualifications (4.24)—appropriate disclaimers and qualifications should be included in the valuation report, being designed to inform the client of the level of reliance that can be placed on the report and whether further action is required, as considered further in ANZPGP201 Disclaimer Clauses and Qualification Statements (API, 2021b); and
- signing the report (4.25)—the valuation report shall be signed by the person who conducts the valuation, who must be the person who inspects the property. Where a valuation report is counter-signed, the capacity in which the counter-signatory is signing must be clearly stated to avoid any misunderstanding by anyone relying on the report as to whether the counter-signatory has inspected the property and the extent of involvement in the valuation process.

As with inspections, experience through the regularity of report writing allows the valuer to become familiar with the listed items and to identify a property where greater attention to a specific item may be needed in the valuation report. For example, the legal description may be an old form of title such that a commentary may be required on the valuation implications.

5.3.3.4 Summary—reporting

The valuation report under IVS103 should contain no surprises, being entirely consistent with that agreed between the valuer and the client in the *Scope of Work*, having only a minimal list of required inclusions. VPS3 notably extends and amplifies the list of inclusions in the report to ensure transparency and consistency with the agreed terms of engagement, with the list further extended in ANZVGP111.

5.3.4 Summary—the valuation process

The process of instructing, undertaking and reporting valuations is clearly and consistently cascaded through IVS, RICS and API publications, emphasising transparency and the inter-related nature of the three activities. Effectively, only that which is agreed upon between the valuer and the client should then happen during the valuation and subsequently appear in the valuation report.

5.4 API—residential property valuation

In an Australian context, the valuation of some residential property for certain lenders for secured lending purposes represents a significant exception to the instructing, undertaking and reporting framework considered previously.

By agreement between the API, its members and certain lenders, the following levels of advice may be provided:

- long form reports (full on-site physical inspection by the valuer and all relevant enquiries undertaken);
- PropertyPRO pro-forma reports (short form template style report, full on-site physical inspection by the valuer and limited enquiries as per the API PropertyPRO Supporting Memorandum);
- Restricted Assessment pro-forma reports (short form template style report, 'drive-by' (kerbside) external inspection only by the valuer and limited enquiries as per the API Restricted Assessment Supporting Memorandum); and
- Desktop Assessment (no physical inspection by the valuer, no formal enquiries and limited reporting as per the API Residential Desktop Assessment—Memorandum for First Mortgage Purposes) (source: www.API.org.au, accessed 12 May 2023).

As is evident, such levels of advice rely on proprietorial agreements and reports such that readers should contact the API for further information.

5.5 Valuer's professional risk

The availability and cost of professional indemnity insurance for valuers in Australia have been a major issue for many years, and it is in the interests of all practising valuers to minimise the number of claims and potential settlements and so minimise future insurance premia.

The seminal text by Joyce and Norris, *Valuers Liability* (1994), provided a watershed in the recognition and management of a valuer's professional risk and was followed by the API's Risk Management Module program, which has led to much greater awareness of risk by practising valuers in Australia.

IVS101, 102 and 103, VPS1, 2 and 3 and ANZVGP111 provide the practising valuer with an opportunity to minimise risk in the valuation process. By prescribing that which should be within an instruction from a client to a valuer, that which should be considered when undertaking the valuation and that which should be included within the valuation report, the valuation process is made more transparent for the valuer and the client so reducing the risk of any key element being omitted or misunderstood.

While carefully following the relevant standards, practice standards and guidance papers will not magically eradicate risk from the valuation process, it will contribute to a significant reduction and allow the practising valuer to focus more closely on the high-risk judgmental inputs to valuation methodology.

5.6 Summary and conclusions

Chapter 1 outlined the structure of the property asset class, examining the traditional characteristics of property (including heterogeneity, durability, illiquidity and so forth) and the traditional risks of property (including location, building, tenant risk and so forth) through the lenses of systematic, unsystematic and idiosyncratic risk, so aligning property valuation with capital market theory.

Chapter 2 considered the evolution of property valuation in Australia, the role of the valuer and the diverse activities of the valuation profession, followed by a detailed examination of the inter-acting framework provided by valuation standards and ethical standards promulgated by IVSC, RICS and API.

Chapter 3 explored concepts of value and normative and positive definitions of value, dissecting the International Valuation Standards' definition of market value with a reconciliation to the concept of market value in *Spencer v Commonwealth* (1907) and examining such contemporary valuation issues as valuation lag, variance, accuracy, negligence and valuer rotation.

Chapter 4 introduced International Financial Reporting Standards and International Accounting Standards with a detailed examination of the key provisions of International Valuation Standards, the RICS Red Book and API guidance papers that impact on valuation practice in Australia.

This chapter outlined conceptual approaches to the valuation process with a review of the self-supporting process of instructing, undertaking and reporting valuations under the International Valuation Standards, RICS Red Book and API guidance papers, examining how this process inter-relates to the choice of valuation approach, valuation method and the purpose of the valuation.

While formulated almost 50 years ago, Graaskamp's (1977) approach to the valuation process exhibits a significant amount of commonality with Whipple (2006) and also with IVS101, 102 and 103, with the former being more conceptual and the latter being more prescriptive. Effectively, the principles of the valuation process are well established and enduring, with fine-tuning of the detail occurring as time passes.

Transparency and communication are the core of instructing under IVS, RICS and API publications, encouraging a dialogue between client and valuer to ensure that both fully understand what is to be provided in the valuation and any limitations on its use before it is undertaken or reported.

The level of detail for undertaking a valuation varies significantly between IVS, RICS and API, with IVS providing high-level requirements for the valuer to follow while RICS introduces greater detail, viewing inspection as a risk management process, with API advocating a far more detailed approach through the provision of a list of 26 items to note during the inspection process.

Similarly, the level of detail for reporting a valuation varies significantly between IVS, RICS and API, with IVS echoing the *Scope of Work* in the valuation report with only a minimal list of required inclusions. RICS extends and amplifies the list of inclusions, which is further extended in ANZVGP111. However, common to all three publications is the requirement to ensure transparency and consistency with the agreed terms of engagement, providing a valuation report that is fit for purpose.

The next chapter will address the market approach to valuation through the comparative method of valuation, including the key steps of accumulation, analysis, adjustment and application of comparable sales evidence to the subject property being valued, with an example.

Chapter 7 considers the income approach to valuation addressed through the static methods of the capitalisation of income and the profits methods of valuation, including an examination of the key inputs for each method with examples and a consideration of both marriage value and the surrender and renewal of leases.

Chapter 8 considers the income approach to valuation addressed through the dynamic method of the discounted cash flow method of valuation, including an examination of the key inputs and a focus on the derivation of the discount rate and consideration of the role of sensitivity and scenario analysis, with examples.

Chapter 9 considers the cost approach to valuation addressed through the replacement cost, reproduction cost, summation and residual or hypothetical development methods of valuation.

Finally, Chapter 10 concludes the book with a consideration of future perspectives, including the role of uncertainty, data, automated valuation models, artificial intelligence, optionality, environmental, social and governance issues, retail and office space use and indigenous issues.

References

API (2021a) *ANZVGP111—valuation procedures—real property*, Australian Property Institute, Deakin.
API (2021b) *ANZPGP201—disclaimer clauses and qualification statements*, Australian Property Institute, Deakin.
Graaskamp, JA (1977) *Appraisal of 25 North Pinckney*, Landmark Research, Madison.
IVSC (2021) *International valuation standards*, International Valuation Standards Council, London.
Joyce, L and Norris, K (1994) *Valuers liability*, 2nd edition, Australian Institute of Valuers and Land Economists, Deakin.
RICS (2021) *RICS valuation—global standards*, Royal Institution of Chartered Surveyors, London.
Whipple, RTM (2006) *Property valuation and analysis*, Lawbook Co, Sydney.

6 Market approach to valuation

6.1 Introduction

This book is an introduction to the fundamentals of property valuation, outlining the principal methods of property valuation in Australia within the context of International Valuation Standards, bridging the gap between traditional property valuation methods and the modern era of global valuation governance.

Chapter 1 outlined the structure of the property asset class, examining the traditional characteristics of property (including heterogeneity, durability, illiquidity and so forth) and the traditional risks of property (including location, building, tenant risk and so forth) through the lenses of systematic, unsystematic and idiosyncratic risk, so aligning property valuation with capital market theory.

Chapter 2 considered the evolution of property valuation in Australia, the role of the valuer and the diverse activities of the valuation profession, followed by a detailed examination of the inter-acting framework provided by valuation standards and ethical standards promulgated by IVSC, RICS and API.

Chapter 3 explored concepts of value and normative and positive definitions of value, dissecting the International Valuation Standards' definition of market value with a reconciliation to the concept of market value in *Spencer v Commonwealth* (1907) and examining such contemporary valuation issues as valuation lag, variance, accuracy, negligence and valuer rotation.

Chapter 4 introduced International Financial Reporting Standards and International Accounting Standards with a detailed examination of the key provisions of International Valuation Standards, the RICS Red Book and API guidance papers that impact on valuation practice in Australia.

Chapter 5 outlined conceptual approaches to the valuation process with a review of the self-supporting process of instructing, undertaking and reporting valuations under the International Valuation Standards, RICS Red Book and API guidance papers, examining how this process inter-relates to the choice of valuation approach, valuation method and the purpose of the valuation.

This chapter seeks to address the market approach to valuation through the comparative method of valuation, including the key steps of accumulation, analysis, adjustment and application of comparable sales evidence to the subject property being valued, with an example.

Chapter 7 considers the income approach to valuation addressed through the static methods of the capitalisation of income and the profits methods of valuation, including an examination of the key inputs for each method with examples and a consideration of both marriage value and the surrender and renewal of leases.

Chapter 8 considers the income approach to valuation addressed through the dynamic method of the discounted cash flow method of valuation, including an examination of the key inputs and a focus on the derivation of the discount rate and consideration of the role of sensitivity and scenario analysis, with examples.

DOI: 10.1201/9781003397922-6

Chapter 9 considers the cost approach to valuation addressed through the replacement cost, reproduction cost, summation and residual or hypothetical development methods of valuation.

Finally, Chapter 10 concludes the book with a consideration of future perspectives, including the role of uncertainty, data, automated valuation models, artificial intelligence, optionality, environmental, social and governance issues, retail and office space use and indigenous issues.

This book is based on those standards and guidance documents published in IVSC (2021) and RICS (2021) and on the API website (accessed January to May 2023). Given their nature, standards and guidance documents are dynamic, being regularly updated and with the most recently published versions replacing previously published versions. Accordingly, readers should not rely on this book as a current statement of a standard or guidance document and should visit www.ivsc.org, www.rics.org and/or www.api.org.au to find the most recent version.

As an introductory textbook on property valuation methods in Australia, this book is a companion to Australia's leading advanced valuation textbook, *Principles and Practice of Property Valuation in Australia,* edited by the same author and also published by Routledge, which is a deeper analysis of key principles underlying property valuation and current techniques and issues in the practice of property valuation for major sectors of the Australian property market.

Traditional valuation texts, such as Millington (2000), consider five methods of valuation:

- the comparative (or comparison) method;
- the income (or investment or capitalisation) method;
- the profits (or accounts or treasury or receipts and expenditure) method;
- the contractor's (or summation or cost) method; and
- the residual (or hypothetical development) method of valuation.

This chapter addresses the market approach and the comparative method of valuation.

The principles of the market approach to valuation and the comparative method of valuation will be considered through the following key elements:

- *Adams* approach to the comparative method (6.3.1):

  - *Adams* accumulation (6.3.1.1);
  - *Adams* analysis (6.3.1.2);
  - *Adams* adjustment (6.3.1.3);
  - *Adams* application (6.3.1.4);

- IVSC approach to the comparative method (6.3.2);
- RICS approach to the comparative method (6.3.3); and
- API approach to the comparative method (6.3.4),

followed by a worked example of the application to the assessment of market value.

6.2 Comparative method of valuation

The market approach to valuation is one of the three principal valuation approaches recognised by IVSs and is grounded in economic theory, being based on the economic principle of price equilibrium whereby the value of a property interest is indicated by comparison to identical or similar property interests for which price information is available, with the comparative method of valuation being one of the five methods of valuation cited in such traditional texts as Millington (2000).

At the heart of the comparative method of valuation is comparison, such that the level of similarity of the comparable transactions to the subject property is fundamental. If the level of similarity is high, the method is explicit, transparent and reliable. If the level of similarity is low, the level of judgment in adjustment and application is higher so that the method is less explicit, less transparent and less reliable.

As Isaac and O'Leary (2012) note:

> There is no escaping the fact that comparison lies at the very heart of the valuation process because prices arrived at in the market are irrefutable evidence that somebody was willing to pay whatever it was to acquire a particular interest in property.

(page 66)

The comparative method of valuation can be applied to those types of property interests for which comparable evidence is available upon which to base an assessment and which exhibit a high level of homogeneity. It is the most commonly used method for capital value assessments of owner-occupied residential property (not investment property), including land, houses and apartments.

The method may also be applied to capital value assessments of residential development land and agricultural land, though great care is required in determining the level of similarity given the wide range of relevant variables such as nature of development consent or productive capacity, respectively.

In rental value assessments, the method may be applied to residential, office, retail and industrial property primarily, though it may be applied to any rental property type for which comparable transaction evidence is available.

Owner-occupied residential property, residential development land and agricultural land may each exhibit a high level of homogeneity, particularly in location, built envelope (if any), planning controls, tenure and so forth. They may also exhibit frequent sales transactions, providing a potentially wide range of sales evidence from which comparisons may be drawn.

Similarly, residential, office, retail and industrial property lettings may exhibit high levels of homogeneity with frequent leasing transactions providing a potentially wide range of rental evidence from which comparisons may be drawn.

The comparative method of valuation is preferred as the conventional method of valuation by the Courts, with other valuation methods to be used only when comparable sales are not available (*Graham Trilby Pty Ltd v Valuer General* [2009] NSW LEC 1087 at 41[*Trilby*]; *Redeam Pty Ltd v South Australian Land Commission* [1977] 40 LGRA 151 at 156; *Riverbank Pty Ltd v Commonwealth* [1974] 48 AJLR 483 at 484; *Marroun v Roads and Maritime Services* [2012] NSWLEC 199 at 196; *El Boustani v Minister Administering the Environmental Planning and Assessment Act* 1979 [2012] NSWLEC 266 at 23; *Tenstat Pty Limited v Valuer General/Woolworths Limited v Valuer General* [2012] NSWLEC 1361 at 35).

Further, in an Australian context, Court decisions provide extensive guidance to the principles of the comparative method of valuation, which may be considered in association with guidance from IVSC, RICS and API.

6.3 Comparative method of valuation—principles

The comparative method of valuation seeks to assess the value of a property interest by comparing the subject property interest to recent transactions of similar property interests. While the concept is simple, the application is often challenging.

The properties chosen for comparison should be similar to the subject property in terms of location, size, construction type, planning, tenure and so forth, with the comparable transactions being within a period (ideally) of 12 months prior to the date of valuation.

For example, if the subject property interest is a three-bedroom timber house, sales within the last 12 months of other three-bedroom timber houses in close proximity to the subject property will be most helpful. A sale two years ago of a six-bedroom brick house located five kilometres from the subject property is likely to be less helpful.

In periods of market volatility, the period that is considered recent may be less than 12 months. In rapidly rising or falling markets, values may change significantly in three or six months such that sales from 12 months ago may be of limited assistance.

In the event of no sales evidence, the valuer should consider carefully whether this means that the market has not moved or that there have just been no sales. Even if there are no sales in a sub-market, the sub-market may have moved, and regard should be given to sales activity in surrounding sub-markets and inferences drawn. The adoption of the IVS definition of market value (adopted by RICS and API) allows the valuer to consider what a hypothetical purchaser would pay a hypothetical vendor, and it is unlikely that a hypothetical vendor would accept a lower value for his/her property if, despite the absence of sales in the subject property sub-market, properties in surrounding sub-markets have shown increases.

6.3.1 Adams *approach to the comparative method*

As the comparative method of valuation is the preferred method of the Courts, it will be considered through the lens of the NSW Land & Environment Court decision in *Adams v Valuer General* [2014] NSWLEC 1005 (*Adams*), which established four sequential steps, being:

* accumulation;
* analysis;
* adjustment; and
* application

of potentially comparable sales transactions (para 29). While *Adams* focuses on comparable sales transactions, the principles are equally applicable to comparable leasing transactions.

6.3.1.1 Adams—accumulation

The accumulation step is described in *Adams* as follows:

> *The accumulation of potentially genuinely comparable sales seeks to identify and establish a pool of relevant comparable sales from which information may be deduced concerning the value of the subject property.*

> (para 32)

Reflecting the heterogeneity of property, it is preferable at this stage in the process to include as many sales as possible in the sample for consideration, provided each shares similar characteristics to the subject property and so is a relevant comparable sale, as the sample size is likely to be diminished during the course of undertaking the following steps.

For the effective application of the comparative method of valuation, extensive, detailed and accurate information about comparable sales is essential. In the past, valuation firms maintained meticulous file records of property sales, which provided a significant source of competitive advantage. Today, it is common to rely on online data sources with, in an Australian context, Domain, Realestate.com.au and State Valuer General websites being popular.

While there is no maximum or minimum ideal number of comparable sales, several are preferable. Unless directly comparable, one or two may be too few to form a view of the market, whereas more than six may be challenging to comprehend appropriately. However, a paired comparison of two sales may be helpful to identify the effect of a particular characteristic or the impact of time and market changes.

To fully understand the context of comparable sales, it may be necessary to contact the vendor's agent or other valuers, reinforcing the importance of networks and personal contacts for the valuer to verify sales and gather more information.

6.3.1.2 Adams—analysis

The analysis step is described in *Adams* as follows:

> *The analysis of potentially genuinely comparable sales provides a common basis of measurement by seeking to convert all potentially comparable sales to a common basis of expression such as a unitary rate (rate per square metre, rate per hectare, etc), improved or unimproved (through allowance for the absence or existence of improvements, etc) and so forth.*
>
> (38)

The unitary rate should be that commonly used in the market for that type of property, and it is important that the same unitary rate is adopted for all comparable sales in the sample to permit comparison to be made on a common basis.

While land sales may be analysed on a common basis of rate per sqm or rate per hectare, residential property sales may not require analysis except where they lack a common basis, such as being partially improved or improved with a dilapidated or derelict dwelling.

6.3.1.3 Adams—adjustment

The adjustment step is described in *Adams* as follows:

> *The adjustment of potentially genuinely comparable sales acknowledges the fact that no two properties are ever identical and seeks to convert those potentially comparable sales to a hypothetical expression of value as a unitary rate in the context of the subject property through the reflection of differences (such as size, location, use, date, etc.) between the respective potentially comparable sales and the subject property.*
>
> (40)

> *Because properties are never identical, explicit and/or implicit adjustment for differences is obviously necessary, but caution is required through making as few adjustments as possible, in a consistent manner, to ensure the reliability of the comparable sale when related to the subject property, with too much adjustment potentially rendering the comparable sale unsafe to use.*
>
> (41)

> *Therefore, as a matter of general valuation principle, fewer adjustments may be preferred to more adjustments, and smaller adjustments may be preferred to larger adjustments in rendering comparable sales safe for use.*
>
> (42)

Very significantly, the Court noted that "Caution in adjustment is required as too much adjustment renders the use of comparables unsafe" (para 44), indicating that no comparable transaction is necessarily irrelevant though care is required with the level of adjustment required as too much adjustment may render the comparable transaction of limited relevance (considered further at para 57).

Further, smaller adjustments are preferred to larger adjustments, and explicit adjustments are preferred to implicit adjustments, such that particular caution is required with large implicit adjustments (para 46).

Having accumulated a pool of potentially genuine comparable sales and analysed each on a common unitary rate basis, the comparable sales require adjustment for differences in those aspects that are of relevance to the property type. For example, for most properties this may include land area, planning and tenure, with residential property transactions potentially requiring adjustment for location and views and office-letting transactions potentially requiring adjustment for floor level and aspect. Those aspects of relevance to different property types are considered further, in what follows.

Miller's (1956) research into working memory suggests *the magical number seven, plus or minus two,* to be the number of pieces of information that an individual can receive, process and remember. Therefore, a matrix plotting each comparable sale as columns and around seven aspects for adjustment as rows may be capable of comprehension.

Each cell in the matrix will contain an adjustment, which may be a percentage, a description (such as superior, comparable, inferior), an arrow or other form of comparison, but must be consistently adopted by the valuer and must be explicit.

Case law suggests that, for adjustment by percentages, the total adjustment should be no more than +/-30% for the comparable sale to be safe for use, and adjustments should follow a common pattern (for example, 2.5%, 5%, 7.5%, 10% or 2%, 4%, 6%, 8%) when judgementally based, with adjustments such as +1.5% or -6.33% requiring clear supporting evidence.

Importantly, while the matrix approach affords transparency and fosters logical relativity of adjustments, Shapiro et al. (2019) note that the level of adjustment is subjective and requires the valuer to have relevant market experience in order to form a judgment.

A matrix approach to adjustment is one of several approaches identified by Whipple (2006):

- **review and intuition**, being a *mental process* that *somehow ends up with an estimate of value,* but *no link is made between the quoted sales and the value estimate* (page 262). This is, effectively, little more than assertion based on experience which, as it cannot be explained, lacks credibility and is subject to increasing criticism by the Courts;
- **construction of an adjustment grid,** which may be qualitative or quantitative, addressing some of the issues plaguing review and intuition, with a matrix approach suggested previously based on *Adams*;
- **quality point rating,** by which factors contributing to value to the most probable buyer are identified and weighted (for example, in a suburban office building: age 0.10; location 0.45; physical condition 0.10; and occupancy potential 0.35—total 1.00), then given a score from 1 to 5 for each factor for each comparable sale, with the scores then summed to give a total weighted score for each comparable sale. The subject property is then subject to similar weighting of factors contributing to value and the mean of the comparable sales applied to derive an estimate of value; and
- **regression analysis,** which is generally more helpful where there is a large data set from relatively homogenous property.

Kininmonth (2022) considers the importance of technology in adjusting comparable sales, particularly locational analysis which is under constant change. The author notes that Google maps, with the ability to apply layers of information, enhances the valuer's ability to quickly review both geographical features and man-made infrastructure at a point in time and over time via time-lapse satellite and high-resolution aerial photography. Kininmonth notes that such locational analysis enhances the valuer's ability to determine the weighting of locational attributes as determinants of value.

Those variables requiring adjustment will vary between property sectors, with residential, office, retail and industrial property each having a range of variables that impact value. Following Wyatt (2023), the variables for adjustment may include:

6.3.1.3.1 RESIDENTIAL

Tenure—freehold, strata or community title, leasehold
Legal constraints—easements, covenants
Location—proximity to schools, shops, parks, train station, bus stops
Amenity of area
Nature—detached house, duplex, terrace—high-rise apartment, low-rise apartment
Views
Aspect—north/south facing or east/west facing
Size
Number of bedrooms
Number of bathrooms
Quality of finishes in kitchen and bathroom
Garage/car port or parking for apartments
Garden
Planning zoning and permitted uses
Age, physical condition
Construction type—walls, roof, structure, external, internal
Heating and/or air conditioning
Gas and/or electricity service
Energy efficiency and environmental performance
Transaction date, passage of time and changes in market

6.3.1.3.2 OFFICE

Tenure—freehold, strata or community title, leasehold
Legal constraints—easements, covenants
Location—proximity to train stations, bus stops, other offices, support facilities such as retail
Accessibility
Nature—high-rise tower, low-rise office building, office above retail, campus-style
Views from upper floors
Size/net lettable area
Parking
Planning zoning and permitted uses
Age, physical condition, whether refurbished or not
Construction type—walls, roof, structure, external, internal, ceilings
Number of levels

Configuration

Services—air-conditioning, heating, ventilation, lifts, fire safety, lighting, toilets, end-of-trip facilities, kitchen, delivery access/loading facilities

Availability of three-phase electricity

Foyer quality and corporate image

Level of natural light on office floor

Office floor-to-ceiling height

Flexibility and adaptability

Energy efficiency and environmental performance

Transaction date, passage of time and changes in market

6.3.1.3.3 RETAIL

Tenure—freehold, strata or community title, leasehold

Legal constraints—easements, covenants

Location—proximity to train stations, bus stops, major roads

Accessibility

Nature—shopping centre (super-regional, regional, sub-regional, neighbourhood), within a row of shops, freestanding shop

Size and dimensions of retail space

Parking

Planning zoning and permitted uses

Age, physical condition, whether refurbished or not

Construction type—walls, roof, structure, external, internal

Number of levels

Configuration

Services—air-conditioning, heating, ventilation, lifts, escalators, fire safety, lighting, toilets, delivery access/loading facilities

Availability of gas and three-phase electricity

Energy efficiency and environmental performance

Transaction date, passage of time and changes in market

6.3.1.3.4 INDUSTRIAL, WAREHOUSE AND LOGISTICS

Tenure—freehold, strata or community title, leasehold

Legal constraints—easements, covenants

Location—proximity to city, major arterial roads and state highway network, railways, ports and airports

Accessibility

Nature—part of estate, independent freestanding building

Size/floor area

Surrounding land for truck manoeuvring, parking

Planning zoning and permitted uses

Age, physical condition, whether refurbished or not

Construction type—walls, roof, structure, external, internal, wall/roof lining

Clear height, floor to roof (eaves height)

Clear span and absence of columns

Floor loading

Loading docks

Flexibility and adaptability

Number of levels, level of office space provision

Configuration

Services—heating, ventilation, lifts, fire safety, lighting, toilets, kitchen

Availability of gas and three-phase electricity

Energy efficiency and environmental performance

Transaction date, passage of time and changes in market

6.3.1.4—Adams—application

The application step is described in *Adams* as follows:

> *The application of those potentially genuinely comparable sales to the subject property seeks to determine the value of the subject property through a consideration of the relevance (such as being limited, indirect or direct) of the unitary rate derived from those adjusted comparable sales relative to the subject.*
>
> (para 56)

and:

> *While all comparable sales evidence may be considered relevant and so cannot be disregarded, the level of relevance of different comparable sales to the subject property may vary leading to the valuer attributing differing weight to different comparable sales.*
>
> (para 57)

Having accumulated a pool of potentially genuine comparable sales, analysed each to a common unitary rate basis and then adjusted each to a hypothetical expression of value as a unitary rate in the context of the subject property through the reflection of differences, the adjusted comparable sales require application to the subject property through a consideration of their individual relevance and the resulting weight to be given to each.

While no sale is irrelevant, those with the greatest similarity to the subject may be rated as of direct relevance, those with lower similarity may be rated as of indirect relevance, and those of limited comparability may be rated as of limited relevance. The application step may give the greatest weight to those comparable sales of direct relevance in determining the range of value for the subject property, which should then broadly accord with those comparable sales of indirect or limited relevance to which less weight is attributed.

6.3.1.5 Summary—Adams approach to the comparative method

The great benefit of the decision in *Adams* is that it provides a four-step approach to making the comparative method of valuation transparent, logical and explicit. Significantly, while *Adams* still requires the use of judgment by the valuer, it moves the comparative method of valuation away from being based on assertion and implicit assumptions.

6.3.2 IVSC approach to the comparative method

IVS105 *Valuation Approaches and Methods* (IVSC, 2021) refers to the comparative method of valuation as the comparable transactions method, also known as the guideline transactions method (30.1) or, where the comparable transactions involve the subject property, the prior transactions method (30.2).

In the absence of transactions, the valuer may consider listing or offer prices (the comparable listings method), but this should not be the sole indicator of value with careful thought given to weight (IVSC, 2021, IVS105, 30.3).

Anecdotal, "rule of thumb" or heuristic valuation benchmarks should not be given substantial weight unless it can be shown that buyers and sellers place significant reliance on them (IVSC, 2021, IVS105, 30.16).

6.3.2.1 IVSC—key steps

Consistent with *Adams*, IVS105 (IVSC, 2021) identifies the key steps in the comparable transactions method to be:

- identify the units of comparison (such as $ psm) that are used by participants in the relevant market;
- identify the relevant comparable transactions and calculate the key valuation metrics for those transactions;
- perform a consistent comparative analysis of qualitative and quantitative similarities and differences between the comparable assets and the subject asset;
- make necessary adjustments, if any, to the valuation metrics to reflect differences between the subject asset and the comparable assets;
- apply the adjusted valuation metrics to the subject asset; and
- if multiple valuation metrics are used, reconcile the indications of value (30.6).

6.3.2.2 IVSC—accumulation of comparable sales

Consistent with *Adams*, IVS105 (IVSC, 2021) states that a valuer should choose comparable transactions within the following context:

- evidence of several transactions is generally preferable to a single transaction or event;
- evidence from transactions of very similar assets (ideally identical) provides a better indication of value than assets where the transaction price requires significant adjustments;
- transactions that happen closer to the valuation date are more representative of the market at that date than older/dated transactions, particularly in volatile markets;
- for most bases of value, the transactions should be "arm's length" between unrelated parties;
- sufficient information on the transaction should be available to allow the valuer to develop a reasonable understanding of the comparable asset and assess the valuation metrics/comparable evidence;
- information on the comparable transactions should be from a reliable and trusted source; and
- actual transactions provide better valuation evidence than intended transactions.

6.3.2.3 IVSC—analysis and adjustment of comparable sales

Consistent with *Adams*, IVS105 (IVSC, 2021) states that a valuer should analyse and make adjustments for any material differences between the comparable transactions and the subject asset, with common differences warranting adjustment for property assets including but not being limited to:

- material characteristics (age, size, specifications, etc.);
- relevant restrictions on either the subject asset or the comparable assets;
- geographical location and related economic and regulatory environments;
- unusual terms in the comparable transactions;
- differences related to marketability and control characteristics of the comparable and subject asset; and
- ownership characteristics (type of interest) such as legal form of ownership (30.8),

to which IVS400 *Real Property Interests* (IVSC, 2021) adds:

- the respective locations;
- the permitted use or zoning at each property;
- the circumstances under which the price was determined and the basis of value required;
- the effective date of the price evidence and the valuation date; and
- market conditions at the time of the relevant transactions and how they differ from conditions at the valuation date (50.4),

noting that property interests are generally heterogeneous (50.1), with the oft-quoted row of terrace houses or row of industrial units that have identical physical characteristics still having differing locations.

IVS410 *Development Property* (IVSC, 2021) notes that the two main approaches to the valuation of development land are the market approach and the residual method (40.1), with the approach to be used requiring the exercise of judgment depending on the required basis of value and specific facts and circumstances such as the level of recent transactions, the stage of development of the project and movements in the property markets since the project started (40.3).

IVS410 (IVSC, 2021) further notes that some types of development property can be sufficiently homogenous and frequently exchanged in a market for there to be sufficient data from recent sales to use as a direct comparison (50.1). This is most likely to occur for residential and small office, retail or industrial development property, with the comparative method unlikely to be suitable for larger or more complex office, retail or industrial development property or smaller properties displaying heterogeneity (50.2) or for development property where work has commenced, as partially completed development properties rarely transact in the market (50.3), though may be suitable for establishing the value of a completed property as one of the inputs into the residual method (50.4).

6.3.3 RICS approach to the comparative method

Consistent with *Adams*, VPS 5 *Valuation Approaches and Methods* in the RICS Red Book (RICS, 2021) notes:

> The market approach is based on comparing the subject asset with identical or similar assets (or liabilities) for which price information is available, such as comparison with market transactions in the same, or closely similar, type of asset (or liability) within an appropriate time horizon.

(2)

The RICS Professional Standard *Comparable evidence in real estate valuation* (RICS, 2023) states, as recommended best practice, that comparable evidence should be:

- comprehensive—there should be several comparables rather than a single transaction or event;
- very similar or, if possible, identical to the item being valued;
- recent, i.e., representative of the market on the date of valuation;
- the result of an arm's-length transaction in the market;
- verifiable;
- consistent with local market practice; and
- the result of underlying demand, i.e., comparable transactions have taken place with enough potential bidders to create an active market (page 5).

However, there may be a limited number of available comparable transactions and a lack of up-to-date evidence due to infrequent trading, sale prices being influenced by a special purchaser, a lack of similar or identical evidence given the heterogenous nature of property and property markets often being not fully transparent with limitations on publicly available information necessitating analysis and interpretation (RICS, 2023).

6.3.3.1 RICS—hierarchy of comparable sales evidence

RICS (2023) notes the following sources of comparable evidence:

- market evidence:
  - direct transactional evidence of a sale or letting, being open market transactions close to the date of valuation;
  - publicly available information, being information published by a government or other recognised authoritative source through the press or online;
  - published databases by large property firms or research organisations;
  - asking prices, though caution is required as they may differ substantially from the agreed final transaction price; and
  - historic evidence that predates the date of valuation, with the acceptable extent of predating depending on market conditions;
- indices, such as those produced by MSCI or by large property firms; and
- automated valuation model data,

with great care required to verify the data by detailed examination.

In terms of relative weight, RICS (2023) provides the following hierarchy, which is capable of application to comparable sales and comparable lettings:

Category A—direct comparable evidence:

Contemporary, completed transactions of near-identical properties for which full and accurate information is available (may include the subject property);
As previously mentioned, but for similar properties;
As previously mentioned, but where full data may not be available;
As previously mentioned, but where properties are being marketed and offers made.

Category B—general market data:

Published sources, commercial databases;
Other indirect evidence, such as indices;
Historic evidence;
Demand and supply data for rent, owner-occupation and investment.

Category C—Other sources:

Transactions from other real estate sectors and locations;
Other background data (interest rates, stock market movements).

For lettings, such as office space or industrial buildings, lease-related transactions may also be informative, such as lease renewals, rent reviews, sub-lettings and assignment of leases where a premium is paid (positive or negative).

However, regard must be given to the effect of the terms of the lease that may impact value (such as the tenant's improvements in lease renewal or any specified assumptions in rent review). In terms of relative weight, lease renewals may be considered most informative, then rent reviews and sub-lettings with assignments considered least informative (Wyatt, 2023).

6.3.3.2 *RICS—analysis and adjustment*

Consistent with *Adams*, the RICS Professional Standard *Comparable evidence in real estate valuation* (RICS, 2023) notes that raw comparable data requires conversion into useable comparable evidence. This requires establishing a common basis of measurement and adjustment to allow for differences in the various factors that may affect value, which may be quantitative or qualitative, based on the valuer's experience and knowledge of the local market, with a matrix format often assisting the valuer's judgement.

6.3.4 *API approach to the comparative method*

API guidance papers referring to the comparative method of valuation include:

*   ANZVGP111 *Valuation Procedures—Real Property* (API, 2021a);
*   ANZVGP110 *Considerations when forming an opinion of value when there is a shortage of market transactions* (API, 2021b); and
*   AVGP301 *Rental Valuations and Advice* (API, 2023).

6.3.4.1 *API—accumulation, analysis and adjustment*

Consistent with *Adams*, ANZVGP111 *Valuation Procedures—Real Property* (API, 2021a) addresses the accumulation, analysis and adjustment steps. Accumulation may be of *relevant market transactions* and *other market indicators,* with the extent of accumulation being *appropriate to the type of property and report* (6.1). Accumulation may comprise *several comparable sales,* but *a much wider range of data may be considered,* being *recent transactions* with comments if more than six months has elapsed since the sale or less months if the market is changing rapidly (6.1).

Curiously, despite the issues arising from the cognitive bias of anchoring identified in behavioural finance, section 6.3 requires research and consideration of the subject property selling price in relation to other sales evidence, the state of the market and the definition of market value to identify apparent inconsistency for which an explanation should be sought and included in the report.

Relevant market transactions should be analysed with the extent of analysis being *appropriate to the type of property and report* (6.1). Concerning adjustment, if sales are *not directly comparable as to date of sale or other factor, but in the same locality*, an explanation should be provided (6.1).

6.3.4.2 API—shortage of comparable sales transactions

The objective of ANZVGP110 *Considerations when forming an opinion of value when there is a shortage of market transactions* (API, 2021b) is to guide valuers *with forming a professional opinion as to the value of an asset* or leasing rental *when there is a shortage of market transactions available for use as valuation inputs as at the date of valuation* (1.1). Where there is a shortage of transactional evidence, the valuer should *compile as much evidence as reasonably necessary to assist the formation of an opinion of the market value* (3.0).

While *evidence* is not defined, section 4.0 provides a non-exhaustive list of *information sources* that *may assist* in forming *an opinion of adjustments that may be necessary when applying prior transactional evidence,* including:

* prior transactions (empirical historical data) and market information (4.1);
* new mandatory codes and legislation, such as regulations introduced for COVID (4.2);
* market intelligence from market participants including *buyers, sellers, agents, researchers and valuers* (4.3);
* market transactional data and information on economic and market activity (4.4);
* unsettled market transactions/heads of agreement or transactions that failed to settle/heads of agreement that failed to proceed (4.5);
* observations from previous crisis events, such as bushfires, earthquakes, pandemics and the GFC (4.6);
* observations of the stock market with a focus on the REIT market (4.7); and
* market research from reputable sources, though the opinion of another person or entity should not simply be adopted, but the valuer should form their own opinion giving weight to the available market research (4.8),

with the source of valuation inputs to be explained in the valuation report (5.3).

6.3.4.3 API—rental valuations and advice

AVGP301 *Rental Valuations and Advice* (API, 2023) considers market evidence (6.4), calculation of gross effective rent (6.5), method of comparison (6.6) and GST (6.7), providing the following hierarchy for the weight that is to be placed on market evidence:

* a new lease to a new tenant;
* a market rent agreed between landlord and tenant at a mid-term review or exercise of option;
* a market rent set by determination at a mid-term review or exercise of option;

- new lease to sitting tenant on expiry of a prior lease, with consideration to be given to whether a premium rent was agreed in reflection of goodwill or an existing fit out; and
- evidence of passing rents for sitting tenants (6.4).

The treatment of incentives is addressed in section 6.5, where gross effective rent is defined as *the actual liability for rent and outgoings after adjustments for any incentives to the face rent are taken into account* (6.5) being the appropriate unit of comparison unless directed otherwise under a specific lease (6.6). Any incentives should be converted into a periodic equivalent over the term of the lease (6.5) with a cash flow approach claimed to be most accurate whereby:

- the monthly cash flow, including incentives, is expressed and the net present value calculated;
- the monthly cash flow excluding incentives is expressed and the net present value calculated; and
- *it is then a simple matter of determining, at what initial rent the net present value without the incentives, equals the net present value with the incentives* (6.5)

with the discount rate for non-escalated cash flows being the equivalent of the capitalisation rate and that for escalated cash flows being the equivalent of the internal rate of return (6.5).

Finally, section 6.7 notes that *the basis of GST treatment should be the manner in which the market participants treat GST for the type of property and lease in accordance with GST legislation.*

6.3.4.4 API—residential mortgage valuation practice

While the comparative method of valuation is most commonly applied to residential property for secured lending purposes (such as mortgage lending), in Australia, this may be impacted by arrangements between valuers, API and lenders, which were considered in Chapter 5.

6.3.5 Summary—comparative method of valuation

The principles of the market approach to valuation and the comparative method of valuation were considered through the following key elements:

- *Adams* approach to the comparative method (6.3.1):
    - *Adams* accumulation (6.3.1.1);
    - *Adams* analysis (6.3.1.2);
    - *Adams* adjustment (6.3.1.3);
    - *Adams* application (6.3.1.4);
- IVSC approach to the comparative method (6.3.2);
- RICS approach to the comparative method (6.3.3); and
- API approach to the comparative method (6.3.4),

with a worked example of the assessment of market value in what follows.

There is a manifest similarity between *Adams*, IVSC, RICS and API concerning the principles of accumulation, analysis, adjustment and application. Each consistently contribute to making the comparative method of valuation logical, transparent and explicit. Significantly, while each still requires the use of judgment by the valuer, they move the comparative method of valuation away from being based on assertion and implicit assumptions.

Clients and readers of valuation reports can trace the valuer's logic through the implementation of the four steps of accumulation, analysis, adjustment and application in a transparent manner, which increases confidence in the assessment of value. As with many aspects of valuation, the judgments involved in the use of *Adams* may differ between two valuers, but neither may necessarily be wrong.

6.4 Comparative method of valuation—practice

As the comparative method of valuation is the preferred method of the Courts, it will be considered through the lens of the NSW Land & Environment Court decision in *Adams,* which established four sequential steps:

* accumulation;
* analysis;
* adjustment; and
* application

of potentially comparable sales transactions (para 29). Such an approach is consistent with the IVSC, RICS and API approaches to the comparative method.

The following worked example applies the comparative method of valuation to fictitious properties for the purposes of illustration only, and the data therein should not be adopted unchanged by readers undertaking valuations.

6.4.1 Outline of example

You are instructed to assess the market value of a three-bedroom house with a double garage on a 600 sqm block of land at a valuation date of 30 June 2023. The exterior of the house is of brick construction, and the interior is in fair condition. The house is in an outer suburb, located close to schools, train station and shops.

6.4.2 Outline of comparative method—accumulation

The accumulation step is described in *Adams* as follows:

> *The accumulation of potentially genuinely comparable sales seeks to identify and establish a pool of relevant comparable sales from which information may be deduced concerning the value of the subject property.*

> (para 32)

Reflecting the heterogeneity of property, it is preferable at this stage in the process to include as many sales as possible in the sample for consideration, provided each shares similar characteristics to the subject property and so is a relevant comparable sale, as the sample size is likely to be diminished during the course of undertaking the following steps.

Your search of internal records, relevant databases and websites identifies six potential genuinely comparable sales:

Sale 1

The sale of a three-bedroom house with a double garage on a 600 sqm block of land, three months before the valuation date, for $774,000. The exterior of the house is of timber construction, and the interior is in poor condition. The house is in the same outer suburb, located around 1 km from schools, train station and shops.

Sale 2

The sale of a two-bedroom house with no garage on a 400 sqm block of land, four months before the valuation date, for $790,000. The exterior of the house is of timber construction, and the interior is in fair condition. The house is in the same outer suburb, being within 200 m of the subject property, close to schools, train station and shops.

Sale 3

The sale of a three-bedroom house with a double garage on an 800 sqm block of land, two months before the valuation date, for $1,040,000. The exterior of the house is of brick construction, and the interior is in good condition. The house is in the same outer suburb, located around 400 m from schools, train station and shops.

Sale 4

The sale of a two-bedroom house with a double garage on a 600 sqm block of land, six months before the valuation date, for $900,000. The exterior of the house is of timber construction, and the interior is in good condition. The house is in the same outer suburb, located close to schools, train station and shops.

Sale 5

The sale of a three-bedroom house with no garage on a 700 sqm block of land, one month before the valuation date, for $970,000. The exterior of the house is of brick construction, and the interior is in fair condition. The house is in the same outer suburb, located about 500 m from schools, train station and shops.

Sale 6

The sale of a four-bedroom house with a double garage on a 1,000 sqm block of land, six months before the valuation date, for $1,175,000. The exterior of the house is of brick construction, and the interior is in very good condition. The house is in an adjacent outer suburb, located about 2 kms from schools, train station and shops.

6.4.3 Outline of comparative method—analysis

The analysis step is described in *Adams* as follows:

> *The analysis of potentially genuinely comparable sales provides a common basis of measurement by seeking to convert all potentially comparable sales to a common basis of expression such as a unitary rate (rate per square metre, rate per hectare, etc), improved or unimproved (through allowance for the absence or existence of improvements, etc) and so forth.*

(38)

The unitary rate should be that commonly used in the market for that type of property, and it is important that the same unitary rate is adopted for all comparable sales in the sample to permit comparison to be made on a common basis.

In this example, the accumulated comparable sales are all improved residential properties, which provides a common basis of measurement. However, unlike the subject property and other comparable sales, Sale 2 and Sale 5 do not have a garage. Also, the comparable sales took place between one and six months before the valuation date.

Issues such as the absence of a garage and the impact of market changes over time may be addressed either in the analysis step or in the adjustment step. For the purposes of illustration in this example, the absence of a garage in Sale 2 and Sale 5 will be addressed in the analysis step by the addition of $40,000 to the sale price, representing the valuer's understanding of the cost of building a double garage in the relevant suburb:

Sale 2	Sale price	$790,000
	+ garage	$40,000
	Analysed sale price	$830,000
Sale 5	Sale price	$970,000
	+ garage	$40,000
	Analysed sale price	$1,010,000

Therefore, adopting an analysed sale price of $830,000 for Sale 2 and $1,010,000 for Sale 5 provides a common basis of expression for all the comparable sales for use in the adjustment and application steps.

The impact of market changes over time may be addressed by increasing/decreasing the comparable sale price in the analysis step or in the adjustment step. Such an increase/decrease should be based on market evidence, such as from the analysis of paired sales or from data published by a reputable agency or research group. For the purposes of this example, it is assumed that there has been no market movement over the six-month period leading to the valuation date, so no amendment to the sale prices of the comparable properties is required.

6.4.4 Outline of comparative method—adjustment

The adjustment step is described in *Adams* as being the reflection of differences (such as size, location, use, date, etc.) between the respective potentially comparable sales and the subject property within the following guidelines:

- fewer adjustments may be preferred to more adjustments;
- smaller adjustments may be preferred to larger adjustments; and
- explicit adjustments are preferred to implicit adjustments.

Following Miller (1956), a matrix plotting each comparable sale in columns and around seven aspects for adjustment in rows may be capable of comprehension. Adjustments should be consistently made and be explicit. When adopting percentages, case law suggests the total adjustment should be no more than +/-30% for the comparable sale to be safe for use, and adjustments should follow a common pattern (for example, 2.5%, 5%, 7.5%, 10% or 2%, 4%, 6%, 8%) when judgementally based, with adjustments such as +1.5% or -6.33% requiring clear supporting evidence.

6.4.4.1 Overview of comparable sales

A review of the comparable sales suggests the following:

Sale 1

The timber construction, internal condition and location are all inferior to the subject property. Therefore, the subject property would be expected to sell for a higher price than Sale 1.

Sale 2

The fewer bedrooms, smaller block size and timber construction are all inferior to the subject property. Therefore, the subject property would be expected to sell for a higher price than Sale 2.

Sale 3

The location is inferior to the subject property, but the block size and internal condition are superior to the subject property. The relativity of the differences will determine if the subject property would be expected to sell for a lower price or higher price than Sale 3.

Sale 4

The fewer bedrooms and timber construction are inferior, but the internal condition is superior to the subject property. The relativity of the differences will determine if the subject property would be expected to sell for a lower price or higher price than Sale 4.

Sale 5

The location is inferior, but the block size is superior to the subject property. The relativity of the differences will determine if the subject property would be expected to sell for a lower price or higher price than Sale 5.

Sale 6

The location is inferior, but the larger number of bedrooms, block size and very good internal condition are superior to the subject property. The relativity of the differences will determine if the subject property would be expected to sell for a lower price or higher price than Sale 6.

6.4.4.2 Adjustment matrix

Adopting an adjustment basis of 2.5% increments (not because accuracy to 0.5% can be assured but reflecting a common pattern of incremental increases), the previously mentioned inferior and superior aspects of the comparable sales to the subject property may be quantified as shown in Table 6.1.

Readers will note from Table 6.1 that the greater the difference between the comparable sale and the subject property, the greater the level of adjustment, with adjustments being applied

Table 6.1 Adjustment matrix

	Sale 1	Sale 2	Sale 3	Sale 4	Sale 5	Sale 6
Location	+5%	0%	+2.5%	0%	+2.5%	+10%
Land size	0%	+5%	−5%	0%	−7.5%	−10%
Bedrooms	0%	+7.5%	0%	+7.5%	0%	−10%
Internal condition	+10%	0%	−5%	-5%	0%	−10%
External construction	+7.5%	+7.5%	0%	+7.5%	0%	0%
Total	+22.5%	+20%	−7.5%	+10%	−5%	−20%

Source: Author

consistently across each of the comparable sales. Further, none of the adjustments sum to more than 30% for a given comparable sale, indicating that the accumulated comparable sales are safe for use.

The issues of inferiority and superiority should be viewed through the lens of making the comparable sale less or more valuable than the subject property. For example, a larger block size will make Sale 3 more valuable than the subject property (adjustment to Sale 3 price -5%), whereas poor internal condition will make Sale 1 less valuable than the subject property (adjustment to Sale 1 price +10%).

The adjustments from Table 6.1 are applied to the analysed sale prices in Table 6.2:

Table 6.2 Adjusted sale price matrix

	Sale 1	Sale 2	Sale 3	Sale 4	Sale 5	Sale 6
Analysed sale price	$774,000	$830,000	$1,040,000	$900,000	$1,010,000	$1,175,000
% Adjustment	+22.5%	+20%	−7.5%	+10%	−5%	−20%
Adjusted sale price	$948,150	$996,000	$962,000	$990,000	$959,500	$940,000

Source: Author

Therefore, the adjusted comparable sale prices for use in the application step range from $940,000 to $996,000.

6.4.5 Outline of comparative method—application

The application step is described in *Adams* as follows:

> *The application of those potentially genuinely comparable sales to the subject property seeks to determine the value of the subject property through a consideration of the relevance (such as being limited, indirect or direct) of the unitary rate derived from those adjusted comparable sales relative to the subject.*
>
> (para 56)

and:

> *While all comparable sales evidence may be considered relevant and so cannot be disregarded, the level of relevance of different comparable sales to the subject property may vary leading to the valuer attributing differing weight to different comparable sales.*
>
> (para 57)

Therefore, the adjusted comparable sales require application to the subject property through a consideration of their individual relevance and the resulting weight to be given to each. While no sale is irrelevant, those with the greatest similarity to the subject property may be rated as of direct relevance, those with lower similarity may be rated as of indirect relevance and those of limited comparability may be rated as of limited relevance.

The application step may give the greatest weight to those comparable sales of direct relevance in determining the range of value for the subject property, which should then be broadly in alignment with those comparable sales of indirect or limited relevance to which less weight is attributed.

Having regard to their similarity to the subject property, the level of percentage adjustment and the resulting adjusted comparable sale prices, the following levels of relevance may be proposed:

Direct relevance	Sale 3, Sale 5
Indirect relevance	Sale 4
Limited relevance	Sale 1, Sale 2, Sale 6

Giving the greatest weight to those comparable sales of direct relevance, the range of value for the subject property is $959,500 to $962,000, from which the market value of the subject property may be assessed at $960,000.

As a final quality control check, the valuer should step back and consider the assessment of $960,000 to ensure that it is in alignment with the comparable sales evidence—effectively asking the fundamental question, *does this valuation make sense?*

6.4.6 Summary—comparative method of valuation

The adoption of the accumulation, analysis, adjustment and application steps from *Adams*, being consistent with IVSC, RICS and API, may appear to be a lengthy and involved process, but it is simply making the comparative method of valuation logical, explicit and transparent, giving clients and readers of valuation reports greater confidence in the assessment of value. As a valuer's experience increases, the speed at which the process can be undertaken will increase, and the valuer's ability to spot inconsistencies and anomalies will also increase.

6.5 Summary and conclusions

Chapter 1 outlined the structure of the property asset class, examining the traditional characteristics of property (including heterogeneity, durability, illiquidity and so forth) and the traditional risks of property (including location, building, tenant risk and so forth) through the lenses of systematic, unsystematic and idiosyncratic risk, aligning property valuation with capital market theory.

Chapter 2 considered the evolution of property valuation in Australia, the role of the valuer and the diverse activities of the valuation profession, followed by a detailed examination of the inter-acting framework provided by valuation standards and ethical standards promulgated by IVSC, RICS and API.

Chapter 3 explored concepts of value and normative and positive definitions of value, dissecting the International Valuation Standards' definition of market value with a reconciliation to the concept of market value in *Spencer v Commonwealth* (1907) and examining such contemporary valuation issues as valuation lag, variance, accuracy, negligence and valuer rotation.

Chapter 4 introduced International Financial Reporting Standards and International Accounting Standards with a detailed examination of the key provisions of International Valuation

Standards, the RICS Red Book and API guidance papers that impact on valuation practice in Australia.

Chapter 5 outlined conceptual approaches to the valuation process with a review of the self-supporting process of instructing, undertaking and reporting valuations under the International Valuation Standards, RICS Red Book and API guidance papers, examining how this process inter-relates to the choice of valuation approach, valuation method and the purpose of the valuation.

This chapter addressed the market approach to valuation through the comparative method of valuation, including the key steps of accumulation, analysis, adjustment and application of comparable sales evidence to the subject property being valued, with an example.

With the comparative method of valuation being one of the most widely used methods of valuation, through repetitive use, its implementation becomes second nature to the practising valuer who develops an instinct for assessing value using the method. As a valuer's experience increases, the speed at which the process can be undertaken will increase and the valuer's ability to spot inconsistencies and anomalies will also increase.

While some valuers may resist a formalised approach to the comparative method, favouring a reliance on art or judgment, not only the Courts but also the regulators and the professional bodies all prefer a formalised approach which, not surprisingly, is of a broadly consistent nature. From a risk management perspective, the adoption of a formalised approach by valuers reduces the risk in the valuation process and the risk to the valuer of inadvertent error or inconsistency in judgment.

Within a formalised approach, there still remains the need for valuer judgment, expressed as adjustment for the relativity between variable aspects of the comparable sales and the subject property. The level of adjustment is subjective and requires the valuer to have relevant market experience and local knowledge in order to form a judgment. However, implementation of a formalised process makes the comparative method of valuation transparent, logical and explicit such that clients and readers of valuation reports can trace the valuer's logic through the implementation of each of the four steps in a transparent manner, increasing confidence in the assessment of value.

It may be ironic that a theoretically robust implementation of the comparative method, resisted by some valuers, may save the careers of many valuers. While the comparative method works best for homogenised property sub-sectors with frequent sales, such sub-sectors are most exposed to the replacement of valuers by technology and AVMs. It is in the valuation of heterogenous property sub-sectors, where there may be fewer directly comparable sales, that a theoretically robust implementation of the comparative method may be most useful and where the exercise of judgment and knowledge of the local market that can only be provided by a valuer and not by technology, may be most helpful.

The next chapter will consider the income approach to valuation addressed through the static methods of the capitalisation of income and the profits methods of valuation, including an examination of the key inputs for each method with examples and a consideration of both marriage value and the surrender and renewal of leases.

Chapter 8 considers the income approach to valuation addressed through the dynamic method of the discounted cash flow method of valuation, including an examination of the key inputs and a focus on the derivation of the discount rate and consideration of the role of sensitivity and scenario analysis, with examples.

Chapter 9 considers the cost approach to valuation addressed through the replacement cost, reproduction cost, summation and residual or hypothetical development methods of valuation.

Finally, Chapter 10 concludes the book with a consideration of future perspectives, including the role of uncertainty, data, automated valuation models, artificial intelligence, optionality, environmental, social and governance issues, retail and office space use and indigenous issues.

References

API (2021a) *ANZVGP111 valuation procedures—real property*, Australian Property Institute, Deakin.

API (2021b) *ANZVGP110 considerations when forming an opinion of value when there is a shortage of market transactions*, Australian Property Institute, Deakin.

API (2023) *AVGP301 rental valuations and advice*, Australian Property Institute, Deakin.

Isaac, D and O'Leary, J (2012) *Property valuation principles*, Palgrave Macmillan, Basingstoke.

IVSC (2021) *International valuation standards*, International Valuation Standards Council, London.

Kininmonth, D (2022) 'Residential property valuation', in Parker, D (Ed) *Principles and practice of property valuation in Australia*, Routledge, Abingdon.

Miller, GA (1956) 'The magical number seven, plus or minus two: some limits on our capacity for processing information', *Psychological Review*, Vol 63, No 2, pp. 81–97.

Millington, A (2000) *An introduction to property valuation*, Routledge, Abingdon.

RICS (2021) *RICS valuation—global standards*, Royal Institution of Chartered Surveyors, London.

RICS (2023) *RICS professional standard: comparable evidence in real estate valuation*, RICS, London.

Shapiro, E, Mackmin, D and Sams, G (2019) *Modern methods of valuation*, Routledge, Abingdon.

Whipple, RTM (2006) *Property valuation and analysis*, Lawbook Co, Sydney.

Wyatt, P (2023) *Property valuation*, Wiley Blackwell, Chichester.

7 Income approach to valuation—static

7.1 Introduction

This book is an introduction to the fundamentals of property valuation, outlining the principal methods of property valuation in Australia within the context of International Valuation Standards, bridging the gap between traditional property valuation methods and the modern era of global valuation governance.

Chapter 1 outlined the structure of the property asset class, examining the traditional characteristics of property (including heterogeneity, durability, illiquidity and so forth) and the traditional risks of property (including location, building, tenant risk and so forth) through the lenses of systematic, unsystematic and idiosyncratic risk, so aligning property valuation with capital market theory.

Chapter 2 considered the evolution of property valuation in Australia, the role of the valuer and the diverse activities of the valuation profession, followed by a detailed examination of the inter-acting framework provided by valuation standards and ethical standards promulgated by IVSC, RICS and API.

Chapter 3 explored concepts of value and normative and positive definitions of value, dissecting the International Valuation Standards' definition of market value with a reconciliation to the concept of market value in *Spencer v Commonwealth* (1907) and examining such contemporary valuation issues as valuation lag, variance, accuracy, negligence and valuer rotation.

Chapter 4 introduced International Financial Reporting Standards and International Accounting Standards with a detailed examination of the key provisions of International Valuation Standards, the RICS Red Book and API guidance papers that impact on valuation practice in Australia.

Chapter 5 outlined conceptual approaches to the valuation process with a review of the self-supporting process of instructing, undertaking and reporting valuations under the International Valuation Standards, RICS Red Book and API guidance papers, examining how this process inter-relates to the choice of valuation approach, valuation method and the purpose of the valuation.

Chapter 6 addressed the market approach to valuation through the comparative method of valuation, including the key steps of accumulation, analysis, adjustment and application of comparable sales evidence to the subject property being valued, with an example.

This chapter seeks to consider the income approach to valuation addressed through the static methods of the capitalisation of income and the profits methods of valuation, including an examination of the key inputs for each method with examples and a consideration of both marriage value and the surrender and renewal of leases.

DOI: 10.1201/9781003397922-7

Chapter 8 considers the income approach to valuation addressed through the dynamic method of the discounted cash flow method of valuation, including an examination of the key inputs and a focus on the derivation of the discount rate and consideration of the role of sensitivity and scenario analysis, with examples.

Chapter 9 considers the cost approach to valuation addressed through the replacement cost, reproduction cost, summation and residual or hypothetical development methods of valuation.

Finally, Chapter 10 concludes the book with a consideration of future perspectives, including the role of uncertainty, data, automated valuation models, artificial intelligence, optionality, environmental, social and governance issues, retail and office space use and indigenous issues.

This book is based on those standards and guidance documents published in IVSC (2021) and RICS (2021) and on the API website (accessed January to May 2023). Given their nature, standards and guidance documents are dynamic, being regularly updated and with the most recently published versions replacing previously published versions. Accordingly, readers should not rely on this book as a current statement of a standard or guidance document and should visit www.ivsc.org, www.rics.org and/or www.api.org.au to find the most recent version.

As an introductory textbook on property valuation methods in Australia, this book is a companion to Australia's leading advanced valuation textbook, *Principles and Practice of Property Valuation in Australia,* edited by the same author and also published by Routledge, which is a deeper analysis of key principles underlying property valuation and current techniques and issues in the practice of property valuation for major sectors of the Australian property market.

Traditional valuation texts, such as Millington (2000), consider five methods of valuation:

- the comparative (or comparison) method;
- the income (or investment or capitalisation) method;
- the profits (or accounts or treasury or receipts and expenditure) method;
- the contractor's (or summation or cost) method; and
- the residual (or hypothetical development) method of valuation.

This chapter addresses the income approach, the income (or investment or capitalisation) method of valuation and the profits (or accounts or treasury or receipts and expenditure) method of valuation.

The principles of the income approach to valuation will be considered through the following key elements:

- capitalisation of income method—perpetuities (7.3.1);

  - representative single period income (7.3.1.1);
  - reversionary income (7.3.1.2);
  - capitalisation rate (7.3.1.3);
  - formulae for income capitalisation (7.3.1.4);
  - voids (7.3.1.5);
  - rounding off (7.3.1.6);

- capitalisation of income method—annuities (7.3.2)

  - short term leasehold interests (7.3.2.1);
  - long term leasehold interests (7.3.2.2); and

- profits method of valuation (7.3.3),

followed by worked examples of the application of each to the assessment of market value, together with a consideration of marriage value and the surrender and renewal of leases.

7.2 Income approach to valuation

The income approach to valuation is one of the three principal valuation approaches recognised by IVSs and is grounded in economic theory, being based on the economic principle of anticipation of benefits. IVS105 (IVSC, 2021) defines the income approach as follows:

> *The income approach provides an indication of value by converting future cash flow to a single current value. Under the income approach, the value of an asset is determined by reference to the value of income, cash flow or cost savings generated by the asset.*
>
> (40.1)

The income approach is, therefore, premised on the existence of an income—either actual through the leasing of a property by an owner/landlord to an occupier/tenant or imputed/hypothetical in the case of an owner-occupied property. Given the vast portfolios of office, retail, industrial and other property owned by institutions (superannuation funds, insurance companies, REITs, wholesale property funds and so forth) as investments to provide income return and capital growth, the income approach is widely used by the valuation profession.

As well as being premised on a return, the income approach is also premised on the risk associated with that return. IVS105 (IVSC, 2021) notes that a fundamental basis for the income approach is that investors expect to receive a return on their investment and that such a return should reflect the perceived risk of that investment (40.4).

IVS105 (IVSC, 2021) notes that the income approach should be applied and afforded significant weight under the following circumstances:

- the income-producing ability of the asset is the critical element affecting value from a participant perspective; and/or
- reasonable projections of the amount and timing of future income are available for the subject asset, but there are few, if any, relevant market comparables (40.2).

Further, IVS105 (IVSC, 2021) notes that the income approach may be applied and afforded significant weight where:

- the income-producing ability of the subject asset is only one of several factors affecting value from a participant perspective;
- there is significant uncertainty regarding the amount and timing of future income related to the subject asset;
- there is a lack of access to information related to the subject asset; and/or
- the subject asset has not yet begun generating income but is projected to do so,

though the valuer should consider whether any other approaches can be applied and weighted to corroborate the value indication from the income approach (40.3).

VPS5 *Valuation approaches and methods* in the RICS Red Book (RICS, 2021) notes:

> *The income approach is based on capitalisation or conversion of present and predicted income (cash flows), which may take a number of different forms, to produce a single*

current capital value. Among the forms taken, capitalisation of a conventional market-based income or discounting of a specific income projection can both be considered appropriate depending on the type of asset and whether such an approach would be adopted by market participants.

(2)

IVS105 (IVSC, 2021) also notes:

In some circumstances for long-lived or indefinite-lived assets, DCF may include a terminal value which represents the value of an asset at the end of the explicit projection period. In other circumstances, the value of an asset may be calculated solely using a terminal value with no explicit projection period. This is sometimes referred to as the income capitalisation method.

(50.3)

There are, therefore, essentially two valuation methods within the income approach, being the conversion of future cash flow to a single current value by either:

- the application of a multiplier to the cash flow, being the static income approach known as the income, investment or capitalisation method which is considered in this chapter; and
- discounting the future cash flow to a present value amount, being the dynamic income approach known as the discounted cash flow method, which is considered in the next chapter.

IVS400 (IVSC, 2021) notes that the income approach may be applied to an actual or estimated income that either is or could be generated by the owner of the interest. In the case of investment property, such income may be in the form of rent (or other payment such as licence fee), and for an owner-occupied building, it may be the assumed rent base or what it would cost the owner to lease equivalent space (60.1).

Income such as rent and licence fees from offices, retail or industrial property should be distinguished from income that is closely tied to a particular use or trading activity generated by a building that is suitable for only that type of trading activity, such as a hotel, pub, bar, restaurant, nightclub, petrol filling station, casino, cinema, theatre and various other forms of leisure property. The use of a property's trading potential to indicate its value is usually addressed by the profits method of valuation (IVSC, 2021, IVS400, 60.2).

7.3 Income method of valuation—principles

The income method of valuation will be considered through the:

- capitalisation of income method for perpetual income streams (7.3.1);
  - representative single period income (7.3.1.1);
  - reversionary income (7.3.1.2);
  - capitalisation rate (7.3.1.3);
  - formulae for income capitalisation (7.3.1.4);
  - voids (7.3.1.5);
  - rounding off (7.3.1.6);

- capitalisation of income method for annuity income streams (7.3.2);
  - short term leasehold interests (7.3.2.1);
  - long term leasehold interests (7.3.2.2); and
- profits method of valuation (7.3.3).

7.3.1 Capitalisation of income method—perpetuities

Freehold property is capable of being held in perpetuity, with the net income from a freehold property investment valued as being receivable in perpetuity.

Baum et al. (2018), in their seminal text, succinctly define capitalisation as follows:

Capitalisation is the expression of future benefits in terms of their present value.

(page 128)

A previous edition of IVS's usefully described the capitalisation method as:

where an all-risks or overall capitalisation rate is applied to a representative single period income

(IVSC, 2013, para 60, page 24)

where the income stream is likely to remain constant (or consistent with the market), and the capitalisation rate is based on the time cost of money and the risks and rewards attached to the income stream (Parker, 2016).

This identifies the two key variables within the capitalisation method as the multiplier or capitalisation rate (known as the "all risks" rate in the UK and the "overall" rate in the US) and a representative single period income. The concept of multiplying a single period income figure by a single rate to assess value leads to the method being known as a static method. While apparently deceptively simple, each variable masks a myriad of complex issues (Parker, 2016).

With only two dependent variables, the capitalisation method may be most appropriate for adoption where there is a stable property in a stable property market with stable comparable sales transactions where each has a relatively simple risk profile. This effectively limits the use of the capitalisation method to simpler, smaller properties for which there is a substantial pool of comparable sales evidence in a deep market and valuers should take great care in attempting to apply the capitalisation method to complex, larger properties and/or markets of limited depth (Parker, 2016).

As will be considered in what follows, the assessment of a representative single-period income is heavily dependent on heuristics, and the assessment of the capitalisation rate is heavily dependent on valuer judgement, such that the reliability of the capitalisation method is inverse to the complexity of the investment property being valued and/or the stability of the market within which it is situated (Parker, 2016).

Effectively, therefore, the capitalisation method of valuation is best suited to simpler, smaller, stable properties in stable markets, with complex, larger, less stable properties in less stable markets better suited to valuation by the discounted cash flow method (Parker, 2016).

The capitalisation method may be applied to properties with an existing income stream (known as investment properties), to vacant properties where a potential income stream may be assessed or to owner-occupied properties where a notional income stream may be imputed (being the income stream that the owner foregoes by occupying the property rather than leasing it to another party).

Baum et al. (2018) note that:

> *The strongest critics of the capitalisation approach argue that it fails to specify explicitly the future income flows and patterns assumed by the valuer, and that the capitalisation rate which is growth implicit fails to identify income risks which should be stated explicitly.*

(page 135)

To this, Isaac and O'Leary (2013) cite the common response:

> *The defence is said to be that valuation is an art and not a science and that the valuer should be trusted to exercise judgment and experience when selecting an appropriate yield for a particular property.*

(page 20)

Isaac and O'Leary (2013) further note that, in an age where there are legitimate expectations that decision-making should be objective and transparent, it is not surprising that the method comes under scrutiny.

7.3.1.1 Representative single period income

Assessment of a representative single period income requires the valuer to determine the hypothetical current market level of gross income, outgoings or expenses, and net income with regard to transactions of comparable property in the relevant market and then apply a series of heuristics, including:

- assuming that the single period income will comprise the constant income;
- assuming that the single period income will comprise the income in perpetuity;
- assuming that the useful life of the property will be in perpetuity;
- making manually calculated income allowances for currently vacant space and/or space occupied at more/less than current market income levels;
- making percentage or similar adjustments for possible future vacancy and possible future incentives; and
- linking future tenant retention and leasing strategies to an assessment of possible capital losses for deduction

and so forth, each of which may have no firm grounding in transactions of comparable property in the relevant market but accumulate to impact one of the two key multipliers in the capitalisation method of valuation. Accordingly, a small variation in any or all of the market-derived and heuristic inputs may result in a significant variation in the assessment of the representative single period income and so in the assessment of value (Parker, 2016).

The capitalisation method generally deduces the representative single period income from the Full Rental Value (FRV) or the Estimated Rental Value (ERV), being the market rent of the property as defined by IVSs. For simplicity, this text will adopt market rent.

The market rent may be the same as (rack rented), greater than (under-rented or reversionary) or less than (over-rented) the rental passing under a lease. If the market rent is the same as the rental passing, that rental may be converted to a single period representative income and capitalised in perpetuity. If the market rent is greater or lesser than the rental passing, the rental would be converted to a single period representative income and capitalised up to market rent review or lease expiry with a reversion to market rent which would be converted to a single period representative income and capitalised in perpetuity, deferred for the period until the rent review or lease expiry.

The difference between market rent and single representative period income comprises deductions for any recurrent periodic costs or expenses (not one-off capital expenses that are considered later in the capitalisation method) that an investor/owner may have to pay under the lease and which are generally known in Australia as outgoings.

Outgoings include statutory charges (such as rates, land tax, emergency services levy, etc.), insurance, maintenance costs (such as lifts, air-conditioning, lighting, etc.), security costs, cleaning costs, management costs and ongoing repairs, which are the landlord's responsibility.

The deduction of outgoings from market rent produces the single representative period income or net income of the property, which may then be capitalised at an appropriate capitalisation rate.

In some parts of the world, leases may be referred to as full repairing and insuring leases (FRI—where the tenant has the responsibility to repair and insure the entire property) or internal repairing leases (IRT—where the tenant is only responsible for internal repairs). In Australia, it is common for the owner to have the obligation to repair the exterior of the property and for the occupier to have the obligation to repair the interior of the property. However, the valuer should carefully read the lease document to ascertain where the obligation for repairs sits and reflect this in either outgoings or capital allowances.

7.3.1.2 Reversionary income

It was noted previously that where the market rent is greater or lesser than the rental passing, the rental would be converted to a single period representative income and capitalised for a term up to market rent review or lease expiry with a reversion to market rent, which would be converted to a single period representative income and capitalised in perpetuity, deferred for the period until the rent review or lease expiry.

Conventionally, the term income would be capitalised at a lower rate than the reversion income—say 7% for the term and 7.5% for the reversion—to reflect the greater perceived security of the term income. However, as Isaac and O'Leary (2013) note:

> There is no mechanism or formula which can be used to engineer these yield adjustments and it requires judgment on the part of the valuer, underlining the fact that this type of valuation is more of an art than a science.
>
> (page 24)

Such an approach is conventionally known as a term and reversion valuation. For completeness, though not usually adopted in Australia, an alternative is the layer approach or core and top slice approach, whereby the passing single representative period income is capitalised in perpetuity, and the increase is also capitalised in perpetuity but deferred until realised. The layer approach or top slice approach assumes an upward-only rent review so the passing single representative period income (core) can never fall. Readers are referred to Wyatt (2023) for further explanation of the layer approach or top slice approach if required.

Where there are rent reviews to other than market rent, such as CPI rent reviews or fixed increases, these would be similarly reflected in a series of capitalisations of rent passing converted to a single period representative income at each review until lease expiry when there would be a reversion to market rent which would be converted to a single period representative income and capitalised in perpetuity, deferred for the periods covered by the various rent reviews. A similar approach is adopted for the treatment of rent-free periods and other incentives commonly found in the leasing of investment property.

It may be possible that the reversion to market rent may be at some point in the future, perhaps after a three-yearly open market rent review under a lease or after five years of annual CPI-linked rent reviews under a lease. Importantly, the capitalisation method does not attempt to escalate market rent or any deductions into the future so that the market rent that is finally capitalised in perpetuity is the market rent as at the date of valuation. While this may appear illogical and counterintuitive, it is yet another feature of the simplistic assumptions underlying the capitalisation method, with any potential for rental growth or decline above or below current market rent being addressed within the capitalisation rate selected. The capitalisation rate within the capitalisation method is, therefore, growth implicit and may be contrasted to the discounted cash flow method, which is growth explicit (see Chapter 8).

7.3.1.3 Capitalisation rate

TIP1 (IVSC, 2012) defines the capitalisation factor as follows:

> *The multiple applied to a representative single period income to convert it into a capital value*

(TIP1, 1)

and the capitalisation rate as follows:

> *The return represented by the income produced by an investment, expressed as a percentage.*

(TIP1, 2)

Assessment of the capitalisation rate requires a significant exercise of judgement by the valuer. The valuer should determine the capitalisation rate with regard to transactions of comparable property in the relevant market, deduced through analysis of the capitalisation rates exhibited by such transactions and then adjusted by applying professional judgment to reflect differences between such transactions and the subject property in order to assess the appropriate capitalisation rate for application to the subject property.

Reflecting the significant role of professional judgement in the assessment of the capitalisation rate, two equally experienced valuers may assess two different capitalisation rates for the same property. While neither is necessarily wrong, even a small variation in capitalisation rate may result in a significant variation in the assessment of value, potentially compounded by variations in the assessment of representative single period income (Parker, 2016).

The capitalisation rate (or all risks rate) is a single multiplier encompassing an enormously wide range of risk and return issues, including the relativity of property as an asset class to other asset classes (such as shares or bonds), the relativity of one property sector to another (such as offices to retail property), the relativity of one property to another (such as one office property to another) and the specific characteristics of the individual property being valued.

The capitalisation rate indicates the return on capital provided by a property investment— such as an investment priced at \$1,000,000 providing a net income of \$100,000 pa generates a return on capital of 10%pa. However, somewhat confusingly, the capitalisation rate may be alternatively expressed as a reciprocal referred to as Years Purchase (YP) (being 100/capitalisation rate) which represents the number of years that would be required to provide a return of capital to the investor—such that 100/10 provides a YP of 10, indicating it will take ten years of net income of $100,000 pa to provide a return of the capital invested of $1,000,000.

The capitalisation rate should be distinguished from the initial yield of a property investment, which is the annual return to the investor from the initial net income generated by a property investment relative to the capital value paid for a property—such as a net income of $70,000 pa generated by a property investment for which $1,000,000 was paid is showing an initial yield of 7%. If the property's initial net income is market rent, then the capitalisation rate and the initial yield will accord. If the market rent is above the property's initial net income, then the initial yield will be lower.

Similarly, each should be distinguished from the exit yield of a property investment, which is the annual return to the investor from the net income generated by a property investment in the last year of ownership relative to the capital value for which the property was sold—such as a net income of $150,000 pa generated in the last year by a property investment which was sold for $1,875,000 shows an exit yield of 8%.

While not generally considered in Australia, concepts of equivalent yield and equated yield are commonly considered in the UK, with readers referred to Baum et al. (2018) and Isaac and O'Leary (2012, 2013) for a deeper consideration.

7.3.1.4 Formulae for income capitalisation

The most commonly required valuation formula is to calculate the value of a cash flow in perpetuity at a given rate of interest, which is usually expressed as *Years Purchase in perpetuity* or *YP perp*. As the name suggests, it represents the number of years required to repay capital invested by annual net income, with the *YP* or multiplier being the reciprocal of the rate of return. Therefore, an investment of $100 million producing an annual net income of $5 million will provide a return of capital in 20 years and a return on capital of 5% pa. Accordingly, *YP perp at 5%* is 100/5 or 20.

Similarly, the value of an investment property producing annual net income of $5 m in perpetuity at a rate of return or capitalisation rate of 5% is:

Net income	$5.00 m pa
YP perp at 5%	× 20
Capital value	$100.00 m

The calculation of the value of a cash flow for a given number of periods at a given rate of interest is usually expressed as *YP x years at y%*, being calculated using the present value of $1 pa formula, which may be expressed as:

$$PV\$1pa = \frac{1 - (1+i)^n}{i}$$

Therefore, the multiplier for a cash flow for five years at 5%, usually expressed as *YP 5 years at 5%*, will be 4.3295.

The calculation of a right to a cash flow in perpetuity after a given number of periods at a given rate of interest is usually expressed as *PV $1 for x years at y%*, calculated using the present value formula, which may be expressed as:

$$PV\$1 = \frac{1}{(1+i)^n}$$

Therefore, the multiplier for the present value of a cash flow in perpetuity, which is available after five years at 5%, usually expressed as *PV 5 years at 5%*, will be 0.7835.

While these formulae may be easily calculated using a calculator or Excel, *Parry's Valuation and Conversion Tables* (Davidson, 1978) have provided ready reckoner tables of multipliers for over a century.

7.3.1.5 Voids

Voids are a break or gap in continuous net income from a property and may occur, for example, when:

- a property is currently vacant and anticipated to take one year to be leased with a six-month rent-free incentive; or
- a property is anticipated to be vacant, such as a property which is leased with the lease expiring in two years and, on expiry, the property is expected to be vacant and to take one year to lease with a six-month rent-free incentive.

Effectively, this is a variation on the term and reversion approach through the inclusion of a deferral, so that, in the previous examples:

- the commencement of the assumed income in perpetuity is deferred for one and a half years; and
- the passing rent is capitalised for two years, with the reversion capitalised in perpetuity deferred for three and a half years.

Alternatively, the capitalisation rate may be adjusted to reflect the prospect of voids, though the availability of comparable evidence upon which to base such an adjustment may be very limited.

7.3.1.6 Rounding off

The conventional approach in valuation is to round off the capital value once only at the end of the capitalisation process. While the market rent may be a rounded number, each stage of a reversionary valuation should not be rounded off, but the exact totals summed and the sum thereof should then be rounded off with a level of precision adopted by market participants.

For example, the sum of each stage of a reversionary valuation for a small office building may be $1,519,500, which may be rounded to $1.5 million, whereas a larger shopping centre where the sum is $374,850,000 may be rounded to $375 million.

7.3.1.7 Summary—capitalisation of income method—perpetuities

Freehold property is capable of being held in perpetuity, with the net income from a freehold property investment valued as being receivable in perpetuity. The capitalisation of income method for perpetual income streams was considered through the:

- representative single period income;
- reversionary income;
- capitalisation rate;
- formulae for income capitalisation;
- voids; and
- rounding off,

emphasising the importance of and inter-relationship between the net income and the capitalisation rate in the capitalisation of income method.

7.3.2 Capitalisation of income method—annuities

Freehold property is capable of being leased to a tenant who then holds a terminable leasehold interest for a fixed period of time, which may be of value. The net income payable under a terminable leasehold interest for a fixed period of time is in the nature of an annuity, commonly arising in Australia in two scenarios:

- a short-term leasehold interest; or
- a long-term leasehold interest.

A leasehold interest will only have value if the lease is capable of being assigned (sold), such that the common provision in leases that assignment is permitted with the lessor's prior written consent, such consent not to be unreasonably withheld, to a party of no lesser financial and operational capacity is essential. If the lease is not capable of being assigned (sold), there is no interest to be valued and the lease is of no value.

7.3.2.1 Short-term leasehold interests

An example of a short-term leasehold interest may be a valuation for the sale of a lease of a small shop that has three years unexpired of a five-year lease term at a fixed rent that is below market rent. The difference in rent passing and market rent (profit rent) for three years is in the nature of an annuity. The payment of the capital value of the profit rent by an incoming tenant may be referred to as payment of a premium, but this should be distinguished from the payment of a premium by a tenant to secure a new tenancy in periods of low vacancy (a reverse incentive).

Millington (2000) describes the basic calculation for the valuation of such a leasehold interest as follows:

	Market rent
Less	Rent paid under lease
=	Profit rent to lessee
x	Multiplier
=	Capital value

Profit rent should be distinguished from the profits method (considered further on) and only arises where a leasehold interest is at a rent below market rent for the period to the earlier of open market rent review or lease expiry.

The multiplier is usually the YP for the period of receipt, so, as the remaining period of the lease reduces, the capital value will fall.

7.3.2.2 Long-term leasehold interests

An example of a long-term leasehold interest might be the lease of a block of land for 99, 125 or 999 years by an institution, such as a government or church, to an investor who then builds an office building on the land which is rented out to tenants. At the end of the lease, the land will return to the institution and the investor will be left with no interest (in reality, there would be complex issues to address concerning the transfer or demolition of the office building, but these are ignored for convenience).

Unlike a freehold interest that may be valued in perpetuity, a leasehold interest is for a fixed period, being the unexpired term of the lease only, and so is in the nature of an annuity. Accordingly, the basic calculation for the valuation of such a long-term leasehold interest may be described as follows:

	Market rent/net income for office building
Less	Rent paid under lease for land
=	Income to lessee
x	Multiplier reflecting length of lease unexpired
=	Capital value of leasehold interest

Traditionally, leasehold interests were valued on a dual rate basis to reflect not only the capitalisation rate but also an allowance for a sinking fund which would accumulate to the valuation amount by the expiry of the lease, thereby providing the leaseholder with a return on and return of capital. In reality, leasehold investors rarely set up a sinking fund and typically accepted a notionally higher rate of return instead. Generally, in Australia, such a dual-rate methodology is not adopted, and a single capitalisation rate or YP is applied, based on analysis of the limited number of leasehold transactions available for consideration, which reflects the absence of return of capital.

Further, the limited number of leasehold transactions generally results in leaseholds being valued using a capitalisation rate related to the freehold rate and not from the analysis of leasehold transactions. For example, if the capitalisation rate for a freehold property was considered to be 6%, then the capitalisation rate for the same property if it was a long leasehold might be considered to be 7–8%.

7.3.2.3 Summary—capitalisation of income method—annuities

Freehold property is capable of being leased to a tenant who then holds a terminable leasehold interest for a fixed period of time. The net income payable under a terminable leasehold interest for a fixed period of time is in the nature of an annuity, which, if below market rent, may result in a short-term leasehold interest or a long-term leasehold interest being of value.

7.3.3 Profits method of valuation

While also referred to as the accounts or treasury or receipts and expenditure method of valuation, for the purposes of this book, the method will be referred to as the profits method of valuation.

The profits method is generally adopted where the type of property is inextricably linked to the business that operates therein, such as a hotel, pub, bar, restaurant, nightclub, petrol filling station, casino, cinema, theatre and various other forms of leisure property. Such properties are often owned rather than leased, so evidence of leasing transactions may be limited and are generally sold fully fitted out as operational entities, such that evidence of sales requires careful analysis. Accordingly, the profits method seeks to examine the economic fundamentals of the business as the source of value of the property by capitalising the estimated future trading potential rather than net income (Wyatt, 2023).

Baum et al. (2018) note that, given the possible combinations of trading style, lease and use, the profits method provides a way of assessing the value of an outlet on its potential merits and so has much to offer but relies heavily on the expertise and skill of the valuer. The valuer must acquire the knowledge and experience of the market or sub-market they wish to work in when adopting the profits method of valuation and apply the same to make relatively subjective assessments (page 307).

IVS400 (IVSC, 2021) notes that, when adopting the profits method of valuation, the valuer should comply with the requirements of IVS200 *Business and Business Interests* and IVS210 *Intangible Assets* (60.3).

IVS200 *Business and Business Interests* (IVSC, 2021) requires that the capitalisation or discount rate applied must be consistent with the type of income or cash flow used, which may be on a pre-tax, post-tax or another basis (60.3). Further, in estimating the appropriate capitalisation rate or discount rate, factors such as the level of interest rates, rates of return expected by participants for similar investments and the risk inherent in the anticipated benefit stream are to be considered (60.5).

Helpfully, IVS200 (IVSC, 2021) also suggests that using historical financial statements of a business entity to estimate future income or cash flow of the business allows the valuer to determine historical trends over time through ratio analysis, which may inform an assessment of risks inherent in the business and the prospects for future performance (60.7).

However, IVS200 (IVSC, 2021) notes that adjustments may be appropriate to reflect differences between the actual historical cash flows and those that would be experienced by a buyer of the business interest on the valuation date, such as:

- adjusting revenues and expenses to levels that are reasonably representative of expected continuing operations;
- presenting financial data of the subject business and comparison business on a consistent basis;
- adjusting non-arm's length transactions (such as contracts with customers or suppliers) to market rates;
- adjusting the cost of labour or of items leased or otherwise contracted from related parties to reflect market prices or rates;
- reflecting the impact of non-recurring events from historic revenue and expense items (such as strikes or weather) though reasonably anticipated non-recurring revenues or expenses in the past or future should be reflected; and
- adjusting inventory accounting to compare with similar businesses' accounting approach or to more accurately reflect economic reality (60.8).

IVS210 *Intangible Assets* (IVSC, 2021) notes that the value of an intangible asset may be determined by reference to the present value of income, cash flows or cost savings attributable to the intangible asset over its economic life (60.1). While intangible assets may not frequently require consideration in the application of the profits method, IVS210 provides guidance on five income approach methods (60.5) to which readers are referred for further detail:

- excess earnings method (60.6–60.17);
- relief from royalty method (60.18–60.21);
- premium profit method or with-and-without method (60.22–60.28);
- greenfield method (60.29–60.32) and
- distributor method (60.33–60.35).

VPGA4 *Valuation of individual trade related properties* in the RICS Red Book (RICS, 2021), considered further in what follows, provides advisory (not mandatory) guidance on the profits method of valuation when applied to the valuation of an individual property on the basis of trading potential (1.2). The profits method applies to property that is designed or adapted for a specific use, and the resulting lack of flexibility usually means that the value of the property interest is intrinsically linked to the returns that the owner can generate from that use. The value, therefore, reflects the trading potential of the property which may be contrasted with generic property (such as office, retail or industrial) that can be occupied by a range of different business types (1.3).

Millington (2000) notes that the profits method is generally only used when there is some kind of monopoly attached to a property, which may be legal or factual. Legal monopoly may arise from some legal restraint to competition, such as a liquor licence. Factual monopoly arises where there is some factor, other than legal, that restrains competition, such as a mountaintop site with only enough land for one café.

While properties such as hotels, pubs, bars, restaurants, nightclubs, petrol filling stations, casinos, cinemas, theatres and various other forms of leisure properties meet the specific use and adaptation criteria for the application of the profits method, other types of property such as car parks, garden centres, caravan parks, self-storage and purpose-built student housing may exhibit less specific use and adaptation may suit valuation by other methods (1.4).

Application of the profits method in VPGA4 (RICS, 2021) is premised on the assumption that the current trade related use will continue. However, where the property may have an alternative use that may have a higher value, an appropriate comment should be made in the report. If an alternative use value is provided, the report should comment that the valuation takes no account of the costs of business closure, disruption or other costs associated with realising this value (1.7).

7.3.3.1 *VPGA4 Valuation of individual trade related properties*

VPGA4 *Valuation of individual trade related properties* in the RICS Red Book (RICS, 2021) notes that valuers who prepare valuations of trade related properties usually specialise in a particular market, such as theatres and cinemas or hotels, pubs and bars, as knowledge of the operational aspects of the property and of the industry as a whole are fundamental to understanding the market transactions and the analysis required (1.5). Further, it is important that the valuer is regularly involved in the relevant market for the class of property, as practical knowledge of the factors affecting the particular market is also required (3.3).

The profits method is explained as a four-step process in VPGA4:

- **Step 1**: An assessment is made of the FMT that could be generated at the property by an REO.
- **Step 2**: Where appropriate, an assessment is made of the potential gross profit resulting from the FMT.

- **Step 3**: An assessment is made of the FMOP. The costs and allowances to be shown in the assessment should reflect those of the REO—which will be the most likely purchaser or operator of the property if offered in the market.
- **Step 4**:
  - **Step 4a**: To assess the market value of the property, the FMOP is capitalised at an appropriate rate of return, reflecting the risks and rewards of the property and its trading potential. Evidence of relevant comparable market transactions should be analysed and applied.
  - **Step 4b**: In assessing market value, the valuer may decide that an incoming new operator would expect to improve the trading potential by undertaking alterations or improvements and reflect these in the Step 1 FMT such that an appropriate allowance should be made to reflect the costs of completing works and the delay in achieving FMT. Similarly, any allowances for repairs and/or decoration should be made.
  - **Step 4c**: To assess the market rent for a new letting, the rent payable on a rent review or the reasonableness of the actual rent passing, an allowance should be made from the FMOP to reflect a return on the tenant's capital invested in the operational entity (such as trade inventory or working capital). The resultant sum is referred to as the divisible balance and is apportioned between the landlord and tenant with regard to the respective risks and rewards, with the landlord's proportion representing the annual rent (3.1).

The various acronyms are defined as follows:

- **FMT**: fair maintainable turnover—the level of trade that an REO would expect to achieve on the assumption that the property is properly equipped, repaired, maintained and decorated (2.5). Baum et al. (2018) note that this is the annual turnover capable of being achieved without over-trading or under-trading having regard to the target audience, being a forward-looking assessment (which may or may not align with historical trading and accounts information considered by the valuer) that should be cross-checked against turnover from comparable evidence. The adoption of the trading potential of an REO means that a property landlord is not penalised for the under-trading of a poor tenant, and a tenant is not penalised for over-trading;
- **REO**: reasonably efficient operator—this is a concept whereby the valuer assumes that the market participants are competent operators, acting in an efficient manner, of a business conducted on the premises. It involves estimating the trading potential rather than adopting the actual level of trade under the existing ownership and it excludes personal goodwill (2.10); and
- **FMOP**: fair maintainable operating profit—this is the level of profit, stated prior to depreciation and finance costs relating to the asset itself (and rent, if leasehold), that the REO would expect to derive from the FMT based on an assessment of the market's perception of the potential earnings of the property. It should reflect all costs and outgoings of the REO, as well as an appropriate annual allowance for periodic expenditures, such as decoration, refurbishment and renewal of the trade inventory (2.4).

When preparing a trade related property valuation, it is essential that the valuer reviews the cumulative results of the different steps of the valuation process, having regard to the valuer's general experience and knowledge of the market (3.4).

An assessment of FMT should exclude any positive or negative turnover and cost impacts that are solely attributable to the personal circumstances or skills, expertise, reputation and/ or brand name of the existing operator (6.3), with the actual trading performance compared to similar types of trade related property and styles of operation (6.4).

Any anticipated changes in competition and the general impact that this may have on profitability and value should be identified in the valuation report (6.6), together with the impact of external influences (such as the construction of a new road or changes in relevant legislation) on trading potential and hence value (6.7).

The capitalisation rate adopted for the valuation of the property as an investment will differ from that of the property with vacant possession. The investment rate of return will generally be determined by market transactions of similar trade related property investments, with careful analysis required given the differing characteristics of trade related property and the wide variety of lease terms (9.3).

Wyatt (2023) helpfully provides further clarification of the profits method as follows:

Estimate	Fair maintainable turnover (FMT)—actual trading accounts may not be relevant
Deduct	Cost of sales (purchases and adjustment for change in value of stock)
=	Gross profit
Deduct	Operating costs (energy costs, rates, insurance, maintenance, marketing, etc.) and wage costs
=	Net profit
Deduct	Remuneration to operator
Deduct	Interest on capital invested, stock and consumables
=	Fair maintainable operating profit (FMOP)
Then either	(1) capital valuation—capitalise adjusted net annual profit at an appropriate freehold or leasehold yield; or
	(2) rental valuation—apportion adjusted net annual profit between rent and profits (the divisible balance)

The profits method is a relatively simple approach to a complex valuation, with Wyatt (2023) noting the following simplifying premises:

- an assumption that the business will at all times be effectively and competently managed, operated and promoted and that it is properly staffed, stocked and capitalised;
- that the valuation includes land, buildings, trade fixtures, fittings, furnishings and equipment associated with the business and assumes they are working and owned outright;
- inclusion of the market perception of inherent trading potential, including transferable goodwill (attached to the property);
- an assumption that advance bookings and order books can be transferred;
- an assumption that existing licences, consents, permits, certificates and registrations can be obtained and renewed;
- an assumption (usually) that trade inventory is included;
- an assumption that personal goodwill is excluded; and
- an assumption that wet and dry consumable stock and any badged items and the value attached to the brand name should be separately identified (page 197).

Baum et al. (2018) note that the process of undertaking a profits method valuation, following the steps outlined previously, involves a significant amount of detail and so may be very time-consuming. While short-hand measures may be used as a cross-check, such as rent/value per cinema seat, restaurant cover, barrel of beer sold, litre of petrol sold and so forth, the consistent analysis of comparable sales in imperfect submarkets is challenging.

The profits method may be a static approach (as described previously) or a dynamic approach based on a discounted cash flow assessment, which may be more suitable for larger or more complex trade related properties (RICS, 2021, VPGA4, 3.2).

Wyatt (2023) provides a more detailed explanation of the application of the profits method to the following types of trade-related property in the UK market:

- hotels, guest houses, bed and breakfasts and self-catering accommodation (page 219)—however, readers should note that McIntosh and Milsom (2022) provide a more detailed explanation of hotels and leisure properties in the Australian market;
- restaurants, pubs and nightclubs (page 221);
- care homes (page 225)—however, readers should note that Towart (2022) provides a more detailed explanation of care homes in the Australian market;
- petrol filling stations (page 227);
- serviced offices (page 229);
- data centres (page 230); and
- student accommodations (page 231),

with Baum et al. (2018) providing a further explanation of the application of the profits method to the following trade related property in the UK:

- cinemas and theatres (page 303);
- golf courses (page 304); and
- racecourses, racetracks and stadia (page 304).

As previously noted, valuers who prepare valuations of trade related property will usually specialise in a particular market, such as theatres and cinemas or hotels, pubs and bars, as knowledge of the operational aspects of the property and of the industry as a whole are fundamental to understanding the market transactions and the analysis required.

Accordingly, the previous is an introductory explanation of the profits method only with considerably greater knowledge and detail required to apply the method in practice, which is usually gained through experience working in such trade related property and/or alongside a competent specialist valuer.

7.3.4 Summary—income method of valuation

The income method of valuation was considered through the:

- capitalisation of income method for perpetual income streams (7.3.1);

  - representative single period income (7.3.1.1);
  - reversionary income (7.3.1.2);
  - capitalisation rate (7.3.1.3);
  - formulae for income capitalisation (7.3.1.4);
  - voids (7.3.1.5);
  - rounding off (7.3.1.6); and

- capitalisation of income method for annuity income streams (7.3.2);
  - short-term leasehold interests (7.3.2.1); and
  - long-term leasehold interests (7.3.2.2),

together with a consideration of the profits method of valuation (7.3.3).

The following section seeks to apply each of the key elements of the capitalisation of income method and the profits method of valuation to the assessment of market value through worked examples.

7.4 Income methods of valuation—practice

The following worked examples apply the capitalisation of income method and the profits method of valuation to fictitious properties for the purposes of illustration only, and the data therein should not be adopted unchanged by readers undertaking valuations.

7.4.1 Capitalisation of income method

As an apparently quick and simple method of valuation, the capitalisation of income method of valuation was used almost exclusively in decades past for the valuation of investment properties in Australia. While it is still used today for smaller properties, it is usually used in association with the discounted cash flow method for major investment properties (such as super-regional shopping centres and premium office towers), reflecting their greater complexity, the challenges of forecasting variable cash flows into the future and the increasingly sophisticated demands of institutional clients (Parker, 2016).

Examples of the application of the capitalisation of income method of valuation will be considered for perpetual income streams and annuity income streams in what follows.

7.4.1.1 Outline of example—perpetuity

You are instructed to assess the market value of:

- Property A—a small industrial building of 2,500 sqm NLA which is leased to Tenant A for a term of five years for $100 psm pa with no rent reviews with three years of the lease term unexpired—being a rack-rented or fully rented investment; and
- Property B—a large industrial building of 10,000 sqm NLA which is leased to Tenant B for $60 psm pa for a term of ten years with six years of the lease term unexpired—being a reversionary investment.

7.4.1.2 Outline of capitalisation of income valuation—perpetuity

Property A (rack-rented or fully rented investment) and Property B (reversionary investment) will be considered sequentially.

7.4.1.2.1 PROPERTY A—RACK-RENTED OR FULLY RENTED INVESTMENT

Your accumulation, analysis, adjustment and application of comparable market rentals in the small industrial property sub-market indicate a current market rental value of $100 psm pa to be applicable to the subject property.

Your analysis of the lease to Tenant A finds that the tenant pays all outgoings, so no deduction for unrecoverable outgoings is required.

Your accumulation, analysis, adjustment and application of comparable sales transactions and discussions with investors active in the small industrial sub-market lead you to conclude that a capitalisation rate of 8% is applicable to the subject property.

In this example, the representative single period income is the passing rental, which is the same as the market rental, being $100 psm pa or $250,000 pa. As the tenant pays all outgoings, no deduction for unrecoverable outgoings is required.

Further, as the passing rental is the same as the market rental, there is no reversionary income.

The applicable capitalisation rate is 8%, and there are no voids, so the capitalisation of income valuation would be undertaken as follows:

Value =	Market rent	= $250,000	= $3,125,000
	Capitalisation rate	0.08	

Alternatively, the Years Purchase or YP may be applied, being the reciprocal of the capitalisation rate and an expression of the number of years of net income required to recoup the present value or outlay:

Net income	$250,000
x YP in perpetuity at 8%	12.5000
Valuation	$3,125,000

As the valuation is a round number, no rounding off is required.

7.4.1.2.2 PROPERTY B—REVERSIONARY INVESTMENT

Your accumulation, analysis, adjustment and application of comparable market rentals in the large industrial property sub-market indicate a current market rental value of $80 psm pa to be applicable to the subject property.

Your analysis of the lease to Tenant B finds that the tenant pays all outgoings, so no deduction for unrecoverable outgoings is required.

Your accumulation, analysis, adjustment and application of comparable sales transactions and discussions with investors active in the industrial sub-market lead you to conclude that a capitalisation rate of 7% is applicable to rack rented investments like the subject property.

In this example, the representative single period income is the market rental, being $80 psm pa or $800,000 pa. As the tenant pays all outgoings, no deduction for unrecoverable outgoings is required.

The reversionary income is the increase from lease rental to market rental ($60 psm pa to $80 psm pa or $600,000 pa to $800,000 pa) at the end of the lease in six years' time.

The applicable capitalisation rate is 7% for a rack rented investment and there are no voids. Conventionally, the term income is considered safer, and the reversionary income is considered riskier (particularly if there is a long time period before the reversion is realised), reflected by a change in the capitalisation rate applied, which is usually based on valuer judgment rather than market evidence.

The capitalisation of income valuation would be undertaken as follows:

Term		
Term rent passing	$600,000	
YP 6 years at 6.5%	4.8410	$2,904,600
Reversion:		
Reversion to market rent	$800,000	
YP perpetuity at 7%	14.2857	
Deferred 6 years		
(PV $1 for 6 years at 7%)	0.666342	$7,615,330
Valuation		$10,519,930

As the valuation is not a round number, rounding off is required, which, in this example, would be rounding to $10.50 million.

7.4.1.3 Outline of example—annuity—short-term leasehold interest

You are instructed to assess the market value of the unexpired portion of a lease of a small retail building of 1,500 sqm NLA, which is leased to Tenant C for $300 psm pa for a term of five years with no rent reviews and three years of the lease term unexpired.

7.4.1.4 Outline of capitalisation of income valuation—annuity—short-term leasehold interest

Your accumulation, analysis, adjustment and application of comparable market rentals in the small retail property sub-market indicate a current market rental value of $400 psm pa to be applicable to the subject property.

Your analysis of the lease to Tenant C finds that the tenant pays all outgoings, so no deduction for unrecoverable outgoings is required.

Your accumulation, analysis, adjustment and application of comparable sales transactions and discussions with retailers active in the small retail property sub-market lead you to conclude that a capitalisation rate of 9% is applicable to the subject property.

In this example, the representative single period income is the market rental, being $400 psm pa or $600,000 pa. As the tenant pays all outgoings, no deduction for unrecoverable outgoings is required.

The profit rent ($150,000 pa) is the difference between the lease rental and market rental ($300 psm pa and $400 psm pa or $450,000 pa and $600,000 pa) for the three-year unexpired period of the lease term.

The applicable capitalisation rate is 9%, and there are no voids.

The capitalisation of income valuation would be undertaken as follows:

Profit rent	$150,000
YP 3 years at 9%	2.5313
Valuation	$379,695

As the valuation is not a round number, rounding off is required, which, in this example, would be rounding to $380,000.

7.4.1.5 Outline of example—annuity—long-term leasehold interest

You are instructed to assess the market value of the freehold interest in a 1,500 sqm block of land in the CBD, upon which a CBD office building has been constructed by the ground lessee, which is leased on a ground lease to Tenant D for $10,000 pa for a term of 99 years with no rent reviews and 66 years of the lease term unexpired.

7.4.1.6 Outline of capitalisation of income valuation—annuity—long-term leasehold interest

Your accumulation, analysis, adjustment and application of comparable market ground rentals in the CBD land sub-market indicate a current market ground rental value of $50,000 pa to be applicable to the subject land.

Your analysis of the lease to Tenant D finds that the tenant pays all outgoings, so no deduction for unrecoverable outgoings is required.

Your accumulation, analysis, adjustment and application of comparable sales transactions and discussions with investors active in the CBD land sub-market lead you to conclude that a capitalisation rate of 7.5% is applicable to the subject land.

In this example, the representative single period income is the market rental, being $50,000 pa. As the tenant pays all outgoings, no deduction for unrecoverable outgoings is required.

The reversionary income is the increase from lease rental to market rental ($10,000 pa to $50,000 pa or $40,000 pa) at the end of the lease in 66 years' time.

The applicable capitalisation rate is 7.5%, and there are no voids. Conventionally, the term income is considered safer, and the reversionary income is considered riskier (particularly if there is a long time period before the reversion is realised), reflected by a change in the capitalisation rate, which is usually based on valuer judgment rather than market evidence. Further, for long-term leasehold interests, the existence or absence of rent reviews to provide growth in the income stream is a significant consideration.

In this example, if there were regular ground rental reviews in the ground lease, then the enhanced security contention for the term income may result in a capitalisation rate of 6.5% being applied for the term and 7.5% for the reversion. However, reflecting the lack of growth in the ground rent for the next 66 years, investors may offset the impact of security with the desire for a higher return and seek 8.5% for the term.

The capitalisation of income valuation would be undertaken as follows:

Term		
Ground rent passing	$10,000	
YP 66 years at 8.5%	11.7107	$117,107
Reversion:		
Reversion to market rent	$50,000	
YP perpetuity at 7.5%	13.3333	
Deferred 66 years		
(PV $1 for 66 years at 7.5%)	0.0084536	$5,635
Valuation		$122,742

As the valuation is not a round number, rounding off is required, which, in this example, would be rounding to $125,000.

7.4.1.7 Summary—capitalisation of income method

The examples of the capitalisation of income method sought to address those valuation scenarios most commonly arising in Australia, being the valuation of a freehold net income stream in perpetuity (both rack rented and reversionary), a short-term leasehold income stream and a long-term leasehold income stream, the latter being in the nature of annuities.

7.4.2 Profits method

The profits method is generally adopted where the type of property is inextricably linked to the business that operates therein, such as a hotel, pub, bar, restaurant, nightclub, petrol filling station, casino, cinema, theatre and various other forms of leisure property. Accordingly, the profits method seeks to examine the economic fundamentals of the business as the source of value of the property by capitalising the estimated future trading potential rather than net income (Wyatt, 2023).

7.4.2.1 Outline of example

You are instructed to assess the market value of the freehold interest in a hotel with 20 bedrooms, a bar and a restaurant. You have been provided with the last five years' accounts for the hotel, which you consider to be a reasonable estimate of fair maintainable turnover (FMT).

7.4.2.2 Outline of profits valuation

Your analysis of the last five years' accounts allows you to form an estimate of FMT for the accommodation, bar and restaurant and to form an estimate of costs of sale, operating costs and wage costs together with remuneration to operator and interest on capital invested, stock and consumables.

Your accumulation, analysis, adjustment and application of comparable sales transactions and discussions with investors and operators active in the hotel market lead you to conclude that a capitalisation rate of 10% is applicable to the subject property.

Following Wyatt (2023), the profits method of valuation would be undertaken as follows:

Estimate	Fair maintainable turnover	Accommodation	$750,000
	(FMT)	Bar	$75,000
		Restaurant	$50,000
		Total	$875,000
Deduct	Cost of sales (purchases and	Purchases	($60,000)
	adjustment for change in value	Adj for depreciation	($15,000)
	of stock)	in value of stock	($75,000)
		Total	
=	Gross profit		$800,000
Deduct	Operating costs (energy costs,	Operating	($75,000)
	rates, insurance, maintenance,	Wages	($250,000)
	marketing, etc.) and wage costs	Total	($325,000)
=	Net profit		$475,000
Deduct	Remuneration to operator		($75,000)

(Continued)

Deduct	Interest on capital invested, stock and consumables	Furniture, fixtures, fittings, equipment	($350,000)
		Stock (avg)	($125,000)
		Cash-1 month	
		working capital	($25,000)
		Operator's capital	($500,000)
		Annualised at 10%	($50,000)
=	Fair maintainable operating profit (FMOP)		$350,000
Capital valuation	Capitalise adjusted net annual profit at an appropriate capitalisation rate	YP in perpetuity at 10%	$3,500,000

Following Wyatt (2023), if the value of the business as a whole is also required, then the value of the inventory, stock and cash can be added to the value of the property:

Capital value of property	$3,500,000
Value of inventory	$350,000
Avg value of stock for year	$125,000
Cash	$25,000
Capital value of business	$4,000,000

7.4.2.3 Summary—profits method

The previous example is a very simplified version of a complex valuation task that requires the valuer to have a detailed knowledge of both the relevant industry being valued and the operation of businesses within that industry.

Unless the valuer is experienced in the valuation of properties within the specific sub-market, such as hotels, pubs, bars, restaurants, nightclubs, petrol filling stations, casinos, cinemas, theatres and various other forms of leisure property, then assistance should be sought from a valuer expert in that specific sub-market (with client consent in the scope of works and acknowledgment in the valuation report).

7.5 Marriage value

The RICS Red Book (RICS, 2021) defines marriage value as follows:

An additional element of value created by the combination of two or more assets or interests where the combined value is more than the sum of the separate values.

(page 11)

A commonly adopted example is the combination of a freehold interest with a ground lease interest, where the value of the freehold unencumbered interest is greater than the sum of the value of the freehold subject to the ground lease and the value of the ground lease.

If marriage value is realised through such a combination of interests, the division of the marriage value between the parties holding the respective interests depends on their respective negotiating strengths.

7.5.1 Outline of example

You are instructed to assess the marriage value in the freehold and leasehold interests in a small suburban office building of 5,000 sqm, which is leased to Tenant E for $750,000 pa for a term of 25 years with no rent reviews and 15 years of the lease term unexpired.

7.5.2 Outline of marriage value calculation

Your accumulation, analysis, adjustment and application of comparable market rentals in the small suburban office property sub-market indicate a current market rental value of $300 psm pa to be applicable to the subject property.

Your analysis of the lease to Tenant E finds that the tenant pays all outgoings, so no deduction for unrecoverable outgoings is required.

Your accumulation, analysis, adjustment and application of comparable sales transactions and discussions with investors active in the small suburban office property sub-market lead you to conclude that a capitalisation rate of 6% is applicable to freehold rack rented investments like the subject property, with 7% applicable to leasehold investments.

In this example, the representative single period income is the market rental, being $300 psm pa or $1,500,000 pa. As the tenant pays all outgoings, no deduction for unrecoverable outgoings is required.

The reversionary income is the increase from lease rental to market rental ($150 psm pa to $300 psm pa or $750,000 pa to $1,500,000 pa) at the end of the lease in 15 years' time.

The applicable capitalisation rate is 6% for a freehold rack-rented investment, and there are no voids. Conventionally, the term income is considered safer, and the reversionary income is considered riskier (particularly if there is a long time period before the reversion is realised), reflected by a change in the capitalisation rate, which is usually based on valuer judgment rather than market evidence.

In this example, if there were regular rental reviews in the lease, then the enhanced security contention for the term income may result in a capitalisation rate of 5.5% being applied for the term and 6% for the reversion. However, reflecting the lack of growth in the rent for the next 15 years, investors may offset the impact of security with the desire for a higher return and seek 6.5% for the term.

The assessment of marriage value in the freehold and leasehold interest may be undertaken as follows:

Valuation of freeholder's present interest:

Term		
Term rent passing	$750,000	
YP 15 years at 6.5%	9.4027	$7,052,025
Reversion:		
Reversion to market rent	$1,500,000	
YP perpetuity at 6%	16.6667	
Deferred 15 years		
(PV $1 for 15 years at 6%)	0.4172651	$10,431,648
Valuation		$17,483,673

Valuation of leasehold interest:

Profit rent	$750,000	
YP 15 years at 7%	9.1079	
Valuation		$6,830,925

Valuation of freeholder interest after purchase of lease:

Market rental	$1,500,000	
YP perpetuity at 6%	16.6667	
Valuation		$25,000,000

Assessment of marriage value:

Value of freeholder interest after purchase of lease	$25,000,000
Less:	
Valuer of freeholder's present interest	($17,483,673)
Value of leasehold interest	($6,830,925)
Marriage value	$685,402

Accordingly, the freeholder could pay the leaseholder (Tenant E) the value of the leasehold interest plus up to $685,402 to marry the freehold and leasehold interests by the leaseholder surrendering its interest to create a freehold investment with a value of $25 million.

While marriage value may commonly arise in the UK property market, where leases are generally longer, with 25 years common, the generally shorter leases in Australia, with 5–10 years common, mean that marriage value rarely arises. For a deeper consideration of marriage value, readers are referred to Shapiro et al. (2019) and Wyatt (2023).

7.6 Surrender and renewal of leases

Where a tenant, such as a major retailer, holds a lease that is expiring in a few years' time and wishes to extend or renew their lease to protect their business, the tenant may approach the landlord seeking a surrender and renewal of its lease. The parties would anticipate the tenant surrendering the balance of its existing lease and simultaneously taking a new lease on similar terms for a further period. By so doing, the tenant achieves security of tenure and the landlord achieves security of income, increasing the value of the investment property.

Where the rent under the existing lease is below market rent, which would be payable on lease renewal, the tenant will have a lease of value. Where the lease renewal increases the value of the property investment, the landlord will enjoy a value uplift if the lease is renewed. Accordingly, it is in both parties' interests to agree to a lease renewal and negotiate a payment between themselves, reflecting the respective value increases.

Shapiro et al. (2019) note that a calculation is usually undertaken from each parties' viewpoint as follows:

- estimate the value of each parties' interest in the property assuming that no alteration to the current lease occurred; and
- estimate the value of each parties' interest in the property assuming that the proposed extension or renewal was granted,

with the difference between the two figures representing the negotiation range with the agreed amount payable as a capital sum or a new lease rent adjustment (page 197).

7.6.1 Outline of example

Following the example in section 7.5.2, assume Tenant E wishes to surrender its lease and take a lease renewal at market rental.

7.6.2 Outline of surrender and renewal calculation

The assessment of surrender and renewal value in the freehold and leasehold interest may be undertaken as follows:

Leasehold (Tenant E's) point of view:	
Proposed interest:	
Lease renewal at market rental, so no profit rental	$0
Present interest:	
As above	$6,830,925
On this basis, Tenant E will loose	$6,830,925
Freehold (landlord's) point of view:	
Proposed interest:	
As above	$25,000,000
Present interest:	
As above	$17,483,673
On this basis, the landlord will gain	$7,516,327

Accordingly, the freeholder could negotiate to pay the leaseholder (Tenant E) up to $7,516,327 to surrender its leasehold interest and take a new lease at market rental.

While surrender and renewal negotiations may commonly arise in the UK property market, where leases are generally longer, with 25 years common, the generally shorter leases in Australia, with 5–10 years common, mean that surrender and renewal negotiations rarely arise. For a deeper consideration of surrender and renewal valuation, readers are referred to Shapiro et al. (2019) and Wyatt (2023).

7.7 Summary and conclusions

Chapter 1 outlined the structure of the property asset class, examining the traditional characteristics of property (including heterogeneity, durability, illiquidity and so forth) and the traditional risks of property (including location, building, tenant risk and so forth) through the lenses of systematic, unsystematic and idiosyncratic risk, so aligning property valuation with capital market theory.

Chapter 2 considered the evolution of property valuation in Australia, the role of the valuer and the diverse activities of the valuation profession, followed by a detailed examination of the inter-acting framework provided by valuation standards and ethical standards promulgated by IVSC, RICS and API.

Chapter 3 explored concepts of value and normative and positive definitions of value, dissecting the International Valuation Standards' definition of market value with a reconciliation to the concept of market value in *Spencer v Commonwealth* (1907) and examining such contemporary valuation issues as valuation lag, variance, accuracy, negligence and valuer rotation.

Chapter 4 introduced International Financial Reporting Standards and International Accounting Standards with a detailed examination of the key provisions of International Valuation Standards, the RICS Red Book and API guidance papers that impact on valuation practice in Australia.

Chapter 5 outlined conceptual approaches to the valuation process with a review of the self-supporting process of instructing, undertaking and reporting valuations under the International Valuation Standards, RICS Red Book and API guidance papers, examining how this process inter-relates to the choice of valuation approach, valuation method and the purpose of the valuation.

Chapter 6 addressed the market approach to valuation through the comparative method of valuation, including the key steps of accumulation, analysis, adjustment and application of comparable sales evidence to the subject property being valued, with an example.

This chapter considered the income approach to valuation addressed through the static methods of the capitalisation of income and the profits methods of valuation, including an examination of the key inputs for each method with examples and a consideration of both marriage value and the surrender and renewal of leases.

The static capitalisation of income method is deceptive in its simplicity. While using only a net income stream and a capitalisation rate may appear easy, every aspect of the property has then to be reflected in either the income stream or the capitalisation rate. Hence, the capitalisation rate effectively becomes the medium reflecting all aspects of growth and risk in the income stream.

The capitalisation of income method is heavily dependent on valuer judgment, with small differences in the capitalisation rate making potentially large differences in the assessment of value. Where capitalisation rates are in the order of 7% or higher, the scope remains for valuer judgements to be expressed through incremental changes of 0.25% in the capitalisation rate. However, when capitalisation rates are in the order of 3% to 6%, expressing valuer judgment becomes much harder as the impact of a 0.25% change is significantly greater, while the ability to determine if a capitalisation rate should be 3.1% or 3.2% is not only challenging but also highly impactful on the assessment of value.

It is now well established that DCF is the appropriate method of valuation for large, multi-tenanted investment properties, with the dynamic nature of the method better suited to reflect the complexity of the cash flows generated by such assets. Accordingly, the capitalisation of income method today is more appropriate for smaller properties with fewer tenants, although its role as a check method for an assessment of value by DCF continues.

It is now almost 50 years since Greenwell's (1976) criticism of the capitalisation of income method as incorrect, illogical and by deduction leading to inaccurate valuations, to which the RICS responded by establishing a research programme into valuation methods and publishing *Guidance Notes on the Valuation of Assets* in 1976, the original RICS Red Book. Remarkably, despite the exponential development in the complexity of interests arising from investment property over the last 50 years, the use of the capitalisation of income method still persists.

The next chapter will consider the income approach to valuation addressed through the dynamic method of the discounted cash flow method of valuation, including an examination of the key inputs and a focus on the derivation of the discount rate and consideration of the role of sensitivity and scenario analysis, with examples.

Chapter 9 considers the cost approach to valuation addressed through the replacement cost, reproduction cost, summation and residual or hypothetical development methods of valuation.

Finally, Chapter 10 concludes the book with a consideration of future perspectives, including the role of uncertainty, data, automated valuation models, artificial intelligence, optionality, environmental, social and governance issues, retail and office space use and indigenous issues.

References

Baum, A, Mackmin, D and Nunnington, N (2018) *The income approach to property valuation*, Routledge, Abingdon.

Davidson, AW (1978) *Parry's valuation and conversion tables*, Estates Gazette, London.

Greenwell, W (1976) 'A call for new valuation methods', *Estates Gazette*, Vol 238, pp. 481–484.

Isaac, D and O'Leary, J (2012) *Property valuation principles*, Palgrave Macmillan, Basingstoke.

Isaac, D and O'Leary, J (2013) *Property valuation techniques*, Palgrave Macmillan, Basingstoke.

IVSC (2012) *TIP1—discounted cash flow*, International Valuation Standards Council, London.

IVSC (2013) *International valuation standards 2013*, International Valuation Standards Council, London.

IVSC (2021) *International valuation standards*, International Valuation Standards Council, London.

McIntosh, R and Milsom, W (2022) 'Leisure property valuation', in Parker, D (Ed) *Principles and practice of property valuation in Australia*, Routledge, Abingdon.

Millington, A (2000) *An introduction to property valuation*, Routledge, Abingdon.

Parker, D (2016) *International valuation standards: a guide to the valuation of real property assets*, Wiley-Blackwell, Chichester.

RICS (2021) *RICS valuation—global standards*, Royal Institution of Chartered Surveyors, London.

Shapiro, E, Mackmin, D and Sams, G (2019) *Modern methods of valuation*, Routledge, Abingdon.

Towart, L (2022) 'Retirement and aged care property valuation', in Parker, D (Ed) *Principles and practice of property valuation in Australia*, Routledge, Abingdon.

Wyatt, P (2023) *Property valuation*, Wiley Blackwell, Chichester.

8 Income approach to valuation— dynamic

8.1 Introduction

This book is an introduction to the fundamentals of property valuation, outlining the principal methods of property valuation in Australia within the context of International Valuation Standards, bridging the gap between traditional property valuation methods and the modern era of global valuation governance.

Chapter 1 outlined the structure of the property asset class, examining the traditional characteristics of property (including heterogeneity, durability, illiquidity and so forth) and the traditional risks of property (including location, building, tenant risk and so forth) through the lenses of systematic, unsystematic and idiosyncratic risk, so aligning property valuation with capital market theory.

Chapter 2 considered the evolution of property valuation in Australia, the role of the valuer and the diverse activities of the valuation profession, followed by a detailed examination of the inter-acting framework provided by valuation standards and ethical standards promulgated by IVSC, RICS and API.

Chapter 3 explored concepts of value and normative and positive definitions of value, dissecting the International Valuation Standards' definition of market value with a reconciliation to the concept of market value in *Spencer v Commonwealth* (1907) and examining such contemporary valuation issues as valuation lag, variance, accuracy, negligence and valuer rotation.

Chapter 4 introduced International Financial Reporting Standards and International Accounting Standards with a detailed examination of the key provisions of International Valuation Standards, the RICS Red Book and API guidance papers that impact on valuation practice in Australia.

Chapter 5 outlined conceptual approaches to the valuation process with a review of the self-supporting process of instructing, undertaking and reporting valuations under the International Valuation Standards, RICS Red Book and API guidance papers, examining how this process inter-relates to the choice of valuation approach, valuation method and the purpose of the valuation.

Chapter 6 addressed the market approach to valuation through the comparative method of valuation, including the key steps of accumulation, analysis, adjustment and application of comparable sales evidence to the subject property being valued, with an example.

Chapter 7 considered the income approach to valuation addressed through the static methods of the capitalisation of income and the profits methods of valuation, including an examination of the key inputs for each method with examples and a consideration of both marriage value and the surrender and renewal of leases.

DOI: 10.1201/9781003397922-8

This chapter seeks to consider the income approach to valuation addressed through the dynamic method of the discounted cash flow method of valuation, including an examination of the key inputs and a focus on the derivation of the discount rate and consideration of the role of sensitivity and scenario analysis, with examples.

Chapter 9 considers the cost approach to valuation addressed through the replacement cost, reproduction cost, summation and residual or hypothetical development methods of valuation.

Finally, Chapter 10 concludes the book with a consideration of future perspectives, including the role of uncertainty, data, automated valuation models, artificial intelligence, optionality, environmental, social and governance issues, retail and office space use and indigenous issues.

This book is based on those standards and guidance documents published in IVSC (2021) and RICS (2021) and on the API website (accessed January to May 2023). Given their nature, standards and guidance documents are dynamic, being regularly updated and with the most recently published versions replacing previously published versions. Accordingly, readers should not rely on this book as a current statement of a standard or guidance document and should visit www.ivsc.org, www.rics.org and/or www.api.org.au to find the most recent version.

As an introductory textbook on property valuation methods in Australia, this book is a companion to Australia's leading advanced valuation textbook, *Principles and Practice of Property Valuation in Australia,* edited by the same author and also published by Routledge, which is a deeper analysis of key principles underlying property valuation and current techniques and issues in the practice of property valuation for major sectors of the Australian property market.

Traditional valuation texts, such as Millington (2000), consider five methods of valuation:

- the comparative (or comparison) method;
- the income (or investment or capitalisation) method;
- the profits (or accounts or treasury or receipts and expenditure) method;
- the contractor's (or summation or cost) method; and
- the residual (or hypothetical development) method of valuation.

This chapter addresses the income approach and the discounted cash flow method, being a modern method within the income approach post-dating the traditional methods listed.

The principles of the discounted cash flow method of valuation will be considered through the following key elements:

- type of cash flow (8.3.1);
- explicit forecast period (8.3.2);
- cash flow forecasts (8.3.3);
- terminal value (8.3.4);
- discount rate (8.3.5):

  - observed or inferred rates/yields (8.3.5.1);
  - build-up method (8.3.5.2):

    - risk-free rate plus a risk premium (8.3.5.2.1);
    - capitalisation rate plus growth (8.3.5.2.2);

  - capital asset pricing model (8.3.5.3);
  - weighted average cost of capital (8.3.5.4);

- present value (8.3.6);
- net present value (8.3.7);
- internal rate of return (8.3.8); and
- formulae for DCF (8.3.9),

with a worked example applying each of the key elements to the assessment of the market value of a multi-tenanted CBD office building.

8.2 Income approach to valuation

The income approach to valuation is one of the three principal valuation approaches recognised by IVSs and is grounded in economic theory, being based on the economic principle of anticipation of benefits. IVS105 (IVSC, 2021) defines the income approach as follows:

> *The income approach provides an indication of value by converting future cash flow to a single current value. Under the income approach, the value of an asset is determined by reference to the value of income, cash flow or cost savings generated by the asset.*
>
> (40.1)

The income approach is, therefore, premised on the existence of an income—either actual through the leasing of a property by an owner/landlord to an occupier/tenant or imputed/hypothetical in the case of an owner-occupied property. Given the vast portfolios of office, retail, industrial and other property owned by institutions (superannuation funds, insurance companies, REITs, wholesale property funds and so forth) as investments to provide income return and capital growth, the income approach is widely used by the valuation profession.

As well as being premised on a return, the income approach is also premised on the risk associated with that return. IVS105 (IVSC, 2021) notes that a fundamental basis for the income approach is that investors expect to receive a return on their investment and that such a return should reflect the perceived risk of that investment (40.4).

IVS105 (IVSC, 2021) notes that the income approach should be applied and afforded significant weight under the following circumstances:

- where the income-producing ability of the asset is the critical element affecting value from a participant perspective; and/or
- where reasonable projections of the amount and timing of future income are available for the subject asset, but there are few, if any, relevant market comparables (40.2).

Further, IVS105 (IVSC, 2021) notes that the income approach may be applied and afforded significant weight when:

- the income-producing ability of the subject asset is only one of several factors affecting value from a participant perspective;
- there is significant uncertainty regarding the amount and timing of future income related to the subject asset;
- there is a lack of access to information related to the subject asset; and/or
- the subject asset has not yet begun generating income but is projected to do so,

though the valuer should consider whether any other approaches can be applied and weighted to corroborate the value indication from the income approach (40.3).

VPS5 *Valuation approaches and methods* in the RICS Red Book (RICS, 2021) notes:

> *The income approach is based on capitalisation or conversion of present and predicted income (cash flows), which may take a number of different forms, to produce a single current capital value. Among the forms taken, capitalisation of a conventional market-based income or discounting of a specific income projection can both be considered appropriate depending on the type of asset and whether such an approach would be adopted by market participants.*

(2)

There are, therefore, essentially two valuation methods within the income approach, being the conversion of future cash flow to a single current value by either:

- the application of a multiplier to the cash flow, being the static approach known as the investment method or capitalisation method, which was considered in the previous chapter; and
- discounting the future cash flow to a present value amount, being the dynamic approach known as the discounted cash flow method (DCF) which is considered in this chapter.

The application of DCF to property valuation was pioneered by Dr. Michael Greaves at the University of Reading in the mid-1970s and taught to undergraduate students there from the late 1970s. However, it was not until around twenty years later, following greater availability of computers, advances in spreadsheets and institutional client acceptance, that DCF became widely used in the valuation profession internationally.

TIP1 (IVSC, 2012) states that the DCF method can be used to value most assets that generate cash flows and may provide a better indication of value than other methods where cash flows are likely to fluctuate from period to period in the short term, such as fluctuations to rental income generated by an investment property due to leasing terms (TIP1, 4).

IVS400 notes that the income approach may be applied to an actual or estimated income that either is or could be generated by the owner of the interest. In the case of investment property, such income may be in the form of rent (or other payment such as licence fee) and for an owner-occupied building, it may be the assumed rent based on what it would cost the owner to lease equivalent space (IVSC, 2021, IVS400, 60.1).

The DCF method can be used to determine different bases of value, such as market value or investment value as defined in IVS or fair value for financial reporting purposes as defined in IFRS13 (IVSC, 2012, TIP1, 31).

Where the DCF method is used in conjunction with one or more other valuation methods, TIP1 (IVSC, 2012) recommends that the valuation report contains either a reconciliation between the respective results or a clear rationale for preferring one method as the better indicator of value (TIP1, 44).

Shapiro et al. (2019) note three applications of the DCF method:

- to find the present value or market value of an investment;
- assessment of net present value where the market price or cost of the investment is known; and

- assessment of the internal rate of return of an investment where the market price or cost of the investment is known.

While a DCF may be undertaken on a calculator or constructed in Excel, sophisticated software packages are available through a range of providers, including Forbury, ARGUS, CoStar and Yardi, with large international valuation firms often having in-house software packages.

8.3 Discounted cash flow method of valuation—principles

The principles of the DCF method of valuation will be considered through the following key elements:

- type of cash flow (8.3.1);
- explicit forecast period (8.3.2);
- cash flow forecasts (8.3.3);
- terminal value (8.3.4);
- discount rate (8.3.5):

    - observed or inferred rates/yields (8.3.5.1);
    - build-up method (8.3.5.2):

        - risk free rate plus a risk premium (8.3.5.2.1);
        - capitalisation rate plus growth (8.3.5.2.2);

    - capital asset pricing model (8.3.5.3);
    - weighted average cost of capital (8.3.5.4);

- present value (8.3.6);
- net present value (8.3.7);
- internal rate of return (8.3.8); and
- formulae for DCF (8.3.9).

TIP1 (IVSC, 2012) defines the DCF method as follows:

A method within the income approach in which a discount rate is applied to all future projected cash flows to estimate present value.

(3)

IVS105 (IVSC, 2021) succinctly defines the DCF method as follows:

Under the DCF method the forecasted cash flow is discounted back to the valuation date, resulting in a present value of the asset.

(50.2)

TIP1 (IVSC, 2012) defines present value as follows:

The value, as of a specified date, of a future payment or series of future payments discounted to the specified date (or to time period zero) at an appropriate discount rate.

(3)

IVS105 (IVSC, 2021) outlines the DCF method as follows:

The key steps in the DCF method are:

- *choose the most appropriate type of cash flow for the nature of the subject asset and the assignment (ie, pre-tax or post-tax, total cash flows or cash flows to equity, real or nominal, etc),*
- *determine the most appropriate explicit period, if any, over which the cash flow will be forecast,*
- *prepare cash flow forecasts for that period,*
- *determine whether a terminal value is appropriate for the subject asset at the end of the explicit forecast period (if any) and then determine the appropriate terminal value for the nature of the asset,*
- *determine the appropriate discount rate, and*
- *apply the discount rate to the forecasted future cash flow, including the terminal value, if any* (50.4).

IVS400 (IVSC, 2021) adds:

The discount rate in a discounted cash flow model will be based on the time cost of money and the risks and rewards of the income stream in question.

(60.4)

Echoing IVS105, TIP1 (IVSC, 2012) identifies the following key inputs for the DCF method:

- determination of the explicit period over which the cash flows will be forecast;
- cash flow forecasts for that period;
- the asset value at the end of the forecast period (terminal value); and
- an appropriate discount rate to apply to the forecasted future cash flows, including the terminal value (6).

The use of DCF to determine market value should make use of market evidence, with all inputs based on market-derived data if possible. Where there is insufficient market data, inputs should reflect the thought processes, expectations and perceptions of investors and other market participants as best they can be understood (IVSC, 2012, 32).

TIP1 notes that all valuation inputs and assumptions should have regard to the conceptual framework for market value in IVS, with sufficient research undertaken to ensure that the cash flow projections or expectations and the assumptions upon which the DCF is based are appropriate, likely and reasonable for the subject market (IVSC, 2012, 34).

Noting that while cash flows may be:

- fixed or variable;
- gross or net of tax;
- gross or net of debt finance costs; or
- reflective or non-reflective of anticipated inflation or deflation,

TIP1 emphasises that cash flows and discount rates should be internally consistent (IVSC, 2021, 37). Therefore, a net of tax cash flow should be discounted by a net of tax discount rate or a nominal cash flow should be discounted by a nominal discount rate, requiring great care in the analysis of comparable transactions to ensure consistent application.

Very significantly, TIP1 (IVSC, 2012) states:

> *As a technique, the DCF method should not be judged on the basis of whether expected future income is proven to be correct or not after the event but rather on the degree of market support for the expectation at the valuation date.*

(32)

Concerning reporting consistent with the requirements of IVS103 (IVSC, 2021), TIP1 (IVSC, 2012) advises that consideration be given to the following for inclusion:

- the source of the prospective financial information used to construct the cash flows;
- the explicit forecast period, including the commencement date of the cash flow and the number, frequency and term of the periods employed;
- the components of the cash inflows and cash outflows grouped by category and the rationale behind their selection;
- the derivation of, or rationale for, the discount rate; and
- the basis of the terminal value calculation,

together with commentary on the possible impact of changes in assumptions to the valuation result which may be in the form of sensitivity analysis (IVSC, 2012, 43).

8.3.1 *Type of cash flow*

In Australia, the market value of investment property using DCF will usually be determined using the nominal whole cash flow for the asset in Australian dollars on a pre-tax basis for a ten-year period, disregarding financing, being contractual cash flows for known periods and forecasts for the balance. This generally reflects the participants' viewpoints as institutional investors, as the type of cash flow chosen should be in accordance with the participants' viewpoints (IVSC, 2021, IVS105, 50.6).

However, as IVS105 (IVSC, 2021) explains, alternative types of cash flow may be appropriate for some valuation tasks and the following must be considered (50.5):

- whole or partial interest cash flow—while the whole cash flow is usually considered, partial interest cash flow, such as cash flow to equity, may be considered;
- pre-tax or post-tax—if a tax rate is applied, it should be consistent with the basis of value and usually a participant tax rate rather than an owner-specific tax rate;
- nominal vs. real—a real cash flow excludes inflation expectations, whereas a nominal cash flow includes inflation expectations. If the cash flow incorporates an expected inflation rate, the discount rate should also include an adjustment for inflation;
- currency—the choice of currency may have an impact on assumptions for inflation and risk, with section 50.7 providing guidance on undertaking a valuation in a currency that differs from the currency used in the cash flow projections; and
- type of cash flow contained in the forecast—a cash flow forecast may represent contractual cash flows, most likely cash flows, expected cash flows (being probability-weighted scenarios) and so forth.

Importantly, as IVS105 (IVSC, 2021) states:

> *In addition, the discount rate and other inputs must be consistent with the type of cash flow chosen.*

(50.5)

Where a cash flow forecast is provided by an owner or prospective owner to be used in estimating market value, it should be tested against market evidence and expectations (IVSC, 2012, TIP1, 33).

8.3.2 Explicit forecast period

The cash flow period selected is dependent on the purpose of the valuation, the nature of the asset, the information available and the required basis of value (IVSC, 2021, IVS105, 50.8). In Australia, valuations of investment property for financial reporting purposes using DCF will usually adopt a ten-year forecast period.

Valuers should consider the following when selecting the explicit forecast period in the context of property valuation (IVSC, 2021, IVS105, 50.9):

- the life of the asset;
- a reasonable period for which reliable data is available on which to base the projections; and
- the minimum explicit forecast period which should be sufficient for an asset to achieve a stabilised level of growth, after which a terminal value can be used.

TIP1 adds that the selection criteria for the explicit forecast period will depend on:

- the purpose of the valuation;
- the nature of the asset;
- the information available;
- the required bases of value; and
- the accepted norm among market participants for the length of the forecast period, where the required basis is the market value (IVSC, 2012, TIP1, 8).

The explicit forecast period should have regard to the participants and the intended holding period for a particular investor should not be the only consideration in selecting an explicit forecast period and should not impact the value of an asset unless the objective of the valuation is to determine investment value (IVSC, 2021, IVS105, 50.11).

Care is required where a major lease expiry or capital expenditure is forecast to occur just before or just after the end of the cash flow forecast period. For example, if a whole building lease is due to expire in Year 11, consideration should be given to using a 15- or 20-year cash flow period, rather than ten year, in order to better reflect the impact.

8.3.3 Cash flow forecasts

TIP1 defines cash flow as follows:

> *Cash that is generated over a period of time by an asset, group of assets, or business enterprise.*

(3)

IVS105 (IVSC, 2021) notes that cash flows for explicit forecast periods will be constructed using prospective financial information (PFI), being projected income or inflows and projected expenditure or outflows (IVS105, 50.12). Regardless of the source of the PFI, the valuer must analyse and evaluate both the information and the underlying assumptions and the appropriateness for the valuation purpose, with PFI for the determination of market value reflecting that anticipated by market participants, whereas PFI for the determination of investment value may reflect that anticipated by a particular investor (IVS105, 50.13). The projected cash flow should capture the amount and timing of cash inflows and outflows from the perspective appropriate to the basis of value (IVS105, 50.15) and anticipated by participants (rather than accounting income and expenses that may reflect depreciation, amortisation and changes in working capital) (IVS105, 50.18).

TIP1 (IVSC, 2012) helpfully advises:

> *The cash flow model should be constructed so as to adequately capture scheduled future events, eg contract terminations, contract reviews on the dates on which they fall due, or expected future events that are expected to trigger changes to the cash inflows and outflows on the dates they are expected to occur.*
>
> (TIP1, 9)

While the cash flow forecast in Australia is usually ten years and the cash flow period is usually monthly (reflecting the monthly rent payment cycle usual in Australian investment property leases), IVS105 (IVSC, 2021) notes that the cash flow should be divided into suitable periodic intervals (such as weekly, monthly, quarterly or annually) with the choice of period depending on the nature of the asset, the pattern of the cash flow, the data available and the length of the forecast period (IVS105, 50.14). However, the valuer must ensure that seasonality and cyclicality are appropriately considered in the cash flow, if necessary (IVS105, 50.19).

IVS105 (IVSC, 2021) provides the valuer with a choice of four bases for the cash flow forecast:

- the contractual or promised cash flow—the usual basis for the valuation of investment property in Australia;
- the single most likely set of cash flows—which may incorporate the contractual cash flow followed by estimates of forecast cash flow, commonly used in Australia for investment property;
- the probability-weighted expected cash flow; or
- multiple scenarios of possible future cash flow (IVS105, 50.16).

Different types of cash flow often reflect different levels of risk, and so may require different discount rates, with particular care required if a probability-weighted expected cash flow is adopted (IVS105, 50.17).

TIP1 (IVSC, 2012) advises that forecasted cash flow estimates need to be based on appropriate assumptions, with market value reflecting those that would be anticipated by market participants, whereas investment value may reflect the reasonable forecasts from the perspective of a particular investor (TIP1, 11).

The cash flow will usually comprise two elements, income and expenses/outgoings:

- income may include the current rent, rent reviews, lease renewals, periods of vacancy, new lettings, relettings and expenses/outgoings recoveries, usually based on a forecast rental growth rate applicable when contractual increases under leases do not apply; and

- expenses/outgoings may include building outgoings and any fees and costs associated with undertaking rent reviews, lease renewals, lettings and so forth, as well as a wide range of owner expenses, including capital expenditure (Baum et al., 2018).

Prospective capital expenditure included in the cash flow should have a sound evidentiary basis. It should be noted that cash flows in the earlier years of the forecast period have a greater impact on the present value, net present value or internal rate of return than cash flows in the later years of the forecast period.

Further, it is the convention to commence a cash flow with period 0 (period zero or Year 0), being the period before the first period in which income and expenditure cash flows occur. Year 0 is, therefore, the period in which the NPV or the acquisition cost of the property should be specified.

8.3.4 *Terminal value*

The valuation of investment property that is held freehold usually assumes that income will be received in perpetuity. Therefore, while the explicit forecast period in Australia will usually be ten years, the cash flow will theoretically continue on in perpetuity with the period beyond the explicit forecast period being reflected in the year ten terminal value—effectively being an assumed sale of the asset at the end of year ten at the then forecast market value of the asset. The terminal value is then discounted back to the valuation date, usually using the same discount rate as applied to the forecast cash flow (IVSC, 2021, IVS105, 50.20).

TIP1 (IVSC, 2012) defines terminal value as follows:

The value at the end of an explicit forecast period of all remaining projected cash flows.

(3)

IVS105 (IVSC, 2021) notes:

In some circumstances for long-lived or indefinite-lived assets, DCF may include a terminal value which represents the value of an asset at the end of the explicit projection period.

(50.3)

TIP1 (IVSC, 2012) notes that if the DCF method is being used to estimate market value, the terminal value can be equated to the market value of the asset at the end of the explicit forecast period. For investment value, the terminal value will reflect the value to the particular investor of continuing to hold the asset indefinitely beyond the end of the forecast period (TIP1, 15).

The following should be considered by the valuer in determining terminal value:

- whether the asset is deteriorating/finite-lived in nature or indefinite-lived, as this will influence the method used to calculate a terminal value;
- whether there is future growth potential for the asset beyond the explicit forecast period;
- whether there is a pre-determined fixed capital amount expected to be received at the end of the explicit forecast period;
- the expected risk level of the asset at the time the terminal value is calculated;
- for cyclical assets, the terminal value should consider the cyclical nature of the asset and should not be performed in a way that assumes "peak" or "trough" levels of cash flows in perpetuity; and

- the tax attributes inherent in the asset at the end of the explicit forecast period (if any) and whether those tax attributes would be expected to continue into perpetuity (IVSC, 2021, IVS105, 50.21).

While the terminal value of investment property in Australia would usually be calculated using the market approach/exit value (being usually the capitalisation method based on the estimated net income in the year following the end of the explicit forecast period—in Australia, this would usually be capitalising Year 11 estimated net income), IVS105 notes any reasonable method may be used with other common methods including the assumption of consistent future growth (the Gordon growth model, further explained in TIP1, section 18) or salvage value (for deteriorating or finite lived assets) (IVSC, 2012, TIP1, 50.22).

Wyatt (2023) notes that the capitalisation rate used to calculate terminal value:

> *is usually higher than initial yields on comparable but new and recently let property investments because it must reflect the reduction in remaining economic life of the property and the higher risk of estimating cash flow at the end of the holding period*
>
> (page 190)

having regard to any allowance for refurbishment or other capital expenditure in the cash flow during the holding period.

8.3.5 Discount rate

TIP1 (IVSC, 2012) defines the discount rate as follows:

> *A rate of return used to convert a future monetary sum or cash flow into present value.*
>
> (TIP1, 3)

IVS105 (IVSC, 2021) succinctly notes:

> *The rate at which the forecast cash flow is discounted should reflect not only the time value of money, but also risks associated with the type of cash flow and the future operations of the asset*
>
> (IVS105, 50.29)

identifying the two key elements of a discount rate, being the reflection of time and the reflection of risk. Further, the discount rate must be consistent with the type of cash flow (IVSC, 2021, IVS105, 50.30).

The development of the discount rate should be influenced by the objective of the valuation:

- if the objective of the valuation is to establish the market value, the discount rate may be derived from observations of the returns implicit in the prices paid for real property interests traded in the market between participants or from the hypothetical participants' required rates of return; and

- if the objective of the valuation is to establish the value to a particular owner or potential owner based on their investment criteria, the rate used may reflect their required rate of return or their weighted average cost of capital (IVSC, 2021, IVS400, 60.5).

Consistent with IVS400, TIP1 (IVSC, 2012) advises:

> *The discount rate applied is dependent on the basis of value required, the type of asset or the cash flows utilised. Where the objective of valuation is to estimate market value, the discount rate should reflect market participants' views of risk. If the objective is to esti-mate investment value, the discount rate will reflect the target rate of return that a specific investor requires having regard to the risks inherent in the asset.*
>
> (23)

The appropriate discount rate may be developed by any reasonable method, including:

- observed or inferred rates—being a common approach in Australia, where regard is given to analysed discount rates from transactions of comparable property;
- a build-up method—such as a risk-free rate plus a risk premium, as is commonly adopted in Australia and recognised in IVS400, 60.6;
- a capital asset pricing model—which may provide assistance in a transparent assessment of a risk premium; or
- a weighted average cost of capital—which may provide assistance in an assessment of invest-ment value for a particular party (IVSC, 2021, IVS105, 50.31).

TIP1 (IVSC, 2012) advises that:

> *The build-up method involves determining the appropriate risk free rate, normally based on a long dated government bond deemed to be free of default risk, and then calculating the additional risk premium to reflect market risks and asset specific risks.*
>
> *The risk premium for real property will reflect factors such as the investment risks associated with the real property market compared to the risk free investment and risks specific to the particular property and property interest.*
>
> *The latter typically will include consideration of the certainty and security of the income and expenditure that will be incurred by an owner, and the certainty of the timing of future changes to the cash flows.*
>
> *Factors such as the quality of the building and its location, the quality of the tenant(s) and the terms of the leases(s) all impact on the risk premium.*
>
> (TIP1, 29)

The discount rate should reflect the nature of and the risks embedded in the forecast cash flows (TIP1, 24). However, double counting should be avoided, such as the explicit reflection of vacancies at lease expiry in the cash flow as well as the reflection of the risk of vacancies in the discount rate.

The discount rate selected should be corroborated by reference to the internal rate of return, a weighted average return on assets or valuation based on other approaches, such as the market approach or the capitalisation method (IVSC, 2021, IVS105, 50.32).

Significantly, IVS105 requires that the valuer must:

- document the method used to develop the discount rate and support its use; and
- provide evidence for the derivation of the discount rate, including the identification of the significant inputs and support for their derivation or source (IVSC, 2021, 50.34),

so making the development of the discount rate an explicit and transparent process rather than an unsubstantiated assertion.

The discount rate must capture the risk underlying the forecast cash flow assumptions and their achievability (IVSC, 2021, IVS105, 50.36), with such risk being assessable by regard to comparison with prior years, qualitative factors, value indications from other approaches such as the market approach and other ways (IVSC, 2021, IVS105, 50.37).

Consistent with IVS105, 50.34 (IVSC, 2021), if the valuer determines that risk is not appropriately reflected in the forecast cash flow or discount rate, then either the forecast cash flow or discount rate must be adjusted with the rationale documented. IVS105, 50.38 prescribes detailed requirements for support for the rationale and for documentation, which ensures that the development of the discount rate remains an explicit and transparent process.

8.3.5.1 Observed or inferred rates/yields

Developing the appropriate discount rate from observed or inferred rates is a common approach in Australia, where regard is given to analysed discount rates from transactions of comparable property. However, care should be taken in such analysis as it is unlikely that discount rates from comparable transactions can be decomposed to expose every element of risk reflected in the discount rate. Such analysis will, however, provide an insight into how the market views risk. As Isaac and O'Leary (2013) note:

Investment transactions will provide a means for deducing the tone of risk perception prevalent in the market for particular types of property assets.

Identifying the appropriate risk premium is therefore a process based on judgment and interpretation. It is not something that can be generated from a standard formula or read from a sliding scale of values.

(page 176)

Effectively, the exercise of judgment required to adjust comparable capitalisation rate evidence for application to the subject property being valued also applies to the adjustment of comparable discount rate evidence (or, more precisely, the risk premium within the discount rate) for application to the subject property being valued.

8.3.5.2 Build-up method

Developing the discount rate through the build-up method may be undertaken in two principal ways:

- the risk-free rate plus a risk premium; and/or
- the capitalisation rate plus growth,

which are considered further on.

8.3.5.2.1 RISK FREE RATE PLUS A RISK PREMIUM

Developing the discount rate through the build-up of the risk free rate plus a risk premium is commonly adopted in Australia and recognised in IVS400:

> *An appropriate discount rate may also be built up from a typical "risk-free" return adjusted for the additional risks and opportunities specific to the particular real property interest.*
>
> (IVSC, 2021, IVS400, 60.6)

Following Baum et al. (2018), the risk free rate plus risk premium approach may be expressed as:

$$R = RFR + RP$$

where:

R = discount rate or required return

RFR = risk free rate

RP = risk premium

TIP1 (IVSC, 2012) defines the risk free rate as follows:

> *The rate of return available in the market on an investment free of default risk.*
>
> (TIP1, 3)

for which, in Australia, the Commonwealth ten-year bond rate is usually adopted, then defines the risk premium as follows:

> *A rate of return added to a risk free rate to reflect risk.*
>
> (TIP1, 3)

Estimating the risk premium, therefore, requires the identification and quantification of risk in the asset being valued. Chapter 1 considered risk in the context of property valuation, noting that the risk inherent within an asset may be asserted to be a combination of systematic risk, unsystematic risk and idiosyncratic (or specific) risk.

Systematic risk comprises those risks endemic to the system, generally considered to be economic risks, such as inflation, which cannot be diversified away in a portfolio. Unsystematic risk comprises those risks that are common to an asset class or sub-set of an asset class, such as regulatory planning risk, which potentially can be diversified away in a portfolio. Idiosyncratic or specific risk comprises those risks that are specific to an individual asset, such as location, which can also potentially be diversified away in a portfolio (Parker, 2011).

TIP1 (IVSC, 2012) defines market risk or systematic risk as follows:

> *Risk that affects an entire market not just a specific company or asset. Market risk cannot be diversified. Also referred to as systematic risk.*
>
> (3)

TIP1 (IVSC, 2012) defines unsystematic risk as follows:

> *Risk that is specific to a company or asset. Can be diversified*
>
> (3)

though, in finance theory, unsystematic risk is usually considered to be those risks that are common to an asset class or sub-set of an asset class, with idiosyncratic or specific risk being those risks that are specific to an individual asset.

Modern portfolio theory asserts that, by combining properties within a portfolio, the impact of unsystematic and idiosyncratic risks may be significantly reduced or neutralised through diversification, in theory, though the significance of unsystematic and idiosyncratic risk in practice for property renders this challenging (Parker, 2011). It was contended in Chapter 1 that unsystematic risk and idiosyncratic risk were likely to be greater for property than for shares and bonds, and their complete neutralisation through diversification may be unlikely.

This contention is evident when considering the risks inherent between different property sectors (such as retail vs. office), between different property sub-sectors (such as grade A office vs. grade C office) and between individual properties (such as 1 Farrer Place vs. 1 Bligh Street in Sydney).

In the valuation process for DCF, the consideration of relative risks arises when contemplating a pool of analysed comparable sales and making adjustments to determine an appropriate discount rate for application or, more precisely, an appropriate risk premium for application—which of the risks are common to all properties in the pool and which are different between properties and so require recognition in the risk premium through the adjustment process?

Inherent within making adjustments to comparable sales is that risks for consideration are from the perspective of individual properties within one property sub-sector only. The adjustment process does not consider retail vs. office risks or grade A vs. grade C office risks but considers the risks between individual properties such as 1 Farrer Place vs. 1 Bligh Street in Sydney.

As considered in Chapter 1, Table 1.1 provided a matrix showing how the fundamental characteristics of property and the wide range of risks arising from property that impact upon the risk return profile of property may be classified as systematic, unsystematic or idiosyncratic in the context of individual office properties such as 1 Farrer Place, Sydney and 1 Bligh Street, Sydney.Table 1.1 showed that if considering the adjustment of the discount rate (or, more precisely, the risk premium within the discount rate) from an analysed comparable sale at, for example, 1 Farrer Place, Sydney, for application to the valuation of 1 Bligh Street, Sydney:

- risks listed in the systematic risks column will be common to both properties and reflected in the discount rate of each; and
- risks listed in the unsystematic risks column will be common to both properties and reflected in the discount rate of each; but
- risks listed in the idiosyncratic or specific risks column will differ between each property and so require reflection in the adjustments made to the discount rate (or, more precisely, the risk premium within the discount rate).

Accordingly, the valuer would focus most closely on the differences in location, building quality, tenant profile, legal issues and technology between 1 Farrer Place, Sydney, and 1 Bligh Street, Sydney, when determining the adjustment to be made to the discount rate (or, more precisely, the risk premium within the discount rate) from 1 Farrer Place, Sydney, for application in the valuation of 1 Bligh Street, Sydney.

Table 1.1 Risk classification matrix

Systematic Risks	*Unsystematic Risks*	*Idiosyncratic or Specific Risks*
Risks affecting all office properties in the Sydney CBD	*Risks affecting all grade A office properties in the Sydney CBD*	*Risks differing between 1 Farrer Place vs. 1 Bligh Street specifically*
Taxation risk	Public policy risk	Legal risk
Compulsory acquisition risk	CSR and sustainability risk	Technology risk
Demographic risk	Security risk	Location risk
Economic risk	Supply/demand risk	Building risk
	Sentiment risk	Tenant risk
	Planning risk	
	Fashion risk	

Source: Author

Wyatt (2023) helpfully notes:

> *Risks that relate to income can be handled by adjusting the cash flow. Risks that relate to the security of the land and property as an investment should be handled by adjusting the discount rate—the higher the perceived risk, the higher the discount rate or yield, all else equal.*

(page 189)

This also emphasises the importance of not double counting risk—such as by having a vacancy allowance in the cash flow while also adjusting the discount rate for vacancy risk.

8.3.5.2.2 CAPITALISATION RATE PLUS GROWTH

Developing the discount rate through the sum of the capitalisation rate and a growth rate is commonly adopted in Australia.

Baum et al. (2018) note the following derivation from Gordon's Growth Model:

$$K = R - G$$

where:
K = capitalisation rate
R = required return or discount rate
G = growth in rents

Further, as noted previously:
$$R = RFR + RP$$

where:
$$K = R - G$$

and combining equation (1) and (2):

   K = RFR + RP—G

where:

RFR = risk free rate

RP = risk premium

which illustrates the interlinked and interrelated nature of each of these key valuation inputs.

   It should be noted that this approach focuses on the addition of an allowance for rental growth only to the capitalisation rate. With the potential for capital growth reflected in the capitalisation rate, K, only the potential for rental value growth, G, should be added to the capitalisation rate to derive the discount rate.

8.3.5.3 Capital asset pricing model

Developing the discount rate through the application of the capital asset pricing model, while theoretically possible, is not commonly adopted in Australia.

   For a deeper consideration of the capital asset pricing model, readers are referred to Brown and Matysiak (2000) and Rowland (1997).

8.3.5.4 Weighted average cost of capital

Developing the discount rate through the application of the weighted average cost of capital, while theoretically possible, is not commonly adopted in Australia.

   For a deeper consideration of the weighted average cost of capital, readers are referred to Brown and Matysiak (2000) and Rowland (1997).

8.3.6 Present value

Shapiro et al. (2019) note that one application of the DCF method is to find the present value of a series of future cash flows generated by an investment.

   TIP1 (IVSC, 2012) defines present value as follows:

   The value, as of a specified date, of a future payment or series of future payments discounted to the specified date (or to time period zero) at an appropriate discount rate.

(3)

This is the most common use of DCF by valuers in an Australian context, where future cash flows are discounted to a present value.

8.3.7 Net present value

Shapiro et al. (2019) note that one application of the DCF method is the assessment of net present value where the market price or cost of the investment is known.

   TIP1 (IVSC, 2012) defines net present value as follows:

   The value, as of a specified date, of future cash inflows less all cash outflows (including the cost of investment) calculated using an appropriate discount rate.

(3)

For investment value purposes, where the market price or cost of the investment is known and included in the cash flow, following the application of the discount rate or target rate of return, a net present value will be derived. If the net present value is positive, the investment returns exceed the discount rate or target rate of return. If the net present value is negative, the investment returns do not achieve the discount rate or target rate of return.

An investor may decide to proceed with the investment if the net present value is positive, as the investor's target rate of return has been achieved, or not to proceed (or, alternatively, to renegotiate) if the net present value is negative, as the investor's target rate of return has not been achieved.

Net present value is commonly used by major investors in Australia to determine whether an investment offered for sale at a nominated price will provide an acceptable level of return.

8.3.8 *Internal rate of return*

Shapiro et al. (2019) note that one application of the DCF method is the assessment of the internal rate of return (IRR) of an investment where the market price or cost of the investment is known.

TIP1 (IVSC, 2012) defines the IRR as follows:

The discount rate at which the present value of the future cash flows of the investment equals the acquisition cost of the investment.

(3)

which is further explained as follows:

The IRR is the discount rate at which the net present value of all the cash flows, including the cost of acquisition equals zero

(TIP1, 30)

noting that the IRR may be used to evaluate an investment in terms of an investor's own hurdle rate or cost of capital (TIP1, 30). The IRR represents an annualised rate of return throughout the life of the cash flow period (Baum et al., 2018).

For investment value purposes, where the market price or cost of the investment is known and included in the cash flow, the IRR may be found as that discount rate which results in a net present value of zero following iteration at various different discount rates using a calculator or by using the IRR function in Excel.

Essentially, the IRR is that return that will be generated by the investment at a given market price or cost. If the IRR achieves or exceeds the investor's discount rate or target rate of return, an investor may decide to proceed with the investment as the investor's target rate of return has been exceeded. If the IRR does not achieve or exceed the investor's discount rate or target rate of return, the investor may decide not to proceed (or, alternatively, to renegotiate) as the investor's target rate of return has not been achieved.

IRR is commonly used by major investors in Australia to determine whether an investment offered for sale at a nominated price will provide an acceptable level of return.

8.3.9 *Formulae for DCF*

Traditionally, introduction to valuation textbooks would include the mathematical formulae for calculating the requisite DCF functions such as PV, NPV and IRR, allowing readers to manually prepare a DCF using a calculator.

Currently, in Australia, a DCF would most likely be prepared using either a sophisticated software package available through providers such as Forbury, ARGUS, CoStar and Yardi or an in-house software package within a large international valuation firm. Alternatively, a DCF may be prepared in an Excel spreadsheet, as in the example given further on.

Care should be taken with inputs such as rent, which may be payable in advance or in arrears and may be monthly, quarterly or annually. Sophisticated software packages usually offer options for selection for each alternative, but vigilance is required when constructing an Excel spreadsheet and entering the relevant data.

In the UK, where quarterly payments and payments in advance or arrears are greater issues, the traditional introduction to valuation textbooks provides detailed instruction concerning the mathematical formulae required. Readers seeking to understand the mathematical formulae for calculating the requisite DCF functions are referred to Baum et al. (2018) for a deeper consideration.

8.3.10 Summary—Discounted Cash Flow method of valuation

The principles of the DCF method of valuation were considered through the following key elements:

- type of cash flow (8.3.1);
- explicit forecast period (8.3.2);
- cash flow forecasts (8.3.3);
- terminal value (8.3.4);
- discount rate (8.3.5):

  - observed or inferred rates/yields (8.3.5.1);
  - build-up method (8.3.5.2):

    - risk free rate plus a risk premium (8.3.5.2.1);
    - capitalisation rate plus growth (8.3.5.2.2);

  - capital asset pricing model (8.3.5.3);
  - weighted average cost of capital (8.3.5.4);

- present value (8.3.6);
- net present value (8.3.7);
- internal rate of return (8.3.8); and
- formulae for DCF (8.3.9).

The following section seeks to apply each of the key elements of the DCF to the assessment of the market value of a multi-tenanted CBD office building through a worked example.

8.4 Discounted cash flow method of valuation—practice

The following worked example applies the DCF method of valuation to a fictitious CBD office investment property for the purposes of illustration only, and the data therein should not be adopted unchanged by readers undertaking a DCF valuation.

8.4.1 Outline of example

You are instructed to assess the market value of a CBD office building of 50,000 sqm NLA, which is ten years old and leased to four tenants, A, B, C and D, on the following basis:

Tenant	NLA SqM	Passing Rent	Rent Review	Lease Expiry
A	20,000 sqm	$750 psm	5 yearly market rent review in Year 3 and 8	2 years after end Year 10
B	10,000 sqm	$750 psm	No rent review	End Year 2
C	15,000 sqm	$750 psm	No rent review	End Year 6
D	5,000 sqm	$750 psm	No rent review	End Year 3

Your accumulation, analysis, adjustment and application of comparable market rentals in the CBD office sub-market indicate a current open market rental value of $1,000 psm to be applicable to the subject property with forecast rental growth of 5%pa.

Your analysis of outgoings costs in the subject property and recovery provisions under the leases indicate an annual unrecoverable outgoings cost of $150 psm pa, which will grow by the annual rate of inflation, which you have assessed at 3%pa.

Your analysis of the CBD office sub-market outlook leads you to estimate that it will take six months to relet the space occupied by Tenant B and Tenant D for a term of ten years each but 12 months to relet the space occupied by Tenant C for a term of five years, with reletting costs being approximately 10% of the first year's rent for each.

Given the imminent lease expiries following the end of the cash flow in ten years' time, you consider an upgrade of the foyer and services, in an attempt to retain tenants, will be required at an estimated cost of $50,000,000.

Your accumulation, analysis, adjustment and application of comparable sales transactions and discussions with investors active in the CBD office sub-market lead you to conclude that a discount rate of 10% is applicable to the subject property and that an appropriate capitalisation rate for the subject property would be in the order of 5%.

8.4.2 Outline of Excel spreadsheet

Table 8.1 comprises a DCF in a simple Excel spreadsheet format. Time is on the horizontal axis rows from Year 0 to Year 11, and the key variables are on the vertical axis columns comprising:

- gross cash flows, tenant by tenant, summed;
- deductions for unrecovered outgoings;
- deductions for reletting costs;
- deductions for capex; and
- net cash flow.

The open market rental growth is calculated at the top of the Excel spreadsheet, being the current open market rental value of $1,000 psm applicable to the subject property with forecast rental growth of 5%pa.

This is a highly simplified DCF Excel spreadsheet for a CBD office building, and readers may expect to include greater complexity in their valuation spreadsheets to reflect the complexity of the CBD office sub-market.

Table 8.1 DCF method of valuation—worked example

		Year 0	Year 1	Year 2	Year 3	Year 4	Year 5	Year 6	Year 7	Year 8	Year 9	Year 10	Year 11
Market rental value psm			$1,000	$1,050	$1,103	$1,158	$1,216	$1,276	$1,340	$1,407	$1,477	$1,551	$1,629
Tenant A	20,000 sqm		$15,000,000	$15,000,000	$22,050,000	$22,050,000	$22,050,000	$22,050,000	$22,050,000	$28,142,008	$28,142,008	$28,142,008	$28,142,008
Tenant B	10,000 sqm		$7,500,000	$7,500,000	$5,512,500	$11,025,000	$11,025,000	$11,025,000	$11,025,000	$11,025,000	$11,025,000	$11,025,000	$11,025,000
Tenant C	15,000 sqm		$11,250,000	$11,250,000	$11,250,000	$11,250,000	$11,250,000	$11,250,000	$0	$21,106,506	$21,106,506	$21,106,506	$21,106,506
Tenant D	5,000 sqm		$3,750,000	$3,750,000	$3,750,000	$2,894,063	$5,788,125	$5,788,125	$5,788,125	$5,788,125	$5,788,125	$5,788,125	$5,788,125
Gross Cash Flow			**$37,500,000**	**$37,500,000**	**$42,562,500**	**$47,219,063**	**$50,113,125**	**$50,113,125**	**$38,863,125**	**$66,061,640**	**$66,061,640**	**$66,061,640**	**$66,061,640**
Less unrecovered outgoings			−$7,500,000	−$7,725,000	−$7,956,750	−$8,195,453	−$8,441,316	−$8,694,556	−$8,955,392	−$9,224,054	−$9,500,776	−$9,785,799	−$10,079,373
Less reletting costs:													
Tenant B					−$1,102,498								
Tenant C										−$2,110,649			
Tenant D						−$578,811							
Less capex												−$50,000,000	
Terminal value												$1,400,000,000	
Net Cash Flow		**$0**	**$30,000,000**	**$29,775,000**	**$33,503,252**	**$38,444,800**	**$41,671,809**	**$41,418,569**	**$29,907,733**	**$54,726,937**	**$56,560,864**	**$1,406,275,841**	**$55,982,267**
PV													
PV at 10%	$759,610,044	$0	$30,000,000	$29,775,000	$33,503,252	$38,444,800	$41,671,809	$41,418,569	$29,907,733	$54,726,937	$56,560,864	$1,406,275,841	
NPV													
Net Cash Flow		−$760,000,000	$30,000,000	$29,775,000	$33,503,252	$38,444,800	$41,671,809	$41,418,569	$29,907,733	$54,726,937	$56,560,864	$1,406,275,841	
NPV at 10%	−$354,505												
IRR													
Net Cash Flow		−$760,000,000	$30,000,000	$29,775,000	$33,503,252	$38,444,800	$41,671,809	$41,418,569	$29,907,733	$54,726,937	$56,560,864	$1,406,275,841	
IRR	9.99%												

Source: Author

8.4.2.1 *Type of cash flow*

Consistent with the usual approach adopted in Australia, the value of investment property using DCF will usually be determined using the nominal whole cash flow for the asset in Australian dollars on a pre-tax basis, being contractual cash flows under the leases for known periods and forecast cash flows for the balance.

8.4.2.2 *Explicit forecast period*

Consistent with the usual approach adopted in Australia, the value of investment property using DCF will usually be determined using a ten-year forecast period. Year 0 is included to allow for the inclusion of the acquisition cost of the property in the NPV and IRR calculations, with Year 11 included to facilitate the calculation of the terminal value.

8.4.2.3 *Cash flow forecasts*

In this simplified example, the cash flow forecasts have been limited to:

- gross cash flows, tenant by tenant, summed;
- deductions for unrecovered outgoings;
- deductions for reletting costs;
- deductions for capex; and
- net cash flow.

8.4.2.3.1 GROSS CASH FLOW, TENANT BY TENANT, SUMMED

For each tenant, the contractual cash flow is included up to rent review or lease expiry. In the case of rent review (Tenant A), the rent is increased to the market level at rent review in Year 3 and Year 8. In the case of Tenants B, C and D, following lease expiry, there is a loss of rent during the reletting period, followed by an increase to market at the start of the new lease. For simplicity, incentives and outgoings lost due to vacancy have been disregarded.

8.4.2.3.2 DEDUCTION FOR UNRECOVERED OUTGOINGS

Tenants are assumed to contribute to the cost of some outgoings, leaving the owner with a shortfall for unrecovered outgoings. Your analysis of outgoings costs in the subject property and recovery provisions under the leases indicate an annual unrecoverable outgoings cost of $150 psm pa, which will grow by the annual rate of inflation, which you have assessed at 3%pa.

8.4.2.3.3 DEDUCTION FOR RELETTING COSTS

Your analysis of the CBD office sub-market outlook leads you to estimate that reletting costs will be approximately 10% of the first year's rent for each tenant, which is included as a deduction in the Excel spreadsheet.

8.4.2.3.4 DEDUCTION FOR CAPEX

Allowances for capital expenditure may be for known items (such as lift replacement) or for anticipated items (such as refurbishment or upgrades). As each of the leases in the subject property will expire 2–2.5 years after the end of Year 10, there is a significant potential future vacancy risk which may be reflected either in the capitalisation rate adopted in the terminal value and/or in an allowance for capital expenditure to upgrade the subject property in the hope of retaining tenants or finding new tenants more quickly should they vacate at lease expiry (with due caution to avoid double counting).

You have determined that a foyer and services upgrade should be allowed in the cash flow for Year 10, and your discussions with architects, designers, engineers and builders suggest that an allowance of $50,000,000 would be appropriate. It should be noted that an allowance of such magnitude should be borne in mind by the valuer when considering the capitalisation rate in the assessment of terminal value, with due caution to avoid double counting.

8.4.2.3.5 NET CASH FLOW

Net cash flow is the sum of gross cash flow less deductions for unrecovered outgoings, reletting costs and capex. When terminal value is included, Years 1 to 10 in the net cash flow row are the amounts discounted to find the present value of the subject property.

8.4.2.4 Terminal value

The terminal value is calculated by capitalising the Year 11 net cash flow by an appropriate capitalisation rate, adjusting for any reversions and including the terminal value in Year 10, effectively assuming a sale of the subject property at the end of Year 10.

Your analysis of recent sales transactions and discussions with investors active in the CBD office sub-market lead you to conclude that an appropriate capitalisation rate for the subject property in the current market would be in the order of 5%. Conventionally, allowing for deprecation and obsolescence, a 0.5% adjustment may be made to the capitalisation rate adopted to determine the terminal value for this type of property, which would result in 5.5% being adopted for the subject property.

However, as a significant allowance of $50,000,000 for foyer and services upgrade has been allowed in the net cash flow, your experience suggests that depreciation and obsolescence and possible tenant risk may be reduced such that you retain a capitalisation rate of 5% for the determination of terminal value and include this in the Year 10 cash flow, thus also avoiding double counting.

8.4.2.5 Discount rate

Your analysis of recent sales transactions and discussions with investors active in the CBD office sub-market lead you to conclude that an observed or inferred discount rate of 10% is applicable to the subject property.

Your analysis and discussions also lead you to conclude that an appropriate capitalisation rate for the subject property in the current market would be in the order of 5%, and your analysis of market rentals in the CBD office sub-market indicates forecast rental growth of 5%pa. Applying the build-up method of the capitalisation rate (5%) plus rental growth rate (5%pa) indicates a discount rate of 10%, which supports the observed or inferred discount rate.

With the prevailing ten-year Commonwealth Government bond rate being 4%, applying the build-up method of risk free rate plus risk premium suggests that if the discount rate is 10%, the risk premium is 6%. Your analysis of recent sales transactions and discussions with investors active in the CBD office sub-market lead you to conclude that this is a reasonable risk premium for the subject property.

8.4.2.6 *Present value*

Applying the Excel function to derive present value using a discount rate of 10% to the net cash flow for Years 1 to 10, =NPV(0.1,E23:N23), provides an assessment of present value that may be rounded to provide an assessment of value of $760 million.

8.4.2.7 *Net present value*

The calculation of net present value inserts the rounded assessment of present value in Year 0 and then applies the Excel function to derive net present value to the net cash flow for Years 0 to 10, =NPV(0.1,D26:N26), providing an assessment of net present value of -$354,505.

In the example, the net present value is marginally negative, indicating that acquisition at the assessed value will provide a return marginally below 10%. If a different acquisition cost were to be adopted, a different net present value would arise, which may be positive or negative.

8.4.2.8 *Internal rate of return*

The calculation of the internal rate of return inserts the rounded assessment of present value in Year 0 and then applies the Excel function to derive the internal rate of return to the net cash flow for Years 0 to 10, =IRR(D30:N30), providing an internal rate of return of 9.99%.

In the example, the internal rate of return is very slightly below the discount rate (target rate), reflecting that the present value was rounded up rather than down in the assessment of value. To achieve its target rate (discount rate), an investor may, therefore, seek to negotiate a slightly lower acquisition cost. If a different acquisition cost were to be adopted, a different internal rate of return would arise, which may be above or below the discount rate (target rate).

8.4.2.9 *Sensitivity analysis*

The use of an Excel spreadsheet allows for quick and easy sensitivity analysis for each of the key variables. For example, the sensitivity of the assessment of value to changes in the rental growth rate from 5% to, say, 4%, 4.5% and 5.5% can be easily observed. Similarly, the sensitivity of the assessment of value to changes in the capex allowance from $50 million to $45 million or $40 million can also be easily observed.

However, regard should be given to interaction effects, such as how changing the rental growth rate may impact the discount rate or how changing the capex allowance may impact the capitalisation rate used in the assessment of terminal value.

As with the use of sensitivity analysis generally, while it is a helpful tool to better understand the dynamics of the cash flow, too much application can lead to analysis paralysis where the sheer volume of value assessments generated serves to confuse rather than to clarify.

8.4.2.10 *Scenario analysis*

The use of an Excel spreadsheet also allows for quick and easy scenario analysis. Whipple (2006) advocates the consideration of at least three scenarios, the most likely scenario, an optimistic scenario and a pessimistic scenario, which *should not be chosen without thought or reason* (page 365) and be underpinned by sound rationale.

While the worked example provided may be considered the most likely scenario, an optimistic scenario might see a higher open market rental value, a higher rental growth rate and a lower capex allowance while a pessimistic scenario might see a lower open market rental value, a lower rental growth rate and a higher capex allowance. Each of these scenarios will have a consequential effect on the capitalisation rate and discount rate adopted with all changes, as Whipple advocates, to be underpinned by sound reasoning.

As there is generally limited market information to rely upon beyond that for the most likely scenario, it is prudent to only make small changes to key variables for the optimistic and pessimistic scenarios, as larger changes may be difficult to support with market information.

As with the use of scenario analysis generally, while it is a helpful tool to better understand the dynamics of the cash flow, too much application can lead to analysis paralysis where the sheer volume of value assessments generated serves to confuse rather than to clarify.

8.4.1.11 Summary—discounted cash flow method of valuation—practice

The principles of the DCF method of valuation were considered through a worked example including the following key elements:

- type of cash flow;
- explicit forecast period;
- cash flow forecasts
- terminal value;
- discount rate:

  - observed or inferred rates/yields;
  - build-up method:

    - risk free rate plus a risk premium;
    - capitalisation rate plus growth;

- present value;
- net present value; and
- internal rate of return.

The worked example serves to highlight not only the dynamic nature of the DCF method, where numerous variables may be easily changed but also the interactive nature of the DCF method, where changes to one variable may have consequential impacts on other variables and a magnified impact on the resulting assessment of value.

8.5 Summary and conclusions

Chapter 1 outlined the structure of the property asset class, examining the traditional characteristics of property (including heterogeneity, durability, illiquidity and so forth) and the traditional risks of property (including location, building, tenant risk and so forth) through the lenses of systematic, unsystematic and idiosyncratic risk, aligning property valuation with capital market theory.

Chapter 2 considered the evolution of property valuation in Australia, the role of the valuer and the diverse activities of the valuation profession, followed by a detailed examination of the inter-acting framework provided by valuation standards and ethical standards promulgated by IVSC, RICS and API.

Chapter 3 explored concepts of value and normative and positive definitions of value, dissecting the International Valuation Standards' definition of market value with a reconciliation to the concept of market value in *Spencer v Commonwealth* (1907) and examining such contemporary valuation issues as valuation lag, variance, accuracy, negligence and valuer rotation.

Chapter 4 introduced International Financial Reporting Standards and International Accounting Standards with a detailed examination of the key provisions of International Valuation Standards, the RICS Red Book and API guidance papers that impact on valuation practice in Australia.

Chapter 5 outlined conceptual approaches to the valuation process with a review of the self-supporting process of instructing, undertaking and reporting valuations under the International Valuation Standards, RICS Red Book and API guidance papers, examining how this process inter-relates to the choice of valuation approach, valuation method and the purpose of the valuation.

Chapter 6 addressed the market approach to valuation through the comparative method of valuation, including the key steps of accumulation, analysis, adjustment and application of comparable sales evidence to the subject property being valued, with an example.

Chapter 7 considered the income approach to valuation addressed through the static methods of the capitalisation of income and the profits methods of valuation, including an examination of the key inputs for each method with examples and a consideration of both marriage value and the surrender and renewal of leases.

This chapter considered the income approach to valuation addressed through the dynamic method of the discounted cash flow method of valuation, including an examination of the key inputs and a focus on the derivation of the discount rate and consideration of the role of sensitivity and scenario analysis, with examples.

While the Australian valuation profession debated for many years whether DCF was a method of valuation or a form of analysis, institutional clients had long adopted the method for multi-tenanted investment property and eventually required that their valuers do the same. Today, DCF is the principal method of valuation for multi-tenanted investment property and the use of sophisticated software packages available through providers such as Forbury, ARGUS, CoStar and Yardi or in-house software packages within large international valuation firms is commonplace.

DCF is a dynamic method of valuation, the ten-year forecast cash flows contrasting starkly with the single period cash flow adopted in the capitalisation of income method. The use of a ten-year cash flow allows the interaction of the discount rate and terminal capitalisation rate with the market rental and rental growth rate to be fully explored by the valuer. Such exploration serves to challenge the validity of assumptions underlying the choice of the discount rate, terminal capitalisation rate, market rental and rental growth rate as, unless they are each appropriately calibrated, a rational assessment of market value will not result.

Conversely, the inclusion of multiple variables such as the lease cash flows, market rentals, vacancies, reletting, discount rate and terminal capitalisation rate creates the potential for inconsistency in assumptions and the double counting of risk. A common issue is the adoption of a high rental growth rate together with extensive periods of vacancy for reletting, which is logically inconsistent or the adoption of a high-risk premium within the discount rate with high-risk allowances in the cash flow (such as vacancy for reletting) which is potentially double counting risk.

While preparation of a DCF in an Excel spreadsheet allows the valuer to fully observe each of the interactions between key variables, the widespread use of sophisticated software packages such as Forbury, ARGUS, CoStar and Yardi and in-house software packages within large international valuation firms means that valuers are less able to observe the interactions between key variables therein. It is, therefore, vitally important that valuers understand how such software packages work and the exact meaning of each input and each function, with such understanding often gained through replicating an Excel spreadsheet DCF in the software package and trailling iterations of the inputs and functions until the software package achieves the same result as the Excel spreadsheet.

The next chapter will consider the cost approach to valuation addressed through the replacement cost, reproduction cost, summation and residual or hypothetical development methods of valuation.

Finally, Chapter 10 concludes the book with a consideration of future perspectives, including the role of uncertainty, data, automated valuation models, artificial intelligence, optionality, environmental, social and governance issues, retail and office space use and indigenous issues.

References

Baum, A, Mackmin, D and Nunnington, N (2018) *The income approach to property valuation*, Routledge, Abingdon.

Brown, GR and Matysiak, GA (2000) *Real estate investment: a capital market approach*, Pearson Education Limited, Harlow.

Isaac, D and O'Leary, J (2013) *Property valuation techniques*, Palgrave Macmillan, Basingstoke.

IVSC (2012) *TIP1—discounted cash flow*, International Valuation Standards Council, London.

IVSC (2021) *International valuation standards*, International Valuation Standards Council, London.

Millington, A (2000) *An introduction to property valuation*, Routledge, Abingdon.

Parker, D (2011) *Global real estate investment trusts: people, process and management*, Wiley-Blackwell, Chichester.

RICS (2021) *RICS valuation—global standards*, Royal Institution of Chartered Surveyors, London.

Rowland, PJ (1997) *Property investments and their financing*, Thomson, Sydney.

Shapiro, E, Mackmin, D and Sams, G (2019) *Modern methods of valuation*, Routledge, Abingdon.

Whipple, RTM (2006) *Property valuation and analysis*, Lawbook Co, Sydney.

Wyatt, P (2023) *Property valuation*, Wiley Blackwell, Chichester.

9   Cost approach to valuation

9.1 Introduction

This book is an introduction to the fundamentals of property valuation, outlining the principal methods of property valuation in Australia within the context of International Valuation Standards, bridging the gap between traditional property valuation methods and the modern era of global valuation governance.

Chapter 1 outlined the structure of the property asset class, examining the traditional characteristics of property (including heterogeneity, durability, illiquidity and so forth) and the traditional risks of property (including location, building, tenant risk and so forth) through the lenses of systematic, unsystematic and idiosyncratic risk, so aligning property valuation with capital market theory.

Chapter 2 considered the evolution of property valuation in Australia, the role of the valuer and the diverse activities of the valuation profession, followed by a detailed examination of the inter-acting framework provided by valuation standards and ethical standards promulgated by IVSC, RICS and API.

Chapter 3 explored concepts of value and normative and positive definitions of value, dissecting the International Valuation Standards' definition of market value with a reconciliation to the concept of market value in *Spencer v Commonwealth* (1907) and examining such contemporary valuation issues as valuation lag, variance, accuracy, negligence and valuer rotation.

Chapter 4 introduced International Financial Reporting Standards and International Accounting Standards with a detailed examination of the key provisions of International Valuation Standards, the RICS Red Book and API guidance papers that impact on valuation practice in Australia.

Chapter 5 outlined conceptual approaches to the valuation process with a review of the self-supporting process of instructing, undertaking and reporting valuations under the International Valuation Standards, RICS Red Book and API guidance papers, examining how this process inter-relates to the choice of valuation approach, valuation method and the purpose of the valuation.

Chapter 6 addressed the market approach to valuation through the comparative method of valuation, including the key steps of accumulation, analysis, adjustment and application of comparable sales evidence to the subject property being valued, with an example.

Chapter 7 considered the income approach to valuation addressed through the static methods of the capitalisation of income and the profits methods of valuation, including an examination of the key inputs for each method with examples and a consideration of both marriage value and the surrender and renewal of leases.

DOI: 10.1201/9781003397922-9

Chapter 8 considered the income approach to valuation addressed through the dynamic method of the discounted cash flow method of valuation, including an examination of the key inputs and a focus on the derivation of the discount rate and consideration of the role of sensitivity and scenario analysis, with examples.

This chapter seeks to consider the cost approach to valuation addressed through the replacement cost, reproduction cost, summation and residual or hypothetical development methods of valuation.

Finally, Chapter 10 concludes the book with a consideration of future perspectives, including the role of uncertainty, data, automated valuation models, artificial intelligence, optionality, environmental, social and governance issues, retail and office space use and indigenous issues.

This book is based on those standards and guidance documents published in IVSC (2021) and RICS (2021) and on the API website (accessed January to May 2023). Given their nature, standards and guidance documents are dynamic, being regularly updated and with the most recently published versions replacing previously published versions. Accordingly, readers should not rely on this book as a current statement of a standard or guidance document and should visit www.ivsc.org, www.rics.org and/or www.api.org.au to find the most recent version.

As an introductory textbook on property valuation methods in Australia, this book is a companion to Australia's leading advanced valuation textbook, *Principles and Practice of Property Valuation in Australia,* edited by the same author and also published by Routledge, which is a deeper analysis of key principles underlying property valuation and current techniques and issues in the practice of property valuation for major sectors of the Australian property market.

Traditional valuation texts, such as Millington (2000), consider five methods of valuation:

- the comparative (or comparison) method;
- the income (or investment or capitalisation) method;
- the profits (or accounts or treasury or receipts and expenditure) method;
- the contractor's (or summation or cost) method; and
- the residual (or hypothetical development) method of valuation.

This chapter addresses the cost approach, the contractor's (or summation or cost) and the residual (or hypothetical development) methods of valuation.

The principles of the cost approach to valuation will be considered through the following key elements:

- cost method components (9.3.1):

  - capture of all costs (9.3.1.1);
  - depreciation (9.3.1.2);
  - land (9.3.1.3);

- replacement cost method of valuation (9.3.2):

  - contractor's method of valuation (9.3.2.1);
  - Australian summation method of valuation (9.3.2.2);
  - reinstatement cost method of valuation (9.3.2.3);

- reproduction cost method of valuation (9.3.3);
- summation method of valuation (IVS) (9.3.4); and
- residual or hypothetical development method of valuation (9.3.5),

followed by worked examples of the application of each to the assessment of value.

9.2 Cost approach to valuation

The cost approach to valuation is one of the three principal valuation approaches recognised by IVSs and is grounded in economic theory, based on the economic principle that a buyer will pay no more than the cost to obtain an asset of equal utility, whether by purchase or construction, as defined in IVS105 (IVSC, 2021):

> *The cost approach provides an indication of value using the economic principle that a buyer will pay no more for an asset than the cost to obtain an asset of equal utility, whether by purchase or by construction, unless undue time, inconvenience, risk or other factors are involved. The approach provides an indication of value by calculating the current replacement or reproduction cost of an asset and making deductions for physical deterioration and all other relevant forms of obsolescence.*

(60.1)

IVS400 (IVSC, 2021) succinctly notes of the cost approach:

> *It may be used as the primary approach where there is no evidence of transaction prices for similar property or no identifiable actual or notional income stream that would accrue to the owner of the relevant interest.*

(70.3)

IVSC TIP2 (IVSC, 2012) expands on this as follows:

> *The cost approach is applicable when there are limited transactions due to the specialised nature, design or location of the asset, or where the asset itself does not produce a cash flow or the cash flows associated with it are not separable from the business using it. The cost approach is therefore typically used as the primary valuation approach when the market or income approaches cannot be applied.*

(14)

Applying the limited transactions principle, a useful test for the adoption of the cost approach is to consider if the asset is regularly traded in the market. Public buildings such as sports stadia, opera houses, town halls, museums, libraries, hospitals, places of worship, convention centres, crematoria, law courts, power stations, prisons, public swimming pools and public toilets or major operating facilities such as car manufacturing plants, oil refineries, steel works, airports and so forth rarely trade and so may be suited to the cost approach.

IVS105 (IVSC, 2021) identifies several circumstances where the cost approach should be applied and afforded significant weight:

- where participants would be able to recreate an asset with substantially the same utility as the subject asset without regulatory or legal restrictions, and the asset could be recreated quickly enough that a participant would not be willing to pay a significant premium for the ability to use the asset immediately (60.2(a))—such as a simple timber home in a developing country without planning or building regulations which could be constructed quickly with the cost being less than buying a house close by;
- where the asset is not directly income generating and the unique nature of the asset makes using an income approach or market approach unfeasible (60.2(b))—such as the properties listed previously which are not regularly traded and are not directly income producing; and/or

- where the basis of value being used is fundamentally based on replacement cost, such as replacement value (60.2©)—for example, valuations for insurance purposes which may be fundamentally based on replacement cost;

and several circumstances where the cost approach may be applied and afforded significant weight, subject to corroboration by other approaches:

- where participants might consider recreating an asset of similar utility, but there are potential legal or regulatory hurdles or significant time involved in recreating the asset (s60.3(a))—such as historic public buildings in developed countries with planning and building regulations;
- where the cost approach is used as a reasonableness check to other approaches (s60.3(b))—such as the market approach or the income approach; and
- where the asset was recently created, such that there is a high degree of reliability in the assumptions used in the cost approach (s60.3(c)).

Such property may be considered specialised property, which the RICS Red Book (RICS, 2021) Glossary defines as:

> *A property that is rarely, if ever, sold in the market, except by way of a sale of the business or entity of which it is part, due to the uniqueness arising from its specialised nature and design, its configuration, size, location or otherwise.*

IVSC TIP2 (IVSC, 2012) does, however, caution that the fact that an asset can be regarded as specialised should not automatically lead to the conclusion that the cost approach should be adopted (15). Further, care is required where the asset is clearly redundant or obsolete and therefore has no utility, as a buyer would not recreate it, and therefore, the value may be very low (reflecting scrap or salvage value) or zero (17).

Where there is evidence of market transaction prices or an identifiable income stream, the cost approach may be used as a secondary or corroborating approach (IVSC, 2021, IVS400, 70.4).

IVS105 (IVSC, 2021) notes three cost approach methods:

- the replacement cost method that indicates value by calculating the cost of a similar asset offering equivalent utility;
- the reproduction cost method that indicates value by calculating the cost of recreating a replica of the asset; and
- the summation method that calculates the value of an asset by the addition of the separate values of its component parts (70.1),

similar to the contractor's (or summation or cost) method of valuation, which is one of the five traditional methods of valuation. Further, the residual (or hypothetical development) method of valuation, being one of the five traditional methods of valuation, includes cost data and so may be considered within the IVS concept of the cost approach.

Wyatt (2023) validly cautions against the careless intermingling of concepts of cost and concepts of value, with cost being a production-related concept and value being an exchange or use-related concept. Mixing notions of value and notions of cost is akin to trying to mix oil and water. Notions of value and notions of cost do not sit well together, and the result is a curious expression that is neither a pure expression of value nor a pure expression of cost.

Following Whipple (2006), Wyatt (2023) notes that the cost approach assumes that value is derived from an additive relationship between land value and building costs, which is questionable as each may merge to provide an undifferentiated stream of utility, the value of which is greater than their sum and for which the contribution of each is impossible to determine. Essentially, only when there are no exchange or use-related value inputs available should the valuer consider a cost approach to valuation.

9.3 Cost methods of valuation—principles

For clarity, the principles of the cost approach to valuation will be considered through the three methods identified in IVS105 (IVSC, 2021) and two of the five traditional methods of valuation, the contractor's (or summation or cost) method and the residual (or hypothetical development) method, as follows:

- cost method components (9.3.1):

  - capture of all costs (9.3.1.1);
  - depreciation (9.3.1.2);
  - land (9.3.1.3);

- replacement cost method of valuation (9.3.2):

  - contractor's method of valuation (9.3.2.1);
  - Australian summation method of valuation (9.3.2.2);
  - reinstatement cost method of valuation (9.3.2.3);

- reproduction cost method of valuation (9.3.3);
- summation method of valuation (IVS) (9.3.4); and
- residual or hypothetical development method of valuation (9.3.5),

9.3.1 Cost method components

For the cost methods of valuation, IVS105 (IVSC, 2021) notes some common considerations, including the capture of all costs, deprecation and underlying land value.

9.3.1.1 Capture of all costs

IVS105 (IVSC, 2021) emphasises that the cost approach should capture all of the costs that would be incurred by a typical participant (70.10), including direct and indirect costs such as:

- direct costs:

  - materials; and
  - labour;

- indirect costs:

  - transport costs;
  - installation costs;
  - professional fees (design, permit, architectural, legal, etc.);
  - other fees (commissions, etc.);
  - overheads;

- taxes;
- finance costs (e.g., interest on debt financing—further detailed in IVSC TIP2 para 30 (IVSC, 2012)); and
- profit margin or entrepreneurial profit to the creator of the asset, such as return to investors (70.11),

with IVSC TIP2 (IVSC, 2012) adding marketing, sales and leasing commissions and the cost of holding the property after construction is completed but before stable occupancy is achieved (28). Common to other valuation approaches under IVSs, the impact of tax is ignored.

While the actual costs incurred in creating the subject asset or a comparable reference asset may be available and provide an indicator of cost, adjustments may be needed to reflect cost fluctuations between the date that the costs were incurred and the valuation date and any atypical or exceptional costs or savings that would not arise in creating an equivalent asset (IVS105, 70.14 (IVSC, 2021)).

9.3.1.2 Depreciation

In the context of the cost approach, IVS105 (IVSC, 2021) notes that deprecation refers to adjustments made to the estimated costs to reflect the impact of any obsolescence affecting the subject asset (80.1), including the principal categories of physical, functional and external or economic obsolescence (80.2):

- physical obsolescence being any loss of utility due to the physical deterioration of the asset or its components resulting from its age or usage;
- functional obsolescence being any loss of utility resulting from inefficiencies in the subject asset compared to its replacement, such as its design specification or technology being outdated; and
- external or economic obsolescence being any loss of utility caused by economic or locational factors external to the asset, which may be temporary or permanent (IVS105, 80.2).

Physical obsolescence can be addressed in two ways:

- curable physical obsolescence, being measured as the cost to fix or cure; and
- incurable physical obsolescence, being measured as the proportion of expected total life consumed (IVS105, 80.5 (IVSC, 2021)).

Functional obsolescence may take two forms:

- excess capital cost where changes in design or construction result in the availability of a modern equivalent asset for lower capital cost; and
- excess operating cost where improvements in design or excess capacity result in the availability of a modern equivalent asset with lower operating costs (IVS105, 80.6 (IVSC, 2021)).

IVSC TIP2 (IVSC, 2021) provides examples of functional obsolescence as an industrial building with a ceiling height different from that required by most users or an office building with many individual rooms separated by structural walls resulting in an inflexible layout (52).

Economic obsolescence may arise when external factors affect an asset, such as:

- adverse changes to demand for the products or services produced by the asset;
- oversupply in the market for the asset;
- disruption or loss of supply of labour or raw material; and
- the asset being used by a business that cannot afford to pay a market rent for the asset and still generate a market rate of return,

being deducted after physical obsolescence and functional obsolescence (IVS105, 80.7 (IVSC, 2021)).

IVSC TIP2 (IVSC, 2021) provides an example of economic obsolescence as a deterioration in location because of changes in local infrastructure, environmental conditions or demographics (59).

Further, IVSC TIP2 (IVSC, 2012) notes that, for some classes of assets, a regular pattern or profile of depreciation can be determined over the life of the asset, thus enabling an appropriate rate of deprecation at the valuation date to be determined with typical deprecation profiles including:

- straight line, being the same proportion of the original cost deducted for each period of the estimated life of the asset;
- diminishing value, being the deduction of a constant percentage rate from the cost at the start of the previous period over the estimated life of the asset; and
- S-curve, being the deduction of different percentage rates for each period over the estimated life of the asset, such as higher rates in the initial period reducing over the estimated life of the asset (69).

IVS105 (IVSC, 2021) further encourages consideration of both the physical life and economic life of the asset. Physical life is how long the asset could be used before it would be worn out beyond economic repair, assuming routine maintenance. Economic life is how long the asset is anticipated to generate financial returns or provide a non-financial benefit in its current use (80.3).

9.3.1.3 Land

Application of the cost approach generally requires determination of the value of the underlying land to be added to the depreciated cost of improvements, for which considerable care is required (TIP2, 73 (IVSC, 2012)). The value of the underlying land is determined with regard to its highest and best use (74) using sales evidence from comparable land (76).

Two methods may be used to estimate land value, being either the value of the land that would be required for a modern equivalent asset or the value of the subject land (75). Where the use of the land and the planning requirements are the same (such as a large industrial plant on land zoned for industrial uses), the value on each basis may be likely to be the same (76).

However, where the use of the land is sub-optimal to the planning requirements and its value may be greater for a different permitted use (highest and best use being greater than current use), the value on each basis may be likely to differ and the cost approach may not be the most appropriate valuation approach to adopt (77).

Where the land value for an alternative use is greater than the value of the entire property for the current use, the value attributable to improvements may be zero or negative if demolition and clearance costs may be incurred (78).

9.3.1.4 Summary—cost method components

The key elements for valuation methods within the cost approach are the capture of all costs, deprecation and the underlying land value. Within the context of each of the cost methods of valuation, each of the key elements requires careful consideration with regard to the type of property being valued (public building, major operating facility and so forth) and the purpose of the valuation.

9.3.2 Replacement cost method of valuation

Replacement cost is the cost that is relevant to determining the price that a participant would pay based on replicating the utility of the asset, not the exact physical properties of the asset (IVS105, 70.2 (IVSC, 2021)), adjusted for physical deterioration and relevant forms of obsolescence to provide a depreciated replacement cost (IVS105, 70.3 (IVSC, 2021)).

Hence, the replacement cost method of valuation may also be referred to as the depreciated replacement cost method of valuation (DRC method) or, if the building design is optimised to replicate the utility of the asset, the optimised depreciated replacement cost method of valuation (ODRC method).

The replacement cost method of valuation may also be known as the cost method or the contractor's method in the UK and Commonwealth and the summation method in Australia.

Significantly, IVS105 (IVSC, 2021) notes that the replacement cost is generally that of a modern equivalent asset, being one that provides similar function and equivalent utility to the asset being valued but which is of a current design and constructed or made using cost-effective materials and techniques (70.5).

By way of example, replacement cost for the Sydney Opera House may be based on the cost of replicating an opera theatre, drama theatre, playhouse, concert hall, restaurant and car park in a current design using cost-effective materials and construction techniques. Accordingly, the replacement cost for the Sydney Opera House would be unlikely to include the internationally recognised convex "sails" structure or the current configuration of facilities.

9.3.2.1 Contractor's method of valuation (depreciated replacement cost)

Following Millington (2000), the contractor's method (or cost method, replacement cost method or depreciated replacement cost method) may be summarised as follows:

	Cost of site
plus	Cost of building
=	Total cost of similar property
less	Deprecation allowance, cost of building
=	Value of existing property

Following Wyatt (2023), the summary of the depreciated replacement cost method may be expanded as follows:

Building:

	Building area sqm
x	Building cost $psm
=	Cost of modern building of equivalent utility
+	Fees, as % of build cost

+	Finance costs for build cost and fees over half build period
=	Gross replacement cost of modern building of equivalent utility
x	Depreciation allowance % (age/estimated economic life)
=	Net replacement cost of modern building of equivalent utility

Land:

	Size of site sqm/hectares
x	Land value psm/per hectare
=	Value of land
+	Finance costs for land over build period
=	Cost of land

Replacement cost valuation:

=	Net replacement cost of modern building of equivalent utility
+	Cost of land

9.3.2.2 *Australian summation method of valuation*

The summation method of valuation, as it is understood in Australia, differs from the IVSC summation method of valuation considered in what follows.

Rost and Collins (1990) describe the summation method as follows:

In valuation practice, the term "summation" means an addition of the values of the constituent parts of a property to arrive at its total value.

It is commonly used in valuing house property which does not conform to the kind of pattern needed for use of the direct comparison method

(page 106)

noting that the method may be used with reference to comparable sales:

* to deduce land value where the current value of buildings is known; or
* to deduce the current value of buildings where land value is known,

with the result of either from comparable sales analysis being capable of adjustment and application to the valuation of a subject property.

Rost and Collins (1990) provide the following example of the summation method:

Sale price of the house property	$49,000
Deduct value of site	$13,000
Value of improvements	$36,000

Apportionment of value of improvements:	
Detached garage—at replacement cost less depreciation	$1,000
Fences and sundries	$1,400
House—brick, tiled roof, 3 bedrooms, etc. 150 sqm @ $224 psm	$33,600
Total	$36,000

noting that the current value of the buildings (value of improvements) as deduced from this sale ($224 psm) could be used as a basis for valuing a subject house of comparable age, condition and type, standing on suitably zoned land in a comparable locality, in the absence of comparable sales (page 107). Further, if the current value of buildings is known from the analysis of comparable sales, this could be used as a basis for valuing a subject land parcel of similar characteristics, standing on suitably zoned land in a comparable locality, in the absence of comparable sales.

More recently, Smithson (1997) provides the following example of the summation method:

House			
136 sqm @ $465 psm		$63,240	
Barbecue	$2,500		
Fences	$7,500		
Swimming pool	$9,000		
Paving	$3,500		
Garden	$1,000	$23,500	
Land		$70,000	
Total		$156,740	Say $157,000

As with inputs for the value of land, cost inputs should be evidence-based, such as from Rawlinsons (2023), builders quotes or estimates from reliable online databases.

9.3.2.3 Reinstatement cost method of valuation

In an Australian context, the reinstatement method of valuation is commonly found in the complex and specialist area of valuations for insurance purposes, incorporating elements of the cost approach. ANZVGP104 *Valuations for Insurance Purposes* (API, 2021) provides detailed guidance on the application of the reinstatement method for insurance purposes, defining reinstatement cost as follows:

> *Where property is lost or destroyed, in the case of a building, the rebuilding thereof, or in the case of property other than a building, the replacement thereof by similar property in either case in a condition equal to, but not better or more extensive than its condition when new.*

> *When property is damaged: the repair of the damage and restoration of the damaged portion of the property to a condition substantially the same as, but not better or more extensive than its condition when new.*

> (page 4)

ANZVGP104 notes the two common approaches to estimating reinstatement cost to be:

- an estimate based on building cost guides; and/or
- an estimate based on elemental costs (often provided by a Quantity Surveyor and the preferred alternative for larger, more complex, regional or remote properties).

Allowance may also be required for increasing building costs if the rebuilding period is lengthy and the relevant insurance policy should be checked concerning the inclusion of costs for removal of debris, GST and loss of rent.

Following Dunsford et al. (2022), the reinstatement cost method may be stated as follows:

	Gross building area sqm
x	Construction cost rate $psm including services (air-conditioning, sprinklers, ventilation, lighting, lifts)
+	Architects, engineering and survey fees
+	Extra costs of reinstatement to bring property up to current regulatory requirements
+	Contingency
=	Reinstatement value

ANZVGP104 (API, 2021) notes:

> *Valuations for insurance purposes are a specialised area of valuation practice requiring in-depth experience and knowledge of insurance and the particular property or item of plant and equipment.*
>
> (page 1)

API members are reminded that the API Code of Professional Conduct requires operation within the limits of qualifications and experience, declining instructions where the member does not have competence and the option to work in conjunction with valuers who have the required competence.

For a deeper consideration of the reinstatement cost method of valuation, readers are referred to Dunsford et al. (2022).

9.3.2.4 Summary—replacement cost method of valuation

The replacement cost method of valuation was considered through three expressions:

- the contractor's method of valuation or the depreciated replacement cost method of valuation;
- the Australian summation method of valuation; and
- the reinstatement cost method of valuation as used in an Australian context,

with worked examples provided in what follows.

9.3.3 Reproduction cost method of valuation

Reproduction cost is the cost that is relevant to determining the price that a participant may pay as it is based on recreating a replica of the subject asset, adjusted for depreciation based on physical functional and external obsolescence associated with the subject asset.

Reproduction rather than replacement may be appropriate in circumstances where:

- the cost of a modern equivalent asset is greater than the cost of recreating a replica of the subject asset; or
- the utility offered by the subject asset could only be provided by a replica rather than a modern equivalent (IVSC, 2021, IVS105, 70.6).

IVSC TIP2 (IVSC, 2012) notes that if an asset's exact design and features were an integral part of the benefit that would accrue to an owner, the equivalent utility could only be provided by a reproduction of the subject asset. An example would be an iconic building where the design was of greater importance than the functionality of the accommodation within it (20).

By way of example, the reproduction cost for the Sydney Opera House may be based on the cost of recreating a replica of the existing building, including the internationally recognised convex "sails" structure, adjusted for deprecation.

Following Wyatt (2023), the reproduction cost method may be stated as follows:

Building:

	Subject building area sqm
x	Subject building cost $psm
=	Cost of recreating a replica of the subject building
+	Fees, as % of build cost
+	Finance costs for build cost and fees over half build period
=	Gross replacement cost of replica of the subject building
x	Deprecation allowance % (age/estimated economic life)
=	Net replacement cost of replica of the subject building

Land:

	Size of site sqm/hectares
x	Land value psm/per hectare
=	Value of land
+	Finance costs for land over build period
=	Cost of land

Replacement cost valuation:

=	Net replacement cost of replica of the subject building
+	Cost of land

9.3.4 Summation method of valuation

Under IVSs, the summation method is outlined in IVS105 (IVSC, 2021) and refers to the underlying asset method whereby each component part of the subject asset is valued and summed to reach the value of the subject asset:

> 70.8. The summation method, also referred to as the underlying asset method, is typically used for investment companies or other types of assets or entities for which value is primarily a factor of the values of their holdings.
>
> 70.9. The key steps in the summation method are:
>
> (a) value each of the component assets that are part of the subject asset using the appropriate valuation approaches and methods, and
>
> (b) add the value of the component assets together to reach the value of the subject asset (IVSC, 2021, IVS105).

9.3.5 Residual or hypothetical development method of valuation

One of the five traditional methods of valuation, the residual method or hypothetical development method of valuation, may be used to determine value when a property has development or redevelopment potential and hence latent value. The method may be applied to assess the value of land for development purposes or the value of a property with redevelopment or refurbishment potential.

Wyatt (2023) succinctly states:

The residual method is based on a simple economic concept: the development value of land can be calculated as a surplus or residual remaining after estimated development costs have been deducted from the estimated value of the completed development.

(page 236)

The residual method or hypothetical development method may be summarised as follows (after Millington (2000):

	Value of the completed development (or gross development value or gross realisation)
less	Total expenditure on development, including developer's profit
=	Value of site or property in present condition (residual value)

Following Wyatt (2023), the summary of the residual method or hypothetical development method may be expanded as follows:

Development value:
Net internal area sqm

x	Market rental $psm pa
=	Estimated rental value
x	Net initial yield or capitalisation rate
=	Gross development value before sale costs
–	Sale costs
=	Net development value after sale costs

Development costs:
Site preparation

+	Building costs—$psm x gross internal area
+	External works
+	Professional fees—% building costs and external works
+	Contingency allowance—% building costs
+	Finance on costs and fees for half building period
+	Finance on costs and finance for void period
+	Letting agents fees—% market rental
+	Letting legal fees—% market rental
=	Development costs
+	Developer's profit on development costs—%
=	Total development costs

Net development value less total development costs
–	**Land costs (calculated in reverse order):**
	Developer's profit on land costs—%
+	Finance on land costs over total development period
=	Residual land value before purchase costs
–	Purchase costs
=	**Residual land value after purchase costs**

The residual method or hypothetical development method, therefore, combines notions of value and notions of cost, which is akin to trying to mix oil and water. Notions of value and notions of cost do not sit well together and the result is a curious expression that is neither a pure expression of value nor a pure expression of cost. As Whipple (2006) succinctly states:

> *At the outset we make it clear that this approach to price estimation is logically flawed and it should not be used except in limited cases.*

(page 432)

The residual method or hypothetical development method may be commonly observed in popular television home renovation shows where the contestant (developer) confidently asserts that, after renovation, a house will sell for $1.5 million, the cost of renovations will be $0.25 million, a profit of $0.25 million is required, and therefore the value of the property in its current condition is $1.0 million.

As will be immediately apparent, the method is entirely dependent on the correct assessment of each input, with a variation in any input having a flow-on effect to other inputs. Great skill is required to assess the optimal form of development, the likely value on completion at some point in the future, the costs of development, including professional fees, which may increase during the development period, the costs of letting or selling the property and the fees and interest payable if the development is to be debt funded and that level of profit that a developer would consider appropriate for the level of risk in undertaking the development (after Millington, 2000).

It is not surprising, therefore, that the application of the residual method or hypothetical development method has led to numerous valuation negligence cases, including *Mount Banking Corporation Limited v Brian Cooper & Co* (1992) 35 EG 23 and *Allied Trust Bank Limited v Edward Symmons & Partners* (1993) EGCS 163.

Isaac and O'Leary (2012) caution that a weakness in the residual method of valuation is that all variables are calibrated at that point in time when the valuation is undertaken, even though they reflect variables at points in the future. While it is conventionally assumed that the end value of the project would increase over time and so offset any increase in costs, the Global Financial Crisis of 2007–08 challenged this assumption, leading to greater caution being required (page 119).

The residual method or hypothetical development method may be static (a single period statement of the present value of each input) or dynamic (a multi-period cash flow approach). The critical difference between the static and dynamic approaches concerns the cost of finance, with the static approach relying on heuristic assumptions while the dynamic approach sets out the cash flow in periods over the development, allowing a more accurate assessment of the cost of finance and the resulting amount available for land acquisition. While the method is widely criticised for being dependent on a very large number of variables, it is also widely used, particularly in the assessment of land value for prospective development.

The residual method or hypothetical development method, as stated previously, effectively determines land value as a function of development cost and development profit. The method may be applied to a development where land, for example, is on the market and has an asking price with the method reconfigured as a development viability tool to estimate potential development profitability, as follows:

	Value of the completed development (or gross development value or gross realisation)
less	Total expenditure on development
less	Asking price of site or property in present condition
=	Developer's profit

Baum et al. (2018) refer to such a use of the residual method as a *development appraisal* and the conventional use, as detailed previously, as a *residual valuation*.

For a deeper consideration of the residual method of valuation, readers are referred to RICS (2019).

9.3.6 Summary—cost methods of valuation

The principles of the cost approach to valuation were considered through the following key elements:

- cost method components (9.3.1):

    - capture of all costs (9.3.1.1);
    - depreciation (9.3.1.2);
    - land (9.3.1.3);

- replacement cost method of valuation (9.3.2):

    - contractor's method of valuation (9.3.2.1);
    - Australian summation method of valuation (9.3.2.2);
    - reinstatement cost method of valuation (9.3.2.3);

- reproduction cost method of valuation (9.3.3);
- summation method of valuation (IVS) (9.3.4); and
- residual or hypothetical development method of valuation (9.3.5).

The following section seeks to apply each of the key elements of the respective cost methods of valuation to the assessment of value through worked examples.

9.4 Cost methods of valuation—practice

A succinct summary of the cost approach, which provides overarching guidance to the various cost methods, is provided in IVS104 (IVSC, 2021):

> The first step requires a replacement cost to be calculated. This is normally the cost of replacing the property with a modern equivalent at the relevant valuation date. An exception is where an equivalent property would need to be a replica of the subject property in order to provide a participant with the same utility, in which case the replacement cost would be that of reproducing or replicating the subject building rather than replacing it with a modern equivalent. The replacement cost must reflect all incidental costs, as appropriate, such as the value of the land, infrastructure, design fees, finance costs and developer profit that would be incurred by a participant in creating an equivalent asset.
>
> (70.5)

> The cost of the modern equivalent must then, as appropriate, be subject to adjustment for physical, functional, technological and economic obsolescence. The objective of an adjustment for obsolescence is to estimate how much less valuable the subject property might, or would be, to a potential buyer than the modern equivalent. Obsolescence considers the physical condition, functionality and economic utility of the subject property compared to the modern equivalent.
>
> (70.6)

IVS105 (IVSC, 2021) notes three cost approach methods, being:

- the replacement cost method that indicates value by calculating the cost of a similar asset offering equivalent utility;
- the reproduction cost method that indicates value by calculating the cost of recreating a replica of the asset; and
- the summation method that calculates the value of an asset by the addition of the separate values of its component parts (70.1),

similar to the contractor's (or summation or cost) method of valuation, which is one of the five traditional methods of valuation. Further, the residual (or hypothetical development) method of valuation, being one of the five traditional methods of valuation, includes cost data and so may be considered within the IVS concept of the cost approach.

The following worked examples apply the replacement cost, reproduction cost, summation cost and residual or hypothetical development cost methods of valuation to fictitious properties for the purposes of illustration only, and the data therein should not be adopted unchanged by readers undertaking valuations.

9.4.1 *Replacement cost method of valuation*

The replacement cost method of valuation will be considered through the contractor's method of valuation (depreciated replacement cost), the Australian summation method of valuation and the reinstatement method.

9.4.1.1 *Contractor's method of valuation (depreciated replacement cost)*

IVS105 (IVSC, 2021) notes that the key steps in the replacement cost method are:

- calculate all of the costs that would be incurred by a typical participant seeking to create or obtain an asset providing equivalent utility;
- determine whether there is any depreciation related to physical, functional and external obsolescence associated with the subject asset; and
- deduct total depreciation from the total costs to arrive at a value for the subject asset (70.4).

9.4.1.1.1 OUTLINE OF EXAMPLE

You are instructed to assess the depreciated replacement cost of a church comprising 750 sqm, built in 1920 with an elaborate stone façade and highly decorated interior common to many suburban churches and so not heritage listed.

The church has 50 years of its estimated 150-year life remaining. Construction costs for a modern church providing equivalent utility are $1,800 psm, according to Rawlinsons (2023) and the construction period is estimated to be one year, with professional fees estimated to be 10% of building costs.

Your accumulation, analysis, adjustment and application of comparable land sales in the suburban sub-market indicate a land value of $1,000 psm to be applicable to the church site of 1,500 sqm. The diocese, which owns the church, can borrow funds for construction and land acquisition at an interest rate of 5%pa.

9.4.1.1.2 OUTLINE OF CONTRACTOR'S METHOD OF VALUATION (DEPRECIATED
REPLACEMENT COST)

Following Wyatt (2023), the depreciated replacement cost may be calculated as follows:

Building:

	Building area sqm	750 sqm
x	Building cost $psm	$1,800 psm
=	Cost of modern building of equivalent utility	$1,350,000
+	Fees, at 10% of build cost	$135,000
+	Finance costs for build cost and fees over half build period at 5%	$37,125
=	Gross replacement cost of modern building of equivalent utility	$1,522,125
x	Deprecation allowance 67%	
	(age/estimated economic life assuming straight line depreciation)	($1,019,824)
=	Net replacement cost of modern building of equivalent utility	$502,301

Land:

	Size of site sqm/hectares	1,500 sqm
x	Land value psm/per hectare	$1,000 psm
=	Value of land	$1,500,000
+	Finance costs for land over build period at 5%	$75,000
=	Cost of land	$1,575,000

Replacement cost valuation:

=	Net replacement cost of modern building of equivalent utility	$502,301
+	Cost of land	$1,575,000
=		$2,077,301

Readers should note that the same property may be valued at different amounts using the cost approach, with the depreciated replacement cost method producing $2,077,301 and the reproduction cost method producing $2,691,225 (in what follows). The relativity of net replacement cost to land value in each method highlights the issues in the cost approach concerning mixing concepts of cost and value, with the example also illustrating the impact of the building cost rate and depreciation period chosen on the output of the cost method. The relativity of net replacement cost to land value also raises issues of highest and best use and development potential, which are conveniently disregarded in the example.

9.4.1.2 *Australian summation method of valuation*

The summation method of valuation as it is understood in Australia differs from the IVSC summation method of valuation considered in what follows, summarised by Rost and Collins (1990) as follows:

In valuation practice, the term "summation" means an addition of the values of the constituent parts of a property to arrive at its total value.
It is commonly used in valuing house property which does not conform to the kind of pattern needed for use of the direct comparison method.

(page 106)

9.4.1.2.1 OUTLINE OF EXAMPLE

You are instructed to provide a summation valuation for a three-bedroom brick house with a tiled roof of 300 sqm, having standard finishes and a detached garage. Construction costs for such a house are $2,400 psm, according to Rawlinsons (2023).

Your accumulation, analysis, adjustment and application of comparable land sales in the suburban sub-market indicate a land value of $875 psm to be applicable to the subject site of 600 sqm.

9.4.1.2.2 OUTLINE OF AUSTRALIAN SUMMATION METHOD CALCULATION

Following Smithson (1997), the summation method may be calculated as follows:

House		
300 sqm @ $2,400 psm	$720,000	
Garage	$15,000	
Land	$525,000	
Total	$1,260,000	Say $1,250,000

9.4.1.3 Reinstatement method of valuation

In an Australian context, the reinstatement method of valuation is commonly found in the complex and specialist area of valuations for insurance purposes.

9.4.1.3.1 OUTLINE OF EXAMPLE

You are instructed to provide a reinstatement valuation for a 2,500 sqm warehouse property in a suburban location which is five years old with pre-cast external walls, metal roof, roller shutter doors, amenities, all services except ventilation and sprinklers to the warehouse and an air-conditioned office and showroom to the front elevation. Construction costs for such a warehouse are $1,000 psm, according to Rawlinsons (2023), with professional fees estimated to be 10% of building costs. As land is not included in a reinstatement valuation, no assessment of land value is required.

9.4.1.3.2 OUTLINE OF REINSTATEMENT METHOD CALCULATION

Following Dunsford et al. (2022), the reinstatement cost method may be calculated as follows:

	Gross building area sqm	2,500 sqm
x	Construction cost rate $psm including services (air-conditioning, sprinklers, ventilation, lighting, lifts)	$1,000 psm
=		$2,500,000
+	Architects, engineering and survey fees at 10%	$250,000
+	Extra costs of reinstatement to bring property up to current regulatory requirements	$0
+	Contingency at 10%	$275,000
=	Reinstatement value	$3,025,000

While the building is relatively new and so meets current regulatory requirements and the rebuilding period may be relatively short, the relevant insurance policy should be checked concerning the inclusion of costs for removal of debris, GST and loss of rent. Similarly, the rate found in Rawlinsons (2023) may require adjustment for location (if the building is in a regional or remote location) or site-specific factors (such as slope, access, etc.).

9.4.2 Reproduction cost method of valuation

IVS105 (IVSC, 2021) notes that the key steps in the reproduction cost method are:

- calculate all of the costs that would be incurred by a typical participant seeking to create an exact replica of the subject asset;
- determine whether there is any depreciation related to physical, functional and external obsolescence associated with the subject asset; and
- deduct total depreciation from the total costs to arrive at a value for the subject asset (70.7).

9.4.2.1 Outline of example

You are instructed to assess the reproduction cost of a church comprising 750 sqm, built in 1920 with an elaborate stone façade and highly decorated interior, which is distinctive, recognisable and a local landmark, being heritage listed.

The church has 50 years of its estimated 150-year life remaining. Construction costs for a reproduction church are $4,000 psm, according to Rawlinsons (2023), and the construction period is estimated to be one year, with professional fees estimated to be 10% of building costs.

Your accumulation, analysis, adjustment and application of comparable land sales in the suburban sub-market indicate a land value of $1,000 psm to be applicable to the church site of 1,500 sqm. The diocese, which owns the church, can borrow funds for construction and land acquisition at an interest rate of 5%pa.

9.4.2.2 Outline of reproduction cost method calculation

Following Wyatt (2023), the reproduction cost may be calculated as follows:

Building:		
	Building area sqm	750 sqm
x	Building cost $psm	$4,000 psm
=	Cost of reproduction building	$3,000,000
+	Fees, at 10% of build cost	$300,000
+	Finance costs for build cost and fees over half build period at 5%	$82,500
=	Gross reproduction cost of building	$3,382,500
x	Deprecation allowance 67%	
	(age/estimated economic life using straight line depreciation)	($2,266,275)
=	Net reproduction cost of building	$1,116,225
Land:		
	Size of site sqm/hectares	1,500 sqm
x	Land value psm/per hectare	$1,000 psm

=	Value of land	$1,500,000
+	Finance costs for land over build period at 5%	$75,000
=	Cost of land	$1,575,000

Reproduction cost valuation:		
=	Net reproduction cost of building	$1,116,225
+	Cost of land	$1,575,000
=		$2,691,225

Readers should note that the same property may be valued at different amounts using the cost approach, with the depreciated replacement cost method producing $2,077,301 (mentioned previously) and the reproduction cost method producing $2,691,225. The relativity of net replacement cost to land value in each method highlights the issues in the cost approach concerning mixing concepts of cost and value, with the example also illustrating the impact of the building cost rate and depreciation period chosen on the output of the cost method. The relativity of net replacement cost to land value also raises issues of highest and best use and development potential, which are conveniently disregarded in the example.

9.4.4 Summation cost method of valuation (IVS)

IVS105 (IVSC, 2021) notes that the key steps in the summation cost method are:

- value each of the component assets that are part of the subject asset using the appropriate valuation approaches and methods; and
- add the value of the component assets together to reach the value of the subject asset (70.9).

As the summation cost method comprises the summing of outputs of the application of other valuation approaches and methods, an example may be as follows:

Value of component asset A by comparative method	$1,000,000
Value of component asset B by DCF method	$1,500,000
Value of component asset C by reproduction cost method	$2,500,000
Value of subject asset	$5,000,000

9.4.5 Residual or hypothetical development method of valuation

One of the five traditional methods of valuation, the residual method or hypothetical development method of valuation, may be used to determine value when a property has development or redevelopment potential and hence latent value. The method may be applied to assess the value of land for development purposes or the value of a property with redevelopment or refurbishment potential.

In the context of development property, IVS410 (IVSC, 2021) notes that the market approach and the residual method are the two main valuation alternatives (40.1). The residual method, which is a hybrid of the market approach, the income approach and the cost approach, is described as follows:

> This is based on the completed "gross development value" and the deduction of development costs and the developer's return to arrive at the residual value of the development property.
>
> (IVS410, 40.1(b))

The residual method is notoriously sensitive to relatively small changes in input variables and IVS410, 20.5 requires the valuer to highlight potentially disproportionate effects of possible changes in construction costs or end value or profitability and requires the provision of separate sensitivity analyses for each significant factor (90.2). Envisaging a dynamic or cash flow hypothetical development model, key input variables are listed in IVS410, 90.6 as follows (with further direction on the determination of each given in the paragraphs shown in parentheses):

- completed property value (90.7–90.14 and 100.1–100.2);
- construction costs (90.15–90.22);
- consultants fees (90.23);
- marketing costs (90.24);
- timetable (90.25–90.27);
- finance costs (90.28);
- development profit (90.29–90.34); and
- discount rate (90.35–90.36),

though smaller valuations may be undertaken using a static model (being the residual method, a point-in-time model) such that a discount rate would not be required.

9.4.5.1 Static approach

The residual method or hypothetical development method may be static (being a single period statement of the present value of each input) or dynamic (being a multi-period cash flow approach) (9.4.5.2). The critical difference between the static and dynamic approaches concerns the cost of finance, with the static approach relying on heuristic assumptions while the dynamic approach sets out the cash flow in periods over the development, allowing a more accurate assessment of the cost of finance and resulting amount available for land acquisition.

9.4.5.1.1 OUTLINE OF EXAMPLE

You are instructed to assess the market value of a suburban development site of 1,000 sqm upon which may be constructed an office building with a 3,000 sqm gross floor area and a net internal area of 2,700 sqm.

Your accumulation, analysis, adjustment and application of comparable market rentals in the suburban office property sub-market indicate a current market rental value of $500 psm pa to be applicable to the subject property, with the tenant paying all outgoings.

Your accumulation, analysis, adjustment and application of comparable sales transactions and discussions with investors active in the suburban office sub-market lead you to conclude that a capitalisation rate of 7.5% is applicable to the subject property.

Construction costs for a suburban office building are $2,750 psm, according to Rawlinsons (2023), and the construction period is estimated to be two years, with the following estimates of costs and fees:

- sale costs at $250,000;
- site preparation costs at $50,000;
- external works at $100,000;
- professional fees at 10% of building costs;
- contingency allowance at 10%;
- finance available at an interest rate of 5%pa;

- a void period of 6 months to find a tenant and/or purchaser;
- letting agent's fees at 10% of market rental;
- letting legal fees at 5% of market rental; and
- purchase costs at 6.5%,

with a developer anticipated to seek a profit margin of 20% on development costs.

9.4.5.1.2 OUTLINE OF STATIC RESIDUAL METHOD OR HYPOTHETICAL DEVELOPMENT METHOD OF VALUATION

Following Wyatt (2023), the static residual method or hypothetical development method may be calculated as follows:

	Development Value:			
	Net internal area sqm	2,700 sqm		
x	Market rental $psm pa	$500 psm pa		
=	Estimated rental value		$1,350,000	
x	Net initial yield or capitalisation rate	7.5%	YP 13.3334	
=	Gross development value before sale costs			$18,000,000
-	Sale costs		$250,000	
=	Net development value after sale costs			$17,750,000
	Development costs:			
	Site preparation		$50,000	
+	Building costs—$psm x gross internal area	3,000 sqm x $2,750 psm	$8,250,000	
+	External works		$100,000	
+	Professional fees—% building costs and external	10%	$835,000	
+	Contingency allowance—% building costs	10%	$825,000	
+	Finance on costs and fees for half building period of 2 years	5%pa	$461,750	
+	Finance on costs and finance for void period of 6 months	5%pa	$242,419	
+	Letting agents fees—% market rental	10%	$135,000	
+	Letting legal fees—% market rental	5%	$67,500	
=	Development costs			$10,966,669
+	Developer's profit on development costs—%	20%		$2,193,334
=	Total development costs			$13,160,003
	Net development value less total development costs:			$4,589,997

Land costs:

-	Developer's profit on land costs—%	20%	($764,999)	$3,824,998
-	Finance on land costs over total development period	PV 5% over 2 years (0.9070)	($355,725)	
=	Residual land value before purchase costs			$3,469,273
-	Purchase costs	6.5%	($211,740)	
=	**Residual land value after purchase costs**			$3,257,533

The static approach to the residual method of valuation indicates that the developer could pay up to $3.25 million for the development site and make a 20% development profit if all the estimated inputs to the valuation prove to be correct.

The static approach to the residual method of valuation indicates a land value of approximately $3,250 psm for a suburban site zoned for office development. The developer would be likely to check this valuation by also undertaking a valuation using the comparative method prior to commencing negotiations with the vendor of the development site.

9.4.5.2 Dynamic or cash flow approach

The residual method or hypothetical development method may be static (being a single period statement of the present value of each input) (9.4.5.1) or dynamic (being a multi-period cash flow approach). The critical difference between the static and dynamic approaches concerns the cost of finance, with the static approach relying on heuristic assumptions while the dynamic approach sets out the cash flow in periods over the development, allowing a more accurate assessment of the cost of finance and resulting amount available for land acquisition.

9.4.5.2.1 OUTLINE OF EXAMPLE

The example set out in section 9.4.5.1.1 for the static method is used again for the dynamic cash flow hypothetical development method, but with finance available at an interest rate of 1.25% per quarter.

9.4.5.2.2 OUTLINE OF DYNAMIC CASH FLOW RESIDUAL OR HYPOTHETICAL DEVELOPMENT METHOD OF VALUATION

Following Wyatt (2023), the dynamic cash flow hypothetical development method may be calculated as follows:

- the development period of two years is modelled as eight quarters;
- the net development value and development costs are spread over the eight quarters to reflect their likely level of being incurred, summed to a net cash flow before finance per quarter; and
- the rolling cost of finance is modelled separately, being cumulative over the eight quarters,

as shown in Table 9.1.

Table 9.1 Dynamic cash flow hypothetical development method

1	A	B	C	D	E	F	G	H	I	J	K	L	M
2													
3				**Total**	**0**	**1**	**2**	**3**	**4**	**5**	**6**	**7**	**8**
4	**Net development value after sale costs**			$17,750,000									$17,750,000
5													
6	**Development costs**												
7	Land purchase			-$3,257,533	-$3,257,533								
8	Land purchase costs			-$211,740	-$211,740								
9	Site preparation			-$50,000	-$50,000								
10	Building costs			-$8,250,000			-$1,237,500	-$1,650,000	-$1,650,000	-$1,650,000	-$1,237,500	-$825,000	
11	External costs			-$100,000			-$50,000	-$50,000					
12	Professional fees			-$835,000			-$600,000	-$235,000					
13	Contingency allowance			-$825,000				-$206,250	-$206,250	-$206,250	-$206,250		
14	Letting agents fee			-$135,000									-$135,000
15	Letting legal fee			-$67,500									-$67,500
16	Developers profit			-$2,958,333									-$2,958,333
17	Net cash flow before finance				-$3,519,273	$0	-$1,887,500	-$2,141,250	-$1,856,250	-$1,856,250	-$1,443,750	-$825,000	$14,589,167
18													
19	**Finance**												
20	Opening balance					-$3,519,273	-$3,563,264	-$5,495,304	-$7,705,244	-$9,657,809	-$11,634,780	-$13,223,964	-$14,214,262
21	Interest at 1.25% per qtr					-$43,991	-$44,541	-$68,691	-$96,316	-$120,723	-$145,435	-$165,300	-$358,199
22	Closing balance				-$3,519,273	-$3,563,264	-$5,495,304	-$7,705,244	-$9,657,809	-$11,634,780	-$13,223,964	-$14,214,262	$16,706
23													

Source: Author

Readers will note that a positive balance of $16,706 may be found in cell M22, which is the amount by which the net development value exceeds development costs plus the cost of finance. While this positive balance is impacted by the use of an interest rate of 1.25% per quarter rather than 5%pa, the key influence is the impact of the timing of cash flows in the dynamic cash flow approach compared to the heuristic assumptions of the static approach concerning:

- finance on costs and fees for half building period;
- finance on costs and finance for void period; and
- finance on land costs over total development period.

Accordingly, the dynamic approach suggests that the developer could pay an amount greater than $3.25 million for the development site and still make a 20% development profit if all the estimated inputs to the valuation prove to be correct.

Currently, in Australia, a dynamic cash flow hypothetical development valuation would most likely be prepared using a sophisticated software package available through providers such as Forbury, ARGUS, CoStar and Yardi rather than in an Excel spreadsheet, allowing for very prescriptive modelling of the timing of cash flows and the finance costs arising.

9.4.6 *Summary—cost methods of valuation*

The variations of the replacement cost method, the reproduction cost method, the IVSC summation method and the residual or hypothetical development method of valuation all focus attention not only on the uncomfortable relationship between notions of cost and notions of value within a valuation method but also on the significant impact on assessments of value that may arise from relatively minor changes to input variables, reinforcing the need for great care to be taken by the valuer.

9.5 Summary and conclusions

Chapter 1 outlined the structure of the property asset class, examining the traditional characteristics of property (including heterogeneity, durability, illiquidity and so forth) and the traditional risks of property (including location, building, tenant risk and so forth) through the lenses of systematic, unsystematic and idiosyncratic risk, aligning property valuation with capital market theory.

Chapter 2 considered the evolution of property valuation in Australia, the role of the valuer and the diverse activities of the valuation profession, followed by a detailed examination of the inter-acting framework provided by valuation standards and ethical standards promulgated by IVSC, RICS and API.

Chapter 3 explored concepts of value and normative and positive definitions of value, dissecting the International Valuation Standards' definition of market value with a reconciliation to the concept of market value in *Spencer v Commonwealth* (1907) and examining such contemporary valuation issues as valuation lag, variance, accuracy, negligence and valuer rotation.

Chapter 4 introduced International Financial Reporting Standards and International Accounting Standards with a detailed examination of the key provisions of International Valuation Standards, the RICS Red Book and API guidance papers that impact on valuation practice in Australia.

Chapter 5 outlined conceptual approaches to the valuation process with a review of the self-supporting process of instructing, undertaking and reporting valuations under the International Valuation Standards, RICS Red Book and API guidance papers, examining how this process inter-relates to the choice of valuation approach, valuation method and the purpose of the valuation.

Chapter 6 addressed the market approach to valuation through the comparative method of valuation, including the key steps of accumulation, analysis, adjustment and application of comparable sales evidence to the subject property being valued, with an example.

Chapter 7 considered the income approach to valuation addressed through the static methods of the capitalisation of income and the profits methods of valuation, including an examination of the key inputs for each method with examples and a consideration of both marriage value and the surrender and renewal of leases.

Chapter 8 considered the income approach to valuation addressed through the dynamic method of the discounted cash flow method of valuation, including an examination of the key inputs and a focus on the derivation of the discount rate and consideration of the role of sensitivity and scenario analysis, with examples.

This chapter considered the cost approach to valuation addressed through the replacement cost, reproduction cost, summation and residual or hypothetical development methods of valuation.

The variations of the replacement cost method, the reproduction cost method, the IVSC summation method and the residual or hypothetical development method of valuation all focus attention on the uncomfortable relationship between notions of cost and notions of value within a valuation method. The intermingling of concepts of cost and concepts of value is beset by challenges, with cost being a production-related concept and value being an exchange or use-related concept (Wyatt, 2023). Mixing notions of cost and notions of value is akin to trying to mix oil and water. Notions of cost and notions of value do not sit well together, and the result is a curious expression that is neither a pure expression of value nor a pure expression of cost.

As the examples for replacement cost and reproduction cost illustrated, the same asset may have two different values based on two different sets of assumptions, which reinforces the need for the valuer and the client to agree on the scope of works and on exactly what is required. Clearly establishing with the client what is required before the valuation task is undertaken will minimise risk for the valuer and maximise satisfaction for the client.

As with many methods of valuation, the cost methods risk major changes to the assessment of value from minor changes to input variables, being very sensitive to key input variables such as building cost and depreciation. Further, the number of input variables in the various cost methods increases the risk arising from the cumulative impact of small changes to a large number of variables, reinforcing the need for great care to be taken by the valuer.

The philosophical and practical challenges arising from the cost methods make the cost approach a valuation approach of last resort. Strong preference should always be given to market-sourced inputs to the valuation process, rendering market approaches and income approaches to valuation preferable for application whenever possible.

The next and final chapter will conclude the book with a consideration of future perspectives, including the role of uncertainty, data, automated valuation models, artificial intelligence, optionality, environmental, social and governance issues, retail and office space use and indigenous issues.

References

API (2021) *ANZVGP104 valuations for insurance purposes*, Australian Property Institute, Deakin.

Baum, A, Mackmin, D and Nunnington, N (2018) *The income approach to property valuation*, Routledge, Abingdon.

Dunsford, C, Klenke, M and Grant, A (2022) 'Valuation for insurance purposes', in Parker, D (Ed) *Principles and practice of property valuation in Australia*, Routledge, Abingdon.

Isaac, D and O'Leary, J (2012) *Property valuation principles*, Palgrave Macmillan, Basingstoke.

IVSC (2012) *TIP2—the cost approach to tangible assets*, International Valuation Standards Council, London.

IVSC (2021) *International valuation standards*, International Valuation Standards Council, London.

Millington, A (2000) *An introduction to property valuation*, Routledge, Abingdon.

Rawlinsons (2023) *The handbook*, 41st edition, Rawlinsons, Perth.

RICS (2019) *RICS professional standard—valuation of development property*, Royal Institution of Chartered Surveyors, London.

RICS (2021) *RICS valuation—global standards*, Royal Institution of Chartered Surveyors, London.

Rost, RO and Collins, HG (1990) *Land valuation and compensation in Australia*, Australian Institute of Valuers and Land Administrators, Deakin.

Smithson, A (1997) 'Valuation of residential property', in Westwood, R (Ed) *Valuation principles and practice*, Australian Institute of Valuers and Land Economists, Deakin.

Whipple, RTM (2006) *Property valuation and analysis*, Lawbook Co, Sydney.

Wyatt, P (2023) *Property valuation*, Wiley Blackwell, Chichester.

10   Future perspectives

10.1 Introduction

This book is an introduction to the fundamentals of property valuation, outlining the principal methods of property valuation in Australia within the context of International Valuation Standards, bridging the gap between traditional property valuation methods and the modern era of global valuation governance.

Chapter 1 outlined the structure of the property asset class, examining the traditional characteristics of property (including heterogeneity, durability, illiquidity and so forth) and the traditional risks of property (including location, building, tenant risk and so forth) through the lenses of systematic, unsystematic and idiosyncratic risk, so aligning property valuation with capital market theory.

Chapter 2 considered the evolution of property valuation in Australia, the role of the valuer and the diverse activities of the valuation profession, followed by a detailed examination of the inter-acting framework provided by valuation standards and ethical standards promulgated by IVSC, RICS and API.

Chapter 3 explored concepts of value and normative and positive definitions of value, dissecting the International Valuation Standards' definition of market value with a reconciliation to the concept of market value in *Spencer v Commonwealth* (1907) and examining such contemporary valuation issues as valuation lag, variance, accuracy, negligence and valuer rotation.

Chapter 4 introduced International Financial Reporting Standards and International Accounting Standards with a detailed examination of the key provisions of International Valuation Standards, the RICS Red Book and API guidance papers that impact on valuation practice in Australia.

Chapter 5 outlined conceptual approaches to the valuation process with a review of the self-supporting process of instructing, undertaking and reporting valuations under the International Valuation Standards, RICS Red Book and API guidance papers, examining how this process inter-relates to the choice of valuation approach, valuation method and the purpose of the valuation.

Chapter 6 addressed the market approach to valuation through the comparative method of valuation, including the key steps of accumulation, analysis, adjustment and application of comparable sales evidence to the subject property being valued, with an example.

Chapter 7 considered the income approach to valuation addressed through the static methods of the capitalisation of income and the profits methods of valuation, including an examination of the key inputs for each method with examples and a consideration of both marriage value and the surrender and renewal of leases.

DOI: 10.1201/9781003397922-10

Chapter 8 considered the income approach to valuation addressed through the dynamic method of the discounted cash flow method of valuation, including an examination of the key inputs and a focus on the derivation of the discount rate and consideration of the role of sensitivity and scenario analysis, with examples.

Chapter 9 considered the cost approach to valuation addressed through the replacement cost, reproduction cost, summation and residual or hypothetical development methods of valuation.

This chapter concludes the book with a consideration of future perspectives, including the role of uncertainty, data, automated valuation models, artificial intelligence, optionality, environmental, social and governance issues, retail and office space use and indigenous issues.

This book is based on those standards and guidance documents published in IVSC (2021) and RICS (2021) and on the API website (accessed January to May 2023). Given their nature, standards and guidance documents are dynamic, being regularly updated and with the most recently published versions replacing previously published versions. Accordingly, readers should not rely on this book as a current statement of a standard or guidance document and should visit www.ivsc.org, www.rics.org and/or www.api.org.au to find the most recent version.

As an introductory textbook on property valuation methods in Australia, this book is a companion to Australia's leading advanced valuation textbook, *Principles and Practice of Property Valuation in Australia,* edited by the same author and also published by Routledge, which is a deeper analysis of key principles underlying property valuation and current techniques and issues in the practice of property valuation for major sectors of the Australian property market.

Concluding the book, this chapter will now consider several key future perspectives impacting the valuation process and the valuation profession, including:

- addressing uncertainty in the valuation process;
- the role of data, automated valuation models and artificial intelligence;
- the emergence of optionality;
- the impact of environmental, social and governance issues on valuation;
- value impacts of structural change in retail and office space use;
- the growing significance of indigenous issues in valuation practice; and
- the future of the valuation profession.

10.2 Uncertainty

Uncertainty has traditionally been recognised as inherent in the valuation process, such as in the income method of valuation, where the capitalisation rate can be varied for uncertainty, in the residual method of valuation for development purposes, where the various input variables can be varied for uncertainty or the discounted cash flow method of valuation for investment or development purposes where each variable can be varied to reflect uncertainty.

Further reflection of uncertainty in the valuation process was traditionally recommended by textbooks to be handled through the use of sensitivity analysis, scenario analysis and probability analysis. Sensitivity analysis investigates the impact of uncertainty on key input variables by examining the degree of change in the valuation caused by a change in one or more of the key input variables (Wyatt, 2023). By identifying the key variables in a valuation and then making minor changes to each progressively and observing the sensitivity of the resulting valuation, the valuer can gain an understanding of which variables are the greatest contributors to uncertainty and hence to volatility in value. Baum et al. (2018) recommend the use of *star diagrams* to analyse relative sensitivity, mapping onto a single-line chart the variations in value against changes in specific variables and so providing a quick and easy way to see to which variables the valuation is most sensitive.

Scenario analysis examines the value impact of changes to several inputs at the same time (Wyatt, 2023). Traditionally, combinations of input variables will be selected to represent pessimistic, most likely and optimistic scenarios and the impact on the resultant values observed. The benefit of scenario analysis is that it combines multiple input variables, whereas sensitivity analysis addresses variation in a single variable, allowing the valuer to model and consider combination effects. Probability analysis takes scenario analysis a step further by attaching probabilities of occurrence to each scenario, such as 40% probability or likelihood of the most likely scenario, 30% probability or likelihood for the pessimistic scenario and 30% probability or likelihood for the optimistic scenario from which a weighted average or expected outcome can be calculated. At a more sophisticated level, probabilities may be attached to individual input variables however, caution should be exercised as there may be little evidence upon which to base such assessments.

The reflection of uncertainty in valuation took a major step forward with the publication of *The uncertainty of valuation* by French and Gabrielli (2004), which identified the problem that valuation models are based on comparable information, relying on single inputs that are not probability-driven while uncertainty is probability driven. Having considered the issues underlying uncertainty in valuations, the authors suggest a probability-based model using *Crystal Ball* software to address the shortcomings in current valuation models.

Following on from the stock market crash of 1987, which was the first post-Second World War global contagion event, the global financial crisis of 2007–2009 focused the valuation professional bodies on uncertainty with a further focus engendered by the COVID pandemic of 2020–2023. Each of these global contagion events demonstrated the interconnectedness of the world's equity, debt and property markets, creating periods of great uncertainty both internationally and across the Australian property markets, often with periods of little or no market sales activity in certain property sectors and therefore, little or no evidence on which to base property valuations.

In the aftermath of the global financial crisis and the COVID pandemic, IVSC, RICS and API each issued guidance on uncertainty, which will be considered, respectively, in what follows.

10.2.1 IVSC TIP4—*valuation uncertainty*

In 2013, IVSC issued Technical Information Paper 4 (TIP4), which addresses valuation uncertainty (IVSC, 2013a). While a TIP provides guidance, it does not mandate or prescribe the use of a particular approach with the intent being to provide information to assist an experienced valuer in deciding which is the most appropriate course of action (IVSC, 2013a).

TIP4 is confined to valuation uncertainty arising in valuations on the basis of market value as defined in the IVS Framework or fair value as defined in IFRS13, particularly financial reporting valuations. TIP4 defines valuation uncertainty as follows:

> *The possibility that the estimated value may differ from the price that could be obtained in a transfer of the subject asset or liability taking place on the valuation date on the same terms and in the same market*

(IVSC, 2013a, page 2)

and:

> *valuation uncertainty is concerned only with uncertainties that arise as part of the process of estimating value on a specific date.*

(IVSC, 2013a, page 4)

TIP4 distinguishes valuation uncertainty from risk, with risk being the exposure that the owner of an asset has to potential future losses caused by factors affecting the asset itself or the market in which it trades, such as:

- *a reduction in market prices after the date of acquisition or valuation;*
- *a deterioration in the security of projected future income;*
- *a loss of liquidity compared with other assets;*
- *costs for maintaining or developing an asset being higher than currently anticipated; (and)*
- *the rate of an asset's technical or physical obsolescence being higher than currently antici-pated* (IVSC, 2013a, page 3),

with such risks recognised by informed buyers and reflected in market prices. Further, such risk is capable of quantification by applying statistical techniques to measure historic price movements or through determination of the discount rate for use in a valuation.

The causes of valuation uncertainty fall into three broad categories which are not mutually exclusive, often being interdependent and correlated:

- market disruption—such as a sudden economic or political crisis that causes valuation uncertainty, manifesting through panic buying or selling or a loss of liquidity due to an absence of transactions. (Examples in TIP4 include the collapse of a global financial firm or a severe earthquake that destroys large parts of a CBD). Thus, there is potential for valuation inputs to be available up to the date of the crisis but with limited relevance for valuation dates at or after the date of the crisis and for the impact of the crisis on market participants and prices not being known in the immediate aftermath creating unquantifiable uncertainty;
- input availability—a lack of relevant input data will cause valuation uncertainty, which may arise due to market disruption or due to an asset being illiquid and rarely traded in a market. Where there is a lack of input data, valuers may need to extrapolate inputs from directly observable prices for similar assets or rely on unobservable inputs developed from the best information available;
- choice of method of model—for many asset types, more than one method or model may be commonly used to estimate value, with IVS102 providing for the use of more than one valuation approach or method. However, where such methods or models do not produce the same outcome, following analysis and reconciliation, the selection of the most appropriate method may itself be a source of valuation uncertainty (IVSC, 2013a).

IVS103 requires uncertainty to be disclosed in a valuation report when it is material, with materiality to be considered from two interrelated aspects being whether the potential impact on the valuation figure is significant and whether it is of relevance to an intended user of the valuation. TIP4 suggests consideration of the following to determine materiality:

- whether the valuation is required for internal purposes by the commissioning party or whether it will be disclosed to and relied upon by third parties with the threshold of materiality likely to be lower if the valuation is to be relied on by third parties;
- the extent to which the value of a total portfolio is affected if the valuation uncertainty affects only certain assets within the portfolio, which may involve considering correlation and inter-dependence between the individual assets;
- whether the cause of the uncertainty was known to the commissioning party or to a third party relying on it when the valuation was commissioned; or

- whether the effect of the uncertainty could expose the commissioning party or a third party relying on the valuation to a significant risk of loss (IVSC, 2013a, pages 7–8).

TIP4 suggests a useful test for considering the materiality of valuation uncertainty to be whether failure to disclose the uncertainty in the report would lead a reasonable person to take action in reliance on the reported valuation that they may not have taken if the uncertainty had been disclosed (IVSC, 2013a, page 8).

Where material, valuation uncertainty should be disclosed qualitatively in the valuation report, including an explanation of the source of the uncertainty and the effect it has on the market and/or valuation process. TIP4 cautions that quantitative measures of valuation uncertainty, if provided in addition to qualitative statements, may imply a false precision with the provision of a range of values not generally recommended (IVSC, 2013a, pages 8–9).

10.2.2 RICS VPGA10—matters that may give rise to material valuation uncertainty

The RICS Red Book (RICS, 2021) addresses valuation uncertainty in VPGA10 *Matters that may give rise to material valuation uncertainty* which is advisory, not mandatory, providing additional commentary on matters that may give rise to material valuation uncertainty in accordance with VPS3 paragraph 2.1(o), which requires that a valuation report must provide commentary on any material uncertainty in relation to a valuation where it is essential to ensure clarity on the part of the valuation user.

VPGA10 provides examples of the three most common circumstances in which material valuation uncertainty may arise:

- where the asset has very particular characteristics (being very unusual or even unique) that make it difficult for the valuer to form an opinion of the likely value regardless of the approach or method used, with quantification highly dependent on special assumptions made;
- where the information available to the valuer is limited or restricted, and the matter cannot be sufficiently addressed by adopting one or more reasonable assumptions; or
- market disruption by unique factors such as unforeseen financial, macro-economic, legal, political or natural events proximate to the date of valuation leading to a reduced level of certainty due to inconsistent or absent empirical data or unprecedented circumstances (RICS, 2021, page 134).

Concerning reporting, VPGA10 notes the overriding requirement that a valuation report must not be misleading or create a false impression, with the valuer expressly drawing attention to and commenting on any issue resulting in material uncertainty in the valuation at the specified valuation date. Where material valuation uncertainty exists, it will normally be expressed in qualitative terms, indicating the valuer's confidence in the valuation opinion offered using a suitable form of words (RICS, 2021).

Significantly, VPGA10 states:

> In most cases it is either inappropriate or impractical to reflect material uncertainty in the valuation figure quantitatively, and indeed any attempt to do so might well seem contradictory
>
> (Page 135)

while a sensitivity analysis may be appropriate in *some limited circumstances* for illustration, accompanied by a suitable explanatory comment (RICS, 2021, para 3.3).

VPGA10 notes that it would normally be acceptable for a valuation report to have a standard caveat to deal with material valuation uncertainty, with the expression of a range of values *not good practice* unless specifically requested (RICS, 2021).

10.2.3 *API ANZVGP110—Considerations when forming an opinion of value when there is a shortage of market transactions*

ANZVGP110 *Considerations when forming an opinion of value when there is a shortage of market transactions* addresses valuation uncertainty in the context of limited comparable sales evidence generally rather than following a significant event. The guidance paper is not mandatory and aims to provide information on appropriate practices and their application to assist members in exercising judgment with a view to best practice and competent professional practice (API, 2021).

Interestingly, ANZVGP110 is founded on the premise that primary regard should be given to comparable sales evidence from the period prior to the period of limited comparable sales arising. Accordingly, the focus is on the adjustment of historic comparable sales in the light of the prevailing environment as of the date of valuation.

ANZVGP110 provides a non-exhaustive list of information sources that may assist valuers in forming an opinion of adjustments that may be necessary when applying prior transactional evidence in relation to the prevailing market as at the date of valuation:

- prior transactions (empirical historical data)—which may provide a foundation, recognising that dated market transactions reflect market conditions at the time when prices may be higher or lower than current values;
- new mandatory codes and legislation—such as the leasing codes introduced by Government during the COVID pandemic, with valuers needing to understand the impact of the code on the market in which the property is assumed to transact;
- market intelligence from market participants—following an event that creates significant market uncertainty, the valuer should converse with a wide range of market participants to understand the impact on the market;
- market transactional data—while comparable sales evidence may be limited, the valuer should consider information about market trends such as the amount of stock on the market, median prices and transaction volumes, marketing and selling periods and listing volumes to assist with understanding market conditions as at the valuation date;
- unsettled market transactions—including transactions that have not yet settled or that failed to settle may add to the understanding of the prevailing market as at the date of valuation;
- observations from previous crisis events—such as bushfires, earthquakes, pandemics and the global financial crisis may provide indicators of how a market recovers;
- observations of the stock market—announcements to the Stock Exchange by property holding entities can be a valuable source of information about market conditions in certain sectors; and
- market research from reputable sources—such as credible market research from reputable researchers and/or organisations that may provide input for the valuer to consider (API, 2021).

ANZVGP110 identifies the following for consideration by the valuer with appropriate commentary when preparing a valuation report in a situation where there is a shortage of market transactions (API, 2021):

- valuation methodology—including a detailed explanation of why the methodology was adopted;

- disclosure of significant market uncertainty—including a statement whether this results in a more subjective opinion of value or significant valuation uncertainty, possibly supported by a sensitivity analysis;
- sources of valuation inputs—explanation of the methodology adopted, including the source of valuation inputs;
- risk analysis—valuers should reflect changing conditions in risk ratings and commentary, possibly including a SWOT analysis, with analysis and reporting of risk being critical issues in the valuation. (It should be noted that ANZVGP110 does not distinguish between risk and uncertainty, unlike IVSC TIP4.);
- selling methods and periods—if the subject property is impacted, such as the impact on residential selling methods and periods during the COVID pandemic;
- leased property considerations—such as the impact of economic uncertainty on tenancy risk in leased property; and
- valuation sensitivity analysis—with ANZVGP110 noting:

There may be circumstances where the provision of a sensitivity analysis indicating a range of values would be of assistance. A single valuation must still be provided.

(API, 2021, 5.7)

10.2.4 Summary

Following consideration of the traditional valuation process responses to uncertainty through sensitivity analysis, scenario analysis and probability analysis, global contagion events, including the 1987 stock market crash, the 2007–2009 global financial crisis and the 2020–2023 COVID pandemic, were contended to demonstrate the interconnectedness of the world's equity, debt and property markets creating periods of great uncertainty both internationally and across the Australian property markets.

The responses of IVSC, RICS and API to such global contagion events were considered, with the respective guidance documents published offering a way for the valuer to think through the relevant issues impacting value without being caught up in the hysteria of the event and emphasising the importance of transparency and disclosure of material uncertainty.

10.3 Role of data, automated valuation models and artificial intelligence

The last two decades have seen an exponential rise in the availability and quality of property data, which is fundamental to the application of artificial intelligence and automated valuation models to property valuation.

By 2018, Baum et al. (2018) had identified two contemporary phases of property technology (*Prop Tech*) evolution, with *Prop Tech 1.0* emanating from the dot com boom of the late 1990s and *Prop Tech 2.0* emerging in the later 2010s.

Prop Tech 1 created a large number of information and analytical businesses, which were then weakened by over-capacity, attacked by market leaders and subsequently swallowed by survivors such as Co-Star and Argus (Baum et al., 2018). In an Australian context, Cougar and Estate Master were each developed by Australian entrepreneurs, gained widespread market use in Australia, and were then swallowed by global market leaders.

Prop Tech 2 is still evolving with extremely intelligent, often very young, entrepreneurs backed by billions of dollars of expert investment working extremely hard to change the way real estate is traded, used and operated, with many failing and losing a lot of money but some surviving successfully and having a radical impact on what is a slow-moving, conservative industry Baum et al. (2018). Baum et al. (2018) note that *it would be surprising, to say the least, if this burst of activity . . . does not lead to significant change in the process of valuation* (page 338).

Automated valuation models seek to relate data representing the attributes of comparable properties to their sale prices in order to forecast the likely sale price of a subject property. This is most easily understood in the context of residential property, where the number of bedrooms, bathrooms, garages and so forth may be used as a guide to the sale price. Automated valuation models are most effective for homogenous markets and so suit, for example, broad acre residential subdivisions or rows of terrace houses but are less suitable for heterogenous markets such as residential property with water views or commercial, retail and industrial property.

Automated valuation models based on multiple regression analysis for residential property have been taught in valuation courses at the world's leading universities for over 40 years. Over the last two decades, the availability and quality of residential property data has increased exponentially, and the number of software houses and major lenders developing and using automated valuation models has also increased exponentially.

While the valuation profession may currently choose to spend its time debating the semantics of whether an automated valuation model is really a valuation, the major lender client base—seeking faster, cheaper forms of risk management for residential mortgage lending—is unlikely to care as they continue to increase their use of automated valuation models.

It is no longer a case of considering when the use of automated valuation models will become widespread because it already is, but how quickly the valuation profession can adapt to move from dependence on residential mortgage valuation work to building successful businesses based on other forms of valuation services.

Artificial intelligence is starting to have a major impact on the world of business, with the Australian financial press, at the time of writing, obsessed with the implications of *ChatGPT* for revolutionising the way business is done. While acknowledging the credibility limitations of Wikipedia, the following provides a succinct summary of artificial intelligence as expressed through *ChatGPT*:

> **ChatGPT** *is an artificial intelligence (AI) chatbot developed by OpenAI and released in November 2022. The "Chat" in the name is a reference to it being a chatbot, and the "GPT" stands for generative pre-trained transformer—a type of large language model (LLM). ChatGPT is based upon OpenAI's GPT-3.5 and GPT-4 foundational GPT models, and has been fine-tuned (an approach to transfer learning) for conversational applications using both supervised and reinforcement learning techniques.*

> *ChatGPT launched as a prototype on November 30, 2022, and garnered attention for its detailed responses and articulate answers across many domains of knowledge. Its propensity to confidently provide factually incorrect responses has been identified as a significant drawback. In 2023, following the release of ChatGPT, OpenAI's valuation was estimated at US$29 billion. The advent of the chatbot has increased competition within the space, accelerating the release of Google's chatbot Bard (based initially on LaMDA and then PaLM), and Meta's foundation model LLaMA, from which chatbots are being developed by others.*

> (Source: https://en.wikipedia.org/wiki/ChatGPT, downloaded 23 May 2023)

Baum et al. (2018) consider artificial intelligence in the context of the most recent iteration of automated valuation models, noting that it *will probably be successful in modelling house prices through the intelligent, real-time re-estimation of several simultaneous regression models being supplied with a continuous feed of house price data* (page 338). The authors further note the US product, CityBldr (www.citybldr.com), as an application of artificial intelligence gaining acceptance which allows users to enter their property information and perform an online highest and best use appraisal of their property to check if it has development or redevelopment potential.

The emergence of artificial intelligence provides the Australian valuation profession with an exciting opportunity to plan for its future by identifying those valuation services most at risk and diversifying their business model to embrace other services less at risk. Central to the successful application of artificial intelligence to property valuation is the role of judgment and the importance of local knowledge. Both of these factors may be considered through the example of a residential property with water views where large quantities of high-quality data in an artificial intelligence application may be unlikely to usurp the role of valuer judgment on the impact of view on value and the valuer's local knowledge of the comparable properties' relative views, aspect and accessibility.

10.4 Optionality

Previous editions of IVS included option pricing models as a valuation method falling under the income approach (IVSC, 2013b, para 60, page 24). While the current IVS do not include option pricing models, nascent academic research internationally has been considering the possibility of applying option pricing models and optionality to the valuation process.

Option pricing theory is based on the seminal works of Black and Scholes (1973) and Merton (1973), with subsequent development by others. Significantly, options provide a right but not an obligation to exercise, highlighting the importance of a right in the valuation process. Option pricing models conceptually use a range of variables, such as current market price, strike price, volatility, interest rate and time to expiration, to theoretically value an option contract. From a property valuation perspective, the interplay of current prices, the right to gain or lose from identified variables, risk and time to derive value offers potential for application to investment property.

Optionality is a wider concept of viewing each contributor in the investment property valuation thought process (such as location, tenant, building, etc.) as a right that has a positive or negative value through the lens of its risk contribution to the capitalisation rate or discount rate, with a particular focus on the role of idiosyncratic risk within the risk premium. Optionality was conceptually discussed at a landmark RICS Foundation Global Symposium in early 2012 (*Real Options: The Future of Property Investment and Property Valuation?* RICS Foundation and University of South Australia, Adelaide, 18–20 January 2012) facilitated by the author. Themes in the subsequent publication of their keynote conference paper (Geltner and De Neufville 2012) were further developed in their book (Geltner and De Neufville, 2018):

> the next major leap in real estate thought leadership, being optionality in real estate . . . a new way to conceptualise real estate as a bundle of opportunities with positive or negative contributions to value that can be combined to optimise value to an individual party or to a market.
>
> (Parker in Geltner and De Neufville, 2018, page xiii)

Research into the conceptualisation of a valuation methodology that reflects optionality remains at a nascent stage, with considerable development required before a methodology can be proposed for consideration by the valuation profession. Even after the proposition of a methodology, the adoption of optionality in everyday valuation practice will still be some way off because, as Parker (2016) notes:

> *Generally, with new methods of valuation and as was observed with the development and adoption of discounted cash flow as a valuation method, there is a period of approximately 20 years between development of a method by academia and adoption of a method by practitioners.*

(page 105)

10.5 Environmental, social and governance issues

Environmental, social and governance issues (ESG) are an increasing focus for business generally and may be expected, over time, to impact the property industry and the property market and, thus, the valuation process.

As businesses develop an ESG framework to assess the impact of their business practices and performance on various sustainability and ethical issues, the role of their property holdings within their ESG framework may come into focus.

Environmental issues may include energy usage and efficiency, waste reduction and carbon footprint reduction, which may each have an impact on property holdings. Social issues may include workplace health and safety and community engagement with governance issues, including risk management and accounting integrity and transparency, which may also have an impact on property holdings.

As a starting point to address ESG issues, very extensive research has been undertaken into sustainability and property, which is comprehensively addressed in Wilkinson et al. (2018), including several chapters of direct relevance to Australia:

- sustainable office retrofit in Melbourne (Wilkinson, 2018);
- valuing sustainability in commercial property in Australia (Warren-Myers, 2018);
- green REITs (Parker, 2018);
- sustainability and housing value in Victoria, Australia (Hurst and Wilkinson, 2018); and
- building energy efficiency certificates and commercial property: the Australian experience (Warren, 2018),

as well as chapters of direct relevance to valuation:

- international standards: key to unlocking the value of green buildings? (Elder, 2018); and
- building sustainability into valuation and worth (Sayce, 2018).

The sustainable characteristics (or lack of sustainable characteristics) of a property are now accepted to impact all relevant variables, including gross rent, outgoings, rental growth rates, outgoings growth rates, vacancy periods, capital expenditure allowances, capitalisation rates, discount rates and the reflection of risk—effectively every variable that contributes to an assessment of value. Sustainability cannot, therefore, be ignored in the valuation process, with the gap between the value of buildings with sustainable characteristics and those without continuing to widen. As Baum et al. (2018) succinctly note:

> *sustainability should be an inherent, integrated and consistent component of the income approach.*

(page 331)

10.6 Retail and office space use

The retail and office property investment markets are both facing structural changes that challenge the fundamental issue of how much space is required, where it is required and in what form it is required. Accordingly, the valuation of individual retail and office property investments needs to be within the context of the bigger picture unfolding in the retail and office property occupier markets.

While neighbourhood shopping centres focus on non-discretionary retailing, such as supermarkets, pharmacies, newsagents and food retailers, sub-regional shopping centres include a greater proportion of discretionary retailing, such as women's and men's fashion, jewellers and footwear retailers with regional and super-regional shopping centres also including department stores.

Over the last decade, the popularity of department stores has decreased and the popularity of cafes, restaurants, cinemas and experiential retailing has increased. Accordingly, some regional and super-regional shopping centres are in a process of transition from a department store-anchored retail offering to an experiential-anchored retail offering. However, the transition is slow and challenging, with some department stores having many years unexpired on their lease and a market not yet mature enough to absorb the total floor area reoffered as experiential retailing.

Further, given the nature of the physical-built envelope of a regional or super-regional shopping centre, construction changes are required to effect a transition which is both expensive and time-consuming to make, resulting in considerable uncertainty during the period of transition that affects value. While such an effect may manifest in rentals achievable, a greater impact may be expected within the risk premium in the discount rate or within the capitalisation rate.

Accordingly, the retail property investment sector is currently facing considerable structural change that will manifest in value, with the expertise of a specialist retail valuer required to make an informed comparative judgment between the subject property being valued and the relevant comparable sales within the framework of the stage of transition of each centre.

A significant impact of the COVID pandemic of 2020–2023 was the mass transition of office workers from working in an office to a work-from-home environment. In Australia, as the pandemic eased, a return to the office was not uniform across the country or across different age cohorts of office workers. At the time of writing, daily occupancy rates in office buildings globally have dropped from 80% before the pandemic to a current range of 20–70% (AICD, 2023). In Australia, occupancy rates are reported as highest in Brisbane at 70%, with Sydney at 55% and lowest in Melbourne at 35% (AICD, 2023). Further, millennials are proving far less inclined to return to working in the office and far more inclined to prefer to continue to work from home.

With the office sector having gone through a phase of businesses changing to open plan and agile working, together with the emergence of co-working, before the onset of the COVID pandemic, resulting in businesses generally leasing less office space per employee, the sector now faces further uncertainty as business try to determine if the work from home phase will continue or abate and whether they have sufficient office space or potentially too much office space.

This uncertainty has the greatest impact in the CBD office markets of the major capital cities as a question hangs over the actual level of demand for office space and hence the supportability of existing rents, the prospects for vacancy with potential impact on incentives, future rent and rental growth and the risk premium in the discount rate or within the capitalisation rate.

The physical nature of the built envelope of an office building means that part of it cannot be excised if demand falls but will remain vacant until a new tenant is found. Further, the development period required for the construction and letting of a new office building means that several are already underway and heading for completion, even though demand for office space may be faltering.

Accordingly, the office property investment sector is currently facing considerable structural change that will manifest in value, with the expertise of an experienced office valuer required to make an informed comparative judgment between the subject property being valued and the relevant comparable sales within any given Australian CBD office market.

10.7 Indigenous issues

Indigenous issues are an evolving and complex area of law that has significant implications for property valuation. The existence of native title and its impact on property valuation has evolved since the early 1990s following landmark court decisions, including *Mabo v Queensland* (No 2) (1992) 175 CLR 1, *Wik Peoples v Queensland* (1996) 187 CLR 1 and 3 *Western Australia v Ward* (2002) 213 CLR 1 (API, 2022). More recently, in the context of compulsory acquisition, compensation for cultural loss has emerged as an area of complexity for property valuation.

APGP402 *Native Title Matters* (API, 2022) provides a helpful overview of the issues arising in the valuation of native title land. APGP402 recognises the deep spiritual and cultural connection that First Nations People have to their land throughout Australia, focusing on native title as a form of property rights protected by law that are meaningful and need to be respected, providing the following overview:

Native title is the name given to the legal recognition of the rights that First Nations People hold with respect to their traditional lands and waters under their traditional laws and customs. The common law recognition of native title as a form of property, which is protected by the Australian Constitution, is consistent with any other property rights in Australia. Unlike any other forms of property, however, it does not derive from the Crown and exists independently. This means that native title rights pre-date the Australian legal system but are recognised and protected by Australian law.

Native title may exist irrespective of whether it has been formally recognised, but for all intents and purposes a native title claim needs to be registered with the National Native Title Tribunal (NNTT) or have been determined by the Federal Court (Court) before it will significantly affect other parties.

(API, 2022, page 1)

From a property valuation viewpoint, APGP402 identifies four aspects of native title that make it unique:

- it is exclusively held by First Nations People, and is inalienable (meaning it cannot be bought or sold). It can only legally be interfered with or affected in accordance with the NTA and often only by agreement with the native title holders;

- it can co-exist with certain other property rights (such as Pastoral Leases, mining leases, infrastructure easements and other non-exclusive forms of tenure) and can sometimes affect the validity of already co-existing property rights and can prevent the grant of additional property rights;
- it is recognised, not created, through Court processes and is separate to the Land Titles Office (LTO) system; and
- when recognised by the Court, the Court recognises it as a pre-existing right that has been in existence for hundreds of years. Although there are good technical reasons for this, for many people unfamiliar with native title, it seems like the Court is retrospectively creating a property interest (API, 2022, page 2).

The key points of APGP402 are summarised as follows:

- native title is already determined over almost 50% of Australia and further native title claims are progressing;
- native title exists overwhelmingly in regional, rural and outback Australia but can exist in certain areas in urban and suburban Australia;
- native title generally does not exist on freehold land or exclusive possession leasehold land but can be encountered on most other forms of land tenure;
- native title creates a property right with value;
- native title is different to Aboriginal heritage; and
- certain developments cannot be built unless agreement with native title holders is reached (API, 2022).

Significantly, APGP402 cautions that native title is *incredibly technical* such that great care should be taken when reporting or advising on native title matters, with members always understanding the limits of their knowledge and expertise in relation to native title and seeking or recommending that advice from experts in the field be sourced where required (API, 2022).

In addition to native title, compulsory acquisition may result in the right to compensation for indigenous groups for cultural loss. In the context of the NSW compulsory acquisition legislation, the Valuer General issued a *Review of Forms of Cultural Loss and the Process and Method for Quantifying Compensation for Compulsory Acquisition* (Valuer General, 2022a) followed by a policy (Valuer General, 2022b) to identify potential forms of cultural loss and a process and valuation method for quantifying compensation for cultural loss having regard to the principal case law of relevance, *Northern Territory v Griffiths* (2019) (*Timber Creek*) which, while providing clarification, does not provide clear guidance.

The review identified that forms of cultural loss may include, but not be limited to:

- access;
- residence;
- activities;
- practices;
- ecology;
- sites;
- trauma; and
- progressive impairment,

each having a potentially different number of sub-forms, with each then having a potentially different level of significance (Valuer General, 2022a).

For the quantification of compensation, the Valuer General proposed that regard be given to the claimant's statement of claim and supporting evidence, the acquiring authority's list of issues and the form, the number and the significance of cultural losses when determining compensation for cultural loss, such that a wide range of forms of cultural loss which are many in number and very significant would support the highest level of compensation with fewer forms, lower numbers and lesser significance supporting lower levels of compensation (Valuer General, 2022a).

At the date of writing, while determinations of cultural loss in NSW are being prepared, no final determinations have yet been issued, nor have such determinations been tested in the Land and Environment Court of New South Wales.

As with native title matters, compensation for cultural loss is also incredibly technical such that great care should be taken when reporting or advising on cultural loss compensation matters, with valuers always recognising the limits of their knowledge and expertise in relation to cultural loss compensation and seeking or recommending that advice from experts in the field be sourced where required.

10.8 The future of the property valuation profession?

The future of the valuation profession is as bright as its members choose to make it. Opportunities (glass half full) or threats (glass half empty) for the valuation profession may be considered through the conventional business school framework of people, process and technology.

At the broadest level, the valuation profession in Australia today comprises graduates of property courses from Universities in Australia or overseas, with those practitioners predating the introduction of bachelor's degree courses now approaching retirement. Over the last forty years, the level of valuation, building, planning and law content in University property degree courses has generally declined and the level of investment, finance, data analysis and business subjects has generally increased together with the inclusion of first-year professional orientation and final year professional practice courses. Accordingly, today's graduates entering the professional assessment programs of the relevant professional bodies, as a precursor to joining the valuation profession, do so with a broad but relevant academic education.

To date, the Universities and the relevant professional bodies have been able to work in harmony, with the Universities accommodating the breadth of topics that the professional bodies seek for inclusion if a degree is to be accredited. However, looking forward, as Universities increase their focus on student numbers and homogenisation of courses, their willingness to accommodate the historic breadth of topics may come under pressure. While this may result in graduates with broad property knowledge who are capable of working in a wide range of property roles, their knowledge may be insufficient for the valuation membership of the relevant professional bodies.

Therefore, over time, the relationship between the University and the professional body will change. If the professional bodies wish to maintain the breadth of topics in a degree accredited for valuation, then Universities may cease to be accredited for valuation and scope may exist for TAFEs and technical colleges, which have less focus on student numbers and homogenisation of courses, to provide more valuation graduates for the profession.

Concerning process, it is challenging to see that valuation methodology needs to change, but the way that it is packaged and sold to clients may provide scope for change. The notion of a valuer providing a valuation is a narrow business proposition, with the education, training and professional experience of valuers making them equipped to offer much more through the application of valuation skills, including analysis and judgment, to wider property problems faced by clients. While the valuer who chooses to continue solely as a provider of valuations may see a continued workload into the future, the valuer who embraces the provision of broader advice to clients may see an increasing workload and a greater diversity of tasks.

Technology is likely to have a major impact on property valuation in the future, as considered in the context of artificial intelligence and automated valuation models. Valuers who see a glass half full will embrace technology and adapt their business model to make the most of the opportunities available. Valuers who see a glass half empty will challenge the relevance of technology and focus on the potential risks in an attempt to protect their existing business model. Over time, as has been apparent with the introduction of discounted cash flow and the adoption of automated valuation models, clients will make the decision for valuers and require the use of technology, providing valuers with an opportunity to (or with no alternative but to) adapt their business model. Forward-thinking valuers will adapt their business model in anticipation of making the most of the opportunity, while others will lag and be forced to adapt in response. The choice rests with the valuation profession.

10.9 Summary and conclusions

Chapter 1 outlined the structure of the property asset class, examining the traditional characteristics of property (including heterogeneity, durability, illiquidity and so forth) and the traditional risks of property (including location, building, tenant risk and so forth) through the lenses of systematic, unsystematic and idiosyncratic risk, aligning property valuation with capital market theory.

Chapter 2 considered the evolution of property valuation in Australia, the role of the valuer and the diverse activities of the valuation profession, followed by a detailed examination of the inter-acting framework provided by valuation standards and ethical standards promulgated by IVSC, RICS and API.

Chapter 3 explored concepts of value and normative and positive definitions of value, dissecting the International Valuation Standards' definition of market value with a reconciliation to the concept of market value in *Spencer v Commonwealth* (1907) and examining such contemporary valuation issues as valuation lag, variance, accuracy, negligence and valuer rotation.

Chapter 4 introduced International Financial Reporting Standards and International Accounting Standards with a detailed examination of the key provisions of International Valuation Standards, the RICS Red Book and API guidance papers that impact on valuation practice in Australia.

Chapter 5 outlined conceptual approaches to the valuation process with a review of the self-supporting process of instructing, undertaking and reporting valuations under the International Valuation Standards, RICS Red Book and API guidance papers, examining how this process inter-relates to the choice of valuation approach, valuation method and the purpose of the valuation.

Chapter 6 addressed the market approach to valuation through the comparative method of valuation, including the key steps of accumulation, analysis, adjustment and application of comparable sales evidence to the subject property being valued, with an example.

Chapter 7 considered the income approach to valuation addressed through the static methods of the capitalisation of income and the profits methods of valuation, including an examination of the key inputs for each method with examples and a consideration of both marriage value and the surrender and renewal of leases.

Chapter 8 considered the income approach to valuation addressed through the dynamic method of the discounted cash flow method of valuation, including an examination of the key inputs and a focus on the derivation of the discount rate and consideration of the role of sensitivity and scenario analysis, with examples.

Chapter 9 considered the cost approach to valuation addressed through the replacement cost, reproduction cost, summation and residual or hypothetical development methods of valuation.

This chapter concluded the book with a consideration of future perspectives including the role of uncertainty, data, automated valuation models, artificial intelligence, optionality, environmental, social and governance issues, retail and office space use, indigenous issues and the future of the valuation profession.

With uncertainty now being a certain part of the business environment, valuers have no alternative but to address uncertainty in the valuation process. Global contagion events demonstrate the interconnectedness of the world's equity, debt and property markets, creating periods of great uncertainty both internationally and across the Australian property markets. Usefully, the responses of IVSC, RICS and API through the respective guidance documents published offer a way for the valuer to think through the relevant issues impacting value without being caught up in the hysteria of the event and emphasise the importance of transparency and disclosure of material uncertainty.

The increased use of technology and data by businesses in general and by competitors to valuers in particular means that valuers have no alternative but to embrace data, automated valuation models and artificial intelligence and to respond in a manner that ensures the survival of the valuation profession.

While not challenging the survival of the valuation profession, optionality, ESG, structural changes in retail and office space use and the growing significance of indigenous issues in valuation practice will each require attention and a considered response by the valuation profession.

Finally, the future of the valuation profession is as bright as its members choose to make it by selecting either a viewpoint of opportunities (glass half full) or a viewpoint of threats (glass half empty). Forward-thinking valuers will adapt their business model in anticipation of future changes to make the most of the opportunity, while others will lag and be forced to adapt in response. The choice rests with the valuation profession.

References

AICD (2023, March) 'Office politics', in *Company director*, Australian Institute of Company Directors, Sydney.

API (2021) *ANZVGP110 considerations when forming an opinion of value when there is a shortage of market transactions*, Australian Property Institute, Deakin.

API (2022) *APGP402 native title matters*, Australian Property Institute, Deakin.

Baum, A, Mackmin, D and Nunnington, N (2018) *The income approach to property valuation*, Routledge, Abingdon.

Black, F and Scholes, M (1973) 'The pricing of options and corporate liabilities', *The Journal of Political Economy*, Vol 81, No 3, pp. 637–654.

Elder, B (2018) 'International standards: key to unlocking the value of green buildings?', in Wilkinson, S et al. (Ed) *Routledge handbook of sustainable real estate*, Routledge, Abingdon.

French, N. and Gabrielli, L. (2004) 'The uncertainty of valuation', *Journal of Property Investment & Finance*, Vol 22, No 6, pp. 484–500.

Geltner, D and De Neufville, R (2012) 'Uncertainty, flexibility, valuation and design: how 21st century information and knowledge can improve 21st century urban development (papers 1 and 2)', *Pacific Rim Property Research Journal*, Vol 18, No 3.

Geltner, D and De Neufville, R (2018) *Flexibility and real estate valuation under uncertainty: a practical guide for developers*, Wiley Blackwell, Hoboken.

Hurst, N and Wilkinson, S (2018) 'Sustainability and housing value in Victoria, Australia', in Wilkinson, S et al. (Ed) *Routledge handbook of sustainable real estate*, Routledge, Abingdon.

IVSC (2013a) *TIP4—valuation uncertainty*, International Valuation Standards Council, London.

IVSC (2013b) *International valuation standards 2013*, International Valuation Standards Council, London.

IVSC (2021) *International valuation standards*, International Valuation Standards Council, London.

Merton, RC (1973) 'Theory of rational option pricing', *The Bell Journal of Economics and Management Science*, Vol 4, No 1, pp. 141–183.

Parker, D (2016) *International valuation standards: a guide to the valuation of real property assets*, Wiley-Blackwell, Chichester.

Parker, D (2018) 'Green REITs', in Wilkinson, S et al. (Ed) *Routledge handbook of sustainable real estate*, Routledge, Abingdon.

RICS (2021) *RICS valuation—global standards*, Royal Institution of Chartered Surveyors, London.

Sayce, S (2018) 'Building sustainability into valuation and worth', in Wilkinson et al. (Ed) (2018) Routledge handbook of sustainable real estate, Routledge, Abingdon.

Valuer General (2022a) *A review of forms of cultural loss and the process and method for quantifying compensation for compulsory acquisition*, Valuer General of New South Wales, Sydney.

Valuer General (2022b) *Compensation for cultural loss arising from compulsory acquisition*, Valuer General of New South Wales, Sydney.

Warren, C (2018) 'Building energy efficiency certificates and commercial property: the Australian experience', in Wilkinson, S et al. (Ed) *Routledge handbook of sustainable real estate*, Routledge, Abingdon.

Warren-Myers, G (2018) 'Valuing sustainability in commercial property in Australia', in Wilkinson, S et al. (Ed) *Routledge handbook of sustainable real estate*, Routledge, Abingdon.

Wilkinson, S (2018) 'Sustainable office retrofit in Melbourne', in Wilkinson, S et al. (Ed) *Routledge handbook of sustainable real estate*, Routledge, Abingdon.

Wilkinson, S, Dixon, T, Miller, N and Sayce, S (2018) *Routledge handbook of sustainable real estate*, Routledge, Abingdon.

Wyatt, P (2023) *Property valuation*, Wiley Blackwell, Chichester.

Index

Note: Page locators in **bold** indicate a table.

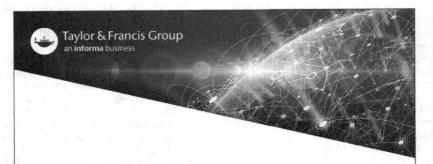

Printed in the United States
by Baker & Taylor Publisher Services